GENIUS AT PLAY

Wind Wizard: Alan G. Davenport and the Art of Wind Engineering

King of Infinite Space: Donald Coxeter, the Man Who Saved Geometry

GENIUS AT PLAY

THE CURIOUS MIND OF JOHN HORTON CONWAY

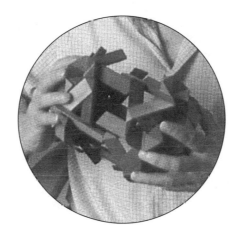

SIOBHAN ROBERTS

BLOOMSBURY

NEW YORK · LONDON · OXFORD · NEW DELHI · SYDNEY

WITHDRAWN

Bloomsbury USA

An imprint of Bloomsbury Publishing Plc

1385 Broadway	50 Bedford Square
New York	London
NY 10018	WC1B 3DP
USA	UK

www.bloomsbury.com

BLOOMSBURY and the Diana logo are trademarks of
Bloomsbury Publishing Plc

First published 2015

© Siobhan Roberts 2015

ISBN: HB: 978-1-62040-593-2
ePub: 978-1-62040-594-9

LIBRARY OF CONGRESS CATALOGING- IN-PUBLICATION DATA
HAS BEEN APPLIED FOR.

2 4 6 8 10 9 7 5 3 1

Designed and typeset by Simon M. Sullivan

Printed and bound in the U.S.A. by Thomson-Shore Inc.,
Dexter, Michigan

The author acknowledges for their financial support the Canada Council
for the Arts and the Ontario Arts Council.

 Canada Council Conseil des arts
for the Arts du Canada

 ONTARIO ARTS COUNCIL
CONSEIL DES ARTS DE L'ONTARIO
an Ontario government agency
un organisme du gouvernement de l'Ontario

To find out more about our authors and books visit
www.bloomsbury.com. Here you will find extracts, author interviews,
details of forthcoming events and the option to sign up for our
newsletters.

Bloomsbury books may be purchased for business or promotional use.
For information on bulk purchases please contact Macmillan Corporate
and Premium Sales Department at specialmarkets@macmillan.com.

For
D.A.B.B.
D.A.B.R.
D.C.N.R.

Simon J. Fraser
4.5.73

Tell all the Truth but tell it slant.
EMILY DICKINSON

CONTENTS

Were he not such an egomaniac, John Horton Conway, archly roguish with a gawky, geeky magnetism, might be writing this book himself. Eyes smiling, hands clasped proudly at his chest, he easily admits,

I do have a big ego!*
    As I often say, modesty is my only vice. If I weren't so modest, I'd be perfect.

Everyone who knows him knows it. Most everyone loves him nonetheless. Conway's is a jocund and playful egomania, sweetened by self-deprecating charm. Based at Princeton University, though having made his name and found fame at Cambridge, he claims never to have worked a day in his life. He purports instead to have piddled away reams and reams of time playing games. Yet he is the John von Neumann Distinguished Professor in Applied and Computational Mathematics. He's a Fellow of the Royal Society of London for Improving Natural Knowledge, a particularly august club, the oldest scientific society in the world—and Conway likes to mention that when he was elected in 1981, he signed the big book of fellows at the induction ceremony and was pleased to see on previous pages the names Isaac Newton, Albert Einstein, Alan Turing, and Bertrand Russell.

Not surprisingly then, considering the company he's keeping, Conway is roundly praised as a genius. "The word 'genius' gets misused an awful lot," says Stanford mathemagician Persi Diaconis. "John Conway

---

* Conway's ego is so sizable that it seemed to demand its own font. This is how you shall encounter him throughout the book.

is a genius. And the thing about John is he'll think about anything. Most mathematicians are analysts or group theorists or number theorists or logicians. John has contributed to every single one of those areas, and yet doesn't fit into any. He has a real sense of whimsy. You can't put him in a mathematical box." He factors large numbers in his head, he pulls π out of a hat (reciting π from memory to 1,111+ digits, that is), and he's been known to carry on his person a few decks of cards, dice, ropes, pennies, coat hangers, sometimes a Slinky, maybe a miniature bicycle, all props he deploys to extend his winning imagination.

"He is among the most charismatic figures in mathematics," says Baron Martin Rees of Ludlow, a former colleague of Conway's at Cambridge and former president of the Royal Society. Biologists speak of a species as "charismatic" for its ability to draw attention to itself. There's a "charismatic walrus" that whistles, growls, and roars on cue into a microphone. Conway looks the part of a walrus, scruffily hirsute, and he seems to take his cue from Lewis Carroll's Walrus: "'The time has come,' the Walrus said, 'To talk of many things. . . .'" Conway likes to talk, and talk and talk and talk. His voice is a rich, gravelly baritone, with a lingering Northern English lilt, that makes anything sound interesting, a voice you can listen to forever—almost. "He was by far the most charismatic lecturer in the faculty," says another Cambridge colleague, Sir Peter Swinnerton-Dyer. "I'm not sure that I can describe how charisma happens. It just is or isn't. And with most mathematicians it markedly isn't."

Still, for Conway, writing his autobiography would be unseemly. Partly because he's an insecure egotist. He very much cares what other people think, and he worries that a self-portrait might come off as *too* egotistical. And partly because he'd have a hard time with "the fiction of humility that the conventional autobiographer must at every moment struggle to maintain," as the occasional biographer Janet Malcolm describes the dilemma. So he'll stick to doing what he does best. Gnawing on his left index finger with his chipped old British teeth, temporal veins bulging and brow pensively squinched beneath the day before yesterday's hair, Conway unapologetically whiles away his hours tinkering and thinkering—which is to say he's ruminating, or maybe he is doing some work, but he'll insist he's doing nothing, being lazy, playing games. Witnessing Conway's gamesomeness over the years, James Propp, a professor of mathematics at the University of Massachusetts Lowell, observed:

"Conway is the rare sort of mathematician whose ability to connect his pet mathematical interests makes one wonder if he isn't, at some level, shaping mathematical reality and not just exploring it. The example of this that I know best is a connection he discovered between sphere packing and games. These were two separate areas of study that Conway had arrived at by two different paths. So there's no reason for them to be linked. But somehow, through the force of his personality, and the intensity of his passion, he bent the mathematical universe to his will."

The hoity-toity Princeton bubble seems an incongruously grand home base for someone so gamesome. The campus buildings are Gothic and festooned with ivy. It's a milieu where the well-groomed preppy aesthetic never seems passé. By contrast, Conway is rumpled, with an otherworldly mien, somewhere between *The Hobbit*'s Bilbo Baggins and Gandalf—a look that should earn him a spot in the online quiz featuring portraits of frumpy old men under the rubric "Prof or Hobo?" He wears faded and frayed chinos, stained with splotches that he camouflages by doodling spirals or crisscrosses over top with his pen. Above the waist he always wears a T-shirt emblazoned with a mathy message, such as:

ARE YOU CRYING?

THERE'S NO CRYING!

THERE'S NO CRYING IN MATH CLASS!

He long ago abandoned his office, which bears no nameplate, but there is a sign he found and repurposed, reading:

CONWAY

$9.99

He was crowded out of these quarters by the wanton mess that accumulated into a full-fledged tip, with multicolored paper polyhedra hanging from the ceiling and gigantic spongy Escher puzzle pieces tiling the floor. His office no longer viable, Conway can usually be found in the mathematics department's third-floor common room. The department is housed in the 15-story Fine Hall, the tallest tower in Princeton, with Sprint and AT&T cell towers on the rooftop. Inside, the professor-to-undergrad ratio is nearly 1:1. With a querying student often at his side, he settles either on a cluster of couches in the main room or, as today, just outside the fray in the hallway, burrowed into a window alcove—I came to think of it as the edifying alcove—furnished with 2 armchairs facing a blackboard. From there he borrows some Shakespeare and addresses a familiar visitor:

Welcome! It's a poor place but mine own!

With clumsy gallantry he clears the spare chair of the day's debris: the *New York Times*, devoured back-to-front with the morning's bagel and coffee; his page-a-day Sudoku calendar; a landslide of loose paper on which he's been running columns of numbers, playing a pointless game he invented about a month ago. Subprime Fibs, he calls it, and he has all the trial-and-error research right there in his filing cabinet, sediments of calculations filed beneath his armchair's seat cushion.

Conway's contributions to the mathematical canon include innumerable games. He is perhaps most famous for inventing the Game of Life in the late 1960s. The *Scientific American* columnist Martin Gardner called it "Conway's most famous brainchild." This is not Life the family board game, but Life the cellular automaton. It is played on a grid, like tic-tactoe, where proliferating cells resemble skittering microorganisms viewed under a microscope. A cellular automaton is a little machine with groups of cells that evolve from iteration to iteration in discrete rather than continuous time—in seconds, say, each tick of the clock advances the next iteration, and then over time, behaving a bit like a transformer or a shapeshifter, the cells evolve into something, anything, everything else.

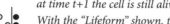

LIFE RULES

BIRTH RULE: *If at time t a cell is dead (empty), and the cell has 3 live (full) neighbors in any direction, then at time t+1 the cell becomes alive.*
DEATH RULE: *If at time t a live cell has 0 or 1 neighbors it dies of isolation, and if a live cell has 4 or more neighbors it dies of overcrowding.*
SURVIVAL RULE: *If at time t a live cell has 2 or 3 live neighbors, then at time t+1 the cell is still alive.*
With the "Lifeform" shown, the five larger cells comprise the "glider" as it moves along the grid—the dark larger cells are live and remains so in the next iteration, the light larger cells are live but die in the next iteration, and the smaller dots are dead cells that in the next iteration come alive.

So the Game of Life is not a game proper. Conway calls it a "no-player never-ending" game. The recording artist and composer Brian Eno once recalled that seeing an electronic Game of Life exhibit on display at the Exploratorium in San Francisco gave him a "shock to the intuition." "The whole system is so transparent," he said, "that there should be no surprises at all, but in fact there are plenty: the complexity and 'organic-ness' of the evolution of the dot patterns completely beggars prediction." And as suggested by the narrator in an episode of the television show *Stephen Hawking's Grand Design*, "It's possible to imagine that some-thing like the Game of Life, with only a few basic laws, might produce highly complex features, perhaps even intelligence. It might take a grid with many billions of squares, but that's not surprising. We have many hundreds of billions of cells in our brains."

Life was among the first cellular automata and remains perhaps the best known. It was co-opted by Google for one of its Easter eggs: type in "Conway's Game of Life" and alongside the search results appear ghostly light-blue cells that gradually overrun the page. Practically speaking, the game nudged the use of cellular automata and agent-based simulations in the complexity sciences, modeling the behavior of everything from ants to traffic to clouds to galaxies. Impractically speaking, it became a cult classic for those keen on no highfalutin application but wasting time. The spectacle of Life cells morphing on computer screens proved dangerously addictive for graduate students in math, physics, and com-puter science, as well as for many upstanding adults, especially those with jobs that provided access to idling mainframe computers. A U.S. military report estimated that the workplace hours lost while nerds clandestinely watched Life evolve on their computers cost millions. Or so one Life legend has it. Another purports that when Life went viral, $\frac{1}{4}$ of all the world's computers were playing.

Yet when Conway's vanity strikes, as it often does, and he opens the index of a new mathematics book, casually checking for . . .

The sacred name of Conway!

. . . he gets peeved that more often than not his name is cited only in reference to the Game of Life. Aside from Life, his myriad contributions to the canon run broad and deep, though with such meandering interests he considers himself quite shallow. He has invented many an idio-syncratic algorithm—for counting stairs while you climb without actually counting, and another for how best to read through a stack of double-sided loose-leaf pages. Then there's his first serious love, geom-etry, and by extension symmetry. From there his promiscuous curiosity has sent him roaming through group theory, knot theory, number the-ory, game theory, coding theory. He proved his chops when he discov-ered what's sometimes called the Conway Constellation—3 among a family of sporadic groups in the ocean of mathematical symmetry. The biggest of his groups, called the Conway group, is based on the Leech lattice, representing a dense packing of spheres in 24-dimensional space where each sphere touches 196,560 other spheres. As Conway once ex-plained to Martin Gardner,

> *There is a lot of room up there.*

He also shed light on the largest of all the sporadic groups, the Mon-ster group, in the "Monstrous Moonshine" conjectures, a paper com-posed frenetically with his eccentric Cambridge colleague Simon Norton. And his greatest masterpiece, in his own opinion at least, is the discovery of a new type of numbers, surreal numbers. The surreals are a souped-up continuum of numbers including the all merely real num-bers—integers, fractions, and irrationals such as π—and then going above and beyond and below and within, gathering in all the infinites and infinitesimals. Again deferring to Gardner's reliable assessment, the surreals are "infinite classes of weird numbers never before seen by man." And they may turn out to have applications in explaining every-thing from the incomprehensible infinitude of the cosmos to the infi-nitely tiny minutiae of the quantum. When Conway found these numbers he walked around in a white-hot daydream for weeks.

What of it, though? Where does all this position him in mathematics' ancient intellectual odyssey toward beauty and truth? Conway on occa-sion sees himself as part of a marching band winding through the streets of time. Then again, unless asked, he rarely if ever stands back to situate himself within the enterprise as a whole. Others have tried. In this age of top-10 lists, the *Observer*, the world's oldest Sunday newspaper, listed Conway in its pantheon of 10 mathematicians whose discoveries have changed our world. But just try to discuss the *Observer's* list with Conway (not to mention another list on which he recently found himself) and he demurs with a vengeance:

> It's nice in one way. It really means that I might be one of the best-known mathematicians in the present day, and this is not quite the same as being the best. And it's probably because of Life. But it's embarrassing. Because people might think I'm behind it in some way. And I assure you I'm not. And it's particularly embarrassing because at least one of those lists doesn't include Archimedes and Newton.

In Conway's view, Archimedes is the preeminent father of mathematics. It was Archimedes who first truly understood the real numbers, and he was the first mathematician to work out the value of π, proving it was between the upper bound of $3\frac{1}{7}$ and the lower bound of $3\frac{10}{71}$. Yet in the *Observer's* ranking, it's not Archimedes but Pythagoras at the top. If not the best mathematician, Pythagoras is perhaps the best-known mathematician of all time, due to his namesake theorem. And generally the list comprises last-name-basis mathematicians who, in their day, appeared in the society pages of science: Euler, Gauss, Cantor, Erdős. Then Conway comes in toward the end, followed by Perelman and Tao, both of whom have been in the news lately. The Russian Grigori Perelman solved the Poincaré Conjecture and refused all the accolades, including the Fields Medal. The University of California's Terence Tao is an expert in prime numbers who accepted his Fields Medal and in 2014 won the inaugural $3 million Breakthrough Prize in Mathematics. Conway's salad days spanned the Sexy '70s and the Excessive '80s. With Perelman and Tao, and Conway even, we are too close to evaluate the long horizon of their contributions, especially by the criteria of whether their pure and abstract math will evolve to find practical application. The verdict on that often takes time, sometimes a long time. The notable exception is John Nash, a colleague of Conway's at Princeton and the subject of the movie and book *A Beautiful Mind*. Nash made contributions in game theory—insights into the forces of chance that play out in our lives day to day—and these were quickly put to use in evolutionary biology, accounting, politics, military theory, and market economics, earning him the Nobel Prize (but in Conway's view, Nash's Nobel work is less interesting than the deep and difficult, albeit less useful, Nash embedding theorem, which states that every Riemann manifold can be isometrically embedded in Euclidean space). Conway has been in the running for the million-dollar Nobel of mathematics, the Abel Prize—which is to say he's been nominated, and the nomination remains on file—with his group theory work being the strongest point in his favor. He has won other big math prizes, but as yet no luck with the Abel. And for the most part any practical implications of his work also remain in waiting. Few doubt that at least some of his gems will find application. The surreals, for instance. "The surreal numbers will be applied," says another Princeton colleague, Peter Sarnak. "It's just a question of how, and when."

When I first proposed a biography to Conway, he nixed the idea out of hand:

Oh god. Never. NO!

I had just finished writing a book about the classical geometer H.S.M. (Donald) Coxeter. Since Coxeter was one his heroes, I'd initially met Conway when I chased him down for an interview at a summer math camp, where he was getting into all sorts of trouble. Every summer he gives over what his colleagues might view as premium research time and spends a couple weeks at camp with precocious young mathematicians. Witnessing him playing endless games with kids, it became abundantly clear that this was his natural milieu; there was no other way he'd rather spend his time. After our math camp meeting, and more Coxeter interviews, Conway ended up vetting the Coxeter manuscript, and along the way, being master of the digression, he managed to talk an awful lot about himself. He talked about crashing overnight at the Kremlin in '66, about attending the burial of Cromwell's skull at Cambridge, about his 3 wives and all the other women, more than he can count (he tried once, during a bout of insomnia). He talked about his triple bypass, his attempted suicide, his ability to twist his tongue into a cloverleaf and 3 other shapes. He's a talker, not a listener. While Coxeter epitomized the reticent and restrained Edwardian gentleman, Conway is the rare man inclined to forthright and global disclosure. However, he was chary, to use a word he likes, about being the subject of a biography. There were too many skeletons in the closet. His answer was NO.

A year or so later, in fall 2006, he suffered a stroke. This gave him a gimpy right side, but he walked out of the hospital with the help of a cane. And easily enough while writing at the blackboard he cultivated his ambidexterity (not so surprising, considering his passion for symmetry). Though all in all he was feeling his mortality much more acutely. A year later again, I arrived in Princeton for a fellowship as a Director's Visitor at the idyllic Institute for Advanced Study—where Einstein ultimately made his home, and where T. S. Eliot visited in 1948, walked the woods, and worked on his play *The Cocktail Party*. The Institute is a heady place, yet very social and, in its way, humble. One mathematician on faculty lives by his bumper sticker cautioning DON'T BELIEVE EVERYTHING YOU THINK. Once settled into my office and apartment, I called John to say hello.

Hey, listen! I've been thinking about that biography . . .

His ego had gotten the better of him. He'd changed his mind, at least provisionally. And no sooner had he acquiesced than he succumbed to the biographee's version of Stockholm Syndrome. He began referring to himself in the third person as "the subject" and signing off his occasional e-mail,

Ever your loyal subject, J.

The loyalty, of course, wouldn't last.

⬙ ⬜ ⬦ ⬡ ⬣

For a time things proceeded smoothly enough. Daily I trekked the mile across town from the Institute grounds up the Springdale hill, past languid herds of deer lounging on the golf course in the morning mist, and down onto campus, often amid the torrential rains queerly common to this part of New Jersey. Conway, happy as a clam, submitted to endless interviews, circling round and round his loops of memories, anecdotes, fables. As the years wore on he greeted me and the damned recording device, as it became known, with mockingly less enthusiasm. He could almost always be found ensconced in his alcove, not working. He hadn't given up all hope for hitting upon more white-hot math like the surreals, but more often than not he was thinkering away with his beloved trivialities, such as the Subprime Fibs—named after the subprime mortgage crisis and the time-honored Fibonacci numbers (the sequence of numbers that begins 0, 1, 1, 2, 3, 5, 8, 13 … with all subsequent numbers being the sum of the previous 2). With that for inspiration, the one and only Subprime Fibs rule he explains to me like this:

> Take 2 numbers, any 2, and write them down. Then add them up. If the sum is a prime number—a number divisible only by 1 or itself—then leave the number alone and write the number down. If the sum is not prime, then divide it by its smallest prime divisor and write down the resulting number. And then take the last 2 numbers written down, add them up, repeat the process, and carry on.

And then, accompanied by some imitation grumbling, he hoists himself out of his armchair and offers a live demonstration on the blackboard, with a disclaimer:

> I know you're not interested, but I'll show you anyway, because you were foolish enough to ask.

Numbers are catnip for Conway, and so is explaining.

> 1 and 1 make 2, and that's prime.
> 1 1 2
> 1 and 2 make 3, and that's prime.
> 1 1 2 3
> 2 and 3 make 5, which is prime.
> 1 1 2 3 5
> 3 and 5 make 8, which isn't prime, so I divide it by the smallest prime I can, which is 2, and I get 4.
> 1 1 2 3 5 4
> 5 and 4 make 9, which isn't prime; divide it by 3 and I'll get 3, which is prime.
> 1 1 2 3 5 4 3

4 and 3 make 7, which is prime.

1 1 2 3 5 4 3 7

3 and 7 make 10, which I can divide by 2.

1 1 2 3 5 4 3 7 5

7 and 5 make 12, which I can divide by 2.

1 1 2 3 5 4 3 7 5 6

5 and 6 make 11, which is prime.

1 1 2 3 5 4 3 7 5 6 11

That's what you do.

What would he call this kind of number game?

A waste of time!

What's fascinating about the rule governing the game, for Conway as the inventor, anyway, is that it's totally stupid. Yet it exists.

I'll tell you what interests me about this—it's really what interests me about mathematics. Nobody else in the whole history of the world has been stupid enough to invent this rule. That's the first thing. But then, if they had, they would find exactly this behavior that I'm finding.

And what I'm conjecturing now is that whatever 2 numbers you start with, no matter how big they are, the sequence ends up in one of 3 particular cycles; it just goes round and round and round. It seems no matter which pair of numbers you start with, it ends up being periodic: it repeats after, say, 18 steps. I can't say it always repeats, because I haven't proved it. But it's as obvious as hell that it always does.

And, how can I say it, even though nobody's ever looked at it—and I'm absolutely sure that nobody's ever looked at it; I mean, it's not inconceivable that somebody's invented it, but why the hell should they have, you know?—but if they had, they would have found this.

That's a curious thing about the nature of mathematical existence. This rule hasn't physically existed in any sense in the world before a month ago, before I invented it, but it sort of intellectually existed forever. There is this abstract world which in some strange sense has existed throughout eternity.

Imagine an uninhabited planet, full of interesting things. You land on it, and it existed for a million years, but no people have ever been there, no sentient beings. There are such places, I'm sure. Go to some remote star and there will be something. But you don't have to go there. You can sit in this very chair and find something that has existed throughout all of eternity and be the first person to explore it.

Conway has no compunction about buttonholing strangers and serving them a rollicking riff on this or any of his many obsessions. Another obsession of late is the Free Will Theorem, in which, he points out, every human being has a vested interest. But usually it's numbers that are the object of his infatuation. He turns numbers over, upside down, and inside out, observing how they behave. Why is it that when you pick a number, any number, then double it, add 6, halve it, and take away the number you started with, your answer is always 3? Above all he loves knowledge, and he seeks to know everything about the universe. Conway's charisma lies in his desire to share his incurable lust for learning, to spread the contagion and the romance. He is dogged and undaunted in explaining the inexplicable, and even when the inexplicable remains so, he leaves his audience elevated, fortified by the failed attempt and feeling somehow in cahoots, privy to the inside dope, satisfied at having flirted with a glimmer of understanding. For his own part, he calls himself a professional nonunderstander. The pursuit is what counts, and chasing after Conway's promiscuous curiosity and probing his ebullient intellect is this book's modus operandi.

> "Promiscuous," by the way, is a funny word. Originally it just meant mixed, maybe well-mixed or something. Then it started being used in the context of swimming pools—"promiscuous bathing" meant men and women could bathe in the same pool, since before they'd had to bathe separately. Then it acquired its odor of sex, "promiscuous behavior," and so on.

△ ⬡ ⬦ ⊗ ⊕

Having asked for it, I could hardly decline the job of writing Conway's biography. I roped him into a fact-finding mission to England; accompanied him to a workshop on the Monster group at Japan's Institute for the Physics and Mathematics of the Universe; shadowed him in Atlanta at an invitation-only conference of mathematicians, magicians, and puzzlers honoring Martin Gardner; tagged along to more summer sessions of math camp where the bright school-age campers, as well as Conway, reveled in "Math Until We Die"; and I served as his travel agent and minder on a trip to Toronto for an appointment with the neuroscientist who studied Einstein's and Coxeter's brains and who is eager to study Conway's, pre- and postmortem.

Meanwhile, mingling with my betters at the Institute for Advanced Study—where the world's best scholars delve deep into the past, the history of humanity, the evolution of the universe—I was ever answering the question of how one writes about a living subject. "If the biographer writes from personal knowledge, and makes haste to gratify the public curiosity, there is danger lest his interest, his fear, his gratitude, or his tenderness overpower his fidelity, and tempt him to conceal, if not to invent," said Samuel Johnson (Conway keeps Boswell's multivolume *Life of Johnson* on his bookshelf, alongside Johnson's *Lives of the Poets*). I tried to heed the warning. Having Conway looking over my shoulder inevitably made his vital signs a liability, mostly for him. I realized this over lunch at the Institute with Heinrich von Staden, the resident authority on ancient science. He told me about the Greek and Roman tradition of vivisection, making public spectacle of strapping a live pig to a plank and cutting him open and observing the mechanics of his beating heart. A fitting metaphor, it seemed, for what this experience would become for Conway.

He tried to mitigate his own suffering with a few conditions: roughly, "Don't Ask, Don't Tell." One wouldn't, or shouldn't, be so crass as to ask Conway too much about *certain* topics, although any information gleaned from other sources was, in theory, fair game. It had to be. Oral history was almost the only resource. Conway keeps no files, no archives, no diaries, no letters. He is impressively inept at the epistolary arts. His pigsties of offices always overflow with unopened mail, and he seldom reads any of his copious e-mail, either. There is a caricature of Conway—an iconic image among a certain crowd—that nicely captures the devilishness he gets away with (see the frontispiece on page vi).

Growing from his head is a topological entity called the "horned sphere." Mathematicians call this form a "pathological example," an entity with properties that are counterintuitive and ill behaved, much like Conway himself. He's a romantic and a rabble-rouser, a utopian and anarchist, all rolled into one. For the most part with the biography he was cooperative, ingratiating, ever willing to talk—except when secondary sources produced an irresistibly salacious anecdote, or worse, telling discrepancies, puzzling difficulties in deciphering fact from fiction, true from false in the faulty towers of memory. At these moments of reckoning it was as if I'd disproved Conway's greatest mathematical masterpiece, debunked the surreal numbers as merely real. He'd shoot me his death stare and say,

Oh, hell. You're not going to put *that* in the book. Are you?!?

Act I

1.

IDENTITY ELEMENTS

Who in the world am I? Ah, that's the great puzzle.
—LEWIS CARROLL

On a late September day in 1956, a skinny 18-year-old left home with a trunk on his back. John Conway wore his hair long and unkempt like a proto-hippie, and although he generally preferred to go barefoot, on this occasion he wore strappy Jesus sandals. He traveled by steam train from Liverpool southeast to Cambridge. As he passed the 5-hour journey, via Crewe with a connection in Bletchley, the not particularly scenic landscape rolling by in a blur of canals and countryside, something dawned on him: here lay a chance for some much-needed self-invention.

In junior school, one of John's teachers had nicknamed him "Mary," since he was such a delicate creature, a bit effeminate. Being Mary made John's life absolute hell until he moved on to secondary school, at the Holt High School for Boys. When the headmaster, A. G. Russell, called each boy into his office and asked what he planned to do with his life, John said he wanted to "read" mathematics at Cambridge. Mathematics has been studied at Cambridge for a long time, according to the website, which also says that its first notable mathematician was the sixteenth century's Robert Recorde, credited with the invention of the equal sign. After loitering for a while with the reprobates at the back of the classroom, John did well enough on the Cambridge entrance exams to receive a minor scholarship and get his name published in the *Liverpool Daily Post*. So instead of Mary, he became known as "the Prof." These nicknames resulted in a terribly introverted teenager, painfully aware of himself and his own suffering. Hence, on the train, he did some meta-thinking. None of his classmates would be joining him at Cambridge. No one would know him. This gave him the audacious idea of transforming himself into a new person: an extrovert! He wondered if he could pull it off. He worried his introversion was too entrenched, but he decided to give it a go. He would be boisterous and witty, he would tell funny stories at parties, he would laugh at himself—that was key.

> Roughly speaking, I was going to become the kind of person you see now. It was a free decision.

Right then, telling me that story, Conway was holding forth in the edifying alcove at the math department, toggling between telling tales and fretting about a big lecture he was due to deliver that night on his latest brainchild, the Free Will Theorem. Conceived in collaboration with his Princeton colleague and friend Simon Kochen, the theorem came about through a casual kicking around of ideas over more than a decade. On August 19, 2004, a Thursday, all of a sudden they realized what they'd achieved. Using a motley combination of quantum mechanics, philosophy, and geometry, they had proven a theorem, almost inadvertently. The simplest statement of their Free Will Theorem is as follows: If physicists have free will while performing experiments, then elementary particles possess free will as well. And this, they reckon, probably explains why and how humans have free will in the first place. It isn't a circular argument so much as it's a spiral argument, a self-subsuming argument, spiraling outward bigger and bigger.

Kochen was the expert in this subject; in his youth he'd done some serious dabbling in the realm of quantum mechanics. Conway's job was not to understand.

> My contribution was *not* understanding all the quantum mechanics stuff. And that was an important contribution. It freed us to think about things in very simple terms.

Obviously, Conway brought a certain brainpower to bear. "He's sui generis," says Kochen. Meaning he's reliably unusual in his approach. And as far as Conway's brain proper is concerned, "It's big," Kochen says. "A lot of people dig deeper and deeper and deeper, use very technical modern machinery. That's not the way John works. He doesn't use too many technical things, not too much apparatus. He works at ground level, the level that he could explain to anyone, using intuition."

> In a fundamental way my job is thinking. You can't see it from the outside. What does the thinking consist of? I think about how to explain whatever I am thinking about to someone. Then I explain it to someone and it doesn't work. So I think about it some more. I tinker with it, with thinking, until I've simplified it. I personally can only understand things after I've thought about them for ages and made them very, very simple.
>
> Most people just understand enough to work. For example, a mechanic doesn't necessarily understand the physics or engineering of how a car works. I'm not putting down a car mechanic. We need practical people. I'm not sure we need theoretical people. Though I'm not going to campaign for my own abolishment.

Conway and Kochen spent a couple of years refining their theorem, readying it for publication in the journal *Foundations of Physics*. With Conway as front man, they also began planning a series of public lectures for fall 2006. They booked the McCosh 50 lecture hall, Princeton's largest classroom, with 446 wooden seats—a creaky 105-year-old venue where Einstein delivered a lecture series on relativity in 1921. Princeton University Press signed the book rights and printed posters to advertise the lectures around campus.

But then things went awry. Conway's wife, Diana, left him. Without her, he floundered. He neglected to take his medication. He suffered his first stroke. The lectures were postponed for more than 2 years. Finally, by March 2009, things were for the most part back on track.

The night before the inaugural lecture, Conway kept himself awake coughing till all hours. I came to this knowledge firsthand. Stealing a page from Margaret Mead's playbook, I'd proposed that I set up camp in Conway's guest room as a full-immersion participant observer. He had no problem with my tailing him 24-7. "My amanuensis," he called me— from the Latin phrase *servus a manu*, a slave at hand. One could let Conway believe what he wanted to believe. Then again, I fetched cough drops and water in attempts to quell his coughing fits, and I carried around his plastic shopping bag full of lecture props, including a book on the Roman poet and philosopher Titus Lucretius and a new braided brown leather belt, a handmade example of knot theory, recently mailed by a friend. He planned to press the belt into service that very evening lest his too-big trousers descend before his audience.

△ ⬜ ⬦ ⊗ ⬢

Assuming his position at the lectern that evening, with his coconspirator Kochen sitting in the front row, Conway opened by barking a greeting cum query at his audience:

WHY ARE YOU HERE TONIGHT?!

He presented 2 answers, with considerable fumbling via PowerPoint (creating the slide presentation had been considerably more challenging for him, intellectually, than constructing the theorem).

1) It was predetermined
2) You chose to come

That really is the problem that faces us.

There was, however, a bigger question: Why was Conway himself there? What business of his was free will? A survey of friends and colleagues on this issue brought rejoinders like "As far as I'm concerned, it's a lot of nonsense." Or "I'm sorry, but I don't understand what John is talking about." The consensus being that he was wandering rather far afield, even for his impressively philandering ken.

Conway, of course, had an answer to the question, by way of a story. Some 65 years earlier, his father had gone to considerable trouble to prove to little John that a radio did not get its information, its sound, from the cord that plugged it into the wall, nor from the wall or the floor by any route, as his son was convinced it did.

My dad borrowed a battery-operated radio set—at that time they didn't basically exist, this was Liverpool in wartime—and he suspended the radio by string from a light fitting. . . . Then he said, "Now watch." He snipped the string. And the radio went on playing music as it fell onto some cushions on the floor—it was in midair and it was still playing music. Well, I didn't understand how that could happen. I still don't understand it, in a sense. We still don't understand how the sun pulls the earth. We don't need an understanding of it. We just accept that it does. The only thing to do is get on with your life. Believe it. Accept it. We don't have to have an explanation for how things happen. They just do.

The radio story was Conway's way of reassuring people that they needn't worry about what they might not understand about the Free Will Theorem. And, he added, almost apologetically:

By the way, we didn't want to prove our theorem. We just wanted to understand what goes on, how the world works. We proved the theorem by accident.

Three axioms make up the guts of the Free Will Theorem. The axioms come from quantum mechanics, which describes the world of the very small, such as elementary particles, and from general relativity, which describes large-scale properties of the universe, such as gravity. But again, the caveat Conway offered, often with throat-clearing asides, was not to worry if you don't understand. He recalled what he once heard the physicist Richard Feynman say about the utter incomprehensibility of quantum mechanics: "If you meet somebody who tells you they understand quantum mechanics, what have you learned? What you've learned is that you've met a liar." Conway has met a few liars. And although he of course doesn't understand quantum mechanics, during the lecture he mentioned the axioms here and there for some ambient scientifica—mood axioms—the postulates in question being "Twin," "Spin," and "Fin." That they rhyme makes them seem at least potentially understandable, in a Lewis Carroll rational nonsense kind of way. From these axioms, and Conway and Kochen's conjuring imaginations, emerged the Free Will Theorem.

And what does "free will" mean? I'm just using this term, "free will"—and many people have said it is a tendentious use of words—to mean that our behavior is not a function of the past.

Precisely how elementary particles demonstrate free will Conway only touched upon in the first lecture. It has to do with an experiment measuring the spin of 2 "Twin" particles, questioning, if you will, the twinned particles about what their spins are. Conway compared this inquisition of the particles to the game Twenty Questions, which he played as a child with his 2 older sisters. John, at the age of about 7, would think of an object and declare it animal, vegetable, or mineral. His sisters would ask questions about the object, and if they succeeded in guessing what it was in 20 questions or fewer, they won. But being a bumptious boy, John displayed no scruples whatsoever when playing this game.

> If I sensed my sisters were getting too close to the object I'd selected, I would change the object. You had to be quite clever to do that. Because you have to select a new object which answers, say, the 7 questions you've already been asked in the same way as the old object did—and is also unlikely to be the kind of object your sisters will think about.

That, he explained, is kind of what the particles do.

> If you ask them this type of "Spin" question, they don't have an answer in mind.
>
> Let's think of that. Let's think of an even cleverer little boy than I was. Very hard to think of a cleverer little boy than I. But think of a cleverer little boy than I was, who never bothers to select an object or an answer in the first place. He just gives the first of so many answers at random and then starts thinking what the object is. Well, that's what the particles do. They don't have answers in mind for each of 33 "Spin" questions that can be asked of them or measured by the experimenters.
>
> Now, a clever enough little boy can answer questions like that on the fly, so to speak, and not be caught out by his sisters. I may say, occasionally I was caught out by my sisters, and there were punishments which I won't bother to describe. But suppose I had a twin brother. In fact, there was a long history of twins in our family. My father was a twin. He had a brother and sister who were twins. I always wished I had a twin brother. And if I had, my sisters would have had a much better chance, because they could insist that my twin and I choose our object together, but then interrogate us separately. If that were the case, we couldn't change the

object. If they chose which one of us they're going to ask about the object, and my twin and I had no chance to transmit information to one another and say, "Hey, quick, I'm changing the object to such and such," well, then we couldn't win. The same happens with the twinned particles. They are tested separately but somehow on the fly they always come up with the same answers.

With that, the Free Will Theorem was essentially QED. Well, not quite. That's an easily digestible analog of the proof, a scientific soupçon. We'll get to the heart of the matter in the not too distant future—we'll revisit the Free Will Theorem intermittently throughout our tortuous journey, treating it like a temporal benchmark, the prevailing present. Most memorable for me during the first lecture was that while Conway took care to avoid getting into any technicalities about the scientific forces at play, he confessed how remarkable he found it that anything could be proven at a mathematical level of precision and exactitude about the nebulous concept of free will.

But, you know, that's what we've done. Our proof is unassailable.

2.

DAZZLING NEW WORLD

As dazzling as first love. I had not imagined there was anything
so delicious . . .

—BERTRAND RUSSELL (on learning Euclid)

Staying at John's house throughout the lecture series, I borrowed his phone for a round of interviews, surveying more of his friends and colleagues who knew not what to make of his latest exploits. Between calls, the phone rang. It was his sister Joan. She'd been trying to get in touch with him since Christmas, but Conway doesn't pick up the phone unless he knows or remembers he's expecting a call. He fails to check messages because he doesn't know how. He'd heard from one of his daughters that Joan was trying to reach him with some bad news. At 82, she'd been diagnosed with breast cancer. Still, it took them ages to connect. Conway either couldn't remember to call, or couldn't remember that Joan's number was hanging on the fridge door, never mind memorizing the number. "You'd think," says Joan, "with a mind like his he could remember those numbers!" I took a message and said I'd get back in touch in the near future for an interview.

About his childhood Conway has select memories, most about the war. Conway remembers his father serving as an air raid warden, and the makeshift telephone system he constructed linking the bomb shelters in their neighborhood, as well as the play version he made for the kids. He remembers his dad carrying him out to their shelter and looking up into the night sky and seeing an entrancing spectacle of spinning lights and balloons, barrage balloons set out by RAF Balloon Command to deter dive bombers. He remembers his mum waking him up on

December 26, 1941, leaning over the bed and saying, "You are 4 today, John Conway." He remembers being evacuated alone to Bangor, Wales. These memories, and a few others, I heard numerous times. I hoped that his sister Joan might be able to retrieve different details, being 10 years her brother's senior. When I called her back, she picked up after a few rings, the television blaring in the background. She started at the very beginning. "He was born on December 26, Boxing Day, in 1937. Well, you probably already have that information," she says, "but it spoiled our Christmas dinner." During our first interview she told me stories for the better part of an hour. During the second, I looked at the telephone's time display: 88 minutes and counting. Talking and talking and talking apparently ran in the family.

In June 1927, their dad, Cyril, 24, married their mum, Agnes, 22, in what Conway suspects was a shotgun wedding. They lived in central Liverpool in a small row of houses just off Penny Lane—as in the Beatles' "Penny Lane," a song that the *Journal of Mundane Behavior* describes as "a portrait of a village virtually teeming with Nowhere Men." Cyril, who smoked like a furnace, was one of those nowhere men, often out of work, picking up odd jobs here and there. He'd left school at 14 to go to work when his father died at 56, leaving his mother a widow with 9 children: 3 sets of twins and 3 singles. He managed to make a decent living playing cards; possessing a photographic memory, he was hired by less talented players who fronted him money, absorbed any losses, and took a sizable cut of his winnings. Not having attended college, he became a lifelong autodidact. He loved science and visited professors at Liverpool University to banter about the latest discoveries. He was also a reader, consuming encyclopedias and encyclopedic works such as Gibbon's *Decline and Fall of the Roman Empire*, as well as a variety of dictionaries. His son, too, became a dictionary reader and logophile at an early age, and he tucked into *Decline and Fall* and was pleasantly surprised by its allusions to sex (all the virgins and concubines, anyway). Conway's mum, who'd worked since age 11, was another great reader. Her tastes ran toward Dickens, and her household was of the Dickensian genre, jolly and convivial despite challenging economic circumstances. Baby Joan, born in 1928, slept in a chest of drawers. By the time the second baby, Sylvia, arrived in 1932, Cyril had a steady job at the Liverpool Institute High School for Boys, working as a technician in the chemistry lab, setting up experiments for students, among them George Harrison and Paul McCartney. At school Mr. Conway was known to be quiet, imperturbable, a background presence, except during the Institute's open house nights, when he always performed a popular spectacle. He'd casually dip his cigarette into a flute of liquid oxygen, lean into the flame of a Bunsen burner for a light, and then with deadpan delivery and perfect timing bring the fag to his mouth with a foot-long flame jetting out. Mr. Conway was a showman. Again, like father, like son.

The family moved into a larger house in a Liverpool suburb in time for John's arrival. Weighing in at 14 pounds 12 ounces, he was not a twin but essentially 2-in-1, with brains to match. Agnes liked to brag about finding her son at the age of 4 sitting on the living room floor and reciting the powers of 2—as Conway himself notes, that's an impressive feat if he got up to 1,024 (2^{10}) but not so much if he reached only 16. Joan takes credit for teaching him to count. He loved to count. And he belligerently and persistently demanded of his sister:

What's more? What's the more?! When does it end?

I mentioned this prophetic tale to Conway. Scowling, he offered some advice:

Don't trust a word Joan says. She always *exaggerates!* The entire family knows it.

Not long after these discussions, Conway and his sister and I stood before their family home in Liverpool, at 8 Fairfield Close, a cul-de-sac, on an overcast September afternoon. By trundling Conway across the Atlantic, I hoped to excavate some more reliable memories. In the event, the Conway family home was there but not there, disguised in fake stone veneer. "Wouldn't recognize it, would ya?" said Joan, who with her short postcancer pixie hair resembled Dame Judi Dench. Meanwhile, Conway's 10-year-old rascal Gareth, also along for the ride on this nostalgia road trip, poked his father's cane down the sewer grate and fished up thick black goopy sludge. And that was that, ho hum, no point in lingering. The Conway family cul-de-sac was memorable only for being a dead end.

⊿ ▢ ⬙ ⬡ ⬢

Our tour of times past also included Conway's old high school, the Holt High School for Boys, and a classmate, Peter Evennett, joined us for the visit. A retired professor of zoology at the University of Leeds, Evennett is also the honorary archivist of the Royal Microscopical Society, and he turned out to be a decent de facto archivist of Conway's adolescence. As soon as they set eyes on each other, Evennett started in with rapid-fire trivia from bygone days, putting Conway on the defensive:

I can't remember anything!!

Evennett remembered John as the school's star mathematician. "You came to school one day with a thing made out of split cane, stuck together with Chatterton's Compound, which is something your father doubtless had at home, black sticky stuff, and you told me it was a 3-dimensional representation of a 4-dimensional cube. Do you remember that?"

No. But it sounds likely.

Conway had not learned about 4-dimensional cubes in math class. The math teacher, Mr. Malone, lent him his copy of *Mathematical Recreations and Essays*, the classic by W. W. Rouse Ball, and updated by Donald Coxeter, who added a full chapter on polyhedra. Conway also got his hands on Coxeter's *Regular Polytopes*, polytopes being multisided geometric figures in any dimension. In 0 dimensions there is 1 polytope, the dot, a solitary point. In 1 dimension there is only the line segment. In 2 dimensions there are an infinite number of regular polygons, and as Coxeter summarized, "Everyone is acquainted with some of the regular polygons: the equilateral triangle which Euclid constructs in his first proposition, the square which confronts us all over the civilized world, the pentagon which can be obtained by making a simple knot in a strip of paper and pressing it carefully flat, the hexagon of the snowflake, and so on." In 3 dimensions there are precisely 5 regular polyhedra, the Platonic solids, admired for their symmetry, particularly by Conway. And here again, Conway insists one can't do better than to consult Coxeter. "The early history of these polyhedra is lost in the shadows of antiquity.

To ask who first constructed them is almost as futile as to ask who first used fire." Coxeter also mentioned that Euclid wrote his book *The Elements* not as a treatise on geometry per se, but rather for the more specialized purpose of supplying devotees with the necessary steps for building all of the 5 regular solids. Euclid begins *The Elements* with a construction for an equilateral triangle and ends with the dodecahedron. The young Conway made it his business to retrace Euclid's steps in *The Elements* from beginning to end, assimilating the proof for how and why there are 5 and only 5 regular polyhedra.

It's really quite easy.

It hinges on fitting together regular shapes within the confines of a given space. Conway explained it to me when he'd just returned from the barber, and he noted that while being sheared to within an inch of his life in the space of about 30 minutes, he had managed to fit in calls from no fewer than 3 women.

Just like the good old days!

In the mathematical exercise at hand we were trying to fit 1-dimensional regular polygons together around a vertex in the limited space of 360 degrees—the mathy crux of it is all in angles.

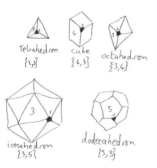

Teliahedron {3,3}   cube {4,3}   octahedron {3,4}

icosahedron {3,5}   dodecahedron {5,3}

In order to form a regular polyhedron, the angles of the component polygons can't sum to 360 degrees or more. The angles of an equilateral triangle are each 60 degrees, so 3 of them total 180 degrees. And if you arrange a total of 4 triangles, 3 around each of 3 vertices, this way you get a tetrahedron. From the regular triangle we get 3 of the Platonic solids—in addition to the tetrahedron, we get the octahedron and the icosahedron. Squares give us the cube, and the regular pentagon gives us the dodecahedron, the fifth and last regular solid. So that's Euclid's argument. There are only 5 regular polyhedra. But then do I understand *why* there are only 5? I can prove it. But *why* is there a proof? I don't know. Do I understand why, if 2 angle bisectors of a triangle have the same length, then the triangle is isosceles? That's a trivial piece of geometry, the Steiner-Lehmus theorem, and it is peculiarly hard. Most proofs of this theorem are indirect—instead of proving that it has to be true, you prove it cannot be false. I call my proof the Schizoid Scissors . . .

Moving right along, and progressing from the 3-dimensional regular polyhedra to the hyperdimensional regular polytopes, in 4 dimensions there are only 6 regular polytopes. But again, why?

Well, apart from the difficulty of understanding how 4-dimensional space can even exist in the first place, once you've accepted that, it's just the same argument. You can fit a certain number of 3-dimensional solids around an edge—in 3 dimensions it's around a vertex, but in 4 dimensions it's around an edge—with a bit of extra room, a bit of rattle, and this rattle you get rid of by folding it down and making it a finite polytope. Instead of triangles and squares, you ask how many tetrahedra or cubes you can stick together at a vertex. The answer is 4 tetrahedra, giving you the simplex, and 4 cubes, giving you the hypercube. So you get the picture. If you understand Euclid's proof in the 3-dimensional case, it's the same proof in the 4- and 5- and 6- and 7- and 8-dimensional cases. In 5 dimensions, there are only 3 finite regular polytopes. In 6 dimensions, 3 again, and it keeps on being 3, 3, 3, 3. Forever.

Actually envisioning polytopes in these abstract dimensions is a more troublesome matter. As Coxeter said, "We can never fully comprehend them by direct observation. In attempting to do so, however, we seem to peep through a chink in the wall of our physical limitations, into a new world of dazzling beauty. Such an escape from the turbulence of ordinary life will perhaps help to keep us sane." In 1955, during Conway's second-to-last year of high school, ordinary or not-so-ordinary life included the film *Blackboard Jungle*, featuring the hit single "Rock Around the Clock"; the FDA's approval of the Salk polio vaccine; Churchill's resignation; the signing of the Warsaw Treaty on Friendship, Cooperation, and Mutual Assistance; the beginning of the Vietnam War; and the launch of the Space Race, with both the United States and

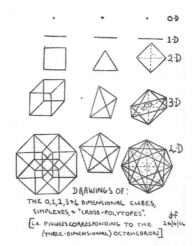

DRAWINGS OF:
THE 0,1,2,3+4 DIMENSIONAL CUBES,
SIMPLEXES, + "CROSS-POLYTOPES".
[i.e. FIGURES CORRESPONDING TO THE
(THREE-DIMENSIONAL) OCTAHEDRON]

Russia building ballistic missiles. In April 1955, an article by Conway appeared in the *Holt School Magazine,* titled "n-Dimensional Regular Polytopes," illustrated with original Conway diagrams but, in his view, containing no original Conway thought; he was channeling Coxeter.

By the next year, according to the magazine's March 1956 issue, Conway was secretary of the Science Society. He reported on his own opening of the society's term with a lecture on calendars and their history: "Conway gave the day's date in most of the chronological systems in use at present, and in many ancient ones . . ." And later in the term he gave a lecture on "Unusual Atmospheric Phenomena." There were no reports of his displaying any interest in the chess or badminton clubs, nor the debating, literary, film, philatelic or aeronautical societies. There was no mention of him on the athletics pages. Conway has never gone in for sports.

> That's true, yes. I believe in exercise: it exists. Do you know that saying
> from Jerome K. Jerome? He wrote *Three Men in a Boat and Idle*
> *Thoughts of an Idle Fellow.* He said: "I love work. I can sit and watch it
> for hours."

Back on the nostalgia trip, Conway's classmate Peter Evennett pulled out his laptop and put on a slide show of photos he'd taken at high school with his Voigtländer Vito B, narrating with a quiz of who's who. "Now then, who can you work out there?"

> Oh god. Don't ask *me.*

Conway was hard pressed to work out himself. Variations on the same continued for the entire visit. Conway grumped about something else he didn't remember, which only greased the memory of his friend.

Conway is top.

"That reminds me," said Evennett, "in one of Mr. Malone's maths lessons he asked you a question, and you said,"

I know, sir. You tell me!

"You cheeky bugger."

But here Conway offered a correction.

No, that was the physics teacher. And he got really mad.

That was as good as it got. Beset with one too many do-you-remember questions, Conway went boom.

I REMEMBER NOTHING!

And he had no interest in remembering. It was as if he'd deliberately wasted no brainpower on committing things to memory over the years, just as he'd wasted no energy on exercising. At best, his memories were like his cane, stowed in the overhead compartment during our plane ride—when he reaches in for retrieval, he finds the item in question has shifted during flight. Our tour of his high school turned out to be about as revealing as our visit to the family home. The main auditorium was now the library, and much of the old school had been demolished to make way for an addition. On our way out at the end of the school day, by happenstance Evennett got talking with the school's math teacher, Lynn Gilford, as she headed to the parking lot, and he thoughtfully made a fuss. "John's a world-famous mathematician, from Princeton, and he's a Fellow of the Royal Society and all sorts of things," said Evennett. "Oh, right?" It wasn't ringing any bells for Mrs. Gilford, who's been teaching math for 40 years. Evennett gave her a hint. "Ever heard of the Game of Life?" he asked. "Yes," she said. He nodded in Conway's direction. "You're joking!" Conway smiled wanly and kept silent. His ego could allow itself to be at most slightly tickled, seeing as Mrs. Gilford had recognized him only for the very bane of his existence.

3.

GYMNASTICS

What mad pursuit? What struggle to escape?
What pipes and timbrels? What wild ecstasy?

—JOHN KEATS

All, however, was not lost, since on a meta level the machinations of the research trip proved illuminating. To rewind the movie reel a bit, Conway and Gareth and I had set off for England about a week before, in September 2009. In an impressive display of parenting, Conway managed to keep Gareth entertained for the 7-hour flight, thanks mostly to the entertainment console with in-flight Sudoku. Supper was served, the cabin lights dimmed, and a voluminous quiet filled the plane, pierced by cheers and jeers from their Sudoku marathon.

> That cannot be a 5, Gareth! There's a 5 over there! . . . Garrrreth. No. It has to be a 7! It *has* to be a 7!

Once we'd landed, Conway, still a British citizen, sprinted through customs with Gareth. I came upon them wrestling with a candy machine in the concourse and we found our bus to Cambridge. Walloped for a while into jet-lagged sleep, Conway revived when we reached the outskirts of town. He started telling tales, the first about the "John Conway Appreciation Society," which we'll hear more about later. We disembarked from the bus at Parker's Piece, a grassy parallelogram of park, and there waiting was our welcoming party, 3 of Conway's 4 adult daughters from his first marriage—Susie, a community gardener and teacher in Nottingham, Annie, who works in Spain as an English teacher, and Ellie, an engineer near Cambridge who enjoys cryptic crosswords. We set out for our accommodations, walking along 1 of 2 paths that bisect the park on the diagonal. Where the paths crossed stood a solitary lamppost bearing a graffiti inscription of its nickname, "Reality Checkpoint." Thus began the research trip.

Cobblestone streets and Gothic academic castles led the way into the heart of town, the university neighborhoods carved through by the River Cam and the bucolic Backs. We checked in to our rooms at Conway's alma mater, Gonville and Caius College (the university being a public body comprised of affiliated departments and faculties and institutes, as well as an unaffiliated federation of 31 privately governed colleges). Then Conway's daughters started organizing his week over an alfresco lunch at a patio restaurant on Trinity Street. "Dad, is there anything you want to do?" asked Annie.

Let me ask my social secretary. Is there anything I want to do?

In addition to the Liverpool trip, there were 2 main items on the itinerary: a reunion with his coauthors of *The Atlas of Finite Groups* and a visit with his best friend at Cambridge, Mike Guy. I'd been warned that meeting Mike might be problematic. Mike had taken to a hermit's life. His father, Richard Guy, another of Conway's coauthors, provided some advice. "As far as contacting Mike is concerned, he is a complete recluse. He has no phone. Since he retired he has no access to e-mail (he didn't reply to it even when he had). He has a house in Orchard Street. . . . He often reads letters sent there but never replies (though one of his nieces successfully got a reply by enclosing a stamped, addressed postcard with a multiple-choice question on it). Louise (my wife) occasionally makes contact by ringing the Champion of the Thames in the evening. This is the pub he visits fairly regularly, but I have the impression that the proprietress isn't very keen on fetching him to the phone and he's not very keen on coming to it." So it would be catch as catch can. And then as we finished lunch, Conway's daughters started squealing at a passerby: "Mike!" "Mike!" "That's Mike!"

It was just like old times, as Annie remarked. She'd think to herself, "There goes somebody looking strange. Ergo, it must a friend of Dad's!"—one of his "sum chums," as his daughters called them. This strange somebody glanced at the group of us and kept going until he caught sight of Conway, whereupon he joined the gathering. Nattily dressed, he also looked a bit ratty, the point of his tie frayed as if it had caught a few times on a cutting board (he is something of a gourmet cook). Despite this dishabille, he was a pleasure to behold. Gorgeous in his youth, he now had a lion's mane of salt-and-pepper hair. And in spite of his mathematical gifts—Conway considered Mike the better mathematician—he never earned his Ph.D. He had given up pure mathematics for the even more antisocial field of computing. He worked nights as a technical officer at the computer lab, where back in the day he'd often run jobs for Conway.

All these years later, it was as if they'd last seen each other the day before yesterday. They were clearly glad to see each other but didn't have much to say. For my benefit, Mike explained that his first name is actually John, but when he first met Conway Mike decided there should be only 1 John, so Mike went by his middle name instead. And he recounted some of their many exploits. Together they had explored everything under the sun, including 4-dimensional polytopes of the Archimedean rather than Platonic variety—the Platonic solids have all the same vertices and the same faces, while the Archimedean solids'

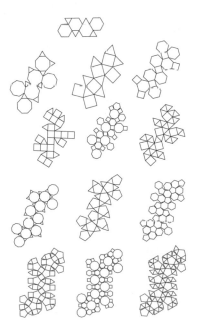

Nets that fold up to form the Archimedean solids.

vertices are all the same arrangements but their faces are various combinations of the regular polygons. Archimedes enumerated all the 3-dimensional solids that came to bear his name, and Conway and Guy enumerated all the 4-dimensional Archimedean polytopes. By their own idiosyncratic method they duplicated previous discoveries: all the polytopes they found had been found before, except one, the grand antiprism.

It would have been a bit disappointing if everything had already been found.

Especially since the problem of enumerating the 4-dimensional Archimedean polytopes was not all that interesting. Why bother, then?

Because it was there. Because we could.

Similar reasoning motivated them on a rainy afternoon to do another enumeration, this time of all the possible solutions to the Soma cube, a 3-dimensional jigsaw puzzle of 7 pieces, each piece comprised of either 3 or 4 cubes, the goal being to fit the 7 pieces together to make one unified 3-by-3-by-3 cube. Seems easy enough, but deceptively so. "Problems worthy of attack / Prove their worth by hitting back"—that ditty is among thousands composed by the Soma cube's creator, the Danish mathematician and inventor Piet Hien.

Do you know his grooks? His little poems, grooks he called them. I remember this line: "A healthy sex life mitigates the lust for other sports." Many of his poems were preoccupied with the bomb, as everybody was in the fifties and sixties. Anyway, he designed this puzzle, a puzzle that doesn't go away after you've solved it, because then there's another way to solve it, and another and another . . .

That rainy Cambridge afternoon, Conway and Guy found 240 ways to fit the Soma cube together, the complete solution. They mapped all the possibilities, with directions, provided you can find at least a single solution to start with, and provided you can find it on their map. Conway pecked out the map in a Balanchinean dance with his typewriter, producing terrain of such complexity that it could easily be mistaken for a subway map of Tokyo.

Tinkering all over tarnation, the pair of them also made what one might call artisanal computers, engineered using knotted embroidery string, marbles, or water. The list could continue, but those were the highlights from a beautiful friendship. This meeting with Mike having been arranged by the gods, the question now was how to meet again? What would be the best way to get in touch? "Don't," Mike said. We set a date for Tuesday next at the pub.

And onward with our itinerary we went. Preparing for the Liverpool road trip, Annie had bought some groceries, getting a 6-pack of Mars Bars for us inconsequentials, and for Conway some bananas— "Something I can feed Father that won't make him go pop." (His favorite snack used to be a cheese sandwich: 2 pieces of cheese with a slab of butter in between.) His daughter Rosie, who lives near Cambridge and runs a small garden farm and is active in environmental issues, had taken the day off work and offered to drive—200 miles, 4 hours. After our stops at the Conway family home and the high school, our caravan made its way 20 minutes south of the city to Conway's sister Joan's home in Chester, where we could all have a relaxed visit. Upon arrival, Conway was confused.

I'm not quite sure WHY I'm here. What am I doing?

The agenda at Joan's was to sort through the counterfactuals, all the stories Joan had told me that her brother dismissed as nonsense. For example, when he was about 7 and she 17, he divined a trick: give him a date, any date, such as March 14, 1879, and he'd instantaneously pronounce what day of the week it was (in this case, Friday). All of a sudden her little brother could do this trick, and then just as suddenly he stopped. He would no longer show off to Joan's friends, calculating their birthdays. "I thought he stopped because he'd forgotten. It was a while before I realized that he decided he didn't want to do it anymore. Because he didn't want to be shown up as being a bit of an oddity." Like the story of the boy who wanted to keep on counting—asking What's the more? When does it end?—this story, when I'd asked Conway about it earlier, did not sit well.

It's nonsense!

He didn't say that in front of Joan. But according to Conway the day-of-the-week trick did not descend upon him with divine inspiration when he was 7. He designed a laborious algorithm when he was about 15. Getting brother and sister together in the same room would help clarify these contradictions, or so I hoped. Joan's place was dark and dank and packed to the rafters. John hoards knowledge, Joan hoards stuff, including a lot of books. Bookshelves lined walls in every room, and shelfless books, stacked horizontally, vertically, and diagonally, marched around the foyer, climbed the staircase, rounded the landing, and ascended to the attic. Conway and Gareth overnighted in the attic after dinner out at a restaurant with a sizable gathering of extended family. The next morning a small subset reconvened in the living room, a shabby-chic Victorian parlor with a blazing gas fireplace and a sideboard overrun with glass and pewter receptacles of all shapes and sizes stuffed with silk fans, feathers, dried grasses, artificial fruit.

Joan rolled out a miscellany of family facts and folklore and after a while the conversation came around to her brother's prodigious skill at naming the day of the week for any given date. "He was 7. I used to show him off to my friends," she said. "I asked him how he did it and he said he didn't know. My clever little brother . . ." I interrupted and asked Conway for his account. He was paying no attention, sitting outside the group, head down, nose in a book of KenKen (yet more arithmetic puzzles, similar to Sudoku). He refused to lift his gaze.

Don't ask me now.

Joan continued on without him. Tea was served, with crackers and cheese. Eventually Annie approached the social reprobate, head still buried in his KenKen. "Dad, we've got to be going soon. So you could take an active interest."

Are you suggesting I put this down?

He kept on with his KenKen. Joan single-handedly kept the stories coming, and only sporadically he piped up,

This is a bitter failure!

He had blown a fuse, finally fed up with the family folklore. No, actually, he was lamenting all his mistakes with the KenKen.

I got everything wrong!

His oblivious mood broke when Annie planted an irresistible query. She wondered whether anyone among this assemblage of relations could do the same tricks with their tongue that her dad could do, and she prodded him to demonstrate. For this he was game.

Wait till I've got the cracker crumbs off my tongue . . .

And then he put his tongue on exhibit, tying it into a "Twist," contorting it into a "Cloverleaf," oscillating between "Thick" and "Thin," and an undulating "Wave." He turned my way and (re)told me the story—one among his repertoire of pre-programmed subroutine tales that he releases whenever the opportunity arises—of how he'd learned to do tongue gymnastics.

I was a student at Cambridge. And I got the *Reader's Digest.* And, you know, it has these things like "It Pays to Increase Your Word Power" and stuff. Well, this time in that spot it had "Are You a Tongue Gymnast?" It said researchers at the University of Maryland had been investigating and found that the ability to do this was hereditary. It gave these 4 exercises and the proportions of people who could do them all—I think the cloverleaf was one in 400. And then it said, so far, nobody has been found who could do all 4.

Naturally, Conway took to standing in front of the bathroom mirror and training his tongue.

You know, it's hard to think what message to send your tongue to get it to do this thing.

After about 3 hours, he found he could do all 4. He wrote a letter to *Reader's Digest* saying he was their man. Nothing happened for 6 months or so.

Then one day I was in my college room with a bunch of friends, toasting muffins against the hot gas fire, and there came a knock on my door, at D2 St. Michael's Court. I opened the door and it turned out to be a reporter and a cameraman from *Reader's Digest*.

An interview for another assignment brought them to Cambridge and their editor asked them to check out this oddball student as well. They said, "We understand you're a tongue gymnast?" He invited them in. The cameraman set up his white umbrellas. John put on a gold-medal performance of tongue gymnastics. Then they all shook hands, business concluded. Once the magazine crew had left, Conway and his friends collapsed in giggles. They looked out the window to see that the same had happened to the crew. Conway kept a lookout, but he never noticed an article in the pages of *Reader's Digest*.

Having taught himself these tongue contortions as a teenager, he dined out on the trick for ages. At a party in Montreal many years later he met a woman who could also do all 4 positions. She was known as "God's girlfriend," not so much for her tongue-twisting prowess as because she was gorgeous and happened to be dating a man with the initials G.O.D. Based on their mutual abilities, plus Conway's ability to be struck dumb by a beautiful woman, he tried to woo away God's gorgeous girlfriend.

I sort of thought it was obvious that she should leave G.O.D. and come to me, but she didn't in the end.

No matter, that night he stole someone else's girlfriend instead. And while the story of the tongue gymnastics had almost everyone giving it a go in the parlor, Joan meanwhile seized upon the stealing-girlfriends story. It triggered something in her memory and she blurted out, "Australian lady!"

Which Australian lady?

"Weren't you one of her gentleman friends at one time? I'm trying to think of her name, she was well known . . ." Conway did his best to ignore this query, nose-diving back into his KenKen. But we shall return to the question of which Australian lady. Suffice it to say, Joan did not let it alone. She did not leave that or any other avenue unexplored. We had to wriggle to get away on time. We had to get home for the first birthday party of Conway's daughter's daughter's daughter—his first great-grand-daughter, Molly, though he is vain and prefers not to utter the "greats" and "grands." The siblings' parting was as perfunctory as their initial meeting, with no emotional frivolity, no embrace. "We don't go in for a lot of kissing," Joan said, adding that this might be their final visit. "The older we get, each meeting could be the last. But we're not sentimental people. We know we all have to die sometime."

Once the car windows were rolled up after the drive-away wave, an enthusiastic debriefing ensued.

I honestly think that when Joan tells a story, an interesting story, the probability that it is true is less than $\frac{1}{2}$. I really think it is strictly more likely to be false than true. That might be a bit unkind, so you can up it to $\frac{1}{2}$ if you like. Since you can't check it, it doesn't damn well matter.

The next morning, back in Cambridge, he chewed over a few of his sister's tall tales. Among the juiciest was that during a visit to Cambridge she'd had an "interesting conversation" with Stephen Hawking, and somehow there was a helicopter involved.

I don't believe this story at all. I really think it's totally invented. I mean, I can't disprove it. But then that is partly the point. She doesn't tell stories that you can disprove easily. Within the family, we know she exaggerates anything. And the stories just get better every year.

Then he smiled, and paused, and looked sheepish.

Well, I do it myself. I know I do. I've been trying to remember things as they were but it's very hard. Sometimes I remember the story better than the facts.

There's a story about Conway's undergraduate career, wherein he and his chums are walking along cobblestoned Trinity Street in October 1957, putting up posters announcing WINNIE IS COMING! The posters went up along King's Parade, Trumpington Street, the fence around Great St. Mary's Church, and scattershot about town:

WINNIE IS WAITING FOR YOU

WATCH OUT FOR WINNIE!

ARE YOU READY FOR WINNIE?

This was 2 decades or so after Alan Turing booted up the computer age with his Automatic Computing Engine, aka ACE, and from there the computer's lineage degenerates into a tangled timeline of acronyms: ENIAC, EDVAC, EDSAC, MANIAC. And then Conway contributed WINNIE, a water computer, a "Water Initiated Numerical Number Integrating Engine." Though it's unlikely it was "Numerical Number"; perhaps it was "Water Initiated Nonchalantly Numerical Integrating Engine," or some such. Conway designed WINNIE based on his close observation of urinal-flushing mechanics. Standing about 6 feet tall, she was engineered from plastic cups, siphons, and circuitous plumbing.

How it worked was this: Standing on the stool, I'd pour 1 unit of water into the cup at the very top. This cup would then be $\frac{1}{2}$ full, and the water would just stay in there, and that indicated the binary notation "1" and registered the numerical value 1.

Then I'd pour in another unit of water into the same cup, filling it up and causing all the water to run out via a little tube halfway up at the side of the cup—that's how a siphon works, when the water starts moving out all of it flows out, and it would all runneth over, $\frac{1}{2}$ of it going into the cup waiting below, indicating now the binary notation "10," for the numerical value 2. Pour in another unit, and the first cup again registered "1" and

With WINNIE, 1957.

the second still holds "1," which gives us a grand total of "11," or 3. Another unit made the first 2 cups empty with the third cup registering "1,"
giving 4. And so on. WINNIE could count to 127, or 64 + 32 + 16 + 8 + 4
+ 2 + 1, or 1111111.

She could also add and multiply. Though as soon as the product of any
calculation exceeded her limit, she started peeing—and in fact she peed
off $\frac{1}{2}$ a cup when any cup received its second allotment and ran over to
the next cup, that was the operating principle. But the peeing happened
en masse at the end. All at once all the cups would runneth over in a
domino effect waterfall, emptying all the cups and clearing all the reser-
voirs to 0 as all the water flushed into a holding tank on the floor. At least
that was where the water was supposed to go.

There was an unfortunate incident when Conway exhibited WINNIE
at the Societies' Fair, the annual fall fair where the university clubs
showed off their wares in the hopes of recruiting new members. Conway
belonged to 2 Cambridge clubs: the Archimedeans, the university math
club, and the New Pythagoreans, the math club associated with his college and about 5 other colleges, including Girton, a women's college
(there were 4 women's colleges at the time).

That's important, the girls. We had to pull in some girls!

Conway and his water computer represented the Archimedeans at the fair, though the unfortunate thing was that WINNIE peed and caused a flood and destroyed a nice piece of the Guildhall's parquet flooring. The Societies Fair was thereafter held elsewhere, in the Corn Exchange. But WINNIE was a popular exhibit, earning a write-up in the Cambridge newspaper. She was a "proof of principle" experiment, an experiment conducted to see if Conway's harebrained idea was workable. Hypothesis: If a urinal-flushing doohickey is properly repurposed, it will power a binary computer. Conclusion: Yes, it will.

WINNIE also provides proof that Conway's laziness doctrine goes way back. His raison d'être as an undergraduate was noodling (as distinct from canoodling; and on that front, he left his virginity back home in Liverpool). He kept busy, but not with what he was supposed to be busy with. His fellow mathematics student David Bailin found Conway intimidating when they met on their first day at Cambridge, since within minutes Conway tackled him with an exposition on the principles and precepts of his very own knot theory. As a teenager he'd studied and enumerated a whole lot of knots—roughly 4,000—specifically the knots having 11 or fewer crossings. This extended the existing knot tables considerably. And he did this all by hand, though he later noted in a paper that the enumeration process was "eminently suitable for machine computation."

Knot theory originated in physics as an (erroneous) model for the atom, but since mathematicians took it up, knot theory has been applied not only to physics but also to biology and chemistry. Conway's theory dated to high school, when he saw a popular math book with a picture of a nice curvy knot, maybe a trefoil knot, and following the picture an explanatory equation:

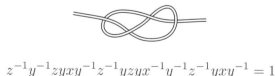

$$z^{-1}y^{-1}zyxy^{-1}z^{-1}yzyx^{-1}y^{-1}z^{-1}yxy^{-1} = 1$$

It intrigued him that something so simple should require such a gnarly equation. He took it as a challenge to learn the history of knots, the what, the why, and the how, which soon gets rather metaphysical.

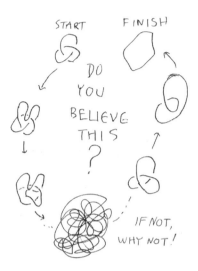

Well, yes, it was a long time before anybody proved that string actually did get knotted. A cord in a bag gets tangled, but does it get knotted? A knot is a knot if it cannot be unknotted, given certain circumstances. It's a tricky problem even to define what "knot" means, let alone determining if a knot is a knot. Here's the problem. Let me draw a sequence . . .

The question is, can this be done? Can we go from "Start" with a knot to "Finish" with an unknot, as the circle is called, without breaking the string? Do you believe this is possible? Do you believe I can get from this trefoil knot, the messy one with, say, a million crossings, to the unknot without breaking the string? If not, why not?

Maybe we can undo this mess midway; maybe there is a terribly complicated way to undo this and it is not a knot. Maybe you can change a knot continuously into an unknot without breaking it or untying the ends. But it takes 1,000 moves. And nobody has ever found the right moves. It is really rather difficult to prove, mathematically, that you can't untangle it.

Any knot in 3 dimensions can easily be unknotted if it is allowed to pass into 4 dimensions, of course! But another difficulty in knot theory is how to tell 2 knots apart. For instance, look at these knots, which are cast in steel medallions on facing gates leading into Cambridge's new Newton Institute for Mathematical Sciences:

The first 2 knots having the same Alexander-Conway polynomial as the unknot.

The knot on the left is the mutation of the knot on the right. Conway discovered the knot on the right. The knot on the left was later discovered by Osaka University's Shin'ichi Kinoshita and Hidetaka Terasaka.

> From my point of view it's a bit of a pity that Kinoshita discovered the other. There is really no difference between these 2 knots. But it's a hard problem, determining if 2 knots are the same. Maybe you could take the trefoil knot down along a funny path to come out to the figure-8 knot . . . ? My interest in knots is really aesthetic, almost sensual. I used to get a great deal of pleasure from drawing knots. So many geometric things are straight lines, flat sides, pointy edges. Knots curve nicely.

Bailin, on the receiving end of Conway's infatuation with knots, wasn't sure what to think. "For a while, I actually wondered if I was doing the right subject," says Bailin, who went on to a career as a physicist at the University of Sussex, with a special interest in string theory. "Because here was this guy who was already an independent mathematician. He had all sorts of interests, but the knot theory I particularly remember. Of course, I subsequently discovered that I was the normal one, and he was abnormal."

"He was always a bit odd," concurs another classmate, Gordon Lord, now a professor emeritus in engineering at Oxford. "He did odd things." He ran an ad in the London *Times*—"Gentleman, starting new religion, seeks converts"—and a few dozen letters came back, one saying, "That is a very good idea. Please let me in on the ground floor." He dreamt up bets for his gullible friend John Basterfield, successfully betting that Basterfield couldn't climb a lamppost on Green Street, a street with no lampposts, and that Basterfield couldn't slip a 10-bob note between pages 7 and 8 of any book (doesn't seem like much of a challenge?—try it), and that Basterfield couldn't think of any 4-letter word in the English language that ended in "-eny" and when Basterfield couldn't, he had him stand on a table and declare "I, John Basterfield, solemnly deny there is any 4-letter word in the English language ending in '-eny.'"

Another of the predilections and preoccupations that kept Conway from his studies was a flexagon binge. It began in December 1956, 2 months into first term, when Martin Gardner published his seminal article in *Scientific American*. "Flexagons," Gardner explained, "are paper polygons, folded from straight or crooked strips of paper, which have the fascinating property of changing their faces when they are flexed." He went on to describe how the "mysteries of flexigation" were discovered (at Princeton, as it happened), and Conway and his friends probed the mysteries further still, with an orgy of flexigation breaking out in Conway's room. Gardiner had focused on the hexaflexagon, a hexagon divided into 6 triangles, and he noted that nobody had found a theory for tetraflexagons, made of 4 square faces. Conway and company set up an assembly line, cutting and taping tetraflexagons together, labeling the square faces so as to track and map each face's migrations. After pinching and pushing and exhausting a tetraflexagon's possibilities, Conway would lob it across the room into a large grape barrel for a wastebasket, and onward the investigations went with yet another tetraflexagon. Barrels and barrels of tetraflexagons later, they found the theory but never bothered to publish.

Falling roughly coextensive with the flexagon furor were the Hungarian Revolution and the Suez Crisis, both occurring in the midst of Conway's first term and inspiring student marches in which he partook. During his second term, his noodling manifested in a meticulous reading of Coxeter's edition of *Mathematical Recreations and Essays*, the loaner he hadn't returned to his high school math teacher, now full of marginalia and frayed at the spine from relentless manhandling. On a Thursday in March, 66 days into 1957, with the end of term and exams fast approaching, Conway took the time to write Coxeter a letter:

Dear Sir,
  Over the past year or so my copy of your edition of Ball's "Mathematical Recreations" has accumulated an astonishing number of notes and

some corrections. Most of these can hardly be said to be suitable for pub-lication in later reprints, but one or two may seem important. . . .

On page 5 he closed with a query about a 4-dimensional polytope:

My absolutely last remark is a question. Where can I find the requisite in-formation required to draw {5,3,3}, or do I have to work out the details for myself? I should be very thankful if you could supply me with some accessible information.

Yours hopefully,
J. H. Conway

The letter now resides in Coxeter's archives at the University of To-ronto Thomas Fisher Rare Book Library. At the very top, in Coxeter's hand, the letter bears the notation "Answered!" Coxeter's reply, deliri-ously received and dearly cherished, has since gone the way of many things that really matter to Conway: lost.

And so our young protagonist's formal studies proceeded lackadaisi-cally, lacking vigor and focus.

Did I ever tell you about the word "lackadaisically"? It dates to about 1600, from people who went around saying "Oh, lack a day, lack a day," bewailing that it wasn't a good day.

He claims to have attended lectures. He definitely attended lectures by visitors. Paul Erdős visited intermittently and gave his talks on "un-solved problems." One of those unsolved problems motivated Conway's paper "On the Distribution of Values of Angles Determined by Copla-nar Points," coauthored with Mike Guy and another Cambridge mate, Hallard Croft, as well as Erdős. This paper gave Conway his Erdős num-ber of 1 (an Erdős number being somewhat like the "6 degrees of Kevin Bacon," but measuring the collaborative connections between mathe-maticians and Erdős—if you failed to collaborate with Erdős himself, but you manage to publish a paper with Conway, then you get an Erdős number 2, and so on). Coxeter also visited Cambridge when Conway was an undergraduate, giving a talk proving the particular cases of a theorem and lamenting that he didn't have a uniform proof that could apply to all cases at once. Conway left the lecture hall and went on his way, trying to work out this problem in his head, and as he crossed Trumpington Street the answer hit him, as did a garbage truck. With the shouts of the garbagemen following him, Conway limped back to the lecture hall, where Coxeter was still taking questions from stragglers.

> And I said, "You nearly killed me!" I told him the story. And ever since then, I've called this theorem "the Murder Weapon."

These extracurricular theorems and papers aside, for the most part Conway did no discernible work. This did not deter him from further cheekiness with his professors. An unmemorable professor of analysis once went on and on and on about something called "Dedekind sections" and none of the students understood a thing and then Conway stood up and said:

Could you manage to prove for us from all that what 2 + 2 make?

The professor retorted, "If you don't know what 2 + 2 make, you shouldn't be in this university." And indeed, toward the end of his first year, his friends bet on whether he would pass or fail his exams. He passed, and handily. He sailed through and earned a first on Part I of the mathematics Tripos—Cambridge's legendarily daunting 3-part course with exams spread over 3 years.

A professor who managed to hold Conway's attention was Abram Samoilovitch Besicovitch, a Russian émigré who spent much of his career at Cambridge. Conway's name became well known among all the math undergraduates because he was always winning the small prizes that Besicovitch offered for solving difficult problems he set and posted on the Arts School notice board. Conway first had him for a seminar course, a small class in which 6 or so students gave the lectures and Besicovitch, the Rouse Ball Professor, sat back and acted as an adjudicating master of ceremonies. When it was Conway's turn to lecture, he decided to prove that π was transcendental—meaning it is not a root of any polynomial non-0 integral coefficients. He took a classical proof from the nineteenth century and tightly compressed this already truncated piece of mathematics into the strict time limit of 60 minutes. When he finished, managing by the skin of his teeth, he looked eagerly at his professor. "Pity," pronounced Besicovitch, explaining that he much preferred the longer proof. Besicovitch instilled fear during his lectures, demanding of his students, "YOU! What was I going to say next?" He also elicited fear for a game he played, a traditional Russian card game, Svoyi Kosiri or "One's Own Trumps." Besicovitch modified the game to make it particularly unforgiving, and thereafter it was known as Besicovitch's Game. Only 2 people had ever beaten him: John E. Littlewood, who occupied the Rouse Ball professorship before Besicovitch, and Harold Davenport, who occupied the position after. Conway and his friends, set on wasting time, paid visits to Besicovitch at his rooms in Trinity College, played him at this game, and never won.

> He would do a sort of simultaneous display. He'd walk around tables and make his moves. And we never beat him. . . . It's a frightening game, in a way. It has the most negative feedback of any game. In other words, it's not a question of making a good move. All moves are bad. You just try to choose the moves that are the least bad.

In his second year, Conway again did very little work, but he did redesign a sundial atop the Gate of Honour tower, and he worked part time as a postman, delivering the mail by bicycle (he relearned to ride in privacy under the cover of darkness, since he'd never learned properly as a boy). And there were a few more forays into activism. The Campaign for Nuclear Disarmament convened the inaugural "Ban the Bomb" march in London's Trafalgar Square over Easter weekend in 1958, and Conway, a pacifist from an early age, participated in a local protest that followed, getting himself arrested with a group of other students. He answered questions put to him by a magistrate and was jailed for 11 days.

> I was imprisoned in the same prison in which John Bunyan was imprisoned about 300 hundred years earlier. . . . I don't think it was literally the same building Bunyan had been in, but it was a pretty old building. So I have a fellow feeling for John Bunyan. Of course, his book is called *The Pilgrim's Progress* and his pilgrim is called Christian. I am not religious, certainly not

so religious as John Bunyan was. So, in some sense, the book is alien to me, except that I recognize the "Slough of Despond," a phrase he used to refer to being depressed.

For Bunyan, the miry slough is "a place as cannot be mended . . . as the sinner is awakened about his lost condition, there ariseth in his soul many fears, and doubts, and discouraging apprehensions, which all of them get together, and settle in this place." For Conway, at one point during his undergraduate years, this was a familiar place. He remembers trying to commit suicide by sticking his head in a gas oven. The smell of the gas so sickening, he couldn't stand it and abandoned the attempt. He can't remember the exact time period or reason for his despair. But he does recall that when the results of Part II of the Tripos exam were posted, he'd dropped to second-class standing, and on the low end of the seconds. This unnerved him, disturbed him, shook his confidence, for a time. Maybe this motivated his suicide attempt?

Could have been. Could I really have gotten so upset about it? I don't know.

At any rate, soon enough the unpleasant effect of taking a second faded. After all, students believed, at this stage, that finishing top of first class would indicate one was trying too hard, not being nearly productive enough in one's extracurricular intellectual pursuits. Ideally, one wanted to achieve a "bottom first," demonstrating a perfect economy of effort. In this regard, Conway was still on the fringe of respectability. His ego, and his indolence, bounced back.

In his third year, however, his recidivism produced deleterious and near disastrous consequences. His supervisor, Christopher Zeeman, known for using catastrophe theory in brain modeling, witnessed this firsthand. I reached Sir Christopher on the phone at his home in Woodstock, Oxfordshire. Did he remember Conway? "Very much so! I used to give him tutorials with David Fowler. They were the most fun tutorials I've ever given! They used to score off each other all the time, full of originality." What was he like back then? "Oh, he was most peculiar. He was shy and gauche." Though what really counted was that Conway had a fertile imagination. He was clever. He was also a slugabed, often making Zeeman and Fowler wait for his arrival at the tutorial. They instituted the habit of confronting the laggard in his college room. They'd open his door and, upon finding him dead asleep, each grab a leg of his bed and dump him out. He had 10 minutes to pull himself together and join them for the session, relocated to the Whim, a coffee shop located practically next door.

Toward the end of term, Zeeman pulled out practice exams from years past. Conway couldn't decipher what the questions asked, let alone how to answer. He'd been swanning around, soaking in the glorious Cambridge springtime, punting down the river and learning to swim (learning to swim by joining the Dampers Club, which took as its members those who while punting accidentally entered the River Cam fully clothed). He went on ambling walks along the riverbank with friends to a pub in the nearby hamlet of Grantchester, and there he invented a drink he named "One of Those," a lethal mix of Guinness stout and brandy. A few weeks before exams, realizing a crisis was at hand, Conway devised the strategy of "Turning Night into Day." He studied all night, slept all day, and passed with honors on Part III of the Tripos. This, however, was not so impressive for someone aspiring to a career in mathematical research. Practically everyone passed with honors. In the ranking of graduates published each year in the *Cambridge Reporter*, a mathematician of any substance was expected to have a little star beside his name indicating he'd made it through this rite of passage "With Distinction." Conway did not. The Laziness Doctrine had gotten the better of him. But how, then, did he continue as a graduate student at Cambridge? His intellectual charm had earned him a protector, that's how. "I had to make a lot of speeches to get him taken on for research," says Zeeman, who wrote a couple of letters as well. "I had to argue on his behalf to the other faculty. I told them he was a genius at pure maths, which he was."

While in Cambridge, I made efforts to take objective measure of more than just Conway's grades. Gonville and Caius College had sent out a circular announcing my research visit, and a number of the natives got in touch, willing to dish. With the noon bells ringing from Great St. Mary's Church not a block away, I arrived at the velvet-curtained office of Michael Prichard, a legal historian, who had done a stint editing the college's volumes of biographical history. Flipping through the set he kept on hand, he confirmed that Conway received his B.A. in 1959, followed by a research scholarship to get him started on his graduate studies, and in November 1962, he was elected a college fellow, receiving 1 of 2 Drosier research fellowships. Prichard had served on the college council when Conway was elected. He didn't remember anything notable about the decision to elect him, but the aftermath stuck in his mind.

Conway was installed as a fellow in a chapel ceremony in December 1962. He was invited to his first event in early January, a formal dinner known as Bishop Shaxton's Solace. His date would be his wife, since a little over a year prior, on September 6, 1961, at the Liverpool registry office, Conway, not yet 24, had quietly wed Eileen Frances Howe, 7 years his senior. His friends weren't even aware he had a steady girlfriend when he'd matter-of-factly returned from a weekend away and announced he was a married man. Soon after, he became a father. Susie was born in May 1962.

On the night of the Shaxton's Solace celebrations, at the appointed hour, the college sat down and said grace. About 30 minutes later, Conway and Eileen appeared at the entrance of the dining room. "John being John," Prichard says, "he had completely misnoted the time, or not noted it at all. So he was arriving late. And with Mrs. Conway, for whom it was the first introduction to the college. She was a bit horrified and he was a bit abashed to find that he'd got the time wrong. And then, far worse was the fact that he'd forgotten to tell the College that he was coming at all. So there was no place. The hall was completely full. The staff said, 'You're not down for dinner.' Then I saw him flee from the room." What a shame, Prichard thought, what a disappointment, for Mrs. Conway in particular. He excused himself from the dinner table and gave chase, just in time to see the couple escape through the front gate. Hollering in their direction, Prichard eventually succeeded in waylaying the Conways. He did his best to persuade them to return. "It was not an easy task, not an easy one at all," he recalls. "And frankly I can't quite remember, but I think I succeeded in getting them back. At least I have the happy memory that I got them in and we squeezed up and made room."

I heard another version of this story later that week when I met Mike Guy at the pub. He had a collection of Conway tidbits ready to recount.

Once Conway turned up in Mike's room and asked for a hammer. When Mike asked why, Conway produced a pack of tacks, epoxy glue, and the dilapidated sandals from his feet. Mike was also impressed by his friend's skills with a needle and thread. He watched him make a doll for one of his children, and another time sew a custom Klein bottle—a bottle with neither an inside nor an outside; an impossible object, somewhat like a torus but with a topological twist—using a quilting of iron-on patches, swaths of bandages, and a zipper that allowed the Klein bottle to unzip into a Möbius strip. And, Mike says, Conway was always, always doing math, and he did it frantically fast. He'd go away for the night worrying over his latest conundrum and come back the next day having worked the whole thing out. What was it like to work with Conway? "Crazy," he says. But the best tidbit, which in keeping with Mike's uncanny kismet came straight off the top and entirely without prompting, was his version of the Shaxton's Solace events. Contrary to Prichard's happy memory, Mike, who'd been deputized to babysit for Susie, remembers that the Conways had made a clean getaway. Not long after they dropped off the baby, they reappeared and explained the mix-up, and then they all went out for drinks.

Christopher Zeeman, who was in attendance at that dinner, concurs with this version of the tale. "The faster Prichard chased him, the faster Conway ran away. Ran all the way down King's Parade and escaped." Did he come back? "No, not for that dinner. He was a little bit naïve about moving into the upper echelons of academic society. Quite a few times I had to rescue him to keep him in the mainstream."

Conway made a fortuitous match for a Ph.D. adviser in Harold Davenport, considered the leader of the internationally respected British school of number theory. And while politically and socially speaking Conway was a radical, Davenport was a conservative. "All changes are for the worse," he'd say. And looking back upon his career and his charges, he said: "I had 2 very good students. Baker"—Alan Baker, later a Fields Medalist—"to whom I would give a problem and he would return with a very good solution. And Conway, to whom I would give a problem and he would return with a very good solution to another problem." At first, at Davenport's recommendation, Conway tried a number theory problem for his Ph.D. thesis. Number theory explores simple conjectures that can be extremely hard to prove. For instance, the French amateur mathematician Pierre de Fermat proved in the seventeenth century that there is only 1 number that is sandwiched directly between a square and a cube: 26, which falls between 25, a perfect square, and 27, a perfect cube. Davenport gave Conway a long-standing open problem, a devil-in-the-details problem about expressing numbers as the sum of fifth powers. The Cambridge mathematician Edward Waring devised the problem in 1770, conjecturing that every number can be expressed as the sum of a certain number of powers: every number is the sum of 4 squares, 9 cubes, 19 fourth powers, 37 fifth powers, and so on. Proofs emerged gradually. The eighteenth century's Joseph Louis Lagrange proved the 4-square theorem, and as per Conway's advice, that is best place to start with an example.

Gimme a number!

Put on the spot, I gave him my favorite number, 7.

That's $2^2 + 1^2 + 1^2 + 1^2$.

Surely there are more difficult numbers. Conway insists there aren't, caviling only slightly.

Well, I suppose there are, but we won't come across them. How about 1,000? 30^2 is 900 and then 10^2 is 100, and 0^2 and 0^2 make it up to 1,000.
Every number is the sum of 4 squares. You never need more than 4 squares. And you never need more than 37 fifth powers. In fact there is only 1 number that needs 37. And that is 223. What's difficult about this is not doing it for any particular number but proving that it can always be done.

Conway met with his adviser every Thursday to discuss his fifth-powers problem. About 10 minutes before their meeting, he'd think of something to say about the problem, making it seem as if he'd been diligently working away on the problem all week. Or he summoned his trademark decoy, the solution to another problem. Because when it came down to it, Conway couldn't muster much enthusiasm for the sum-of-fifth-powers problem. He did no work and no work and no work, which became more and more and more embarrassing. Finally, full of guilt, Conway gave himself the summer. Back home in Liverpool, he worked at the library every day from opening until closing, and 6 weeks later, success. He wrote up his proof professionally, ready for his first Thursday meeting with Davenport at the start of term. "Well now, Mr. Conway, have you been thinking about our problem?" Conway handed it over and Davenport called the meeting to an early close, saying he wanted time to take a thorough look. At their next meeting, Conway was expecting some congratulations. Davenport said, "What you have here is a poor Ph.D. thesis." It didn't provide any new ideas; Conway had just slaved through the necessary work. He took Davenport's advice and never submitted it. Not long after, in 1964, the Chinese mathematician Chen Jingrun published a much better solution to the fifth-powers problem.

> It disappointed me because I suppose I entertained the idea of working it up and publishing it someday, and then I'd have that result to my credit. On the other hand, that would have been a lot of work, and boring work. I was rather relieved not to have to do it.

It should be noted that talk of his solution to the fifth-powers problem makes Conway uncomfortable. He doesn't want this to come off like a "priority claim" planted with his biographer. At any rate, playing against type, Conway then opted for more work. Or, as he points out, it is perhaps more accurate to say he finally hunkered down and did some real work. He dropped that Ph.D. problem and tackled another.

4.

CALCULATE THE STARS

In mathematics you don't understand things. You just get used to them.
—JOHN VON NEUMANN

At this juncture the counting boy who'd asked *What's the more? When does it end?* found his future with infinity. Mathematical logic roused Conway's libido—in the Jungian sense, meaning the free creative or psychic energy that one directs toward personal development. He read the collected works of the German mathematician Georg Cantor, who in the nineteenth century had tackled the mathematically hazardous notion of the infinite.

> Cantor did this absolutely breathtaking thing of keeping on counting. Everybody else counts 0, 1, 2, 3, and you assume that maybe it eventually stops. Cantor counts 0, 1, 2, 3, dot dot dot—actually Cantor started at 1; it was von Neumann who realized it was better to start at 0—but dot dot dot dot, Cantor kept counting.

Cantor created a taxonomy of the very, very large. He described various types or degrees of infinite numbers and encapsulated it all into set theory. "A set," he said, "is a Many that allows itself to be thought of as a One."

When everyone else threw their hands up in despair in grappling with infinity, Cantor remained calm and carried on counting. He began his book *Contributions to the Founding of the Theory of Transfinite Numbers* with an epigraph: *Hypotheses non fingo*—Latin for "I frame no hypothesis." This he borrowed from Newton, who used the phrase in the

43

second edition of *Principia Mathematica* in answering critics who challenged him on the causes of gravity; gravity causes the sun's pull on the earth, but as to what causes gravity apart from the math of kinematics, he offered no hypotheses. In attempting to get my bearings on set theory and infinity, I didn't get far in Cantor's book before I decided to defer to Conway. I called him on his cell phone to set up a meeting. As it rang I could see him coming to with a start, as always when it rings and jerks him back from the land of abstraction to the logistical land of practical nuisances.

Wooooops! Is that me?

Yes, that is your ringing pocket, that black hole attached to your pants. It always seems a lost cause, but miraculously, at the last second, on the tail end of the eighth ring, he commands space-time to cooperate, he lassos and shucks the phone, and there he is:

John Conway! What can I do for you?

Fielding my request for a crash course on infinity, he takes one of his tangential swerves, not entirely off topic.

Did I ever tell you about being able to get within 2 handshakes of Cantor?

Conway gave a lecture at Durham University on Cantor's life and work, and the woman who sponsored the conference, Cecilia Tanner, had met Cantor either in 1904 when she was 5 or 1905 when she was 4 (some combination of 4 and 5, Conway recalls). She was the daughter of the mathematical couple Grace Chisholm Young and William Henry Young. The family lived on a Swiss lake, and when Cantor once came for a visit he politely bent over and shook young Cecilia's hand. Upon hearing this, Conway hastened to shake the elderly Cecilia's hand, thereby positioning himself to within 2 handshakes (and, he adds, he also once shook Bertrand Russell's hand, which gives him a second route to 2 handshakes). That out of the way, we made plans to meet. Finding him in the alcove, I started with a safe general question. The gist of set theory is the study of the infinite, correct?

Well, yes. Infinite numbers. Infinite collections.

The notion of the infinite had tripped up philosophical and theological titans, Aristotle and Thomas Aquinas among them. Mathematicians steered clear of the "horror infiniti," as Cantor put it. The German mathematician Carl Friedrich Gauss—friends with fellow German mathematician Richard Dedekind, a friend and teacher of Cantor's, thus putting Conway within 4 handshakes of Gauss—said that the infinite in mathematics can only be approached, never reached. Gauss being the top mathematician of his time, Conway figures we can take his as the official attitude toward the infinite in the nineteenth century. Before Cantor, that is. Cantor proceeded to do what Gauss said was impossible. Cantor asserted there was an infinite that was "actual" and "complete."

In daily life, one usually comes face-to-face with finite numbers and finite collections. Conway has to his credit a finite collection of 11 published books, and 1 book published in 11 languages—11 is an actual and complete whole number. The rogue Cantor proposed there could be infinite collections, or sets. For example, there are infinitely many integers—the untouched whole numbers, not broken into fractions or decimals.

$$\ldots \;\text{-}4\;\text{-}3\;\text{-}2\;\text{-}1\quad 0\quad 1\quad 2\;\;3\;\;4\;\ldots\;$$

Cantor gave this infinite number of integers a name: Aleph-0, or $\aleph_0$ (pronounced "Aleph-zero").

There are huge numbers of these infinite numbers: Aleph-0, then Aleph-1, then Aleph-2, and so on. And that carries on much longer than you might think. Because the number of these Alephs—the number of infinite numbers—is not Aleph-0; it's not the infinite number of integers, the smallest of the infinite numbers. It's much, much, much much bigger.

The Alephs are a sequence of numbers describing the sizes of progressively larger sets of infinite collections: $\aleph_0, \aleph_1, \aleph_2, \aleph_3 \ldots$ And the Alephs are but one species of infinite numbers that Cantor discovered; he also discovered the Omegas. The Alephs are often called the cardinal numbers, but Conway calls them the "counted" numbers. You could count 0 items in a set, or 167,899,677 items in a set, or $\aleph_0$ items in a set—again, $\aleph_0$ being the smallest infinite number, the number of all the integers, the infinite number of finite numbers.

Cantor's idea won converts, among them the German mathematician David Hilbert, the arbiter of all that was worth doing in mathematics. In 1900, when Hilbert proposed his 23 problems that should define the course of mathematics for the next century, he put at the top of his list the keystone of set theory: Cantor's Continuum Hypothesis, hypothesizing about all the possible sizes of infinite sets. Working from the foundation of $\aleph_0$, the infinite set of all integers, Cantor took an educated guess about which one of the Alephs represents the number of the real numbers—real numbers being the continuum of all the rational numbers, including the whole-number integers and fractions and decimals, as well as all the irrational numbers—like 3.141592 . . . and the number e, the mathematical constant 2.71828182845904523536028747135262

$$\ldots.-4\;-3\;-2\;-1\;\;0\;\;\;1\;\;2\;\;3\;\;4\ldots.$$

$$-{}^{55}\!/_{89} \qquad \sqrt{2}\quad e$$

49775724709369995 . . . —that never repeat or end.

Comparing the real number line to the integer number line, it would seem there are many more real numbers than integers. Cantor proved this to be true. He also proved that the infinite number of real numbers is $2^{\text{Aleph-0}}$—that is, 2 to the power of the infinite set of integers. And then Cantor went one further, guessing that this infinite number of real numbers might be the infinite number that follows directly after $\aleph_0$. He guessed that the infinite number of real numbers would be $\aleph_1$. This was Cantor's Continuum Hypothesis, as yet unproved and perhaps forever unprovable, unless some new set theory axioms are discovered. Conway took a few stabs at it—as he did with another big problem, the related and equally troublesome Axiom of Choice—but he never got anywhere.

Here one might be feeling a bit weak in the knees, all the blood rushing to the head.

You've simply got to get used to this idea. It is a bit mind-blowing. Normally people just say that there are an infinite number of somethings.

Cantor said that there doesn't seem anything wrong with giving this infinite number a name—it's as if he decided to name the number 100 "Albert." And in fact, Aleph-0 is really familiar to everybody, though not
under that name. When you think of any infinite collection of things, you
are probably thinking of the integers, or Aleph-0.

Stars. Are there infinitely many stars?

You probably mean, "Are there Aleph-0 stars?" Of course, we don't know
that there are infinitely many stars. But if there are, their number is Aleph-
0. That means the stars can be numbered and counted. The sun, let's call
it star 0. And then say the pole star is star 1, and then another star is star
2, and so on.

Around the time of our discussion a study came out prompting head-
lines like NUMBER OF STARS IN THE UNIVERSE COULD BE 300 SEXTIL-
LION, TRIPLE THE AMOUNT SCIENTISTS PREVIOUSLY THOUGHT, and
the astronomers said, "It's very important that papers like this are published so that we are reminded how fragile our knowledge of the universe is." The number 300 sextillion—3 trillion times 100 billion, or 3
followed by 23 zeros—is a large integer, but it's nothing compared to $\aleph_0$.
At any rate, just to review, $\aleph_0$ represents the number of integers, and
the integers go on and on and on and on, ad infinitum?

The point is, what you're suggesting in some sense with that question is
that this is an audacious thing to do, to invent a name for this number. But
that is the audacious thing that Cantor did.

"Working" on his new Ph.D. thesis about ordering infinite sets, Conway
slept with Cantor's collected works under his pillow, doubting that he
could absorb all its intricacies consciously. Around the same time he
was also enamored of *Norton's Star Atlas*, another pillow book—and
more on stars here might provide a welcome break from the infinite. As
a boy, Conway had belonged to the Liverpool Astronomical Association; and in Cambridge he joined the British Astronomical Society. He
lived at 35 Chesterton Lane, across the road from Jesus Green, and he

visited the park at night with the purpose of memorizing the names of all the stars.

> It wasn't all the stars, it was all the stars that have individual names. One's got to be a little bit careful. What's a name? You see, Alpha Hercules— that's not a name, it indicates the brightest star in the constellation of Hercules. There are various ways of naming stars, and the oldest way was with a Greek letter followed by the name of a constellation. And then there were names just by numbers, Ursa Major 61, Ursa Major 77, numbering all the stars in the constellation Ursa Major. I memorized the individual star names, such as the stars in Orion: Betelgeuse, Bellatrix, Alnitak, Alnilam, Mintaka, Rigel, Saiph. And so on. Vega is a name, Arcturus is a name, Polaris is a name. Polaris is the pole star. Arcturus is the star that gave its name to the Arctic Circle, because it's always directly above some point on the Arctic Circle—if you draw a line straight down from Arcturus and imagine the spot where the line hits the earth's center, then every day with the rotation of the earth that projection of the star traces out the Arctic Circle.

He lay flat on his back, the star atlas in one hand and a flashlight in the other. He covered the light with a piece of red cloth so his eyes would stay dark-adapted, and he flashed the red light on and off, checking the book, checking the sky. Once, when he took his nose out of the atlas and looked up, he was frightened to see 2, 3 ... 8 men standing in a circle around him. When his eyes adjusted, he was relieved to see that these were policemen, who wanted to know whether his activities involved any combination of public indecency, disturbance, or intoxication.

"Knowledge is power!" That's Francis Bacon's aphorism, which Conway often appropriates. It explains not only his interest in astronomy, but also his interest in flowers, sparked by their connection with the Fibonacci numbers (0, 1, 1, 2, 3, 5, 8, 13...). The daffodil, he noticed, seemed odd, since it displayed 6 petals. According to phyllotaxis, a biological morphology mechanism, the number of petals should correspond to a Fibonacci number. So you'd expect the daffodil to have 5 petals, not 6—until you learn that only 3 of the daffodil's petals are actually petals and the other 3 rogues are protective sepals, which together form a perianth surrounding the corona. In addition to gazing into the heavens at night, Conway wandered around gardens peering into flowers, checking to ensure that the world was functioning as it should.

> If you've got some theory about how things behave, it's reassuring when they behave like that. And it's rather more reassuring when they first appear not to. Because chances are you've made a mistake in your calculations, and then you get worried about it, and you double-check and—oh my god!—you find out what the error was and then the world *is* going according to plan after all.

Auditing the cosmos, Conway feels as if he's in cahoots. At night, if he notices a little cloud obscuring a particular patch of sky, he'll amuse himself by guessing what's behind—perhaps an asterism of 3 stars of second or third magnitude near the first point of Aries, marking the head of the ram. He'll wait until the cloud passes. And then there are the 3 stars. They obeyed.

> Well, they weren't in exactly the position I thought, they might have been up and twisted a bit. But they were the right shape. And I got this really nice feeling. I knew what was behind that cloud—all's right with the world, everything's as it should be. And I was pleased that I knew the sky well enough that I could tell what was behind this little piece of cloud.
>
> Knowledge isn't exactly power, but it sometimes feels like it. Correctly predicting what is behind a cloud, knowing what's going to happen, what's going to be there when the cloud moves away, is, psychologically, rather like ordering it to happen.

Conway's command over mathematical entities, his desire to accumulate enumerations of abstract truths and assert control over the infinite numbers, doesn't seem dissimilar.

> You're right when you say "control of these infinite numbers," or something. I mean, I'm not such a power maniac as I pretend, I hope. I just like knowing things. I really do. And I suppose that is why I do all this mathematical stuff, in a way.

In the photographer Mariana Cook's book *Mathematicians*, Conway's portrait is accompanied by this quotation:

> It's a funny thing that happens with mathematicians. What's the ontology of mathematical things? How do they exist? There's no doubt that they do exist but you can't poke and prod them except by thinking about them. It's quite astonishing and I still don't understand it, despite having been a mathematician all my life. How can things be there without actually being there? There's no doubt that 2 is there or 3 is there or the square root of omega. They're very real things. I still don't know the sense in which mathematical objects exist, but they do. Of course, it's hard to say in what sense a cat is out there, too, but we know it is, very definitely. Cats have a stubborn reality but maybe numbers are stubborner still. You can't push a cat in a direction it doesn't want to go. You can't push a number either.

During yet another meeting at the alcove, with his son Gareth roaming nearby, I asked Conway to push the replay button and contemplate infinite numbers in the context of these comments about the existence of mathematical objects.

> There is a strong sense in which infinite numbers don't exist. There doesn't seem to be anything actually infinite in the real world at all. I don't know, maybe there is. But here are these infinite numbers, and whatever their ontological status is, I'm sure that you know they are not just an invention—I think "discovery" is the right word.
>
> I was studying infinite numbers and one gets to a place where it is not at all clear. There are contradictions that arise, and paradoxes, when you start thinking of infinite collections. So it is not at all clear that infinite collections have any real existence at all.

Still, Conway feels that infinite numbers have some kind of existence, some kind of reality outside Plato's cave. This makes him a Platonist, of sorts, sometimes. Depending on the day, he might blankly confess,

> I'm a Platonist.

Or he might add a caveat:

I'm a Platonist at heart, although I know there are very great difficulties with that view.

Gareth, meanwhile, had disappeared into the common room's computer cave, which prompted further thoughts about reality.

You know roughly what it's like in that room. It has a reality. It's the same now—apart from the fact that somebody's moved a chair or something—from what it was the last time you were in there. And that's what we call reality, somehow. Isn't it? A certain kind of stability. You can go back to the same place and see the same thing, or see what has become of the same thing.

Comparing the 2 standard household pets, cats and dogs, cats do what they want, they have a certain obstinacy. Dogs don't, dogs are friendly and willing to be helpful and they wag their tails and so on. Push a dog and it might sit down. If you push a cat slightly, it pushes back, no matter which direction you push it. Why doesn't it want to go? Why does it automatically decide it doesn't want to go where it's pushed?

Just then Gareth yelled from the computer room, commanding his father's presence.

I don't believe in answering him when he shouts. He has to come.

He came, and reported his Tetris score: 43 to his father's previous score of 21.

Well, that's a bit of a pity, because it means I wasn't as clever as I thought. Go on, let's see if you can improve it.

So cats are more like mathematical entities than dogs?

I'm only saying there is this obstinacy of the real world. It's no good trying to walk through this wall. It just won't let you. Children will scream and wail when they want their mothers to do something, or their fathers. But they won't scream and wail at the wall. They learn really quite quickly that the wall does not respond to screaming. The wall is obstinate. And some of that obstinacy belongs to things like the numbers 2 and 3. Or various other mathematical concepts.

One of his all time favorites is Morley's trisector theorem. It states: "The 3 points of intersection of the adjacent trisectors of the angles of any triangle form an equilateral triangle." It's also known as "Morley's Miracle," on account of the unexpected equilaterality, all angles being 60 degrees. Conway discovered the "indisputably simplest proof" of Morley's theorem, as he himself described to a geometry puzzles newsgroup, and he continues to rave about it to this day:

It's really quite nice. It's one of those things that are simple enough for anybody to understand. It all comes down to the fact that the angles of every triangle total 180 degrees.

With that, he got up to give another demonstration.

I think this is the alcove in which I secreted some chalk.

He flipped open the radiator's control panel, stuck his arm in, and triumphantly pulled forth a full pack of Crayola antidust nontoxic white chalk.

My proof goes like this . . .

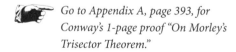 Go to Appendix A, page 393, for Conway's 1-page proof "On Morley's Trisector Theorem."

The point is that mathematical concepts and entities—such as Morley's Theorem and the infinitely many integers—seem to exist independent of a mathematician or a civilian understanding or not understanding their properties. For example, the integers are not a social construct, like art.

Let me rabbit on about this for a bit . . .

I think the numbers 2 and 3 existed before people did. One of the standard examples is that Mars has 2 moons, Phobos and Deimos, and I believe that the statement "Mars has 2 moons" was meaningful and true before there were any human beings to utter it. The fact that we use this particular word "t-w-o" for 2 is obviously a human invention, but I don't think the concept it symbolizes is a human invention. And the truth of Morley's Theorem is not, it seems to me, a social construct. It's not true because people think it's true. Whether it's actually true in the physical world is another matter, because the physical world might not quite match Euclidean geometry. But it's true inside Euclidean geometry, and there is a certain obstinacy about that.

If I came back tomorrow and drew the diagram of Morley's Theorem and found the central triangle had a right angle in it, that would be one of the greatest shocks of my life. Or else I'd start thinking I was going insane again. I don't understand, and I don't think anybody else does either, where the obstinacy comes from. That obstinacy betokens a certain kind of reality of these abstract ideas. And it's harder to understand this reality when you start talking about infinite numbers. But it's got the same character all the time. It is really there. The sense that it is there I don't really understand, even as somebody who has spent my professional life investigating different aspects of this abstract mathematical world and discovering some of them and seeing some of them for the very first time. And. *Yet!* Why does it have whatever reality it has? How can you even describe what kind of reality it has? I don't know. We just shelve it.

Gareth soon returned to report his latest results, a dismal 16.

That's worse than ever! You're no son of mine!

And then the pair of them went off to play Tetris.

△ ▢ ◈ ⊗ ⬡

When Cantor proposed his theory of the infinite he was called a scientific charlatan, a renegade, and a corrupter of youth (Conway has always considered him a role model). Despite the naysayers, set theory provided a much-needed logical foundation for mathematics. All mathematical objects came to be thought of as sets, as collections. And during yet another session on the infinite, I asked Conway for more details on his Ph.D. thesis exploring ways of ordering infinite collections.

Yeah, well, I'm not quite sure it's worth describing.

He proceeded to describe it, in general terms, for the better part of an hour. He began with the ordinal numbers, another new numerical species Cantor discovered. Whereas the cardinals are the "counted" numbers, as Conway calls them, the ordinals are the "ordering" numbers, used to describe the order of things, so it's best to think of them in terms of something that benefits from ordering, like chapters: the first, the second, the third, and so on. And again, in this context Cantor was the first person to consider proceeding, or ordering, or doing the ordered counting, into infinity. The least infinite ordinal he called Omega—say, the *Omega*th chapter—and denoted by the symbol ω.

Cantor kept counting and then he got to Omega, Omega +1, Omega +2, dot dot dot dot . . . And then Omega x 2, and then Omega², with lots and lots of numbers in between. And on and on and on and on.

When talking about infinite sets, Conway is always careful to articulate not merely the usual "and on and on," but rather 4 "and ons," to belabor the point that this scenario really does go for a long, long time. In a valiant attempt to get this across during a lecture, on a nice sunny day he took his class outside and chalked the number line along a sidewalk, along and along and along, ordering the integers in the set Epsilon$_0$, an entity bigger than any we've yet encountered.

If I just write out the names, you'll get the hint: 0, 1, 2, ... Omega, Omega +1 ... Omega +2 ... Omega x 2 ... Omega x 3 ... Omega squared ... Omega cubed ... Omega to the Omega ... Omega to the Omega to the Omega ... Omega to the Omega to the Omega to the Omega ... then Omega to the Omega to the Omega to the Omega to the ZZZUUUUMMMPH ...

The "zumph" translates to a scale break, a drastic catapulting increase in magnitude, and then carrying on with

... Epsilon$_0$, and then Epsilon$_1$ ... Epsilon$_2$ ... Epsilon$_{Omega}$ ... Epsilon$_{Epsilon0}$ ...
and Epsilon ZZZUUUUMMMPH ...

And on and on and on and on. This goes on for so long that a new kind
of number line is warranted, a number line that spirals infinitely inward:

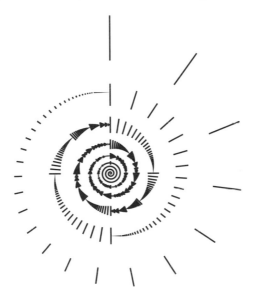

I don't know if you get it, but the first revolution, the first time you go
'round, it's just an Omega. Next time it's Omega Omegas, and then the
next and the next, and then ZZZUUUUMMMPH. Next time you get
'round it's Omega of those, which is Omega cubed. And so on, until you
get to Omega to the power of Omega.

Cantor's ordinals are really the weirdest things. It's absolutely astonishing how long they go on. It's a fantastic thing Cantor did. I think of him in
the same breath as Einstein. They both changed the view of some kind of
universe. With Einstein it was the actual physical universe. With Cantor it
was the conceptual universe of numbers. And now it's a hell of a lot bigger than it was, and it's got a hell of a lot more structure. Before Cantor, I
don't think anybody ever noticed that the infinite wasn't just one number—that there were infinite sets of different sizes. There is the set of integers, and it's infinite. And there's the set of real numbers, and it's infinite.
They are both infinite and they are different sizes. And Cantor was the
first person to think that.

Getting back to the specifics of his thesis, Conway himself eventually came full circle.

In a way, the least said the better.

It was a workmanlike thesis investigating technical questions about ordered sets. For instance, the integers can be ordered in various ways. The usual way is:

(0, 1, 2, 3, 4, 5, 6, 7, 8, 9 ...)

But the integers could also be ordered with evens first, then odds:

(0, 2, 4, 6, 8, 10 ...)   (1, 3, 5, 7, 9, 11...)

Which would be the equivalent of $\omega + \omega$. Or the integers could be ordered by odds, then twice odds, then twice those:

(1, 3, 5, 7, 9 ...) (2, 6, 10, 14, 18 ...) (4, 12, 20, 28, 36 ...)

And that would be $\omega + \omega + \omega$.

By 1964, a couple years longer than it should have taken, Conway finished his Ph.D. thesis, exploring a modest byway of set theory, a tertiary branch in the taxonomy of infinitely many numbers. He titled it "Homogeneous Ordered Sets." He typed it up and submitted it, but the typing was such a mess that the Ph.D. receiving office requested a better copy. He told them,

Forget it! I'll take my business elsewhere!

No, actually, he hired a professional typist, although he thought the final product looked worse, like a too fancy haircut. Never published, this second thesis, like the first, was second-rate.

The story of my life!

5.

NERDISH DELIGHTS

Never let the truth get in the way of a good story,
unless you can't think of anything better.
—MARK TWAIN

Now Conway needed a job. This was a challenge. Not because there weren't jobs to be had, nor because he wasn't qualified. The insuperable obstacle was merely applying. Mercifully, the hiring process for the Cambridge mathematics faculty was then loosey-goosey, somewhere between anarchic and irrational.

The Department of Pure Mathematics, founded the very year Conway received his Ph D , was just setting shop in the old university press warehouse, joining its counterpart the Department of Applied Mathematics and Theoretical Physics, established 5 years before. While Conway and I were in town for the research odyssey, the applied math department was celebrating its semicentennial, culminating in a lecture by Stephen Hawking. Hawking cued up his speech synthesizer and delivered a brief history. Before 1959, he said, when there was no mathematics department proper, professors worked out of their college rooms. The new headquarters, dimly lit and cavernous, had its virtues, being centrally located and occupying a block off Trumpington Street. He also noted, to knowing chuckles, that it had its faults. "But it is often true that the best work is done in crummy buildings." Then he described how he got his start as a cosmologist, and how he developed his own original picture of how the universe worked. "There's nothing like the Eureka moment of discovering something that no one knew before," he said. "I won't compare it to sex, but it lasts longer."

In those early days of departmental flux, the hiring process required nothing so formal as an interview. Conway now had 2 young daughters: the second, Rosie, had been born in July 1963. And in terms of existential pressure, his 60-year-old dad had died that May, from lung cancer (though officially the cause of death was heart failure and coronary arteriosclerosis). Yet as the end of his Ph.D. funding approached, Conway did nothing. He remembers walking down the street and bumping into Ian Cassels, a canny Scot with a serious snuff habit who for a time held the post of the Sadleirian Professor of Pure Mathematics, and also the position of department head. Cassels asked him, "What have you done about a job?"

Er, nothing.

"There's a position opening here, why don't you apply?"

How do I go about it?

"You write me a letter."

What should I say?

Cassels took pity. He offered to write the letter for Conway. He sat down at the side of the road on a stone wall in front of King's College, rummaged through his briefcase, found a pen, pulled out a piece of paper, and began, "Dear Professor Cassels, I wish to apply for . . ." He handed it to Conway and instructed him to sign, and Cassels filed the letter away in his briefcase. Victory was his, Conway was sure. Awhile later he got the news in the mail: "I'm terribly sorry," Cassels wrote. "You didn't get the job." But, he continued, "there is another position coming open next year, and unless you indicate your wishes to the contrary, I shall take your previous letter as a letter of application for that position."

Cassels did not recall this letter transaction when he met me for an interview. He arrived by bicycle looking a bit unkempt, spittle at his mouth and splatters clouding his half-moon gold-rimmed glasses, a widower soldiering on. What he recalls of Conway was that his office was a mess; that he stuffed a cupboard in the common room full of his important books and papers and models; and that he hung out at the department more than most (most mathematicians didn't take to the central headquarters and had to be lured in with free photocopying). He recalls that Conway wasn't one to willingly perform the necessary administrative chores—marking exams, filing grades, et cetera—but if one lorded it over him, he was capable of executing prescribed tasks. Cassels recalls Conway playing games, and that when the first magnetic-card-programmable calculators came out, he programmed his HP-65 to play Dots and Boxes. The calculator allowed only 100 button pushes for any program, and with that Conway made the calculator his most formidable opponent. As to the puzzling letter about the job, that was, well, puzzling. Conway is sure it was Cassels; Cassels isn't so sure; but Conway *is sure* (and he insists on getting the last word). At any rate, in 1964 Conway became an assistant lecturer, taking over the post of mathematical logic upon the retirement of Stourton Steen. "Mathematics," Steen wrote in the introduction to his book *Mathematical Logic*, "is the art of making vague intuitive ideas precise and then studying the result [and] inventing a method whereby our thoughts can be either communicated to others or stored for our own memory."

> **DOTS + BOXES INSTRUCTIONS:** *On a grid of dots (any number of dots as long as n ≥ 3) two players take turns making a single horizontal or vertical line between two unjoined adjacent dots. When a player completes a box she earns a point and marks her initial inside the box and then must take another turn. The winner is the player who takes the most boxes.*

With the teaching job secured, Conway now needed a matching position with a college, to make up the other $\frac{1}{2}$ of his salary. Sidney Sussex College wanted him, and Peterhouse as well. Although he had been a research fellow at Caius, his alma mater couldn't offer him a teaching fellowship because the college had recently appointed a teaching mathematician and didn't have the need or space for another. Peterhouse would be the better fit, its demographic being more mathematically inclined, but Conway was put off by its pretensions. Without any mention of the fellowship, he received an invitation to dine at the college. He was seated near the head of the table next to the Master, who he suspected of surveilling his etiquette. Afterward, adjourning to the "combination room," he was seated next to the bursar and senior tutor, for port and cheese and fruit and further reconnaissance. He got the fellowship offer. But the proposition from Sidney Sussex involved none of that finicky foreplay, and so it was at "Sid Suss" that he made himself at home.

Home meant residing for a good amount of time in dimensions greater than 3. He cultivated this slippery grip on reality in the solitude of the Fellows Garden, where the garden path itself was slippery, the summer's overripe mulberries, heavy with juice, having taken their Newtonian plummet. They made a mushy purple mess underfoot as Conway perambulated contemplatively, and tentatively, wearing a clunky contraption on his head with gangly protrusions emanating from his eyes. While this headdress obscured Conway's view of the mundane 3-dimensional reality, the gadget's purpose was that in doing so it would enhance his ability to see the world in a more awe-inspiring 4 dimensions.

> Seeing multidimensional things has been a slight obsession with me all my life. Or at least apprehending multidimensional things, comprehending them, studying them.

But ask Conway how precisely one intuits 4 dimensions, and depending on his mood he might respond:

None of your business! That's personal!

More likely, though, he'll tell the long story of how he tried to train himself to see 4 dimensions. The first step in his scheme was to coax his faithful friend Mike into making a few short films that would expand the bounds of his spatial perception by depicting computer-generated vignettes of geometrical entities, cubes and so forth, as they rotated and reflected through 4-space. Conway stared at these images and waited for levitation. Nothing happened. His retina was too accustomed to seeing 2 dimensions and inferring 3, and from there it couldn't easily extrapolate to 4. This is what prompted him to get crafty and construct an assistive device, his hyperspace helmet.

Toward the end of the Cambridge trip, Conway and I visited the Sidney Sussex Fellows Garden. The mulberry tree was still there, and the garden as a whole had changed little, although now it was open to the public.

This used to be all locked away, closed to visitors. And you see, it's enclosed by this high wall so nobody can see in. And moreover you can't do too much damage to yourself. I was worried about that. You realize, these weren't glasses I was wearing. It was a complicated helmet with periscopes on it. Let me draw you a picture . . .

You see, my idea was that under normal circumstances our eyes, each eye, sees a 2-dimensional picture. But the 2 pictures differ by what's called parallax, which is always horizontal parallax because your eyes are spaced horizontally apart. If you close your right eye and look at that mulberry tree with your left eye—or you can do it by holding your index finger out in front at arm's length—and then close your left eye and look at it with your right eye, it appears to shift its position slightly, it moves back and forth. That displacement is horizontal parallax.

The point is, we only have a 2-dimensional retina. We have this built-in visual system that can only see 2 dimensions. Each eye sees a 2-dimensional picture and then we get some kind of partial vision of 3 dimensions by having these 2 different eyes which see 2 slightly different pictures that differ ever so slightly by a horizontal parallax.

So I had this great idea of using the notion of "double parallax" to see 4 dimensions. Your left eye's picture and your right eye's picture theoretically could differ not only by horizontal parallax but also by vertical parallax. That makes 4 positions, which would give your eyes the input they need to see in 4 dimensions.

And what generated the vertical parallax was the helmet. I made it out of a crash helmet, cut various bits off, bolted on a visor, and put these army surplus periscopes in place. One of them moved my left eye diagonally downward to the middle of my chin, and the other moved my right eye diagonally up to the middle of my forehead. The net effect was that my eyes were displaced vertically, and to rather more than the usual horizontal displacement, about twice as much.

And then what I did was I just walked around in the Fellows Garden for a few hours every day when I could spare the time. And I gradually got accustomed to vertical parallax, to seeing the mulberry tree displaced vertically instead of horizontally.

There was also the famous day, or famous for me anyway, when I decided I was going to walk out in public, in the center of town. I'm pretty sure it was a Saturday. If I deliberately chose Saturday, I was a fool, because you know there were throngs of shoppers. The streets were crowded. I was getting in everyone's way and people were gawking and kids were yelling, "Mummy! What is that?" When I went out there with this strange helmet on, it was harder. But when I was walking around in here it was all slow motion; nothing was moving, and I could stop and study what things looked like with vertical parallax.

And then my idea was that I would try viewing the 4-dimensional pictures in the films again, using horizontal and vertical parallax. To get my eyes used to it I practiced switching back and forth from horizontal to vertical parallax while I walked around here in the garden. I needed to know that the horizontality wasn't hardwired in. I was unsure as to whether the eyes could be trained to interpret vertical parallax at all. I needed to know that the brain would accept vertical parallax. And it did.

And then after all this training to see vertical parallax, I took the helmet off and watched the film again—trying to use both horizontal and vertical parallax at the same time on my own. But you know, it was a rather coarse pixel screen, and the pictures were rather small, not very well done, and the whole thing really died because this little computer-generated movie wasn't much good. So it didn't really work. I mean, yes, I did see some sort of 4-dimensional stuff. But I think of it as the 4-dimensional fiasco rather than a great success.

Or, as he once put it slightly more optimistically:

I suppose I had a limited amount of success in that quixotic quest. I could see 4 dimensions because I just got used to thinking that way. But there was no hope of going beyond, so what's the point?

At this stage in his career, Conway didn't consider polytopes and this foray into hyperdimensional space as being his quote-unquote "job." Later it would become a more professional undertaking, which he explored by more conventional means, and going well beyond 4 dimensions, initially to 24 dimensions, later to 196,883, and all by brute-force brainpower. Conway never tried LSD, known to induce intensified visual impressions and kaleidoscopic shape shifts. Nor did he eat any magic mushrooms and converse with his geometric friends. And he does Bill Clinton one better, claiming that he doesn't even know what marijuana smells like. Despite having come of age in the sixties, the permissiveness of the prevailing culture never persuaded him to do drugs—he was a straightedge hippie, in that sense. He is the first to admit he wasn't nearly so unimpressionable in the sexual realm.

Of his time at Sidney Sussex, which was brief, Conway has a couple more staple stories he likes to tell. The most fantastic of the bunch he may well have told 100 times or more—I'd heard it again and again. His first wife Eileen had heard it, perhaps in the inaugural telling. And she told it to me when we met at a pub one morning for tea.

Before getting into that, Eileen also had some other anecdotes on offer. Having graduated from Trinity College, Dublin, with a degree in modern languages, French and Italian, she made her future husband's acquaintance at a postwedding party thrown for her friend Shirley, Conway's cousin. "He was an unusual young man, which is what attracted me," she says. For instance? "Well, there is something quite funny, quite sweet, really. John and I went to a restaurant soon after we met and I was standing back waiting for him to open the door. And he said, 'Well, go on, then!' Most young men were opening doors and pulling out chairs and that sort of thing. But it just didn't occur to him. He didn't think that way. There's a door, you're standing in front of me, so why not go in? And it's logical, I suppose."

Once married, they had 4 children, spaced arithmetically if unintentionally 1, 2, 3 years apart. The third, Ellie, arrived before the doctor did, in June 1965. John oversaw the delivery, arriving home just in time and exhausted from that very day finishing his undergraduate supervisions for the term (supervisions were supposed to take an hour each, but Conway's lapsed into hours, until he started setting an alarm clock for the allotted period to prevent himself from talking on and on and on and on). A couple years after Ellie's arrival Eileen announced to her husband, "I'd like another baby before I'm 40." Her husband obliged. After the arrival of Annie, in November 1968, Conway returned to the department and got the standard question: "Had the baby?"

Yes.

"Boy or girl?"

Yes.

"He was being logical," explains Eileen. "It was a boy or a girl. It wasn't a third set." She recalled how he once carried the girls upstairs to bed, all at the same time—Susie on his shoulders, Rosie and Ellie on his hips, Annie in front. "I can still hear the very heavy footsteps. Clomp. Clomp. Clomp. Clomp. He was a very strong young man." He worked on math endlessly and everywhere, with the children crawling all over him. He liked films and books, and he liked it when Eileen played the family piano. But math was his only serious interest. "I was sympathetic but I didn't really understand," says Eileen.

He also liked a good story. And so back to that particularly fantastic tale. Ever the Scouser, Conway came home in the middle of the night and told Eileen about a fabulously odd party he'd just attended. At the behest of Sidney Sussex's Master of College, he and select fellows were summoned to a private dinner, together with the college chaplain and

With Eileen and their 4 girls.

Dr. H. N. S. Wilkinson, who had recently donated to the college the head of Oliver Cromwell, Lord Protector of the Commonwealth and a fellow of the college circa 1616. Following his death in 1658, Cromwell was buried briefly in Westminster Abbey, but when the monarchy that he'd overthrown returned to power, he was exhumed for posthumous hanging and decapitation. His head was set on a spike atop Westminster Hall, and it later went missing, turning up in a museum of curiosities before residing with the Wilkinson family. And now Cromwell's head was to be laid to rest in the college chapel. To hear Conway's telling, it was a raucous night, with a sumptuous dinner and ample drink. The Master led a candlelit procession to the antechapel, where the chaplain gave a brief service, followed by the burial.

With the Cambridge research trip mostly finished, Conway headed back to Princeton and I stopped by Sidney Sussex College to ask after Cromwell's skull. The porter escorted me to the antechapel and pointed to a plaque on the wall: "Near to this place was buried on 25 March 1960 the head of Oliver Cromwell." When I arrived back in Princeton, I asked Conway for more details. Did he see the skull? Where exactly was this dinner? This time, however, my detailed questions were not greeted with his know-it-all enthusiasm.

> Yeeesss. That is a great story, isn't it? And I often tell that story, with myself playing a supporting role. As if I had actually been there.

He made it up. He *wasn't* actually there. Conway hadn't attended the consecration of Cromwell's skull. He'd no doubt heard rumors of the event, and in an opportune moment, when he needed a captivating story to tell, maybe when he needed an alibi, he claimed this tale as his own, because, well, it was a great story. But it made Conway an accomplished fictioneer and a rather unreliable narrator of his own life.

I was both impressed and perplexed by his derring-do. There I was at the Institute for Advanced Study, attempting a finely drawn portrait of my subject, and against my best intentions and best efforts the biography seemed to have gone a bit off the rails. The Cromwell story and perhaps a host of others were, it seemed, figments of his imagination.

Doing my part to contribute to the Institute community, I presented a talk on my predicament, on the elusive nature of biographical truth. Most talks in this neighborhood of the intellectual firmament were more rarefied. One scholar, the fabulously monikered Aristotle Socrates, an astrophysicist, spoke on "Solar Systems Unlike Our Own." Conway was, by comparison, high comedy, in an orbit all his own—prankish, belligerent, hijacking the process, living up to that diabolically wild-horned caricature (see the frontispiece on p. vi). Irving Lavin, the Institute's art historian emeritus, took an interest in the drawing and offered his assistance in deciphering what it said about Conway's antics. Conway was in good company among artists who matched creativity with promiscuity, intellectual and/or interpersonal—Picasso, for example. So maybe Conway's seeming inability to distinguish fact from fiction correlated to his uncanny ability to see mathematics differently and to achieve his idiosyncratically original results. Commenting on the caricature itself, Lavin rummaged around for relevant references and pointed to the sixteenth-century Italian artist Gian Lorenzo Bernini as an early ancestor of artists doing exaggerated comical drawings with massive heads to malign or poke fun at their subjects. He thought the caricature vividly captured Conway as rapscallion. "Very cunning!" says Lavin. Cunning indeed—showing dexterity in artfully achieving one's ends by deceit, evasion, or trickery.

The second Sidney Sussex story Conway likes to spin—this one true (?!)—concerns his resignation in high dudgeon from his fellowship. It turned on a mastership election, an event at Cambridge that is rather like electing the pope, drawn out with political crosscurrents and nastiness. As tradition dictated, Conway and all the other fellows trooped into the Master's Lodge, and when his turn came, he declared, I, John Horton Conway, vote for John Wilfrid Linnett—a chemist and later a vice chancellor of the university. There was no contest, no other contender. At a dinner in college about 6 weeks later, Richard Chorley, a geomorphologist, turned to Conway and asked if he'd heard the latest. Apparently, initially there had been a second candidate in Joseph Grimond, a former leader of the Liberal Party. Rumor had it that some Sid-Suss fellows sent Grimond a letter warning him he would be unwelcome, "unacceptable to the College," as Conway remembered the phraseology. Grimond took the hint and withdrew. Conway, dismayed to hear of this skulduggery, left the dinner table, returned to his college room, and wrote his resignation letter, forfeiting a substantial fraction of his salary in the process.

The next day the Archimedeans held their annual punt party, celebrating the end of exams with a trip along the River Cam to Grantchester. As Peter Swinnerton-Dyer, a mathematician at Trinity College and Conway's elder by about a decade, eased his bulky frame into their boat, he inquired whether Conway might be interested in becoming a fellow at Trinity. Swinnerton-Dyer dropped a few hints, but he didn't have the say-so to make it happen himself. In the end, Conway was welcomed back to Gonville and Caius College. He took a meeting with the Master, the sinologist Joseph Needham. When he arrived at his office, Needham was finishing up some paperwork. "You might be interested in this," he said. It was a university form on which Needham had to indicate what he'd done in the past year: "Nothing." He said he'd been filling out the same form in the same way for several years. He wondered if there was anyone on the receiving end actually reading these forms. His point was that Conway could return to the college on the condition that he do nothing, at least in terms of teaching, for 2 years—Caius couldn't be seen to be poaching a teacher from another college. Conway could hardly object, and he was made a Supernumerary Fellow. Not supernumerary meaning, ahem, super at numbers, but rather as in a supernumerary tooth, exceeding the prescribed number, exceeding what is required or desired, and at that a special honor.

Sandals-in-all-seasons Conway would typically saunter into the math department common room and announce his arrival by slapping his hand on one of the large steel girders in the middle of the room. This sent out a satisfyingly dissonant *dinggggg*. Another day of play now in session.

Phutball (short for "Philosopher's Football") provided eternal amusement. Conway invented this 2-player board game with a Greek chorus of graduate students at his knee, among them Robert Curtis, his first graduate student in group theory. Despite his having invented Phutball, this is not a game at which Conway excels. Like Besicovitch's card game, it is a game governed by negative feedback.

> Every time you take your turn you get this horrible feeling in the pit of your stomach. Because every move is bad. Instead of selecting the move that is best, you select the move that is least bad. And even though it's a board game, and looks nothing like Besicovitch's game, you get the same feeling of your gut seizing up. You make any move and immediately feel you shouldn't have done it, and you think to yourself, Oh god, what have I done?

A de facto Phutball rule allows it that if after a particularly excruciatingly bad move a player requests "Please, may I cry?" and the request is granted—"Yes, you may cry!"—then the move can be taken back and replayed. But even with such concessions, Conway is not very good at Phutball and indeed he is not very good at game playing generally, or at least not very good at winning. Nevertheless, he was the perpetrator of endless gaming sessions in the common room, ultimately elevating games to a suitable subject for serious research investigation, albeit punctuated by spasmodic outbursts whereby he leapt into the air, latched on to a pipe along the ceiling, and swung violently back and forth. This trapeze act hardly made Conway the department's leading acrobat. He was outperformed by Frank Adams, an algebraic topologist and mountaineer who liked to climb under a table without touching the floor. Conway found Adams intimidating, a forbiddingly serious mathematician. Adams, the Lowndean Professor of Astronomy and Geometry, had a reputation for being a hard-ass, a hard lecturer and hard on himself. Colleagues suspected his relentless ambition was to blame for his periodic nervous breakdowns. Adams worked like a man possessed, and this caused Conway unease. He was sure Adams disapproved of his comparatively slothful recreational ethic. And in turn this caused Conway to feel guilty, to worry that he was on the verge of being sacked. Because all he was doing was squatting in the common room playing games, inventing games, reinventing rules to games he found boring.

Conway likes games that move in a flash. He played backgammon constantly, for small stakes—money, chalk, honor—though for all that practice he was not terribly good at backgammon, either. He took too many risks, accepting doubles when he shouldn't and upping the ante to as much as 64 times the original stakes merely to see what would happen, all the while talking math—for example, there was Conway's Piano Problem that asked: What's the largest object that can be maneuvered around a right-angle corner in a fixed-width corridor? (The lower bound for the object's area is $\frac{2}{\pi} + \frac{\pi}{2}$. You can do better. But to find out how much better is very difficult.) He wasn't interested in winning at backgammon so much as he was interested in the possibilities of the game. He liked to play a flamboyant "back game," falling intentionally behind with inexplicably loony plays. Opponents, witnessing such folly, would let their guard down and get careless, gradually losing ground. Then Conway would make his move. Usually this strategy backfired and he lost as expected. Every now and then, depending on the luck of the dice—the element of chance is key in backgammon, and consequently the game defies much mathematical analysis and any pretensions of a serious research agenda—Conway would successfully rush in from behind and pull out a spectacular win.

While Conway was hopelessly addicted to backgammon, some of his colleagues carefully rationed their own allotment, and others abstained outright, fearing that if they submitted at all they'd be sucked in and their research derailed. Other colleagues expressed concern that Conway was setting a bad example and corrupting the souls of graduate students. This, of course, was his plan! One such student was Simon Norton, a child prodigy who had attended Eton College and managed to earn an undergraduate degree at the University of London during his last year of high school. When he arrived at Cambridge, Norton, already a backgammon whiz, easily fell in with the crowd. And a lightning-fast calculator, he became Conway's protégé, working out on all the problems

Conway couldn't solve. He kept tabs on virtually all problems under way by everyone, snooping and eavesdropping and interrupting and bleeting out *"Fallllllssse!!"* when he noticed a mistake. He also had a capacious vocabulary, which the logophile Conway appreciated, at least when Norton deigned to display this talent. For the most part he came across as inarticulate and quiet, except when it came to backgammon. Games often attracted an audience, and the audience heckled and kibitzed. Norton presumptuously assumed the role of umpire and blurted unsolicited adjudications: "The machine says!" meant there was only a single solitary move a player could make. "The dice are no longer needed!" meant the winner was clear and the game might as well be over. At which point Norton snatched away the dice.

During England's 1978–1979 "Winter of Discontent" a general strike and power cuts disrupted daily life, but backgammon continued by candlelight.

Apart from the incessant play, an advantage of squatting in the common room, as Conway came to discern, was free food. He has never been one to formally engage in the ritual called lunch, so he always welcomed the appearance of cookies with coffee and tea, leftover sandwiches after a guest lecture, or spoils of cake and champagne following a Ph.D. defense. And as it happens, the fair division of leftovers is a gamelike problem that, unlike backgammon, can be mathematically analyzed. Conway solved the problem of the "envy-free division" of cake into 3 portions—"envy-free" meaning no one would be left wanting someone else's share rather than their own. He thought this was newsworthy enough that he sat down at his orange typewriter and pecked out a letter to Martin Gardner. Dating back to his jag analyzing flexagons in follow-up to the *Scientific American* column, Conway had made a habit of summarizing his recreational research in lengthy letters to Gardner. He fed a hefty roll of foolscap into his typewriter, like butcher paper, and typed out an on-going stream until it was long enough to send—3 or 4 feet would be long enough, he figures, though one letter Gardner cut up into the equivalent of 11 legal-sized pages.

Conway typically began his letters with a preamble:

> *I got your first parcel of books just before Christmas, and was so de-lighted I spent the next few days reading and re-reading them, particu-larly the Annotated Alice, which is superb. (My wife was very annoyed with you!)*

Then he'd launch into research updates, beginning with, say, his solution for dividing cake, then moving on to a new wire and string puzzle, and then the bulk of the letter given over to:

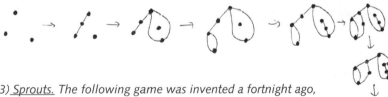

3) Sprouts. The following game was invented a fortnight ago, on a Tuesday afternoon. By Wednesday it had infected our Maths dept beyond recall—even the secretarial staff had suc-cumbed. We started with n spots on a piece of paper. The move is to join two of these spots—which are allowed to be the same spot—by a curve, and then to create a new spot on this curve. The curve must not pass through old spots, nor may it cross old curves, and *at no time may any spot have more than 3 arcs emanating from it*. In normal sprouts a player who cannot make a move loses, so that the ob-ject is to move last—in misère sprouts the last player loses.

Sprouts, invented with graduate student Mike Paterson, became the subject of Gardner's first *Scientific American* column featuring Conway, published in July 1967. Working on the column, Gardner wrote back to Conway with a list of questions, leaving more than ample space for him to fill in the answers, beginning with a question about his name, John H. Conway: "What does the H stand for?"

> *Horton. Why so much space for this? Did you expect something like Hog-ginthebottomtofflinghame-Frobisher-Williamss-Jenkinson?*

Gardner also wanted more details on the genesis of the game. "I predict that it will become such a standard, well known game that it will be of interest to record a few details about the circumstances surrounding its invention," Gardner wrote. "Could you supply a few details? Doodling during a lecture? (If so, what lecture?) Doodling over glasses of beer?"

> *We were doodling long after teatime in the Department common room trying to invent a good pencil and paper game. This was some days after I'd more or less completely analysed the Lucasian game, an old game also with spots, but with no new spots added, so it doesn't "sprout". It originally came from a rather complicated game about folding stamps which [Mike Patterson] had put into pencil and paper form, and we were successively modifying the rules. At one point [Mike] said "why not put a new spot in the middle" . . . and as soon as this was adopted all the other rules were discarded, the starting position was simplified to just n points (originally 3), and sprouts sprouted . . .*
>
> *The day after sprouts sprouted it seemed that everyone was playing it. At coffee or tea times there were little groups of people poring over ridiculous-to-fantastic sprout positions. Some people were already attacking sprouts on Klein bottles and the like, with at least one man thinking of higher-dimensional versions . . . one found the remains of sprout games in the most unlikely places.*
>
> *Whenever I try to acquaint somebody new to the game nowadays, it always seems that they've already heard of it by some devious route. Even my 3 and 4 year old daughters play it with each other, though I can usually beat them.*

And Conway kept the info coming, heading the next month's letter:

IMPORTANT BREAKTHROUGH IN SPROUTOLOGY!

Today, Gardner's prediction about continued interest in the game has proved correct. The World Game of Sprouts Association is "devoted to the discovery of sprouts reality" and to "a serious exploration of the game," and holds an annual championship tournament online. "For humans only" is one of the rules, since extensive computer analysis of the game over the years inspired some to enter their computer programs in the tournament rather than themselves. Conway hadn't heard about the World Game of Sprouts Association, but he was well aware of computers playing the game. Computers were all the rage when he invented Sprouts; computers were a large part of the motivation.

> I was distressed. Computers were being used to solve a number of open problems—computers could solve problems standing for 100 years. We wanted to invent a game that would be hard to analyze by computer.

Although it took a while, in the early 1990s a Bell Labs trio produced a paper documenting a "Computer Analysis of Sprouts," analyzing the winning strategy for games up to 11 spots. "Beyond n = 11 their program was unable to cope with sprouting complexity," Gardner reported back to his readers. Decades later, a French duo wondered whether the 11-spot record was beatable. As a hobby, the students developed software called GLOP—based on the French comic strip character Pif le Chien, who says "Glop" to express satisfaction. They produced a Ph.D. thesis on the subject, and they claimed to have solved Sprouts games up to 44 dots. When Conway heard this he was somewhat curious, if incredulous.

> I doubt that very much. They are basically saying they have done the im-

possible. If someone says they've invented a machine that can write a play worthy of Shakespeare, would you believe them? It's just too complicated. If someone said they'd been having some success teaching pigs to fly . . . Though if they were doing that over in the field behind the Institute, I would like to take a look.

By all outward appearances Conway was blissfully playing his way through the 1960s. Inwardly he worried that his own mathematical soul was withering away. He was doing nothing, had done nothing. He felt he didn't deserve his job. While he was piddling around, friends of his were graduating and finding no work. He felt trapped giving lectures on "Foundations of Logic," which wasn't quite his thing. He also gave a lecture course on automata. As his students would find out when they continued their studies elsewhere—say, at MIT—Professor Conway had worked out his own original proofs and unorthodox terminology, because he wasn't as familiar as he should have been with the published literature. Typical Conway. It was easier to reinvent the wheel. He improvised as he went, hardly ever planning lectures much ahead of time (or in a haze about what he'd planned; at least once he arrived for a morning lecture wearing his dinner suit from a feast in college the night before). Most lecturers would set down a sequential process: theorem 1, lemma 2, theorem 3, lemma 4. Conway would saunter in and say,

Here's this theorem I've been trying to prove—let's see what we can get.

This is a more honest way to lecture, showing the false starts and "stuckedness" that are crucial to the mathematical process. However, it's also a lot more work, for the student and the lecturer both. A student named Andrew Glass, now a Cambridge math professor, once encountered Conway in the photocopy room executing the administrative task of stapling together his sandals. Conway glanced at his student's open notebook and recognized material from his automata course.

Were my lectures anywhere near that coherent?

Coherent or not, Conway's lectures were popular. An announcement appeared in the *Cambridge Reporter* heralding the establishment of the "John Conway Appreciation Society." It specified that the society had no treasurer (as was technically a requirement for Cambridge societies) but that it did have at least one patron, and it asked: "Guess who?"

The smitten students loved him as much for his mind as his silly high jinks, and maybe most of all for his singular hybrid of sophistication, sincerity, and lascivious showmanship. He wore sandals year-round, yes, but often he was barefoot at the blackboard, having kicked off his sandals and flung them into the radiator or the far corners of the room (hence the perpetual mending). He had a homely lecturing style, discussing abstract concepts in terms of ordinary objects such as train cars (and cats and dogs). Sometimes he brought a large turnip and a carving knife to class, and in illustrating his lesson he would transform the tuber a slice at a time from a sphere to a cube to an icosahedron, devouring the scraps as he went.

A student named Edward Welbourne, now a software engineer in Oslo, had heard about Conway even before he took the Foundations of Logic course. He recalls Conway teaching mathematician Kurt Gödel's Incompleteness Theorem, the first humility theorem in mathematics. Proved in 1931, Gödel's theorem stated that in mathematics there will always be undecidable truths, statements that cannot be proved or disproved—and at that, Gödel's theorem would seem to be a good "theme theorem" for this book and the quagmiric enterprise of remembering and telling tales that exist along a sliding spectrum of verifiability, a mirrored hall of truthiness.

In a course on linear algebra, Welbourne recalls the class when Conway proved that for 2 symmetric quadratic forms, both can be simultaneously diagonalized—no small feat. "Doing each takes a moderately tricky piece of computation," says Welbourne. "To do 2 at the same time is thus doubly tricky, like balancing a broom by its handle on one's chin while juggling," which is exactly what Conway did whilst concluding the proof. Conway quibbles that really he balanced a broom on his chin whilst simultaneously balancing a penny on the hook of a coat hanger and then, with an assured centrifugal swoop, he spun this coat hanger contraption around like a helicopter rotor.

All this appreciation for Conway couldn't have suffered, either, from his habit of starting a course by providing the entire curriculum on a single sheet of paper, full of arrows leading from one subject to the next; nor from his habit of finishing courses a class early and using that last session to speed through all 24 lectures, reprising all the proofs. These final lectures became popular, the audience swelling 30 percent beyond its usual size, attracting students from years past who stopped in for a refresher. Then there was the November that Conway finished his course 2 lectures early. He did the traditional 24-classes-in-1 on the Wednesday, which left the Friday class empty. University regulations dictated that as the professor he was obliged to show up, but he told his students that they were not so obliged, and he rather hoped they'd take the hint. As he approached the lecture room that Friday, all was promisingly silent—none of the raucous buzz and chatter of 200 students waiting for proceedings to commence. Thankfully his loyal followers had obeyed. He walked through the door, and thereupon the class leapt out at him screaming "*Surprise!*" The girls were in fancy party dresses, and the boys were on their worst behavior.

Amidst the chaos, Welbourne inflicted a problem on his good professor, just the sort of jeu d'esprit he knew Conway wouldn't be able to resist. "I doubt he would be offended at the suggestion that he's somewhat scatterbrained. Observing him, it always seemed like there were ideas popping into his head all the time, though he was perfectly capable of concentrating on one idea at a time for long periods," says Welbourne, who was right in thinking his problem would appeal to Conway. It had been doing the rounds, from Belgrade to Denmark to England and beyond, and courtesy of Conway it continues.

I'm going to give it to you the way it was given to me. Tell me when you figure out the pattern:

Now, what comes next?

The history of the puzzle dated to a recent International Mathematical Olympiad in Belgrade. The Dutch contingent sicced the puzzle on the British team, and that's how it was imported to Cambridge, according to an account in the Cambridge math journal *Eureka*. "When I first showed this puzzle to one of my friends," the *Eureka* reporter said, "… he thought for some time and then gave an agonized cry, 'I've solved it—but you need a really *twisted* mind to think of that!' I showed it to several arts students, who were all baffled, which is surprising as it requires no mathematical skills beyond counting. From my mathematical friends I got the same response as the initial one; silence and furious thinking for between two and thirty minutes followed by anguished howling. If hideous noises were heard echoing down the corridors of Newnham it was a good bet I'd asked that puzzle again." Conway, however, let out none of these sounds.

> I could not guess it. And I could tell from the way Eddy said it that I was supposed to be able to guess it. In the end he had to tell me the answer.

Once in the know, Conway was helplessly consumed with what he called "The Look-and-Say Sequence." The name gives a clue for solving it. *Look* at the first number, 1. *Say* how many of that number there are— "one 1"—and write that observation down on the next line, numerically as "11." Then look at that number and say the description: "21." And so forth. Immediately following that last lecture before Christmas, Conway flew off to Boston for a conference and he spent the entire flight fiddling with Look-and-Say sequences, trying out different starting strings of numbers.

$$55555$$
$$55$$
$$25$$
$$1215$$
$$11121115$$

He decided to deconstruct things, inserting commas around the phrases of verbal description—this he called "parsing." And as he explained in an article he wrote for the same issue of *Eureka*:

> The numbers in our strings are usually single-digit ones, so we'll call them digits and usually cram them together as we have just done. But occasionally we want to indicate the way the numbers in the string were obtained, and we can do this neatly by inserting commas recalling the commas and quotes in our verbal descriptions, thus:

$$55555$$
$$,55,$$
$$,25,$$
$$,12,15,$$
$$,11,12,11,15,$$

He titled the article "The Weird and Wonderful Chemistry of Audioactive Decay," because by the end of a flight's worth of fiddling, he had augmented the verbal metaphors with chemistry metaphors, devising the Chemical Theorem, which proved that all the numerical sequences generated by this puzzle ultimately settle into exactly 92 shorter sequences, or "common atoms," as he called them. He aligned the 92 common atoms with the then 92 chemical elements of the periodic table: 3 he aligned with uranium, which is atomic number 92; 13 he aligned with protactinium, which is atomic number 91; 1113 he aligned with thorium, atomic number 90; and so on down to hydrogen, atomic number 1, aligned with the Look-and-Say common atom 22. For instance, take the initial sequence

$$1$$
$$11$$
$$21$$
$$1211$$
$$111221$$
$$312211$$
$$13112221$$

All of those things so far are atoms but not common atoms. The next line you get is: 1113213211, or 11132.13211. When you split it like that in the middle you see it's a compound of 2 common atoms—it's hafnium stannide. Hafnium, actually a real element in the world, is, according to my table, 11132. And then 12311 is tin, but in the international table the chemical symbol of tin is Sn, which comes from the Latin root *stannum*.

So 1, after not that many moves, becomes the compound hafnium stannide! This is an example of the second theorem I proved, the Cosmological Theorem, which asserts that after a certain number of moves from the Big Bang—the beginning of the sequence—all the exotic elements, all the things that are not compounds of common atoms, for instance 1, disappear and everything is made of common atoms.

What happens next is if you follow the left-hand portion, hafnium, and you follow the right-hand portion, stannum, they never interfere with each other. The sequence splits as a compound, and if you continue on with the Look-and-Say procedure, the 2 sides never interfere with each other.

11132.13211

311312.11131221

1321131112.3113112211

How, pray tell, did Conway notice such a thing during the ennui of a transatlantic crossing?

It doesn't very much matter. I'm pretty clever. The point is I did notice it. And I can prove it.

Conway proved the Cosmological Theorem over Christmas, and thereafter the Look-and-Say Sequence was renamed by Eileen as "The Problem That Spoiled Christmas"—Conway was always spoiling Christmas. He lost that first proof, which he'd done with his Cambridge friend and collaborator Richard Parker, a mathematician cum computer designer, but he wasn't too upset because that proof was too long, anyway. Mike Guy did a second proof, also eventually lost. And on it went. All the while subsidiary discoveries kept coming. Conway noticed that the sequence grows in length by an approximately constant 30 percent per generation, the 20th and 21st generations being:

111312211312111322212321121113121112131112132112311321322
112111312211312112213211231132132211231131122211311123113
322112111312211312111322111213122112311311123112112322211
213211321322113311213212312311211131122211213211331121321
12312321123113112221121111312211312111312311121123221112132
11322211312113211

311311222113111231133211121312211231131112312111133112111
312211213211312111322211213113122211311112212211113122111213
2113121113222112132113213221133112132123222211231131122211
31112311322311211131122211213211331121321122121332211211
13122113121113222123211211113121112131112132112311231132132211
2111312212321121113122112131112131221121321132113213221123113
112221131112311311121321122112121322321121113122113322113111
221131221

The latter 408 digits are about 1.3 times longer than the former 302 digits. That ratio is called Conway's Constant: If you take 2 consecutive numbers, their ratio converges on or about 1.303577269. . . . But the number never quite settles down—much like Conway himself. And case in point, to this Conway insists on adding:

> The really astonishing thing is that it's a root of an algebraic equation of degree 71!

This sort of signature johnfoolery is what inspired the John Conway Appreciation Society. Not too long ago someone confessed to Conway that he was the society's founder. Conway promptly forgot who it was, though he remembered where the confession took place, at an event held at Windsor Castle, and hence he thought the confessor was probably the event's convener, Baron Martin Rees. Rees was a student around the time Conway began lecturing, so it seemed plausible. Rees says, "I only know of the 'appreciation society' by reputation." He'd never taken any classes with Conway; he was a fan, but not the founding patron. Was Conway's brain again playing tricks? Was Rees thinking twice about his confession? Taking advice from another befuddled biographer, Geoff Dyer, I puzzled over the discrepancies between these rival claims and settled for the conclusion that the truth lay somewhere in the contradiction.

The John Conway Appreciation Society caused at least one of the Cambridge elders some consternation. "Oh dear," he murmured to a colleague at high table. "Should this be a serious concern? It could lead to a bad case of overweening pride!" Those in the know assured the elder that the society was a satirical poke. Yet what was it exactly? Did it exist only in the abstract? It existed in the concrete, but it was an undergraduate society, and undergraduate societies were usually short on formal structure. Simply put, everyone who thought John Conway was a good thing automatically belonged.*

Andrew Glass, the student Conway ran into in the photocopying room, would have belonged. And returning to Conway's question about whether his lectures were anywhere near as coherent as Glass's notebook suggested, the answer was no. When students discussed Conway's lectures, it emerged that a good many of them were spellbound and too intoxicated with wonderment to take notes while their professor held forth. Glass was the exception, and he was copying his notebook for his fellow students. And, as it turned out, for . . .

> Hey, listen. Could you make me a copy of those notes? I'm meant to be writing a book about this stuff and that's obviously what I need.

Conway promised Glass credit, a promise he kept upon the eventual publication of his first book, *Regular Algebra and Finite Machines*, about 5 years later in 1971. That book was the best thing he'd produced to date, and Conway has always liked to note that his publisher, Chapman and Hall, also published Dickens and Trollope. However, as the book long awaited publication, and as he approached age 30, his life's work still

* Recently there was a Facebook reprise of the society, dedicated to social activities of industrial design students globally, "named in honor of the greatest social deviant."

wasn't adding up to much.

Conway's demons tormented his subconscious in what he calls his "Nerd's Nightmare," though it manifested more like a daydream. On a blistering summer's day, Conway walks with pencil and paper in hand along the dusty paths of Trinity College's Great Court quadrangle. The sun's rays beat down and refract through variations in air density that rise from the paths, creating a shimmering desertlike mirage. And then, from the quadrangle's opposite corner, another big burly alpha male mathematician slowly advances into view. Cue the tremolo whistle that presages a duel in *The Good, the Bad, and the Ugly*. It's a mathematicians' shootout. Who's the fastest to draw a stellated icosahedron? Who's the fastest to solve <u>fill in the blank</u>? Conway always found himself in this imaginary predicament without a single mathematically inclined synapse in his head. The Black Blank is how he thinks of this chapter in his life. He was having fun, playing games, but otherwise feeling guilty and depressed.

6.

THE VOW

At any moment there is only a fine layer between the "trivial" and the impossible. Mathematical discoveries are made in this layer.

ANDREY KOLMOGOROV

In August 1966, the International Congress of Mathematicians convened in Moscow. A frightening place, Conway thought. Nonetheless it was there, reclining against a giant cylindrical pillar at least 5 feet in diameter, that he turned a crucial corner.

Moscow State University hosted the proceedings in its palacelike main building, a 32-floor Stalinist skyscraper atop the (then) Lenin Hills. The itinerary involved 2 weeks of nonstop lecture sessions, with a dozen or more lectures running in parallel slots, as well as select invited talks and the Fields Medal ceremony. One of the recipients of the Fields that year, alongside Michael Atiyah, Alexander Grothendieck, and Stephen Smale, was Paul Cohen. Cohen, in 1963, had achieved a glorious result with the Continuum Hypothesis—Cantor's hypothesis about all the possible sizes of infinite sets.* Conway took a look at Cohen's 200-page paper and deemed it the work of an alien being.

In Moscow, the weather was hot and humid, the political climate

---

* Cohen, with his result, proved the "independence" of the Continuum Hypothesis, which in turn meant that he proved the hypothesis *could not* be proved. This was a nice (if slightly perplexing) bookend to the result Kurt Gödel had achieved in 1940. Gödel proved that the hypothesis could not be disproved. So now the state of affairs in set theory had it that the Continuum Hypothesis could neither be proved nor disproved, it was *provably unsolvable,* at least according to the current axioms—leaving the door ajar ever so slightly, since further intuition into sets might open the way for a solution.

chilly—Communism, the Cold War, Vietnam. In February of that year, Brezhnev's Kremlin had displayed its animus toward the intelligentsia, sentencing 2 Soviet authors, Yuli Daniel and Andrei Sinyavsky, to lengthy prison terms in forced-labor camps for writing novels, published in the West under pen names, that satirized the Communist regime. Mathematics seemed a more benign undertaking, removed from political tumult. Yet at the Congress a vociferous contingent of American mathematicians circulated a petition stating, "We the undersigned mathematicians from all parts of the world express our support for the Vietnamese people and their right to self-determination." If the petition passed under Conway's pen he likely would have signed. There were a lot of petitions going around in that day, and he usually signed, and afterwards he usually fretted about having signed, wishing he knew for certain that "the facts" as presented were, in fact, facts.

Against all odds, Moscow turned out to be quite the party. Women were not plentiful among the conferees, but demographics balanced out by factoring in the large contingent of mostly female translators whose job it was to facilitate communication among approximately 5,000 mathematicians from 58 countries. And Moscow or not, it was the sixties.

The story Conway most likes to tell details how he and a few friends worked out a lovely way of getting girls. The method developed as follows: Conway gave a humble little lecture on "regular expressions," part of his study of regular algebras and finite machines. Among the small audience sat a mathematician from Moldova with a special interest in regular algebras. He and Conway spoke a few patchwork words beforehand, and afterward Conway invited the Moldovan man to join his group of friends heading to dinner. For that they needed a translator, so they went to the translators' booth in the basement and enlisted an attractive young woman. The next night, when Conway and his confreres went out for dinner, he went back and requested the same translator, even though the Moldovan mathematician wasn't in attendance. Their translator suggested a few more translators, her girlfriends, who might like to join. This evolved into a reliable algorithm. Request a translator for languages U, V (Olga), languages W, X (Tanya), and languages Y, Z (Natalya), even when the only language spoken among the partygoers was English. Presto, Conway and friends were keeping company with the sweeter sex for the second week of the Congress (the method was only invented, or discovered, midway through). There was nothing untoward about this scenario, Conway assures, everyone was just enjoying themselves immensely.

Between congressional sessions, Conway was leaning against the aforementioned pillar, wolfing down a salami sandwich during a lunch break, when a man approached and asked, "Are you Conway?" The interlocutor was John McKay, then a Ph.D. student at the University of Edinburgh. McKay had on offer a mathematical commodity he thought might be of interest. As Conway came to understand, McKay was forever peddling mathematical unions, people with people, people with ideas. Over time, Conway learned to rebuff these transactions. Yet he has always been grateful that he didn't reject McKay that first time. Conway was in an expansive mood and willing to listen. Present him with a problem he finds compelling, and Conway latches on like a dog to a tasty bone—you've got him, he's yours. If the offering is not to his taste, he'll find it difficult to hide his indifference—he clams up, he disengages, and disengaging is something at which Conway excels.

But on that inaugural meeting, McKay made an offering that piqued Conway's curiosity. It was a mathematical entity known as the Leech lattice—the best lattice for packing spheres in 24 dimensions, with the "lattice" being a set of points and the points being the centers of the spheres. By analogy, consider that the best packing of circles in 2 dimensions is the "hexagonal packing," hexagonal because if you connect the dots of the centers of any 6 circles surrounding a central circle, these central dots connect to form hexagons. This arrangement of circles has 12 symmetries—it can be rotated or reflected in 12 different ways and it looks exactly the same. By extension, then, suspicions were that the Leech lattice might contain an exquisitely large symmetry—a gem emerging from applied mathematics but with provenance in pure.

The pure lineage goes back centuries in a grand mathematical expedition, tanta-

The best 2d sphere packing ... and its lattice

mount to climbing the highest summits or rocketing to the farthest reaches of the universe. Except this expedition's terrain was symmetry and the goal, ultimately, became an exhaustively comprehensive classification—formally called the Classification Project.

The word *symmetry*—"together measuring" or "measuring the same"—had been used since classical times. In the eighteenth century the Swiss mathematician Leonhard Fuller and the German Carl Friedrich Gauss broke the trail for symmetry's systematic study. In 1832, the Frenchman Evariste Galois laid a foundation stone when he coined the term "group," meaning a collection of movements or operations performed on a mathematical entity, an equation, or a geometric solid such as a cube, that preserve its original identity and its symmetry. The cube has a symmetry group of 48. It can be rotated or reflected in 48 ways and still look exactly the same. Galois didn't live long enough to develop his idea of a group, meeting death in a duel at age 20. The night before, he wrote a letter detailing some of his work. "I hope people will be found who profit by sorting out all this mes . . ." From the mess emerged group theory, the mathematical study of symmetry.

Like the integers, there are infinitely many groups, but groups can be collected in families, such as the finite groups and the infinite groups. Infinite groups are ubiquitous and do not submit to any governing theory; there is no end to the interesting examples, thus making them less interesting. Take the infinite symmetries of the sphere, which looks the same no matter which way it is rotated or reflected. Finite simple groups, by contrast, are more uniquely interesting. For instance, there are 60 symmetries that comprise the rotation group of the icosahedron, and this group compounded, or multiplied times 2 so as to include the mirror or reflection group, is the full icosahedral group of 120 symmetries. In this way the finite simple groups came to be regarded as the fundamental, irreducible units of symmetry—all symmetry groups are compounds of simple groups, much as all numbers are products of prime numbers, and all matter is made up of elementary particles. And the groups expeditionists, discovering new groups here and there just as physicists had discovered the particles, by the twentieth century had embarked on the Classification Project, a grand group theory venture seeking to enumerate all the finite simple groups.

And then there's the applied side of the symmetry story. Currently,

This is an Escher trick: If you look casually at Escher's Circle Limit IV, you see a big overall symmetry. The picture has infinitely many symmetries—defined by the symmetry group 4 ∗ 3 in Conway's notation. But in looking more carefully at the angels and devils, and noticing that some of them are less detailed than others and seem to be facing away from us, then you appreciated what's really going on: The image is not quite as symmetric as you first thought; it's only $\frac{1}{4}$ as symmetrical—defined by the symmetry group ∗3333 which is a subset, a subgroup, of the larger overall infinite group.

"supersymmetry" offers a crucial extension to the Standard Model of particle physics, the model explaining the basic building blocks of the universe and the fundamental forces of nature. Symmetry's explanatory power in physics first emerged in the early twentieth century. The German mathematician Emmy Noether proved her theorem showing the connection between symmetry and the conservation laws in physical systems. Einstein wondered, "How can it be that mathematics, being after all a product of human thought independent of experience, is so admirably adapted to the objects of reality?" Communications technology and coding theory also showed connections with symmetry. In 1948, Claude Shannon, at Bell Labs in New York, published his famous paper "A Mathematical Theory of Communication," demonstrating that the optimal coding for minimizing distortion corresponded to a dense packing of spheres—and optimally dense sphere packings are highly symmetrical, generating highly symmetrical lattices. The next year, Marcel Golay, working nearby at the Signal Corps Engineering Laboratories in New Jersey, discovered a family of codes with words that were strings of 24 0s and 1s. And then in the mid 1960s Cambridge mathematics graduate John Leech happened upon the Golay code and took a look. Leech had worked in the industrial sector at the UK electrical engineering firm Ferranti and was by then a lecturer in the computing laboratory at Glasgow University. Ruminating over Golay's code, he discovered a high-density packing of spheres in 24 dimensions, and he developed a slightly outlandish suspicion that the corresponding lattice, henceforth known as the Leech lattice, would be highly symmetrical—so symmetrical that it might contain 1 of those groups hunted by the expeditionists.

By now the expeditionists had classified most of the finite simple groups, groups and subgroups, and arranged them in a periodic table of sorts, into families and subfamilies. And they'd moved onto the trail of some unexpected outliers that did not seem to be part of any known families. Sometimes these outliers are called the "exceptional groups," but Conway prefers to call them "sporadic groups."

> You know what the word "sporadic" means. It's all to do with seeds, or spores, of mushrooms, things like that—when the plant releases its seeds and they float away to land who knows where. It captures the meaning and sense of being isolated, scattered. But it's got another connotation, which means random or irregular, and the sporadic groups are not really random.

Not random so much as rare, and occurring at irregularly scattered intervals. After some investigation it seemed there were only 26 sporadic groups. The challenge was proving there were only 26 and no more—again, similar to physicists undertaking to establish the number of elementary particles. Initially there were a lonesome 5 sporadic groups, the Mathieu groups, discovered by the French mathematical physicist Émile Mathieu in 1861. The largest and most spectacular is M_{24}, and as Conway has said and written on a number of occasions:

This centenarian group can still startle us with its youthful acrobatics.

For a while, Mathieu's groups seemed to be the only sporadic specimens. Then, in 1966, the Croatian mathematician Zvonimir Janko
shocked the world (the math world, at least) when he discovered a group
with 175,560 symmetries, known as J_1—the first new sporadic group
found in over a century. This opened a can of worms, as it were, or a can
of worms crossed with Pandora's box. It made Leech's prospect about his
lattice's gloriously big symmetry not so outlandish after all. Leech knew,
however, that he lacked the expertise to find this group (he was fairly
certain, based on geometric considerations, that he knew the order of
the group to within a factor of 2, but he couldn't prove it). He dangled
the problem under the nose of a few symmetry aficionados, Donald
Coxeter among them, and he spread the word, telling his friend John
McKay. McKay tempted Conway, and Conway eventually took the bait.

I pestered Conway for more details regarding this Moscow meeting with
McKay, but he begged off. He was loath to add any "spurious precision,"
as he came to refer to his embellishments, advertent or accidental.

Still, he can't resist a good story, like the story about the banquet held
inside the splendiferous Kremlin during the Congress's final night. The
food was awful, and the wait for dessert went on forever. When the wait-
ers finally emerged balancing 4-foot-round trays of ice cream, mathematicians mobbed them and plucked bowls from the trays before they
reached the tables. Conway got his ice cream. Later that night, he found
himself back in the dining room, locked out of the university residence
where he was staying. This was the result of more shenanigans involving
the translators, to be sure, but mostly on the part of a friend of Conway's.
A translator had taken a shine to his friend, who was gay, and so in frantically trying to avoid pursuit, the fellow ran smack into a glass door
and knocked himself out. This meant trouble, and the translator disappeared like a shot. The levelheaded Christopher Zeeman was nearby and
called for a doctor. Suddenly the victim awoke and bolted, and Conway
spent the night looking for him. By the time Conway gave up, he was
locked out of his residence. Unsure what to do, he went back to the banquet hall. There was no one there, and the tables were cleared, some with

piles of tablecloths underneath. He grabbed a tablecloth, threw it over a table for privacy, and made a comfy bed beneath for his sleepover in the Kremlin. The next morning he feared he might be arrested as he passed the kiosk at the exit, but he mimed morning-after drunkenness and escaped. He was on a plane back to England within hours. He arrived home in Cambridge to Eileen and his girls with 2 weeks' worth of stubble on his chin. He had forgotten to pack his razor, and therefrom began the beard he's worn ever since.

That was pretty much it for his Moscow mythologizing—though there was also the theorem that inadvertently got proved, and again in the interest of giving credit where credit was due, he published it as follows: "'A Headache Causing Problem,' by Conway (J. H.), Paterson (M. S.), and Moscow (U.S.S.R.)." Luckily, in terms of the Leech-McKay-Conway storyline, I'd unearthed a monograph titled *From Error Correcting Codes Through Sphere Packing to Simple Groups*, which tells the entire tale, starting with Galois. The author, Thomas Thompson of Walla Walla University, had produced the little book as his Ph.D. thesis in 1978, a mere 12 years (rather than a time-and-memory-warping 4+ decades) after the Moscow conference. Thompson conducted a few rounds of transatlantic telephone interviews and quoted Conway at length, recounting verbatim most of what Conway had told me, and much more. This was a nice find, because conversations on the subject often ended with my sources demurring on the details. McKay was certainly no help; his memory was the worst. As Nietzsche said, "The advantage of a bad memory is that one enjoys several times the same good things for the first time," but there are disadvantages as well, especially when there's a biographer on your case. As Conway had taken to remarking:

My memory. My memory is a liar. It's a good liar. It deceives even me.

And pretty much everyone's memories turned out to be liars—even mine was caught out over the 7 years spent trying to reconcile various versions of stories and untangling false from true. Another account of the Moscow story—in a popular history of symmetry, ostensibly drawn from interviews with Conway—describes the same seminal meeting between Conway and McKay, but in this version Conway isn't gallantly lounging against a giant column savoring a salami sandwich, he's "manning a stall handing out bread rolls stuffed with meat." The notion of Conway performing hostess duties seems preposterous. There was a stall handing out meat sandwiches, and Conway gladly wolfed down as many as humanly possible. That sounds more likely. Conway shrugs his shoulders and chalks it up to a transcription error, or some other distortion of a message unsuccessfully sent.

> That's the sort of thing that happens. Mistakes can be of many kinds. You don't really have to blame people for mistakes. You just accept that they are part of life.

So, long story short, I brought Thompson's error-correcting book along during my next visit to the Conway alcove, and we sat there together reading aloud from the page. It said that in those days, Conway wasn't all that interested in sphere packing, nor was he a group theorist. Check, check. He hadn't joined the expeditionists in their classification of the groups, though the book did say that he'd dabbled, he'd tried to verify some of Janko's assertions. Since in addition to finding the sporadic group J_1, Janko also predicted the existence of 2 more. Conway again agreed; he'd done some fiddling with Janko's findings, although not seriously. But unlike others outside the fray, he was not afraid of group theory.

Over the next year or so he tried to interest his friend and Cambridge colleague John Thompson in the Leech lattice. Thompson was the world expert in group theory, and he has the hairy eyebrows to match his deified status (he is not related to Thomas Thompson, author of that little monograph). Conway once wrote him a letter of reference that began: "Being asked to write a letter of reference for John Thompson is like being asked to write a letter of reference for God"—incidentally, Thompson studied theology before switching to math. When Conway knew that Thompson wasn't about to go hunting for this purported group, Conway decided to give it a try. Along the way he continued in his efforts to persuade Thompson, but those overtures went unrequited. Mathematicians were constantly approaching him with what they thought was the next big group, the long-lost group, the Holy Grail of groups. Thompson resisted, but he said that if Conway worked out the symmetries in the group, then he'd take it more seriously.

Thus challenged, Conway set out to discover the group of symmetries for the Leech lattice, the very big number of symmetries that would define this godforsaken group. The 2-dimensional hexagonal circle packing has 12 symmetries; in 4 dimensions, 24 spheres can touch any given sphere and there are 1,152 symmetries; in 8 dimensions, there are 240 spheres and 696,729,600 symmetries; but how many symmetries would operate on Leech's 24-dimensional lattice? Conway warned his wife that he would be working hard to find this number. Because if he found it, it would make his name. Similarly, he'd taken a stab at some of the big problems—not only Cantor's Continuum Hypothesis and the Axiom of Choice, but also Fermat's Last Theorem and the Riemann Hypothesis—never with any high hopes and never with any luck. But every now and then he'd take one of these big problems off the back burner and daydream about the excitement and glory of success, and every so often he even had a few new ideas. This time he cleared the decks and told the kiddies that Daddy wasn't to be disturbed. He set aside Wednesday nights from 6 o'clock to midnight and Saturdays from noon to midnight, for as long as necessary. As he told Thomas Thompson for the monograph:

> On the first Saturday, I had a last cup of coffee and kissed the wife and kids good-bye, went and locked myself in the front room, and started to work.

These remarks startled Conway with their verisimilitude, their ring of truth.

That actually does sound like me!

He expected to keep his house-arrest work ethic for weeks or months or beyond. Locking himself away that first day, he unfurled a roll of wallpaper backing paper, finally making use of the rolls and rolls left behind by the previous tenant. He sketched out all he knew about the problem. By evening, a mere halfway into his Saturday allowance of work time, he'd

figured it out. He'd deduced the Leech lattice's number of symmetries—
that is to say, the order of its group. It was 4,157,776,806,543,360,000. Or
double that. Either-or.

> *It was about 6 in the evening. I telephoned Thompson and dictated this
> order to him saying that it was either this number or twice this number.
> And then he got really terribly excited and a short time later telephoned
> me back with the correct order of the group.*

The double, 8,315,553,613,086,720,000. Thompson still wasn't about
to take it on himself, however. So Conway went back to work. In order
to prove the group existed, he had to corroborate all the coordinates, all
the center points of the hyperspheres that touched any given sphere—no
small task in 24 dimensions. The center point of a sphere in 3 dimensions has 3 coordinates—(x, y, z). The center point of the 24-dimensional
spheres had 24 coordinates—

$$(a,b,c,d,e,f,g,h,i,j,k,l,m,n,o,p,q,r,s,t,u,v,w,x)$$

In order to execute the existence proof, Conway constructed a matrix
of 24 rows and 24 columns for which he calculated all 576 entries. Filling in the matrix was a bit like doing a Sudoku puzzle, but more difficult.

> *It wasn't entirely a routine calculation. But I couldn't quite see how to
> prove that the group generated by this matrix, and some others, was the
> group I was interested in. Anyway, I telephoned Thompson again and told
> him that I had this matrix, but that I was feeling quite exhausted (even
> though it was only 10 o'clock) and was going to bed. I would talk more
> about it tomorrow. Then I hung the telephone up.*

And off to bed he did not go. He thought he should at least take a stab
at the calculations for the proof.

> *The problem was to show that a spanning set would be sent by this ma-
> trix to another spanning set. For some reason I must have had a blind
> spot. Anyway, it suddenly dawned on me as soon as I had finished tele-
> phoning him the second time that I was being stupid. So I wrote down a*

list of 40 vectors such that if the matrix fixed those as a whole, then it was all right. And I checked one of them.

Excited now, he called Thompson back with the latest.

I said, "Well now, look, I've done a fortieth of this thing and I know it's all going to work and so, really now, I'm going to bed."

He went back to work.

Well, how bloody stupid to give up, and so I carried on. At a quarter past midnight, I telephoned Thompson again, saying that it was all done. This group is there. It was absolutely fantastic—12 hours had changed my life. Especially since I had envisioned it going on for months—every 3 days spending 6 or 12 hours on the damned thing.

The next day, Sunday, he met with Thompson and started a discussion that went on for days, weeks, months . . . And news of the discovery traveled around Cambridge, among those inclined to be interested. A physics grad student heard it from his mathematician friends: "John Conway had found a big group!"

Now I wanted to drill down and ask Conway what, exactly, he was doing when he locked himself away.

Well, I'll tell you what happened. These investigations of the Leech lattice were all from the point of view of symmetry—symmetry symmetry symmetry symmetry symmetry.

The Leech lattice is fantastically symmetrical. I think of these things as Christmas tree ornaments, with lots of spikes sticking out, or exquisitely cut gems, and gorgeous symmetry appearing whenever you look. You look at them from one point of view and you see one kind of symmetry. Then it rotates and you are looking along some other axis and you see another kind of symmetry. And to my eye it is tremendously beautiful.

With the Leech lattice, some of the symmetries were obvious, they just permute the coordinates and change the signs of coordinates—rotate and reflect spheres onto one another. I called these the visible symmetries. The difficulty was to prove that there were non-obvious symmetries.

A non-obvious fact was that any of the 196,560 spheres next to the central sphere touches exactly 4,600 other spheres—that was a good hint that there might be other symmetries besides the obvious.

Imagine, for instance, 2 spheres in 24 dimensions touching each other. I worked out the number of spheres that touched both of them and it was 4,600. And then I looked at another pair of spheres that didn't look similar to the previous pair, counted the number of spheres touching both of them—4,600 again. So this constancy of various numbers suggested that the situation was in fact more symmetric than it looked. These coincidences aren't going to happen by accident; they aren't going to happen without there being a reason behind it. The coincidence of getting 4,600 again and again, this pointed to something non-obvious.

All these spheres, each touching 196,560 spheres, were arranged in 3 separate groupings. And these groupings demonstrated the obvious symmetries, but I wanted to find 1 symmetry that united all 3 sets. I wanted to prove that you could pick up the entire configuration and turn it round somehow and that every sphere would fall exactly into the place that was originally occupied by another sphere. And the coincidences, the constancy of certain numbers that popped up—the 4,600—made it look as though there was indeed a unifying symmetry to be found.

After he found the big number, Conway worked with the 24-dimensional coordinates to measure neighboring spheres. But what exactly was he doing, and how? The answer is no more complicated than the Pythagorean Theorem, $a^2 + b^2 = c^2$. The square of the hypotenuse of a right triangle equaling the sum of the squares of the other 2 sides.

Let's think of 2 dimensions again. So you've got the vector whose coordinates are (4,7). To get the length of that vector, take 4^2, which is 16, plus 7^2, which is 49—that gives 65—so the length of that vector is the square root of 65.

Now, on the other hand, take the vector whose coordinates are (8,1). The length of that vector is the square root of 8^2 plus 1^2, which is the square root of—oh my god!—65 again! Because 8^2 is 64 and 1^2 is 1. So those 2 vectors have the same length. They don't look the same. But this is a geometrical thing.

With the Leech lattice I was dealing with 24 coordinates and there were 3 shapes of vectors. One of them had a 3 and lots of 1s.

$$(3,1,1,1,1,1,1,1,1,1,1,1,1,1,1,1,1,1,1,1,1,1,1,1)$$

The other one had 2 4s and lots of 0s.

$$(4,4,0,0,0,0,0,0,0,0,0,0,0,0,0,0,0,0,0,0,0,0,0,0)$$

And the other one had 8 2s and lots of 0s.

$$(2,2,2,2,2,2,2,2,0,0,0,0,0,0,0,0,0,0,0,0,0,0,0,0)$$

So we apply the Pythagorean Theorem. For the first one, 3^2 is 9 and 23 times 1^2 is 23, and 9 and 23 make 32—so the answer is the square root of 32. And you get that with the next coordinate, because 4^2 plus 4^2 is 32, and a lot of 0s. And 2^2 plus 2^2 all the way to 8 terms plus a lot of 0s is also 32. But you know, this is uninteresting. It really is. It is uninteresting to everybody. If you know it, you know it, and it's easy. And if you don't know it, you suspect there might be something interesting in it, and there isn't anything. It's a calculation.

Conway insists that it's crass to pull back the calculatory curtain too far. It's trite, it's trivial, and it defeats the point.

Yes, it's true, my calculations, technically speaking, were using Pythagoras' theorem. But Pythagoras' theorem is more than 2,000 years old, for god's sake. I'm not conscious of using Pythagoras' theorem. All 3 vectors were related by a symmetry. I had to figure out what that symmetry was. To concentrate on the calculation is misleading. It's like asking an artist, "Where did you paint the person's chin? Was it 1-foot-5 above the base of the picture, or 1-foot-6? And how far to the right was it?" Do you understand me? If you're thinking about conceptual things, the measurements don't matter. That's the sense in which I'm saying you're not interested, despite your saying you are. I mean, as long as I can work out the distance from one point to another, I can do my thinking and my geometry and I can see that this is a very regular configuration, then there is no reason for you to be concerned with it.

It's rather unfortunate that we can't just see these things. Because it means that I can only appreciate the beauty of them, truly, after I've have done the calculation. But the calculation isn't the point. The calculation is the scaffolding. And it doesn't matter how I do it, as long as I can do it. Since I can't conjure up 24-dimensional space, I use numbers to do it. The only way I have of studying it, since it's not in our space, is to give coordinates for the points.

For a time I was thinking so geometrically about these things that I used to imagine myself with lots and lots of arms and legs, extra limbs. Because if I have 2 arms and point 'em out, then they both lie in a plane. And I'll use a leg as well, and now they are lying in 3-space. To form an adequate idea, an adequate geometric visualization, of what is going on in 24 dimensions is more or less impossible. In large dimensional space, there are large numbers of directions to point, so you would seem to need quite a lot of arms and legs. I imagined myself stuck in the middle of this space, and trying to understand things, looking up at the stars, pretending they are the lattice points, and just sort of daydreaming.

Anchored by his armchair, Conway waggles his arms and legs around in the space in front of him. And then, speaking of daydreams, he slides off on a tangent:

You know, the question of why the space we are in seems to be 3-dimensional is a very puzzling question. There doesn't seem anything very special about 3-dimensional space. So, why are we living in it?

As is the tradition, Conway's discovery became known as the Conway group. And that group was the largest of 3 simple groups nested together, sometimes collectively called the Conway Constellation. This was the hot mathematical news of the day and earned him a cosmopolitan array of lecture invitations. He flew to Paris, Göttingen, Montreal. During a trip to Montreal there was 8 inches of snow. Conway, as per usual, was wearing only his sandals. He arrived at the venue with wet, red feet and kicked off his frosted leather tangles and yet again lectured barefoot. Finding the group kicked off Conway's jet-set life. He'd fly to New York, deliver a single lecture, turn around, fly back home.

This breakthrough cleared the way for his white-hot discoveries, discoveries summoned via a force that he whimsically, grandiosely, gives a

Shakespearean name—the "Hotspur property," after the character Hotspur in *King Henry IV*.

In act III, Glendower says,

> *I can call spirits from the vasty deep.*

Hotspur replies:

> *Why, so can I, or so can any man;*
> *But will they come when you do call for them?*

For Conway, now they would. And the results came thick and fast. As Samuel Johnson characterized Hotspur, he was at once the comic butt and tragic hero, displaying a noble madness—although "inflated with ambition" and subject to "turbulent desire," Hotspur was "a man able to do much and eager to do more." So was Conway. But it's at this juncture in his lifeline that he made what he calls "The Vow": "Thou shalt stop worrying and feeling guilty; thou shalt do whatever thou pleasest." He surrendered to his peripatetic curiosity and followed wherever it went, whether toward recreation or research, or someplace altogether non-mathematical, such as his longing to learn the etymology of words. "Pandiculate" versus "paniculate." "Ubiety" versus "uberty," "uberous," and "ubigerous"—"ubiety," meaning "whereness," versus "nullibiety," meaning "nowhereness," all of which has next to nothing to do with the ubiquitous use of "ubiquitous." He can also trot out a good riff on the number of words related to the word "number"—

> "Numb" is one of them. "Nemesis" is another. What happens is that "number" is an old Indo-European word, and it originally meant something like "share." The floods came and the land was divided again, and you queued up to get your share. Somebody who is nimble is somebody who is quick at taking their share. "Numb," the past participle of "nim," literally means "taken" or "seized"—deprived of one's senses. And then "nemesis" is basically your share of what fate has in store for you.

Conway's fate was to do all the stuff that he had formerly feared his fellow mathematicians might floccinaucinihilipilificate. "Floccinaucinihilipilification" is perhaps his favorite word. He reckons it's longest word in the Oxford English Dictionary, and he recites nearly verbatim the OED's definition: "the action or habit of estimating as worthless." His telling of its etymology checks out as well. It is a Latin-based word, invented circa 1730 at Eton as a schoolboy's joke. Consulting a Latin textbook, the student found 4 ways of saying "Don't care" and stuck them together: *flocci*, a wisp of wool; *nauci*, a trifle; *nihili*, nothing or something valueless; *pili*, a bit or a whit, something small and insignificant (and then *facere*, to make).

Conway had long maintained, publicly anyway, that all his noodling around, his compulsion for trivialities—memorizing stars, counting petals, playing backgammon—was worthless for all practical purposes. Regardless, he now could be the living, breathing embodiment of "Don't care!"

Before, everything I touched turned to nothing. Now I was Midas, and everything I touched turned to gold.

Act II

7.

RELIGION

Life is far too important to be taken seriously.

—Oscar Wilde

On a frustrating Friday night circa November 1970, Conway watched a spaceship waltz across a screen in the Cambridge Computer Laboratory. He was staring at the screen of a PDP7, an 18-bit programmed data processor with a magnetic core memory and a price tag of $72,000. Friday was his night with the machine. The screen was dismal. The pixels glowed green. He spent hours and hours and hours in that crepuscular room. Door closed, lights out, shades drawn, Conway was making himself blind, exploring his Game of Life. And this was *after* inventing and investigating the game by cruder means, by hand with a Go board and stone counters. Appealing to left brain and right brain both, it was a beautiful invention. Initially even Conway would agree with this assessment. Later he had a change of heart.

A cellular automaton with a simple set of 3 rules,* Life begat alluring, transfixing, infectious complexity. The initial configuration of cells on a theoretically infinite grid determined the configuration of the next generation, which determined the next and the next, and so on. Patterns emerged, seemingly from nowhere. The simplicity belied all the work,

---

* **LIFE RULES REMINDER:**
Birth: *If at time t a cell is dead, and the cell has 3 live neighbors in any direction, then at time* t + 1 *the cell becomes alive.*
Death: *If a live cell has 0 or 1 neighbors it dies of isolation, and if a live cell has 4 or more neighbors it dies of overcrowding.*
Survival: *If a live cell has 2 or 3 live neighbors, then the cell remains alive.*

or again all the play. Creating the game had taken years of tinkering, tweaking the rules at morning coffee, afternoon tea, often all day in between and into the night.

Watching the spaceship, Conway was waiting to see whether the random pattern of cells that he'd put on the grid would continue to grow and move across the screen, whether the configuration might crash into something nearby and with what consequences, whether the cells ultimately faded away and died, or vanished in a flash. As he confessed to Martin Gardner in a letter, Conway was most enamored of the trivial Life-forms, such as the pattern that starts as a cat's face, evolves into a huge grin, and ends as a paw print.

> *Cheshire cats and such are nice—at one time I spent masses of time (far too much!) feeding in pictures like this and watching their behavior.*

But watching that spaceship waltz across the screen, he was getting a bit annoyed at how long it was taking. He was ready to go home. The only thing stopping him was Religion.

Religion was a self-imposed rule that prohibited Conway from shutting off the machine until the fate of a Life-form was clear—he didn't want to kill anything interesting. Life was an approximate simulation of real life, after all. And presumably, if it were played for long enough on a truly infinite grid, some simulacrum of a living creature would crawl out of the "warm little pond," as Darwin called it. Conway doesn't kill spiders, either. He's not a Jain; he doesn't look where he treads so as not to step on an ant. He will escort a bug outdoors. And the same sympathetic sentiment applied to Life. Whereas in regard to all other aspects of religion he abstains, he practiced this Religion with devout faith, and as a result he sometimes stared at the screen for a good hour longer than he wanted.

> It caused some inconvenience. But you know, that's what religious beliefs should do. You should accept whatever happens.

Right then, reminiscing about Life, Conway was still in the edifying alcove on the first day of his lecture series on the Free Will Theorem. I had asked him to recite the highlights of his curriculum vitae. This was partly an effort to distract him from fretting over the size of his audience that night and worrying about his chronic coughing fits. Obligingly, he recited his life's works, as he can do on demand with near perfect replicability—although this time he neglected to mention the Game of Life, until prompted.

With its elegantly minimalistic laws, Life is not only a nice analogue of real life, and even the entire universe. The game's most interesting property is that it's deterministic, predictably unpredictable. The continual evolution of cells is always predestined by what came before, yet what happens even a few steps in the future is unfathomable, too difficult to compute. Even Conway had to sit there in front of the screen and watch. Watch and wait.

And just as the Game of Life is quintessentially deterministic, the Free Will Theorem is quintessentially not.

To me, this ironic incongruity seemed telling, symbolic of something. "The test of a first-rate intelligence," noted F. Scott Fitzgerald, "is the ability to hold two opposing ideas in mind at the same time, and still retain the ability to function."

When I asked Conway, he made nothing of it. There was no symbolism, no ironic asymmetry, nothing profound. A mere 4 decades elapsed between these 2 competing concepts that emerged from his brain. If anything, it's a testament to the only other religion to which Conway subscribes: catholicism, his small c catholic curiosity that reliably leads him hither and thither. Otherwise he is an atheist. And while Conway had vested no ideological faith in the fact that Life was deterministic, he is not so detached from the Free Will Theorem. Conway is wedded to the notion that we really do possess the ability to make choices free from constraints. That said, he hates having to make choices. This he has in common with Cambridge philosopher Ludwig Wittgenstein, a fact Conway learned from the physician he went to as an undergraduate, Dr. Edward Bevan, who had been Wittgenstein's physician and friend. For instance, dining for the first time at the Anchor Pub along the River Cam, Wittgenstein cross-examined the waitress about what dishes were absolutely always available. He wanted to ensure that once he made a selection on this first visit, he would not be bothered with the same tedious task again. Conway feels the same way. Day in and day out, he eats his meals at the same restaurants and orders essentially the same food—dry bagel and black coffee at breakfast, fish with rice for dinner.

> The ordeal of choosing something new is more trouble than the access to greater variety is worth.

His belief in free will, however, extends beyond trivial decisions about what he eats and nontrivial decisions about whom he marries. According to his definition, free will means that one's behavior is not a predetermined function of the past. During all the buzz about the lectures, by contrast, Conway's colleague John Nash revealed he was a "strict determinist." And then there was the little-old-lady question—at a trial-run lecture in Australia, a little old lady had asked him: "God gave us our free will, don't you agree?" It reminded Conway of Napoleon's exchange with Laplace, when the emperor congratulated the mathematician on *Mécanique Céleste*: "I see you haven't made mention of the great architect of the universe." To which Laplace replied, "Your Highness, I had no need of this hypothesis." Neither did Conway. But he dreaded the theological question. His Princeton colleague Joe Kohn, slated to do the introduction at the inaugural lecture, loitered with Conway and Simon Kochen in the common room beforehand and threatened to plant a prickly religious query: "Does the theorem prove God doesn't exist?" Kohn also teased the duo that their real motive was the opposite, that they were secretly attempting to win themselves the million-pound Templeton Prize, awarded "For Progress Toward Research or Discoveries about Spiritual Realities."

Even without Nash and other disbelievers who stayed away, the house was packed for Conway's inaugural lecture. The main lecture room and a second room both overflowed, the aisles jammed with people sitting on the stairs. The audience numbered an estimated 600, the kind of crowd Conway attracted in his heyday—say, when giving a lecture on the Game of Life. Kohn's glowing introduction mentioned that Conway was best known for Life, and that was the last to be heard of it over the 6-week-long series.

Wading slowly into the lecture with a warm-up question, Conway asked of his audience:

Are there any determinists present?

He expected there would be. He'd given talks about the Free Will Theorem at a few academic institutions, where he always asked that question and there were always determinists present. He'd formulated a theory that determinists are better educated than free will thinkers. Free will is the obvious thing to believe. Determinism is subtler. It takes a considerable amount of education to grapple with the metaphysics that makes determinism possible. Determinism is impossible to disprove, and that, Conway said, might be the place to begin, because the impossibility of disproving determinism is a very easy argument . . .

> You go and see a really very interesting movie and you don't know how it's going to turn out. It's exciting. The next day you take a friend to see the same movie. Well, in a way, for you it's determinist, but for your friend it's not. Now that's not the argument I'm talking about, that's just to give you an idea of what the argument really is. The argument is what we call the second-time-around argument. What's to say that we aren't at the second showing of the universe movie? You know? Something went wrong maybe with the initial universe and it's been started again, and we're being fed exactly the same sense impressions as we were the first time around. In that case, the first time around was free, and the second time around is certainly determinist.

All the forces that could be rallied scientifically would fail to distinguish between a deterministic universe and a universe that operated otherwise. Yet science as it evolved tended to point in the determinist direction. By way of example, Conway cited Newton's theory of gravitation and Einstein's theory of general relativity—both are totally deterministic. But starting in the 1920s, the climate of opinion shifted as a result of the emergence of quantum physics, a mathematical machine for predicting the behavior of nanoscopic particles. As a result, more and more people seem to believe in free will. Though some people sit on the fence and waffle.

> There's a guy called Dennis Overbye who writes about science in the *New York Times*. Several times he's published articles in which he says, "Everything we know of science convinces me that the world is deterministic. Nevertheless, I cling to the illusion of free will."

Conway couldn't run his life without "the illusion of free will." His wives past and present might collectively question the degree to which he can run his own life at all. His mother-in-law does his laundry. His finances are a mess; he sought advice from a bankruptcy lawyer and delighted in his name, Mr. Detzky. But to the main point, Conway clarifies that he does not believe in the *illusion* of free will. He doesn't believe there is any *illusion*. He believes we have free will.

For Conway, the alternatives are incredible. If there is no free will and the universe is deterministic, some metaphysical force 13.75 ±0.17 billion years ago mandated John Horton Conway into existence and preordained the Free Will Theorem, as well as his Game of Life, and made Dennis Overbye a reporter who would write a feature about free will without mentioning the Free Will Theorem. As it happened, however, Overbye had tried to get in touch, or Conway had heard secondhand that he'd tried, that perhaps he'd sent an e-mail. Conway was among the earliest e-mail adopters but these days his various accounts are unreliable, either periodically shunned or permanently shuttered, so Overbye's e-mail must have evaporated into the electronic ether. Their meeting of minds clearly wasn't meant to be.

8.

CRITERIA OF VIRTUE

Our life is frittered away by detail . . . Simplify, simplify.
—HENRY DAVID THOREAU

While staying at Conway's place during the lectures, surveying the field of colleagues and friends and trying to figure out what to make of his free will detour, I put Martin Gardner at the top of my To Call list. As much as anyone, Gardner had suffered the full kaleidoscopic battery of ideas exploding like fireworks from Conway's brain. He'd been inundated with those rambling letters, some bearing teasers on the envelope: *NEW NEWS about the Angel Problem!* When Conway began making regular trips to America he took every opportunity to regale Gardner in the flesh, stopping by his house at 10 Euclid Avenue in Hastings-on-Hudson, 20 miles north of New York City. After dinner and their nightly old-fashioned cocktail, Gardner and his wife Charlotte toddled off to bed at a disgracefully early hour. This left Conway stuck alone in the rambling house for what seemed like long winter nights, though he usually visited in the summer. Fortunately, Gardner's attic office was packed with a voluminous library, file cabinets full of column research, and toys tucked away everywhere. Conway once opened a drawer and out jumped a mechanical spider that landed on the table, walked over to the edge, felt around with its legs, then turned and went the other way.

Conway far overstayed any average mortal's welcome, sometimes for an entire week, or 2. And after finally taking his leave, Gardner would exclaim at all the ideas that Conway had tossed forth "in such bewildering profusion . . . I still have my head spinning." Gardner, too, provided fodder, such as a puzzle that had left him puzzled, the dissection of a cube into 6 polycubes. Gardner said nobody knew how many solutions it had. As they sat at a table with the polycube pieces Conway started putting them together. Working away, he thought aloud and asked Gardner to be his deaf ear. "That meant that I had to listen to what he was saying, but I didn't need to understand it. While he was talking and jabbering away he was making notes on a piece of paper with little diagrams, which I didn't understand." In less than an hour, Conway announced there were 13 different solutions. Gardner still dutifully didn't understand, but he was happy to have the answer.

Similarly, Gardner didn't know what to make of the Free Will Theorem, though he expressed faith that Conway must be on to something. He wanted to know more about it, and he looked forward to having Conway and me visit so he could learn about the theorem firsthand (or at least listen). In the meantime, in preparation for our telephone interview, Gardner had jotted down a list of 50 or so notes about Conway that he wanted to go over. "So, should I just rattle on?" He said his first significant mention of Conway in his column had to do with Sprouts, and the next note was about Phutball, both of which we've encountered previously. The third note he'd jotted down detailed the Game of Life. Gardner first learned about Life from Conway in a 12-foot missive sent in March 1970. Conway would come to refer to this as the "fatal letter" that let Life loose on the world. The letter also discussed a game called Hackenbush that he'd been fiddling with over Christmas, as well as other unimpartial games, games wherein the moves available differ for the 2 players. It wasn't until 9 feet into his letter that Conway arrived at an item he'd been tinkering with for ages:

The game of life.
This is something that has been around for years, but at last I've got what I wanted—an apparently unpredictable law of genetics. We start with an infinite array of squares, in some of which are living organisms. The population develops in steps, there being a law of genetics which determines the contents of any square at time t+1 in terms of the contents of it and its 8 neighbours at time t. The problem is to find a good law. What are the criteria of virtue?

Whenever Conway and I discussed Life, his quantitative estimation of "around for years" varied from 18 months to 2 years to perhaps even 3. But to go back even further, Conway recalls that the seed of Life was a book of essays with an orange cover titled *Automata Studies*, published in 1956—that's what inspired his idealist intellectual itch, his *Jugendtraum*, as he calls it, his dream of youth.

An automaton is "something which has the power of spontaneous motion or self-movement," according to the OED, or "a piece of mechanism having its motive power so concealed that it appears to move spontaneously." The earliest known occurrence of the word is in a seventeenth-century play by Francis Beaumont and John Fletcher: "[It] doth move alone, A true automaton." But doth it think? This was the theme of the orange book, as set out by its editors, the father of information theory, Claude Shannon, and the father of artificial intelligence, John McCarthy. "Among the most challenging scientific questions of our time," they stated in the preface, "are the corresponding analytic and synthetic problems: How does the brain function? Can we design a machine which will simulate a brain?" There were 4 essays in the book that discussed just such a machine: a Turing machine. In a thought experiment circa 1935, British logician and computer scientist Alan Turing imagined a machine that was capable of computing any arbitrary calculation. The machine possessed infinite memory capacity courtesy of an infinite tape divided into squares and etched with symbols that provided the input and instructions for the machine to execute infinite calculations. Turing then went one better. He showed that any Turing machine could be programmed to behave like every other Turing machine—it would be a universal machine. Turing's thought experiment captured Conway's imagination, programmed him in a way, planted in his brain the notion and the know-how for investigating new and simple universal machines. Researching the possibilities, he learned that the Institute for Advanced Study's John von Neumann had been possessed of much the same desire. Von Neumann wanted to build a universal constructor, a machine that output other machines, including itself. And as Conway recalls it, von Neumann wondered about the potential for such a machine to colonize the planets, starting with Mars.

It doesn't much matter what planet it is. The thing is it would obviously be fantastically difficult to colonize any planet. The solution was not to send people, but to send machines whose job was to build the necessary infrastructure and make the planet habitable. Mars being the red planet, with rocks rich in iron, the machine would be an iron smelter of sorts, extracting iron and providing fuel for making more machines. The machines it makes are the exact same as itself, the maiden machine. And all the machines do more smelting and make more machines, until you've got an awful lot of machines, millions of the damn things, a hive of machines. I don't know, it sounds like a nightmare almost.

But the point is that with the machines working away, an atmosphere would emerge as a byproduct. After all, the rust is iron oxide, and after you've separated the iron there is a lot of oxygen. So the idea is they develop an atmosphere and put some grass down and make it all nice and homey and cozy. And then after the machines have been working for whatever time it takes, then you send over some people. . . .

Or so Conway had heard, or read, somewhere.

I don't know where I heard it and I don't know how much truth there is in what I'm telling you, actually.

Truth. What is it, anyway? The opposite of falsehood. There's subjective versus objective, relative versus absolute. $1 + 1 = 2$, that's for certain.

Mars or no Mars, it's very much in the spirit of von Neumann. Von Neumann's notion was that one could build a universal constructing machine, a self-replicating robot that built robots that built robots that built robots, and so on. However, the cost of robots building robots would be prohibitive. Von Neumann took a suggestion from his Polish American mathematician friend Stanislaw Ulam and downsized his universal constructor concept to a 2-dimensional abstraction—a cellular automaton with self-replication powered by an algorithm, a mathematical recipe. The action played out on a grid of squares governed by a prescribed set of rules. Each square could be in any of 29 states, and the state of any square was entirely dependent on the state of its 5 neighbors at the previous iteration, which collectively then could be in any of $29^5 = 20,511,149$ possible states. Von Neumann's death in 1957 cut short his work on cellular automata, with his book *Theory of Self-Reproducing Automata* published posthumously. When Conway leafed through the book, he was curious about the 29-state rule, so he flipped to the appendices at the back. There he found 80 pages of grids and tables, as well as a chart translating how von Neumann had programmed his cellular automata to do exactly what he wanted.

> It seemed awfully complicated. What turns me on are things with a wonderful simplicity.

Surely, Conway thought, the machine could be more casually, more lazily, more cleverly designed, i.e. by *not* designing it.

> The idea is you start with some simple set of rules that you can remember. Even though the rules are simple, you hope that the resulting behavior will be rather unpredictable. Because if a machine is behaving in a generally unpredictable manner then probably there will be ways of making it do whatever you want.
> We should go play with a Go board and see it . . .

Conway pushed himself out of his armchair and galumphed from the alcove into the common room. He headed for a foursome of sofas clustered around a table with a board at its center, dropped himself into the cushions, and threw down some stones.

And that's roughly how it went in Cambridge 4 decades ago when he was inventing the Game of Life. He'd bound into the common room and gather up his floating following of graduate students and friends.* They'd throw down some stones and tinker with the possibilities. Over the course of 2 or 3 years, Conway harnessed his disciples' brainpower; they were happy to be exploited, they were game for whatever game was going.

---

* Although the Life disciples never formed a fixed set, Conway's core group of investigators included, at various points in time and in various capacities, Stephen Bourne, Paul Callahan, Mike Guy, Richard Guy, Nigel Martin, Ray Mitchell, Simon Norton, Mike Paterson, Miles Reid, and doubtless countless others.

Usually it wasn't Life, it was backgammon or this or that, chess hardly ever. Conway dislikes chess. He can't stand the waiting while his opponent busily and intently stares at the board thinking. And he objects to its lack of simplicity.

It's not God's game!

He would agree to play chess if and only if his opponent allowed that he could invent his own version of the rules, otherwise he steered clear (his daughters could twist his arm, and he granted them the advantage of immortal bishops). However, he *was* prepared to be interested in Go, an encircling game for 2 players that originated in China more than 2,500 years ago. Even Go wasn't exactly to Conway's taste—it wasn't mathematical. But the black and white stones and gridlike board came in handy when testing the innumerable systems of cellular automata he cycled through before arriving at Life.

Conway and the disciples would throw down some stones, arrange a starting configuration, apply whatever rules held sway that day, and watch what happened.

Let me try and think what typically happened. Somebody would invent a rule, we'd play it during coffee time, and then there would be something wrong with it. The next day there would be some tinkering with that rule and we'd make it a bit better and we'd carry on playing it for a week until we found out what was really wrong with it, and we'd tinker with it again. So probably about once a week we changed the rules and played with a new system. And I'm sure there was a time when a month went by and nobody bothered to play at all. Sometimes we got bored with it. We got bored with Life.

Meanwhile, Conway was, as always, doing other things. He likes to keep various problems on various burners. His recipe for success is to have 4 problems on the go: a big problem, difficult and important, that will probably depress you before it makes you successful; a workable problem, tedious but with a clear strategy so you can always make some progress and feel a sense of accomplishment; a book problem, for the book you're writing or may eventually write; and a fun problem, since life is hardly worth living if you're not having some fun.

This was also around the same time that Conway became smitten with group theory and found his group, and discussions were still ongoing with the god of groups, John Thompson. And even then, Conway was still groping around in the dark with this terrain. That he and Thompson could have an intense intellectual conversation without being entirely simpatico is one of the beauties of mathematics. Mathematics is wedged uneasily between art and science, and within the discipline there are artists and there are scientists. Conway is an artist, Thompson a scientist. Awhile into their regular discussions, Conway remembers Thompson said to him, "You have no idea what I'm talking about, do you?"

No, actually.

"The problem seems to be the character tables. Promise if you don't understand, you'll interrupt me and ask me a question."

Well, that will be every 10 seconds.

"Yes, it will be annoying at first, but it's the only way to do it."

Fleeing these taxing regimes at the end of the day, Conway would fly down the math department's 4 flights of stairs 2 steps at a time, counting his giant plunging leaps: 2, 4, 6, 8, violent spin around the banister; 2, 4, 6, 8, violent spin; 2, 4, 6, 8; gaining momentum and overweening confidence as he went, finally flinging himself through the door at the bottom. He knew the drill so well that once when the lights were out and the stairwell pitch black he closed his eyes and took a running leap. A bad idea, the damn fool concluded, whilst on the centrifugally unstoppable trajectory downward. But he lived to loiter in the common room another day.

Initially, Conway's dream was to find a 1-dimensional universal machine, the simplest of all systems, something that moved along a line

At the wheels of FRACTRAN (as imagined by mathematician David Logothetti).

rather than the 2-dimensional plane of a Go board. He came up with some 1-dimensional prototypes that got him quite close to achieving his *Jugendtraum*, closer even than the Game of Life. He was rather pleased, for instance, with a creation he called FRACTRAN.

At its essence, FRACTRAN is an esoteric programming language— "esoteric" in this context being technical jargon for "joke" and the name FRACTRAN making a joke at the expense of FORTRAN, IBM's Mathematical FORmula TRANslating System, a cumbersome programming language developed in the 1950s. By comparison, FRACTRAN is Spartan in its simplicity. The program, the algorithm, is nothing but a list of fractions. And with that, FRACTRAN could compute anything that's computable. It is "Turing complete."

FRACTRAN became a favorite among Conway's stock of "golden oldie" lectures. He'll strut to the blackboard and with great bravado present his opening gambit. He writes 14 fractions:

$$\begin{array}{cccccccccccccc} A & B & C & D & E & F & G & H & I & J & K & L & M & N \\ \frac{17}{91} & \frac{78}{85} & \frac{19}{51} & \frac{23}{38} & \frac{29}{33} & \frac{77}{29} & \frac{95}{23} & \frac{77}{19} & \frac{1}{17} & \frac{11}{13} & \frac{13}{11} & \frac{15}{2} & \frac{1}{7} & \frac{55}{1} \end{array}$$

Then he gives the basic instructions, the program or operating system for his machine:

First, start with the input 2. Find the first fraction in the row that when multiplied by 2 produces a whole number. You'll get nothing until fraction "M"—since $2 \times \frac{15}{2}$ gives the output 15. Write down that result.

And then repeat. Multiply 15 by the first fraction in the row that will produce a whole number. So, 15 × fraction "N" gives $825 = 3 \times 5^2 \times 11$. Write down that number, so now you've got the sequence 15, 825 . . .

Continue on in this fashion, and—here's the key—keep an eye out for an output number that is a pure power of 2. And watch for a certain pattern to emerge . . .

After 19 steps, the whole-number result is 4, which is 2^2. Success! Conway pauses so his audience can behold this lovely result. Then he proceeds for quite a way before pausing again and casually informing his audience that the next result, the next power of 2 he's looking for, is 2^3. The audience mutters amongst themselves—it seems to be doubling each time—$2^2 = 4$ and $2^3 = 8$—not exactly ho-hum, though only mildly interesting. Pedaling through more and more calculations, after the step 69 Conway finds 2^3. Then he divulges that the next power of 2 he'll find, at the 211th step, is $2^5 = 32$. And then, after quite a while again, he'll get $2^7 = 128$, and then $2^{11} = 2,048$, and then . . .

$$\dots 2^{13} \dots 2^{17} \dots 2^{19} \dots 2^{23} \dots 2^{29} \dots 2^{31} \dots 2^{37} \dots 2^{41} \dots 2^{43} \dots 2^{47} \dots 2^{53} \dots 2^{59} \dots 2^{61} \dots$$

Another murmur in the audience. "What the hell is going on? The machine is generating the prime powers of 2?!"

And that's not all FRACTRAN can do. Conway composed a program of 24 fractions with which FRACTRAN can compute *anything*, and his program of 40 fractions spits out the decimal digits of π until the end of time. Though here's the rub: While the programs are short, the operating times are long. As Conway once explained to an audience,

> With π, it's very inefficient even to get the first digit after the decimal point. Well, you basically have to wait until the universe grows cold. And it's the same for generating the primes. It's astonishingly simple, trouble is it takes a long time to compute—the prime p takes roughly $2p^3$ operations, so to compute the one hundredth prime, you know, will take a mil-

lion operations; to compute the millionth prime will take 10 to the 18 operations or something, which is absolutely huge. So it won't get anywhere in your lifetime, so to speak. You see, what those programs emphasized were shortness of program rather than shortness of the time taken to compute something. I was really concerned with theoretical computation, not practical computation. I'm a very impractical person.

Conway was nevertheless quite happy with FRACTRAN. He wrote up a paper published in an academic journal and sold FRACTRAN like soap powder. He usually calls it his "washing powder paper," though it should really be the "washing machine paper" since it's the machine that's key—

Your Free Samples of FRACTRAN.

Only FRACTRAN Has These Star Qualities . . .

• Gets those functions really clean!
The entire configuration of a FRACTRAN machine at any instant is held as a single integer—there are no messy "tapes" or other foreign concepts to be understood by the fledgling programmer.

• Makes workday really easy!
FRACTRAN needs no complicated programming manual—its entire syntax can be learned in 10 seconds, and programs for quite complicated and interesting functions can be written almost at once.

• Matches any machine on the market!
Your old machines (Turing, Minsky, etc.) can quite easily be made to simulate arbitrary FRACTRAN programs, and it is usually even easier to write a FRACTRAN program to simulate other machines.

• Astoundingly simple universal program!
By making a FRACTRAN program that simulates an arbitrary other FRACTRAN program, we have obtained a simple universal FRACTRAN program.

"It's a really fascinating bugger," raved a math blogger recently (and in 2014 it inspired a set of questions in the final of the British Informatics Olympiad). After providing an intricate explanation, the blogger concluded: "Evil, huh? . . . It's based on one of the most bizarrely elegant concepts of computation I've ever seen." In its simplicity and universality, FRACTRAN was as yet Conway's closest approach to fulfilling his *Jugendtraum*.

> The Prime Producing Machine in a way says it all. You wouldn't expect a list of 14 fractions to know anything about primes!

Fundamentally a game of fractions, FRACTRAN was just another mindless game. The mindlessness was imperative. Still, the word "mindless" sends Conway searching for a better word to describe what he was after with his dream.

> How can I say it? What can I call a designless system? A found system. A random system almost, but it's not random. A thoughtless system. There is no thought behind it, no plan. Unplanned! That's good. Or planless.

The problem with a totally planless system was that Conway would have to live with it long enough to discern the plan that organically emerged from the planlessness. He would have to sit and watch it for hours upon hours when he wanted to go home. He came to regard FRACTRAN as a close approach but a failure. Coding the program with such a long string of fractions was too complicated. Fewer fractions would be better. A few years after he debuted FRACTRAN in class, a student surreptitiously pulled him aside in a supermarket. Silently, the student fished in his shirt pocket and retrieved a speck of paper folded into nearly nothing. Unfolded, it was no bigger than a fortune cookie message, and the message here was mere 13 fractions (also for producing primes). Not a word was spoken. It was understood. Conway had been outdone. Still, he wanted an even simpler system. No finicky fractions. Eventually he decided that finding the idyllic 1-dimensional system was too hard. He gave up.

> I tried and failed.

He took some advice from Samuel Beckett. "Try again. Fail again. Fail better."

△ ▢ ◇ ⬟ ⬢

The Game of Life, similarly, was a planless system, and together with his gang of graduate students Conway had the collective will to live with Life long enough to see what evolved. However, if you ask Conway now about how it all went down, he's liable to get a bit testy. He's sick of Life. He doesn't want to talk about it anymore. He has gone on about it at length over the years, and even lately he recounted the minutiae about how Life's rules evolved for Tanya Khovanova. Khovanova is a freelance mathematician and MIT research affiliate, also a blogger, and she captured some of the details from the primary source himself in a post titled "The Sexual Side of Life":

> We thought in terms of birth rules and death rules. Maybe one day's death rule would be a bit too strong compared to its birth rule. So the next day at coffee time we'd either try to weaken the death rule or strengthen the birth rule, but either way, only by a tiny bit. They had to be extremely well balanced; if the death rule was even slightly too strong then almost every configuration would die off. And conversely, if the birth rule was even a little bit stronger than the death rule, almost every configuration would grow explosively.
>
> What's wrong with that, you might ask? Well, if the "radius" grows by 1 unit per generation, then after 9 or 10 moves, it's off the Go board. We can probably find more Go boards, of course, but after another 20 or so moves it will outflow the coffee table and then it is awfully hard to keep track. We wanted to be able to study configurations for much longer than that, which meant that we had to disallow rules that might lead to linear growth. Of course, we weren't interested in rules that usually led to collapse.

The fight was to find the sweet spot where configurations grew, but not too quickly. By the penultimate try, working with the penultimate set of rules, Conway had trimmed his ambitions. Aiming to improve vastly on von Neumann's 29-state system, and having given up on a 1-state system like FRACTRAN, he had by now also given up on a 2-state system. Conway and his crew had moved on to a 3-state system, and it dripped with sexual innuendo. A cell was empty or full, and if it was full, the cell was occupied with a black or white marker, denoting male or female. Given the male-female component, a Lifer shouted out a name that stuck: "Actresses and Bishops!" The namesake is a comical piece of English idiom—"as the actress said to the bishop"—a rimshot afterthought tacked onto an inadvertently lewd double entendre. Dating as far back as Edwardian times, it was used by Kingsley Amis in his 1954 hit novel *Lucky Jim*, and reprised to good effect by Ricky Gervais in *The Office*.

With Life's Actresses and Bishops, initially the population growth imitated biology, with 2 parent markers giving birth to another marker. Soon it became apparent that this led to linear growth; the birth rule was too strong, and the game quickly outgrew the flotilla of Go grids surfing the Cambridge common room. They changed the birth rule to stipulate that a threesome was necessary for procreation—2 actresses and a bishop or 2 bishops and an actress; and the "weaker sex rule" stipulated that to keep the population in balance, 2 actresses and a bishop produced a baby bishop, and 2 bishops and an actress produced a baby actress. There was also the "sexual frustration rule" stipulating that death ensued if one wasn't touching somebody of the opposite sex. Actresses and Bishops held sway for some time, with more subtle tinkering of the rules. Eventually it became apparent that the sex of the parents had no effect other than to determine the sex of the children, which in the next iteration would have no effect again. Conway's solution to this superfluity was to abolish sex (no metaphor there!). So after all that unsuccessful tinkering with a 3-state system, he'd landed on a 2-state system after all. Never mind male or female, a cell could be live or dead, full or empty, according to the rules that finally stuck. Here's how he initially stated the rules in his letter to Martin Gardner:

i) if an empty cell has just 3 full neighbours at time t, then it will be full at time t+1

ii) unless a full cell has just 2 or 3 full neighbours at time t it will be empty at time t+1

And he noted:

In other words, the population behavior should be unpredictable . . . overpopulation, like underpopulation, tends to kill. A healthy society is neither too dense nor too sparse.

With just the 2 primary states, live or dead, each neighborhood was comprised of 9 cells (including the central cell), meaning there were only 2^9 or 512 possible configurations of states—a considerable improvement on von Neumann's 20,511,149. Conway's system was simpler, as desired. He could live with Life. Now, instead of testing new rules, the investigators went on a biodiversity blitz through the jungle, on the lookout for new Life-forms. The modus operandi had so far been to haphazardly play and remember what happened, with no record keeping. This had its drawbacks. As Conway noted to Gardner:

I had better warn you that it is phenomenally easy to make mistakes.

Now the throwing down of stones became more methodical, documenting a taxonomic tree of Life species. First they ran through all the basic permutations starting with 1 live cell, which in a single generation or tick of time *t* dies of loneliness. As does any arrangement of 2 live cells. A triplet of 3 horizontal adjoined live cells becomes 3 vertical live cells in a single tick, and then these 3 vertical cells flash directly back to 3 horizontal cells in the next tick, and back and forth and back and forth. This became the "blinker," one of a class of configurations called "oscillators."

Some of the tetrominoes, arrangements of 4 adjoined live cells, evolved into another common family of configurations, those that quickly settled into stasis, remaining stable and unchanged, hence they were named "still life." A square of 4 live cells remains a square, in the most ubiquitous still life, the 2-by-2 "block." When 4 live cells are arranged in a row, within 2 ticks they evolve into a 6-celled still life called the "beehive." And beehives arising in sets of 4 earned the name "honey farm."

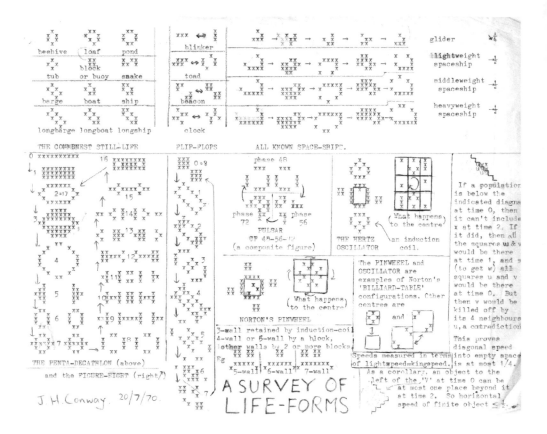

A SURVEY OF LIFE-FORMS

J. H. Conway. 20/7/70.

Over time, a comprehensive "Survey of Life-Forms" amassed, which Conway diligently typed up and sent to Gardner. At this point, however, the enterprise clearly needed to pick up some speed. Slow going was the lot of the Lifers, working on Go boards, reporting their progress with pencil and graph paper, annexing more and more grids to push the frontier into 100s of generations. The task of writing a program to run Life on the PDP7 computer went to Mike Guy, together with another talented computer scientist, Stephen Bourne, who later authored the foundational interfaces for Unix, the Bourne shell. They desperately needed the computer because there was still serious work to be done. There was the matter of Conway's *Jugendtraum*, his quest for universality. There was the big theoretical question that still needed answering: Is Life universal?

To that end, during the summer of 1969—the summer of Woodstock, the first man on the moon, British troops in Northern Ireland, Colonel Muammar el-Qaddafi taking control in Libya—the Lifers were cloistered away, pushing forward on the safari to track the evolution of known animals, and, more important, hunting new specimens to add to the bestiary. New Life-forms were key. In order for Life to be universal, it needed to have among its population creatures that behaved like parts of a computer. Foremost, Life the universal machine needed a medium of information transfer, a medium to carry binary 1s and 0s. It also needed a clock mechanism to emit this information in pulses, as well as something that could be co-opted for logic gates.

But again, querying Conway on these technical details put me in close quarters with the man and his temper. So borrowing again from times past when he was more willing to talk:

> One metaphor that has been with me for a long time is the following: I like to think of a huge abandoned warehouse equipped with logical devices such as AND, OR, and NOT gates. Suppose a maniac lived there who would solder together a big number of these devices just randomly. Then with enough time you could learn how to program this, and it wouldn't take a lot of intelligent design so that the big circuit would be unpredictable and probably even universal.
>
> For instance, you might press a button here and you notice that a little red light comes on, and then you try and understand how these buttons correspond to these things and discover a way of adding 2 numbers. You press a button 5 times and then you do something else, and then you press it 8 times and detect that the answer is 13. And, if the warehouse is big enough, and if the behavior is interesting enough, you gradually learn how to use little bits of it to do whatever you like. So that's the dream. And the question now was how small can you make the warehouse, how simple can you make the connections?

One of the 5-celled pentominos, the "r-pentomino" became a promising source for all the little bits and pieces needed for information transfer. It started out at generation 0 looking like a harmless small letter r— ⌗. Then it swelled in a burst of chaos and didn't stop for more than 1,000 generations, belonging as it did to a family of organisms called methuselahs, patterns with long life spans that grow much bigger than their starting configuration—named after the biblical patriarch said to have lived for 969 years. There is also the Methuselah of wine, a large bottle holding the equivalent of 8 normal-sized bottles. Though beer was the Lifers' beverage of choice, and the 5 o'clock ritual on any given day was to go to the Anchor Pub or the graduate center, buy a round of beer and potato chips, and play bar billiards. In bar billiards, there was a rule stipulating that anyone at any time could declare "binding to . . ." such as "binding to involve the red ball" or "binding to involve the black peg" or "binding to not aim." They'd also played around with the empty chips packets, taking an empty packet, folding it in $\frac{1}{2}$, and tucking it into the next empty packet, then folding that in $\frac{1}{2}$ and tucking it into the next empty packet, and on and on. A theory developed, never disproved, that this packet process never terminates, since even with dozens of empty packets it was always feasible to fold the packet full of packets in $\frac{1}{2}$ and tuck it inside another packet.

They'd all head back to the department eventually and continue on the trail of the methuselah r-pentomino, hoping to happen upon an information stream. The Life computer program was still in the works, so frustration over their lack of success was exacerbated by the fact that the investigators were still working manually. Even 10 generations proved nearly impossible to document accurately without elaborate and diligent checks. In this regard, a force for the good arrived in the form of Richard Guy, Mike's father, who visited nearly every summer. British-born, he had studied mathematics at Cambridge, spending much of his time playing and analyzing chess, composing endgame problems that he published in the *British Chess Magazine*. This led to his intensive games research, considered pivotal in the history of combinatorial game theory. He served in the Royal Air Force during the war and as a meteorologist in Iceland and Bermuda, then lectured for a time at the University of London, as well as in Singapore and in Delhi at the Indian Institute of Technology, before eventually landing at the University of Calgary. A precisian fellow—precise, careful, fastidious, conscientious—qualities of character that the Lifers on the whole lacked. Conway appointed him "blinker watcher," a tedious task. He kept an accounting of blinkers and other debris that splintered off from center stage as the action in the spotlight evolved generation upon generation.

Late in the fall of 1969, as the group was still on the trail of the r-pentomino, the elder Guy's attention to detail paid off. The drama had been building since generation 27, when the scene split, stage left and stage right, each a microcosm of chaos unto itself. At generation 69, Guy noticed an animal that no one had ever seen before. It seemed to be wiggling, skittering, gliding its way diagonally across the board. He hollered to the others: "Come over here, there's a piece that's walking!" This was the first step toward proving Life universal. Conway christened this walking piece the "glider" (though now he wishes he'd called it the "ant"), because after 2 moves its position differs from the starting position by a "glide reflection," a symmetry operation, and at generation 4 it looks exactly the same as it did at generation 0, but it has glided diagonally downward by a single place. And then onward it wiggled . . .

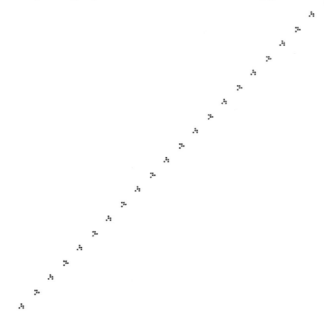

With that wiggling walk, the glider was the first Life-form that wasn't fixed like a still life or repetitive like an oscillating blinker. The glider had a life all its own. And it was the component most needed for a universality proof. The skittering glider provided the information stream. Now Conway just needed a gizmo that reliably emitted gliders, a "glider gun," as he called it. For now, the discovery of the glider secured Life's fate. By the r-pentomino's endgame at generation 1,103, a total of 6 gliders had walked across the board. Conway knew they'd hit upon a system that worked. Up until then Conway had kept his cards close to his chest, perhaps providing Martin Gardner a few tempting hints. When the glider appeared on the scene, then he was ready to crow.

> Then I sent the Fatal Letter off to Martin. And then all hell broke loose. That's why I call it the "fatal" letter.

9

CHARACTER ASSASSINATION

Knowing is not enough; we must apply.
—GOETHE

All hell broke loose when Martin Gardner wrote his October 1970 column about Life. In the column Conway issued a challenge: $50 for the first person to find the piece of circuitry in the computer, the "glider gun," that would all but prove Life universal.

And the pandemonium has continued ever since.

On a local level, as I mentioned, these days talking about Life with Conway can cause considerable perturbation. Without much warning he reaches his threshold and turns testy. It terrifies him that another of his worst nightmares might come true, that his life will in the end be reduced to Life. When we met for another session in the alcove, he tried to prepare me for the hellish consequences, i.e. the wobbly he was about to throw.

Oh god. I don't know whether to tell you now or not.

Oh, sure, get it over with.

Well, it may be upsetting to you. It's upsetting to me, actually. I lay in bed probably about a week ago in the early hours of the morning. And I've decided, I have to say, I'm becoming thoroughly disenchanted with your biography.

It's basically because recently you've been asking me these questions about the Life game. And do you know something? I hate the Life game. I've really realized I hate the damned Life game.

Well, that can go in the book . . .

Let me finish! So I'm scared of the following thing happening. I'm scared of it becoming another one of these, "John Conway, inventor of the celebrated Game of Life . . ." I told you, every time I turn to a book, a new math book, I look up the sacred name and it says: "Conway, Game of Life, pages 34 to 38." And that's roughly all it says. And how can I say it—it's not character assassination, exactly, it's quality assassination. I regard Life as trash, frankly. I mean, it was a real part of my life to have discovered it and so on. And I don't think it should be totally removed. But it seems to be all that I'm known for, among the general public. And I want you, somehow—I wanted you to somehow set the record straight, by not doing the SAME DAMN THING AGAIN!

I mean, god I was quite upset. I was so terrified that I was thinking of saying, so to speak, "Publish and be damned! I don't want anything more to do with it!"

May I speak?

Permission to speak? No, not yet.

You should appreciate something. This was never a big deal as far as we were concerned. This was just a recreation, a game we played. Somehow it became a bit more important later on, or at least it did in the eyes of other people. I never thought of it as very important, I just thought of it as a bit of fun. In fact, in a way I felt ashamed of it. I don't think it counts in the mathematical community, or at least in the serious mathematical community. I don't think any of my Princeton colleagues think this Life game is of any importance. I don't know. In a way it doesn't count for me.

So I wasn't going to cooperate any more in this character assassination, I wasn't going to answer any more questions about Life, roughly speaking. Well, I don't mind answering a few, to tell you the truth. Just let me say . . . How can I say it? Life was a genuine part of my life, and I told you about the *Jugendtraum* and so on. But I really want you to minimize it, rather than maximize it.

Okay. Now speak.

The less said the better. That seemed the best means of assuagement. It's a fool's errand, attempting to reason with Conway when he's in a state.

Conway and I set out on another research trip, to the ninth biennial Gathering for Gardner (G4G9), an invite-only pilgrimage in honor of Martin Gardner that draws about 400 mathematicians, magicians, mathemagicians (a word Gardner coined), puzzlers, jugglers, acrobats, skeptics, philosophers, physicists, linguists, theologians, computer programmers, chaoticians. The incorrigible Gareth again came along, a bright child among children of advanced ages. We landed in the lobby of Atlanta's Ritz-Carlton, all marble and gilt with a modern boho disco vibe, and tumbled into the melee. Gardner's books have titles like *Mathematical Magic Show*, *Mathematical Bewilderments*, *Mathematical Circus*, *Mathematical Carnival*, and the G4G events are the living, breathing incarnation. Conway wrote the foreword for *Mathematical Carnival*, and in doing so he offered a trick:

> *Here is a way to make this book pay for itself quite quickly. Gather 10 or more people together and ask them to say what happens to a riderless bicycle when someone pushes its lower pedal towards the rear (while someone else just stops it from falling). Promise to pay a quarter to everyone who gets it right, provided that anyone who gets it wrong will pay you a quarter. Allow them as much discussion as they like but no experimentation. Then all troop out to find a bicycle and watch it do the uncanny thing that has won me at least a dollar every time I have tried so far.*

Over any given Gardner gathering's 5 days, presentations are packed back to back and strictly limited to 10 minutes, the conference equivalent of speed dating. Participants address a nexus of intellectual jewels, some eminently practical, most purely quizzical. Harvard's Erez Lieberman-Aiden expounded on "Physical Analogues of Spacefilling Curves: How the Human Genome Folds." MIT's Erik Demaine presented his work on the "Conveyor Belt Puzzle Font," inspired by an open problem in computational geometry. The Swedish magician Lennart Green clumsily spilled his deck of cards into a crumpled mess but still managed to deal himself a royal flush, while Canadian magician Lisa Menna talked about the "curiosity-curmudgeon curve" and how it was better to "open a mind with wonder than close it with belief." The 20-something Vi Hart debuted her musical organ function grinder, programmed by her father, freelance mathematical sculptor George Hart, who's also a research professor in engineering at Stony Brook. Gwen Laura Fisher from California, a mathematical bead weaver and designer of "the Conway Bead," presented her research about math anxiety, conducted at the Burning Man Festival. Also in attendance was Caspar Schwabe, a geometry artist from Japan's Kurashiki University of Science and the Arts who inflated a giant multicolored blimp of a stellated icosahedron at dinner, rattling the chandeliers in the Ritz ballroom. And there was Rich Schoeppel, a Utah mathematician and a cryptography superstar of the late 1970s and '80s who designed the "Hasty Pudding Cipher," an also-ran candidate in the competition for selecting the U.S. Advanced Encryption Standard. Finally, one cannot forget Neil Sloane, a steadfast friend of Conway's and a fellow at AT&T in Florham Park, New Jersey. During his presentation Sloane pitched his ever-expanding Online Encyclopedia of Integer Sequences, a database he's been collecting since 1964, first on file cards, then punch cards, then finally the Internet via a moderated wiki run by a nonprofit foundation. Sloane's absolute favorite out of all the encyclopedia's quarter million sequences is the sequence discovered by Colombian mathematician Bernardo Recamán Santos. This sequence contains a pattern of numbers so difficult to decipher that those who've tried have dubbed it "How to Recamán's Life."

These are Conway's people. And to pick up on the theme of wrecking a man's life, his Game of Life is always a favorite on the itinerary at the Gardner gatherings. It's certainly not what Conway talks about. His entry on the program was titled "Untitled Talk" and you can be sure it had nothing to do with you-know-what. Yet Life remains a sustaining obsession for others, both during the formal rapid-fire sessions, such as programmer Tom Rokicki's status report on "Modern Life," and during informal sessions with fans clamoring to pick Conway's brain. Neil Bickford, for one, had been keeping an eye out for his chance to talk to Conway. A self-described "mathematician/programmer/experimenter/puzzler/geek/magician/artist/gamer (mostly 1, 2, and 4)," Bickford had missed a few opportunities already, because whenever an opportunity presented itself he had a nervous attack and chickened out. On the night of the magic marathon he found himself sitting a mere 2 seats away from his target. He shuffled over and introduced himself with a charming stammer. "So," he said, nervously stroking his chin. "May I ask, how did you find the Game of Life?" Conway didn't miss a beat. He summoned his avuncular storytelling tone and delivered an intricate if abridged history. Bickford, aged 12 and a dead ringer for, of course, Harry Potter, was entranced. Meanwhile, Gareth, entranced with his Nintendo DS, sat to his dad's side and was totally oblivious to this transaction. Bickford told Conway that he'd just finished programming his own reinvention of Life, which is what Life aficionados do (there are variants called "Life Without Death" and "Larger than Life" and "Real-Life" and "HighLife"). He asked Conway a few more knowing questions, then floated back to his seat beside his mom. Conway returned to his book of MathDoku without any grumbling or complaining about all those questions on the subject of his *inventio non grata*. For a good cause, he is capable of letting bygones be bygones.

Conway is a mainstay at G4G. He was featured in a documentary tribute to Gardner, covering the second gathering in 1996. "My main interest in magic," Gardner explained in the film, "is because it arouses a sense of wonder about how things operate, about the natural world. The universe is almost like a huge magic trick, and scientists are trying to figure out how it does what it does." In this regard, Gardner called Conway a "creative genius," and he concurred with the creative genius in saying that "Life is one of the stupidest things Conway has ever done." Although the documentary is a Gardner tribute, many of the interviewees veer toward talking about Conway (the doc is mislabeled on YouTube *John Conway on Games and Puzzles*). The mathematician and programmer Bill Gosper said, "He's approximately the smartest man in the world. Conway is frighteningly smart. If he persists with his habit of mentally factoring numbers, future neuroanatomists comparing his brain to Einstein's will find nothing but a gigantic division table." Following more "John Conway is a genius" praise from Stanford mathemagician Persi Diaconis, the film then cuts to the genius himself pulling his trademark tongue tricks, sticking out his clapper and waving it at the camera, thumbs in ears and hands waving as well for added effect. This prompted the interviewer to ask him: "What is the relationship between fun math and serious math?"

> I'm a serious mathematician—I've got a good job here. So I do some serious mathematics but I also do games. And for me they are very similar. You know, when you play a game, if you learn to be good at it, you find what it is you should be thinking about. That is really rather subtle. And that's what we do in mathematics.

Puzzles, for instance. What are puzzles? A puzzle is a little game whereby you prove to yourself that you can do something that you didn't think you could. Conway demonstrated in the doc with another bodily puzzle: Stretch out your arms, twist an arm over the top of the other and clasp your hands together, then bring your hands underneath and through toward your face. Place your index fingers at either side of your nose. Now release the twisting in your arms entirely without letting go of your nose—your right index finger should be touching your right nostril, and your left finger your left nostril. Onscreen it worked out fine for Conway, but he left his interlocutor contorted and confused. Conway now gives away the secret with an explanatory replay:

> I'll tell you how to do it. Put your arms left over right, then clasp your hands. And make sure the left little finger is on top—it all depends on how you cross your arms in the first place. If your left arm is on top then the left little finger has to be on top, but if it's the right arm on top then it's the right little finger. So make sure your left pinkie is on top, and then interlace your fingers properly like that all the way through. Bring your hands under your arms toward your nose, put your index fingers on either side of your nose—put your nose right in there without undoing your index fingers. Now, you can disentangle yourself.
>
> By the way, you crossed left over right arms, now clasp the other way. It feels strange, doesn't it?

This reminded him that he once conducted a chirality census, surveying people's left-right inclinations.

> Everybody has made this decision. Fold your arms. Now fold them the other way. Cross your legs, cross them the other way, et cetera, et cetera, et cetera. One way feels right and one way feels awkward. Once I did an investigation, me and a few students. We called it the Sexual Census—now I think of it as the "Six Different Kinds of Sex." You know, "sex" is really the same basic word as "section"—"sex" refers to the great cutting of humanity and animals, and some plants, into 2 sexes, into 2 parts. Well, it turns out that there are a whole lot of ways of dividing people into 2 groups . . .

But on to other things.

At the Gardner gatherings, Conway (among a handful of others) gets 20 minutes instead of 10 for his talks. All the same, as his turn approached at G4G9 he was worrying about his ability to stay within those temporal bounds. He still didn't know what his "Untitled Talk" would be about. He never likes to decide until the absolute last minute—a strategy he uses for keeping himself fresh and his synapses young. Sometimes he gives his audience a choice of topics and lets them vote. This time, assuming his spot at the lectern, he pronounced his own preference: "The Lexicode Theorem—Or Is It?"

> I'll cast some doubt on this theorem, to say the very least, but all turns out well in the end.

This is another of his golden oldies, and a nice sampling of Conway's brand of not so much performance art as performance mischief. He sets the scene with some definitions. "Lexicode" is shorthand for "integral lexicographic code." "Integral" meaning the code words in this code are strings of integers from 0 onward to infinity, not just strings of 0s and 1s as with binary, and not just strings of 0 through 9 as with decimal notation. "Lexicographic" meaning the code and its words are defined by lexicographic order, as in the ordering of words in a dictionary.

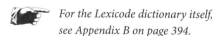 *For the Lexicode dictionary itself, see Appendix B on page 394.*

Conway doesn't get very far, however, in unfurling the fabulous Lexicode before pratfalls and pitfalls appear. At fault, it seems, is the usually simple business of addition. He stumbles upon 2 words that when added together unexpectedly make a word that is *not* in his Lexicode dictionary, as it should be—namely:

$$000111$$
$$+ 001012$$
$$= 001123$$

And there is no 001123 in the dictionary.

> The trouble is, there seem to be some difficulties with this theorem. The sum of those 2 words isn't a Lexicode word, so then the theorem is false. There is something wrong with the Lexicode Theorem. We've got to edit it somehow until it's true. And the best—well, the simplest—cure is to say it's actually, um, not a theorem! So, wait a moment. Perhaps we should call it the "Lexicode Non-Theorem." On the other hand, this is a theorem that I discovered and I have some reasons for wanting it to be true. So let's look at it again . . .

He tries to fix the non-theorem—"fix" as in fix the engine, and "fix" as in fix the race. It's a delicate business. He has to suggest some falsities, but not irretrievably so. He's dissembling. He carefully restates and scrutinizes his statement that the sum of 2 Lexicode words is a Lexicode word, under natural definitions of vector addition and scalar multiplication. And there he finds a loophole:

> It doesn't say *the* natural definitions of addition and multiplication. So maybe it is a different notion of addition on these digits. . . . Oooohhhh, dear. I don't know what the sum of any 2 numbers is now.

If you imagine the multiverse theory of physics, we're now in a parallel universe, as it were, where the laws of arithmetic are ever so slightly askew from the laws of arithmetic we know and love. So now Conway must go back to first principles, strip the thing down to its bones. The first Lexicode word is 000, and since every Lexicode word begins with infinitely many 0s, this might be a good place to start.

I don't even know what 0 + 0 is. Let's do some mathematics. All good
mathematics starts with the word "Let": Let 0 + 0 = z. I rather suspect it's
going to be 0, but perhaps that's a bit naive of me . . .

What's 000000 + 000000? It must be zzzzzz. But all code words begin
with infinitely many 0s.

Aha! So z = 0. FANTASTIC! We have a theorem. We can say: THEO-
REM: 0 + 0 = 0.

Now listen, people, this is serious mathematics going on. Okay, I think
this theorem deserves a number, so I think I'll call it "Theorem 0." We're
getting somewhere here. We now know that 0 + 0 = 0. And it follows
that 0 + n = n for all n.

Since he is successfully deducing theorems from the Lexicode Non-
theorem, Conway decides it's safe to recategorize it as the Lexicode
Axiom. Initially this seems like success, but actually there's some serious
slippage.

There is a little problem. What's 1 + 1? Well it's really easy to tell what 1 +
1 is. What we do is we appeal to the "Lexicode, um, Axiom." Let's see . . .
What do we learn? 1 + 1 = 0.

So much for pinning our certainty of truth on the fact that $1 + 1 = 2$
(as Tarski's Truth Theorem holds, arithmetical truth cannot be defined;
truth cannot be defined in an arithmetical way).

Now the axiom has to be recategorized again.

I think what we should do is call this the "Lexicode Problem," or the
"Lexicode Question"—and finish it with a question mark. The question is:
Is the Lexicode defining a new arithmetic? Let's have a look at it again . . .

It's numerical smoke and mirrors. Nothing adds up. An audience
member interrupts with an observation, to which Conway politely if
absentmindedly turns his attention:

Sorry? Oh. I'm out of time.

He is 38 minutes into his 20-minute talk.

Let me just say, then, that you might like the multiplication a bit better. For example:

$$2 \times 2 = 3$$
$$2^2 = 3$$
$$4^2 = 6$$
$$4^4 = 5$$
$$16^2 = 24$$
$$16^{16} = 17$$
$$256^2 = 384$$
$$256^{256} = 257$$

1, 2, 3 are the cube roots of unity
1, 8, 10, 13, 14 are the fifth roots of unity

All sorts of interesting things happen. Okay, I'll terminate!!!

He takes his seat. For a few seconds, anyway, only to pop back up as the next speaker is about to be introduced. Conway offers a concluding footnote:

By the way, I didn't tell you what the Lexicode Theorem becomes in the end! It becomes a definition, because it does actually define the addition and multiplication. And then, after all, it is a theorem, it just didn't mean quite what you thought. The theorem is true, it really is quite true. But I'm not going to prove it. I'll leave that as an exercise—the "Lexicode Exercise"!

This is a nice example of Conway's alluring esotericism (or not-so-alluring, depending). "Esoteric" was a word that Conway expounded upon later the same day, recounting the time he'd spent a couple decades back attending the First Pythagorean Conference in Spetses, Greece.

Do you know this "esoteric" word? The story about it is that Pythagoras gave his lectures from behind a curtain. Certain students were with him behind the curtain. But only a certain class of student, a select few, were given that knowledge, which was obscured to the others. So if you were really good and passed your exams and all that sort of thing . . . I was about to say if you were a good boy and passed your exams, but there were quite a lot of girls among the Pythagoreans, although it's called the brotherhood; of the 240 known names of people in the brotherhood, 60 were female, which is fantastically good for that period, and it's quite good even for this period. If you were a suitably advanced student, you were allowed behind the curtain with Pythagoras. So "esoteric" means within the curtain or behind the curtain. It meant you could see Pythagoras.

The companion word, the antonym, is "exoteric," knowledge obvious to anyone. Exoterically, the Lexicode turned out to have a mind of its own. Feigning obliviousness, before Conway knew what happened and despite his best efforts, his once wonderful theorem became a non-theorem, then an axiom, then a problem and/or question, and then finally (before its resurrection) it hit rock bottom as a measly definition. Though to this assessment Conway takes offense.

Don't be so concerned to make value judgments. We're just putting it in different categories. There is neither an ascent nor a descent noticed.

Esoterically, and lingering for a moment on the Lexicode's incarnation as a definition, what it defines is a "nimber arithmetic," nimbers being a shadow system of numbers that emerged from a game called Nim. Harvard's C. L. Bouton set down the theory of the game in 1901. His instructions:

The game is played by two players, A and B. Upon a table are placed three piles of objects of any kind, let us say counters. The number in each pile is quite arbitrary, except that it is well to agree that no two piles shall be equal at the beginning. A play is made as follows: The player selects one of the piles, and from it takes as many counters as he chooses; one, two . . . or the whole pile. The only essential things about a play are that the counters shall be taken from a single pile, and that at least one shall be taken. The players play alternately, and the player who takes up the last counter or counters from the table wins.

Nimbers, then, are the values of any Nim heap. They correspond to the ordinal numbers, the ordering numbers, as Conway calls them, numbers that are used to describe the order of things, such as the counters in the piles. But here's the trick: nimbers obey different rules of addition, as defined by the Sprague-Grundy theorem, and different rules of multiplication, as discovered and defined by Conway.

I discovered Nim multiplication when I was a junior fellow at Caius College. I gradually worked out the multiplication table, things like $2 \times 2 = 3$. I was all by myself, lying down on the plush carpet in front of the gas fire in my room, and 4×4 was a sticking block, so to speak. I proved that 4×4 couldn't be 0. And it couldn't be 1. Pause. And it couldn't be 2. Pause . . . And . . . it couldn't . . . be 3 . . . PAUSE . . . No, it couldn't be 4. I'm leaving longer and longer pauses. Nope, can't be 5 . . . Let's try 6. And then, 6, I couldn't disprove. It took me about an hour to come to this conclusion, that I couldn't disprove it. And if I supposed 4 4s were 6, I could work out the entire table up to 15 times 15.

I've just described where I'd got to by the end of the morning. In the afternoon I thought I'd better apply my definition to work out what 4 4s really were. It took me some time and indeed it turned out to be 6. And I still didn't know, by the way, that it all worked, that it was all sort of consistent. For instance, if you double something, and double it again, you should get $3 \times$ it because 2 2s are 3. So you double 7 and get 9, and double 9 and get 14, and indeed 14 is 3×7.

Come again? (As the actress said to the bishop.)

If you double something twice, you should have multiplied it by 2 and then by 2 again, so you should have multiplied it by 3 because 2 2s are 3. The real thing to catch on to is that 2 2s are 3, dammit! So double 7—double meaning multiply by 2—so double 7 and you get 9—obviously! And then you double that again, 2 9s are 14, so 3 7s should be 14, and indeed they are. Um, in fact in this arithmetic, 2 14s are 7, not the other way around.

Anyway, this whole bizarre system of arithmetic sort of seemed to be working . . . I still hadn't at that time proved that it worked, and it took me quite a lot longer to prove it worked. But when I verified from the definition that 4 4s really were 6, I lay on my back and waved my arms and legs in the air and just giggled. For ages. Nobody was there. It just seemed so funny. Holding my belly. Because it was crazy.

△ ▢ ◈ ⊕ ⬡

It's easy to overdose at the Gathering for Gardner. It's a 5-day weekend jammed with talks and events from 8:00 A.M. to 10:00 P.M., with extra-curricular nonsense until way past midnight. Conway is typically the earliest to rise and last to bed, but even he gets overwhelmed, feasting on the buffet of infinitely much to know and lamenting the impossibility of knowing it all, despite the fact that, being a know-it-all, knowing it all is always his aim.

At midday on Saturday, I escaped to my hotel room and tried to get the man of the hour on the phone. Gardner himself attended only the first 2 Gatherings, when he was in his mid-80s. By the time of this ninth Gathering, he had recently turned 95, a milestone celebrated with a weeklong puzzle extravaganza in the *New York Times*. Solving puzzles is pleasurable, he explained to the reporter, due to a happy by-product of evolution. "Consider a cow," he said. "A cow doesn't have the problem-solving skill of a chimpanzee, which has discovered how to get termites out of the ground by putting a stick into a hole. Evolution has developed the brain's ability to solve puzzles, and at the same time has produced in our brain a pleasure of solving problems." And at 95, Gardner hadn't stopped playing with puzzles and tricks. He stopped attending the Gatherings in his honor mostly because he disliked travel. Once, in some subterfuge to elicit his participation, an organizer asked Conway to give Gardner a surprise phone call that would be broadcast through the Ritz ballroom for all to hear. Conway refused. It was too much of a trick to pull even on the master of tricks.

When I called Gardner from my hotel room, he picked up immediately. We confirmed the plans for Conway and me to come visit—anytime, he said; "I'm not going anywhere!" And he recalled a couple of Conway-related Gathering incidents. Dick Hess, author of *Mental Gymnastics*, paused during a presentation and said he wasn't sure his figures were accurate, to which Conway instantaneously heckled:

THEY ARE!

Similarly, Oxford's mathematical physicist Sir Roger Penrose said during a session that he wasn't sure if a certain theorem could be generalized to higher dimensions:

IT CAN!

Back downstairs at G4G9, Conway wasn't heckling so much as doing his usual loitering. For the most part he avoided the talks, instead installing himself on a modernist settee in the foyer outside the main ballroom, where there was always a steady hum of activity, punctuated at times by somebody banging out the Charlie Brown theme song on the piano. Conway received his own private audience, people plying him with mathy doodads and interrogations. A magician friend, Mark Mitton, who works the Park Avenue party scene in Manhattan (and internationally), wanted to continue their ongoing conversation about rope tricks. Conway is always willing to demonstrate—especially when a television camera is pointed his way, as it was during that documentary tribute to Gardner. Holding the rope with both hands, wrapping the rope this way and that around his wrists, seemingly taking himself hostage, he offered a casual commentary.

You know it's impossible to tie a knot without leaving go of the ends of the string . . .

A few beats later, with a fetching flourish, he stares into the camera and concludes with a tease—

. . . the way I just did.

Many of the rope tricks Conway learned over the years he got from Gardner. He recounted for Mitton how Gardner impressed him with a new trick whereby he brashly grabbed hold of a rope, banged his hands together, and . . .

BAM! There was the knot. It was absolutely fabulous. Then he taught me how to do it. And damn it, I forgot. What you have to do is perform a knot trick 10 or 20 times a day for the first 3 days after you learn it, and then 4 times a day for the next week, and then once a day for another week, and then once a week for a month, and then once a month for the rest of your life. And I didn't do all this. After a few days, I realized I hadn't done it, and tried to do it, and I'd forgotten. . . . The hands are where the memory is, as you know.

Mitton, himself a knot trickster extraordinaire, is impressed with how Conway lives in the action of knot permutations. With any knot trick there's the mathematics of it, and then there's the spatial-temporal handling, and both contain so much information that it's impossible to pinpoint wherein resides the magic. "It goes back to the heart of Descartes," says Mitton. "Descartes chooses certainty over truth. The solve is ultimately poetry. John feels his way through the knots kinesthetically, as many magicians do, but he takes it much farther by understanding what he is doing and creating variations, asking 'How many other ways can this be done?' His permutations are fascinating because of the level of variation and the nature of his exploration and play. Kinesthetically, once you do the trick with both hands, performing the chiral reflection of what you just did, going in instead of out, you start to see the process and topology of the knot more clearly." This comes in handy for Conway when he suspects a member of the audience is scrutinizing things carefully and catching on to the trick, because then he can switch to the reverse knot, the reflection. With the scrutineer staring intently at his left hand, the locus of all the action up till then, Conway moves all the action to his right. "The way John follows these possibilities, and just how much he has forgotten, is a bit overwhelming," says Mitton. "The key is to put the correct length of rope into his hands, and then to watch and learn."

At G4G9 Conway also caught up with Bill Gosper, a veteran Life enthusiast who invented Hashlife, an algorithm that runs Life exponentially faster, making it easier to discern the fate of Life-forms in the distant future. Gosper is also a founder of the hacker community, which adopted the Life glider as its emblem ("hacker" as in the programming subculture, not the computer security threat). While Gareth dangled upside down off the back of the settee playing his Nintendo, Conway and Gosper peered at Gosper's laptop and played with Life. They watched a pattern called the Wedge evolve with quadratic growth. "It turns out," explained Gosper, "that quadratically is the fastest anything can grow, because everything is confined to an area by John's speed limit theorem—there is a box that grows at a certain speed, and nothing can get outside that box." They watched as 2 clusters of Corderman switch engines reacted with each other, shooting off gliders. "This device, the Corderman switch engine, by itself will run 12 or so generations and then die," he said. "But 2 of them next to each other will sustain each other." A tongue of gliders extended off to the side. A crystal started to grow. Gosper turned down the speed, all the better to watch the action unfold. "Here comes the main event: *Yeeeeaaaaooooow!* You can see how fast that was on the grand scale of slow." In the grand finale, a switch engine laid a sine wave of blocks, repeatedly, to create a great big wedge, with the population of cells in the billions, soon to be trillions. "The number of digits in the population is almost twice the number of digits in the generation," said Gosper, "which is the meaning of quadratic growth."

This is also the meaning of what it is to be Life addict.

I turned Life off. Gosper did not.

Gosper was once turned down for a job at Sun Microsystems when someone warned the hiring committee that he would probably just hack Life. He caught the bug when he won Conway's $50 challenge, together with a group of hackers at Marvin Minsky's MIT Artificial Intelligence Project. On November 4, 1970, Gosper sent Gardner a Western Union telegram full of numerical coordinates designating how to configure a glider gun on the Life grid, along with the words IS A GLIDER GUN and RUSH REPEAT BACK. Western Union forbade coded messages and Gosper feared they might reject it, but the telegram got through and when Gardner received it he noted at the bottom: "I hope he's right!" For verification, Gardner sent the coordinates off to Robert Wainwright, one of the many fanatics with whom he'd begun a correspondence. Wainwright first explored Life with a checkerboard and a jar of pennies. This soon became too cumbersome. Employed as a systems analyst for Mobil Oil in Manhattan, he had access to an IBM 360/75, then among the largest computers in the United States, so he wrote a Life program and began his more serious investigations, working on various challenges posed in

Gardner's column. When Wainwright first submitted his computer runs for overnight processing at the company, the operators aborted the jobs because they assumed all the outputted Life-forms were a program error, a core dump of gibberish dots. One of those core dumps confirmed Gosper's claim to be true. He had found the glider gun, the first infinitely growing pattern.

Conway was glad Gosper and his colleagues at MIT won the prize, and it was won in exactly the way he hoped. The glider gun emitted a glider every 30 generations. Conway and his Cambridge crew now went into overdrive, putting together the other necessary components—AND gates, OR gates, and both permanent and temporary memory store—all the circuitry and hardware needed to build a computer on the Life screen. As Conway wrote in a 6-foot, single-spaced note he dashed off to Gardner in November 1970:

> _I think the remaining deep problem is the universality of the game_. Can we build up a library of components which we can put together to form a "machine" which can be programmed to perform arbitrary mathematical calculations? The answer I feel is almost certainly "yes," now that the glider gun has appeared. . . . Obviously what's needed here is a detailed study of the interactions of gliders with various objects.

It was a race to universality, Conway's Cambridge team versus Gosper's MIT team, though they weren't really competing. By this time the Life computer program was up and running at Cambridge. Conway had assumed his Friday night habit of screen watching, crashing gliders into gliders. The glider was the smallest in the family of spaceships, the featherweight among a fleet of lightweight, middleweight, heavyweight, and overweight spaceships. And it was in the spaceships' ability to waltz around and smash about that resided all the potential—potential to generate new Life-forms, new computer parts. Less than a month of screen watching later, in December, Conway was back at his typewriter writing to Gardner and making use of the red ribbon for the 3 crucial words:

Mailed Dec 6/70

Dear MG,
    I hope this letter is not too late – mail seems to take a very long time to reach you. I delayed it until now because I wanted to complete my proof that
        LIFE IS UNIVERSAL

What this means is essentially that you can "program" life to perform any kind of calculation—for instance the theorem implies that we can produce a system that emits a stream of gliders in successive groups of sizes 3,1,4,1,5,9,2,6,5,3,5... ! (For ever!)

Which is to say, Life could calculate π. It could calculate anything. In the broadest logical sense, Life was a metaphor for all of mathematics; it contained all of mathematics.

After that, naturally Conway never sat down to formally write up the proof. Practically speaking, what would a Life computer look like? He didn't think any further about that, either. According to one estimate, it would require 10^{13} pixels, i.e. 10 trillion. The screen would span an area about 6 times the size of Monaco, and if you ever managed to hold the entire screen in view, the patterns of Life-forms evolving would read as a hazy twinkling glow, like a galaxy (and as it turned out, the Game of Life became a valuable modeling tool in investigating spiral galaxies). Conway has fantasized occasionally that with such large sampling, primitive Life-forms might crawl out of the snowy noise and say Hello to their creator. But for the most part he was on to other things, other games.

With no published proof proper, the world simply had to take Conway's word for it that Life was universal. Extrapolating and applying to cellular automata in general, this became known as Conway's Presumption, an aphorism of sorts in the theory of computation with various phrasings, such as:

If a lot can happen, everything will happen.

Or:

If a lot is going on, everything can.

Conway, for his part, didn't know it was called Conway's Presumption (formulated as such by his colleague Chaim Goodman-Strauss, professor and department chair at the University of Arkansas).

But I am happy to own it! And I don't remember phrasing it that way, but it's quite a happy way of phrasing it. The way I used to phrase it is this: "If you can't understand what's going on, then probably *everything* is going on."

You know, when you have one of these cellular automata, if you look at it and can predict what will happen from here on in, then you've got some degree of understanding. But if you can't predict, then probably everything is going on. In other words, you can learn to program it to do anything and everything, whatever you want—you can find little spaceships in your cellular automaton. It would mean it was universal.

And that was that. End of story. The chase was over, the conquest complete.

Really, for me it was over.

The first Life column was Gardner's most popular column ever, outdoing even the Flexagons Furor, and it filled *Scientific American* headquarters with mail from far afield, from Moscow, New Delhi, Tokyo. Conway, too, was inundated with mail, one letter arriving in October 1970 from Stan Ulam, whose acquaintance he'd made not long before. Conway had been prepared to dislike Ulam, one of the fathers of the H-bomb, but when they met in the late 1960s Conway found him thoroughly congenial. When Ulam got in touch about Life, he'd been corresponding with Gardner about new ideas for mathematical games, such as "integer-shifting games." He asked Gardner if these games had been studied before. Gardner suggested he ask the expert. And then, as Ulam relayed to Conway, "By a very nice coincidence, a few days after I received Gardner's letter I saw in the latest issue of the *Scientific American* your fascinating game…Some time ago I was playing more complicated games on computers. The two enclosed reprints give some idea of such constructions. . . ." Ulam had devised several cellular automata, investigating various neighborhoods and states and rules. As Conway reported to Gardner:

I knew about the von N stuff, but didn't realize Ulam was the real founder.

Gardner followed up his first column with a second, announcing the "startling new results" concerning universality. He drilled down into automata theory and exercised his powers of prediction: "The most immediate practical application of cellular automata theory," he said, "is likely to be the design of circuits capable of self-repair or the wiring of any specified type of new circuit. No one can say how significant the theory may eventually become for the physical and biological sciences. It may have important bearings on cell growth in embryos, the replication of DNA molecules, the operation of nerve nets, genetic changes in evolving populations and so on. . . ."

The incessant reader response warranted a third installment as well, and Gardner reported some of the more spectacular discoveries sent in by readers. Since personal home computers were still something of a luxury, anyone who had a hard-core hankering to try Life on something more powerful than a game board or graph paper was driven to figure out a way to pilfer computer time at work. One serious hub was at Honeywell (though another was a group of hackers at the University of Waterloo that still did all their investigations by hand). At Honeywell, Gardner recalled, an employee by the name of Charles Corderman programmed a secret switch, variously described in Life lore as a "hot button" or a "boss button," or perhaps a more covertly rigged contraption under his desk operated by a foot pedal or a knee switch—at any rate, some emergency gadget allowing him to change his computer screen in a flash from Life back to the company project he was supposed to be working on.

The Life legend Conway likes to trot out (temperament permitting) pertains to the purported government report about exactly how much time people spent playing Life at work. If the report existed at all, those in the know imagine it as a cautionary memo from DARPA, the Department of Defense's Advanced Research Projects Agency, expressing concern over the millions of dollars Life cost the nation in illicit computer time. As to the legend's veracity, Gosper could only speculate. "My guess is, if there was such a report, that its conclusions were grossly understated. The KGB could not have wrought such sabotage in its wildest dreams. The amount of legitimate computer time stolen from legitimate employers in the seventies was in the hundreds of millions of dollars."

Investigating Life, 1974.

The civilian population, not necessarily inclined to start fiddling and get addicted, also began to take notice. Life was the theme for a year-end crossword in the *Guardian* newspaper, and a photographer from London's *Sunday Times* visited Conway and tried desperately to capture him transfixed by a glowing screen in the dark computer room for an article asking "Is it just a game?" "Life, though it begins with tiddlywinks, ends in a very frightening game. For it opens the door into an eerie world in which abstract mathematical concepts take tangible 'living' shape." This publicity had repercussions in kind. Conway received a letter from a woman who proposed marriage, delirious that she'd finally found her kindred spirit. Another went roughly like this: "Dear Dr. Conway, I have an interesting question. I've asked various scientists but I've never got anything sensible for a response. It occurred to me you might be just the kind of oddball scientist to be able to answer. Here is the question: A spaceship is traveling around the Earth and it takes 2 hours to go around, and now its speed is doubled and it takes 1 hour . . ."

The letter went on, clearly scrawled in high excitement, with the speed doubling yet again and again and again until it was flying around the Earth 10 times a second, or something. And the letter was increasingly in capitals, bigger capitals, more exclamation marks, and finally he said,

"Until it breaks the light barrier." Exclamation mark, exclamation mark, exclamation mark. And then he asked my opinion of what happened next. So a bunch of students and I sat reading this letter. We wrote back a little letter that said, "Thank you. This is a question we have been considering here for some time. The answer is, it turns inside out and flutters slowly downward."

Midmorning on the last day of G4G9, polymath technologist Stephen Wolfram, with a crumpled Kit Kat wrapper in hand, approached Conway at the Ritz settee. He wanted to pick his brain about the Free Will Theorem. "What is the meat of the thing?" He came away unsatisfied, unconvinced that the Free Will Theorem had anything to do with free will. Free will is a subject about which Wolfram has some ideas, originating with his interest in cellular automata and expressed in his book *A New Kind of Science*. With that in mind, I in turn nabbed Wolfram for a chat about all things Conway in the Ritz lobby bar. "I remember 2 very funny stories," he says. "Okay, so one—can I really tell you this story? I think I can. Many years ago . . ." In the late 1980s Wolfram debuted Mathematica, a program that solves any equation entered. Soon it became an indispensable tool for millions of scientists and mathematicians, professors and students, in everything from physics to topology, medical research to weather analysis. But with the launch of Mathematica, trademark infringement litigation ensued, initiated by a long-dormant but reemerging company named Mathematica Policy Research (started in the 1950s by John von Neumann and Oskar Morgenstern). In order to make their case, the litigants had to show that there would be a likelihood of confusion by consumers. As Wolfram recalls, their prime piece of evidence—"the sample of the confused"—was that an individual at the company had attended a dinner party with a bunch of Princeton pooh-bahs, including "a paper-eating mathematics professor named John Conway," and that Professor Conway had been confused by a mention of the von Neumann Mathematica and in his confusion wondered whether it was the same as the Wolfram Mathematica. Wolfram was eagerly anticipating the moment at the trial (which never came, since the case was settled) when Conway took the witness stand and was cross-examined by the defense with the question "Professor Conway, are you ever confused?" Wolfram knows Conway well enough to know that he makes a virtue of being confused. And I've heard him admit as much himself—

I'm confused at various times. In fact, I'm confused at all times. It's a permanent state.

Ask Conway what he is doing tomorrow, and although he can calculate the day of the week for any given date for thousands of years, it usually takes him a while to orient himself and determine the current day of the week.

Wait a minute. What am I doing tomorrow? What *is* tomorrow? What day is it today? I'm confused . . .

That the perpetually confused professor was confused about which Mathematica was which surely wouldn't carry much weight in court. Wolfram's second story also goes to character. In 1993, journalist John Horgan wrote a *Scientific American* article titled "The Death of Proof," casting Wolfram in the antiproof position with the following: "The obsession with proof, Wolfram declares, has kept mathematicians from discovering the vast new realms of phenomena accessible to computers. Even the most intrepid mathematical experimentalists are for the most part 'not going far enough,' he says. They're taking existing questions in mathematics and investigating those. They are adding a few little curlicues to the top of a gigantic structure." Casting Conway as pro-proof, Horgan continued: "Mathematicians may take this view with a grain of salt. Although he shares Wolfram's fascination with cellular automata, Conway contends that Wolfram's career—as well as his contempt for proofs—shows he is not a real mathematician." And then Horgan quotes Conway as saying,

Pure mathematicians usually don't found companies and deal with the world in an aggressive way. We sit in our ivory towers and think.

Soon after the article's publication, Conway wrote Horgan a letter claiming and complaining that his words were taken out of context, copying it to Wolfram with a handwritten addendum of an apology. When Wolfram and I spoke in a follow-up interview by phone, he pulled the letter out of his vast scanned archives and perused its contents while I waited. "I have to say this letter is surprisingly polite toward me." Why surprising? "Because my interactions with Conway have been strange. I would say in some ways strangely competitive, which I find bizarre because I think our objectives are fairly different." While Wolfram could not have cared less about the Horgan article, Conway worried and stewed and lost sleep. He's a vulnerable soul himself, susceptible to minor slights, and in turn he doesn't like to offend.

Wolfram is somewhat disappointed that he and Conway haven't had more interaction. "John is not somebody I know well. He's somebody I've interacted with a bunch of times over the years who I should know better than I do, because we have quite common interests." In addition to their mutual interest in cellular automata, Conway and Wolfram hold in common oversized egos, but beyond that they are a study in contrast. Wolfram, like Simon Norton, was an Eton prodigy. Born in 1959, he published his first paper at age 15 and won a MacArthur fellowship at 21. Then he had a prolonged stint at the Institute for Advanced Study, where he started in earnest his cellular automata studies, doing work that ultimately would reshape the approach to analyzing complex phenomena. He remained at the Institute until 1986, then became a free agent, a scientist entrepreneur. Legend has it that when he left the Institute, he hired moving trucks and absconded at the crack of dawn on a Sunday morning with all the computers containing his research. "Completely false," he says. (Aren't all stories that are too good to be true? Legend also has it that Einstein's archives upon his death were spirited away from the Institute in the dead of night in a fleet of trucks with armed guards.) It wasn't until 2002 that Wolfram self-published his opus, *A New Kind of Science*, proposing a radical vision for exactly that—a new way of doing science inspired by his longstanding love for cellular automata.

When Wolfram first used a computer in 1973 he played around with the Game of Life. Put off by all the trivial "Cheshire-cat-isms," he programmed his own 2-dimensional cellular automaton. Throughout his many years of cellular automata research, he was curious to talk to Conway and get at the more serious side of things. An early meeting took place at a conference on Dynamical Systems and Cellular Automata, in Luminy, France, in September 1983. Wolfram found Conway at lunch regaling mathematicians by demanding their birth dates and bouncing back the day of the week on which they were born. The serious-minded Wolfram found these trivialities maddening. "Eventually I said, 'I can't stand this! Stop doing this! This is just ridiculous!'" He pried Conway away from this silliness and led him to more serious terrain as they took a walk down a rocky path to a cliff overlooking the Mediterranean Sea. "We were able to have a long walk and a nice talk about the fundamental principles of things, which he has plenty to say about." Putting the final touches on his book in the year of the millennium, Wolfram called up Conway to dig deeper at the origins of Life. They spoke for a few hours, though again it took Wolfram a while to get Conway off his trivial bent, his emphasis on the games. "What was kind of funny to me was that the first version of the story was, 'Oh, it's games, blah blah blah blah blah.' The real version was he'd been hired in some position to do logic, and he was interested in a simple enumeration of the recursive functions, and [Life] was something that had come out of that. Which to me was 100 times more interesting. . . . I find that for me, if it sounds too gamelike, I'm not interested."

"I think he is keen to impress people," Wolfram continues. "What he doesn't necessarily do is gauge what is going to impress a given person. And I am much more impressed by hearing about the fundamental stuff than I am in hearing about days of the week for birthdays. I think he cares about what people think, who gets credit for what. And although there is a big layer of playfulness, I think there is . . . competition as well as playfulness in the whole enterprise. It kind of reminds me of a person I knew much better than I know John, the physicist Dick Feynman, who wrote this book called *What Do You Care What Other People Think?* And the funniest part about that book is that [Feynman] cared very deeply about what other people thought, and his whole playful thing was very much a coping mechanism for actually caring quite deeply. Insecure people will often come on very strong and be very aggressive. It is a way of coping with the internal dynamics."

Conway was seduced by Life, and then he abandoned it. Wolfram abandoned academia and founded his company Wolfram Research, allowing him, among other things, to be thoroughly seduced by cellular automata for 2 decades. Not with nothing to show for it. He compiled a list of 256 elementary 1-dimensional cellular automata and named them Rule 0 to Rule 255. He studied all of the rules intensively, running them on a computer program and determining that the prize automaton was Rule 110. He conjectured that this 1-dimensional cellular automaton would be universal. He spoke to Conway about it, and Conway, as is his wont, suggested a name: "LineLife." It wasn't until 1998 that mathematician and computer scientist Matthew Cook, working at Wolfram Research, proved Rule 110's universality. This was big news among a certain crowd, and details spread via the "math-fun" e-mail list. Conway, still then successfully coping with e-mail technology, responded within hours.

Date: Fri, 20 Nov 1998 16:44:11 -0500 (EST)
From: John Conway
Subject: Re: New CA universality theorem: 110 is universal (Cook)

> Matthew Cook has proved that Wolfram's 1D CA rule 110 is universal.

I agree this is very exciting. As far as I know this is the first universality proof for one of Wolfram's automata—is this correct. (I mean "found" automata rather than "designed" ones.) Indeed it might be the first "found" universality after my own one for "life".

It's always been my feeling that the best results would be obtained by learning how to program found things rather than by designing things to be programmable, and I'm very glad to see this striking confirmation. I wish I'd done it myself! (I tried some 1-dimensional CAs, but found it too hard to get anywhere.) Congratulations to Matthew Cook!

> Cook has worked extensively with Wolfram in the past, but got this result alone. Wolfram is glad about the theorem, but would rather have him hold back on publishing his new result until Wolfram's long-awaited book comes out, probably within a year.

I don't think this is entirely proper (though as a request it isn't improper either)—if Cook has any reason to want to publish it earlier, I think he *should feel free to do so—I'm sure Wolfram's book will be a great success in either case.*

John Conway

Wolfram, at this stage still finishing his book, launched a lawsuit, sealing away the Rule 110 results, preventing Cook from publishing or talking about the proof. Conway sympathized with Cook, and he offered to mediate, to give Wolfram a call and try to broker some peace. Cook initially declined the offer, and later changed his mind. He provided the phone number he had for Wolfram, and Conway made the call.

> I telephoned him, and he immediately said that he could better afford to pay the phone bill, so he telephoned back immediately. And then I tried to persuade him not to be such a damned nuisance, though not in those terms. The thing I really didn't like was that I said: "I may have made the situation worse because I gave a lecture here in Princeton about Rule 110." And he said, "Oh yes, I know." Which sort of implied that he'd had a spy there, in a sense, and I didn't like that at all.

In the end, Conway's entreaties didn't make any difference. Wolfram recalled a messy exchange, on the phone and in correspondence, but doubted it was Conway who made the call. "Nobody ever calls me," he says. "I'm unfindable by phone. I've been unfindable by phone for years. Nobody knows my number. I don't even know my number, so there." Conway insists he made the call, and that Wolfram called him back. "Who knows how it was set up," says Wolfram. "If you have access to Conway's archives you'll find some letters related to this there." Conway archives? I told him there was no such thing. "How sad. That makes your job a lot harder."* He tried to make it a bit easier, sending me a few

---

* In the mid-aughts Conway's wife Diana cleared their Princeton house of her husband's junk (which she used to reverently collect) and sent about a dozen boxes to the archives at the American Institute of Mathematics in San Jose, California. Ferreting through the boxes reveals a mishmash: big notebooks and small notebooks, each fractionally filled with the beginnings of a new idea; paper plates (dinner and dessert); a Sears receipt for a TV and other scraps, all covered in numerical musings; the *New York*

choice items from his archive, though understandably he wasn't willing to hand over all the goods. "My relationship to your subject is fairly complicated," he says. "I have a sense of many aspects of him. Some of which I like, some of which I don't." About the "math-fun" e-mail, he says, "That's kind of obnoxious. What a jerk." Yet when Wolfram finally self-published *A New Kind of Science*, in 2002, he sent Conway a complimentary copy with a note playing right to his weakness: "Dear John, You're mentioned more than anyone else in the book . . ." That's how Conway recalls the note. Wolfram, again consulting his archival database, provided confirmation. "The precise quote was: 'You may like to know that among the living you're tied for first place in the index.' (He lost out big-time to people like Alan Turing in the overall count.) I thought the inscription might appeal to his competitive nature."

And looking up the sacred name in the 65-page index, there are a few things to learn. On page 930 there's brief mention of another 2-dimensional cellular automaton that Conway and Cambridge grad student Mike Paterson tested, "an idealization of a prehistoric worm." On page 877 Wolfram bemoans that Conway "treated the system largely as a recreation." And on page 1117 he seems to reprimand Conway's laziness in stopping short of the finish line with a universality proof: "[T]he fact remains that a complete and rigorous proof of universality has apparently still never been given for the Game of Life."

By contrast, in Wolfram's rigorous 1192-page book, the universal Rule 110 (describing Cook's proof) was a prime piece of evidence in support of his grand proposition, a monumental paean to complexity science and cellular automata. As he says in the preface: "Three centuries ago science was transformed by the dramatic new idea that rules based on mathematical equations could be used to describe the natural world. My purpose in this book is to initiate another such transformation, and to introduce a new kind of science that is based on the much more general types of rules that can be embodied in simple computer

---

Times front page from January 1991 with the headline U.S. AND ALLIES OPEN AIR WAR ON IRAQ, and from June 1998, LEWINSKY DISMISSES HER LAWYER; as well as many a math paper such as Peter Sarnak's "Extremal Geometries"; and a lot of unopened mail.

programs." This prompted a journalist to ask, "Are you the next New-ton?" "Maybe," said Wolfram. He had proposed a new law of nature, the principle of computational equivalence, which led many to believe that he was also proposing that the universe is a cellular automaton. The response from scientists and reviewers ranged from apoplectic outrage to fervent skepticism. Where did Conway fall on this score? He enjoyed reading about Rule 110.

> It was quite interesting. I mean, if I'd discovered it myself it would have been a bit better. But then I wouldn't have played with the Life game . . .

Steven Weinberg, a Nobel Prize–winning physicist, wrote a lengthy review essay in the *New York Review of Books* with the headline, "Is the Universe a Computer?" Addressing Wolfram's prefatory remarks, Weinberg said that usually he put books that made such claims on "the crack-pot shelf" of his bookcase. To do so with this book, he said, would be a mistake. "I don't think that his book comes close to meeting his goals or justifying his claims," he wrote, "but if it is a failure it is an interesting one." Especially if Wolfram's work led to the advancement of a clear and simple mathematical statement about complexity. "[I]f Wolfram can give a precise statement of his conjecture about the computational equivalence of almost all automata that produce complex patterns and prove that it is true, then he will have found a simple common feature of complexity, which would be of real interest. In the study of anything outside human affairs, including the study of complexity, it is only sim-plicity that can be interesting."

The Game of Life's applied reach in the study of complexity extends be-yond and beyond—mathematically Life might be easy to dismiss (for Conway especially), but it served as potent fertilizer in the garden of emergent behavior. Given Conway's inclination for checking book in-dexes, an annotated bibliography might be a fitting way to minimalisti-cally survey Life's influence. Searching "Conway Game of Life" on Google Books throws out "about 16,000" hits. We might start with Mi-chael Crichton's sci-fi techno-thriller, *The Lost World*. In the acknowledgments (Conway, page 5), Crichton mentions his indebtedness to Conway; the main character, a mathematician, visits a place called the Santa Fe Institute, refers to the "Game of Life" as a shorthand for a common evolutionary scenario and lectures on "Life at the Edge of Chaos." In real life, the Santa Fe Institute is a hub of complexity science, an early outpost founded in 1984, where cellular automata were used in a process of "evolutionary computation" to design computer programs, as Gardner had predicted they would be. A current professor there, Melanie Mitchell, recently published a popular survey on the subject, *Complexity: A Guided Tour*, wherein Conway is included (pages 149–51, 156) in the procession marching from John Locke through to Alan Turing and Stan Ulam and onward to investigators like MIT's Norman Margolus and Tomasso Toffoli. In their 1980s book *Cellular Automata Machines* (Conway, page 10), Margolus and Toffoli describe their construction of dedicated cellular automata machines that they hoped would gain widespread use among complexity scientists. The exclusive automata architecture allowed the machines to run 1000s of times faster than a general-purpose computer, but then the general-purpose computer got a lot faster in a big hurry, swiftly rendering the hard-to-program cellular automata machines obsolete.

Still, cellular automata proliferated as a tool for investigating complexity. Complexity scientists didn't necessarily use Life itself in their investigations, and they wouldn't likely use any universal cellular automata, because as with FRACTRAN generating π, any universal cellular automaton would be painfully slow for modeling purposes. Instead they custom coded cellular automata to suit their area of study. The Danish theoretical physicist Per Bak ruminated on Conway's Life rule in *How Nature Works: The Science of Self-Organized Criticality* (pages 107–12, 118, 142, 161). Bak developed the "sandpile" cellular automaton, used to study earthquakes, solar flares, mass extinctions, traffic jams, cascades of the "trickle-down" economy, and avalanches of thought in the brain. Similarly, computational social scientist Robert Axtell, together with professor of emergency medicine, environmental health, biostatics, and economics Joshua Epstein, mention Conway's Life as the iconic cellular automaton in their book *Growing Artificial Societies* (page 17), and then detail their cellular automaton "sugarscape," used for modeling trade, combat, seasonal migration, disease transmission, pollution, sex reproduction, and more. Moving from artificial societies to artificial life and artificial intelligence, Carnegie Mellon futurist Hans Moravec first met Life as an undergraduate and says it nudged his work in robotics. In his book *Mind Children: The Future of Robot and Human Intelligence* (Conway, pages 151–58, 175–76), Moravec tells a lengthy fable about "Celltick" creatures and their creator "Newway" and fantasizes about the evolutionary moment when our artificial spawn crawl off the grid and out into our larger universe. Moravec predicts that a human brain equivalent robot will exist by 2040. "Artificial intelligence is basically the idea to have machines able to do everything humans can do, and more, to overcome our limitations," he tells me when I get in touch about his ode to Conway. "There are certain instincts that are no longer appropriate for the way we live. And there are cognitive limitations in our ability to solve problems, so we get into fights instead. Many of these things could be made trivial with robots. Essentially, we are building our own successors."

It occurred to me that Conway has succeeded in building his own successor. Not so much in terms of his animal magnetism, which often gets him into trouble, but certainly in terms of his emotional absenteeism and his cultivated ineptitude that allow him to spend as much time as possible with his math. He confessed to a co-worker that he figured out early on what he could get away with and henceforth tried to exploit his "incompetence" accordingly. As far as all these cellular automata that are descendants of Life or nudged into existence by Life, Conway gets away with a cultivated indifference. One acquaintance was gobsmacked to discover that Conway was less interested in how the Game of Life is used to study spiral galaxies than he was in how to get his name on an asteroid. While Life may pervade the applied domain of complexity, that's simply not Conway's bailiwick. Then again, while imitating life was not his goal, finding artificial life, in a sense, was. And on this subject he's on the record as saying:

> I believe that if you have a large enough configuration you will see evo-
> lution in the plane. What would happen is every now and then there
> would be a creature capable of reproducing itself and then they would
> start to populate the plane. Except the plane is still filled with random
> junk which might kill some of them. So some of them will be better

equipped to survive than others and every now and then they will run into something that hurts and might start a change. Most of these changes will probably be for the worse, but every now and then one of these might be for the better. And then, you know the story. You will probably get evolution happening and you would get creatures that really deserve the name "living."

Many people have produced things of this kind that are closer to real life, such as one with DNA strings in the model. That's counter to my philosophy as it copies the reproductive mechanism that we have. My philosophy is to start with nothing and see if it has its own reproductive system.

Because I am really not interested in a way in what makes us tick. I have always had this idea that it's rather parochial to be too interested in us. What happens when we meet the Martians? By that I mean somebody out there, another form of intelligent life. There is no obvious reason why they are going to use DNA for their method of storing information, reproducing, and so on. They probably have a totally different system.

I feel that the abstract mathematical things that I am interested in are probably closer to the ones the Martians are interested in. . . . I will be very interested to know what the Martians think. Do they actually think in the same way as we do? Will their logic be the same? Drives me nuts! Maybe the Martians don't have the same notion of mathematical existence as we do, but whatever it is, it will be very interesting!

To get back to the literature survey, there's *Cyberfeminism and Artificial Life*, which cites Conway and the Game of Life on page 70; there's *Creation and Evolution: A Conference with Pope Benedict XVI in Castel Gandolfo*, which cites the man and his game on page 40; and there's the forthcoming *Hippie Philosophy and the Building of the Environmental Counterculture*, which makes mention on pages 89–91. The ecopragmatist Stewart Brand tells me he "noticed and admired Conway's Game back then" when it debuted, and by 1986 his *Essential Whole Earth Catalog* advertised Life programs available in the public domain for home computers, Apple and IBM, costing $10 and $8 respectively. And then there's *Game of Life Cellular Automata*, a 637-page fortieth-anniversary collection of articles edited by Life enthusiast Andrew Adamatzky, a computer scientist at the International Center of Unconventional Computing who unsuccessfully beseeched Conway to contribute.

By far the best bookend to this review is Daniel Dennett, philosopher of mind. The Game of Life is a theme he faithfully addresses in his books—in *Freedom Evolves* (pages 36, 42, 46, 48, 50–51, 65); in *Darwin's Dangerous Idea* (pages 166, 171–73, 176, 221–22, 480n, 528); and most recently as a "tool for thinking about free will" in *Intuition Pumps* (pages 359–69, 380).

"I think that Life should be a thinking tool in everybody's kit," says Dennett, "and I've put my actions where my words are, because I teach it to all my students." I went to visit Dennett at Boston University and sat in on his class Philosophy 3: Language and Mind. With 100 or so students assembled for the day's lecture, Dennett first went over the assigned reading, "What Is It Like to Be a Bat?"—a classic essay written in the 1970s by philosopher Thomas Nagel, which concludes that one cannot have an objective approach to subjectivity. What is it like to be the Boston Red Sox? An ant colony? Billions of neurons? What is it like to be John Conway? That's really what we are trying to get at, in a sense. Can we know what it's like to be Conway? Only in the moment, Nagel would argue. Because if we look back, "Conway past" is gone and "Conway present" is a different person. Dennett then segued to Life. "Nagel's paper, famously, flat asserts that we can't know what it's like to be a bat, and I have attributed this to a failure of imagination, not an insight into necessity. We can imagine a great deal about what it's like to be a bat. The more we know about bats, the more we can imagine what it's like to be one." By contrast, he said, "One of the great things about Conway Life is that it's a great imagination extender. It shows in very vivid form how you can get levels of complexity and build up from a very simple underlying physics, if you like, to pattern levels that are really surprisingly sensitive and sophisticated." Dennett continued on to cover the basics of Life, lay out the rules, and emphasize what he considers the most important feature: there are no parts concealed behind the screen, no backstage, no hidden variables; physics in the Life world is entirely transparent. He assigned a problem set, due the following week (starting with a diagonal line of 6 live cells, calculate the next 3 generations). And then he left his students with a warning. "There are people out there who are addicts, Life addicts. So, caution everyone. I'm giving you your first free dose of heroin here. Be careful."

In his book *Darwin's Dangerous Idea*, Dennett describes Life as "a nifty meme." Whereas an idea is passive, a meme is active, it gets passed along like a gene, it is a "virus of the mind." Some memes are beautiful, such as birdsong. Some memes are vicious, such as "Obama is a Muslim." Some memes are raunchy, such as twerking. "A meme spreads quite literally the way a virus spreads," Dennett tells me after class. "A virus doesn't carry its own copy machinery with it. It has to be piggybacked on the cell; it has to commandeer the copy machinery of a cell. And a meme has to commandeer the copy machinery of a brain."

Dennett's brain was first commandeered by Life via Gardner's column in 1970. He was then an assistant professor at UC Irvine, and he became a Life fiddler but not a fanatic. "I fiddled with it, just to fix it in my memory, so that I had, as it were, a working copy of the meme." It wasn't until years later that he noticed Life would make an excellent thinking tool for some of philosophy's perennial topics: consciousness, time, determinism, the physics of the universe. "It's a very nice toy model. Do you know the concept of toy problems? In a number of fields, they look at what they call toy problems, shockingly oversimplified problems which nevertheless can be used to study and think about issues that are too hard to study in the full grubby complexity of the world."

Take determinism. "The Life world has a weird property in that the past is not perfectly readable," Dennett says. "That is, there are configurations in the Life world that do not tell you what preceded them, there are different possible predecessor states. So you can't read the past off the state, to the same degree that you can't read the future off the state. I've made a lot in recent years of the category I call 'inert historical facts.' These are facts that *are* facts, they are definite, but they have left no trace at all in the world as far as we can tell." Maybe that explains the irregular synaptic geometry of Conway's memory—it's riddled with inert facts. "My favorite example of an inert historical fact is that some of the gold in my teeth once belonged to Julius Caesar, or it didn't. Now one of those is true. Either none of the gold in my teeth ever belonged to Julius Caesar, or some of it did. One of those propositions is a true historical fact. I do not think any possible investigation for any amount of money by any expert could ever tell which one of those propositions is true.

Whichever is the truth has simply left no footprints, it's left no finger-prints, it's left no trail. In the Life world, it's very clear that there are lots of inert historical facts. Once that moment has passed, whether that moment was in situation A or situation B is completely unknowable from the current state."

For another example, there's the anthropic principle, an idea that has been nicely encapsulated as such: the more we examine the universe, the more evidence there seems to be that the universe must have known we were coming. "The idea is that physics will have different constants in each universe," Dennett tells me, "just like the variations in Conway Life—change the number of neighbors for birth or death cells, for instance. Some universes will have a life-friendly physics and some won't. The fact that we are in a wonderful life-friendly universe is not surprising. And that is the anthropic principle." Or, as he described in his book *Darwin's Dangerous Idea*:

> [S]uppose that some self-reproducing Universal Turing machines in the Life world were to have a conversation with each other about the world as they found it, with its wonderfully simple physics—express-ible in a single sentence and covering all eventualities. They would be committing a logical howler if they argued that since they existed, the Life world, with its particular physics, had to exist—for after all, Con-way might have decided to be a plumber or play bridge instead of hunting for this world. But what if they deduced that their world was just too wonderful, with its elegant Life-sustaining physics, to have come into existence without an Intelligent Creator? If they jumped to the conclusion that they owed their existence to the activities of a wise Lawgiver, they'd be right! There is a God and his name is Conway. . . . But they would be *jumping* to a conclusion. The existence of a uni-verse obeying a set of laws even as elegant as the Life law (or the laws of our own physics) does not logically require an intelligent Law-giver. . . . What Newton found—and what Conway found—are eternal Platonic fixed points that anybody else in principle could have discov-ered, not idiosyncratic creations that depend in any way on the particularities of the minds of their authors. If Conway had never turned his hand to designing cellular-automata worlds—if Conway had never even existed—some other mathematician might very well

have hit upon exactly the Life world that Conway gets the credit for. So, as we follow the Darwinian down this path, God the Artificer turns first into God the Law*giver*, who now can be seen to merge with God the Law*finder*. God's hypothesized contribution is thereby becoming less personal—and hence more readily performable by something dogged and mindless!

If not intelligently designed, is the universe a computer, a cellular automaton? The reviews of Stephen Wolfram's book took that to be the author's position: "Wolfram believes the universe is a cellular automaton!" But according to Wolfram, this is nothing but a meme. "Somehow there is this meme: 'Wolfram is suggesting the universe is a cellular automaton.' Well, I'm not. Do I think it is worth investigating the possibility that the universe comes from a simple program? Yes. But not the particular simple program that corresponds to cellular automata." As he's said in a TED talk on the subject, "Could it be that somewhere out there in the computational universe, we might find our physical universe? Perhaps there is even some simple rule, some simple program, for our universe. Well, the history of physics would have us believe that the rule for the universe must be pretty complicated. But in the computational universe we've now seen how rules that are incredibly simple can produce incredibly rich and complex behavior. So that could be what's going on with our whole universe."

This genre of ideas is not original to Wolfram. In *A New Kind of Science*'s footnotes, he traces the lineage through René Descartes, Bernhard Riemann, John Wheeler, Roger Penrose, Marvin Minsky, and Richard Feynman. Most directly, he is following on an idea of Edward Fredkin, a professor at Carnegie Mellon and an early pioneer of digital physics. Fredkin suspected as early as the 1950s that the universe is some sort of digital computational process. His friend and colleague Marvin Minsky suggested he take a look at cellular automata. "He told me to look up von Neumann's paper," Fredkin tells me, "and I got that paper and read it and then I was hooked. Immediately I programmed a computer to do it." He investigated a 3-by-3 neighborhood for a time but then turned his attention elsewhere, leaving a Ph.D. student to continue explorations with a 2-state system. Then news broke of Conway's Game of Life. "Annoyance was my first reaction," Fredkin says. "Because I had been working with cellular automata for a long time by then. One of the first things I did was to think about this 3-by-3 neighborhood. But the point is I ignored looking at the 3-by-3 neighborhood. My guess is if I hadn't made that decision I might have discovered the Game of Life. So that was what was annoying."

By the mid-1970s, Fredkin's ideas about the universe as a cellular automaton started to crystallize. During a visit to the UK with his fiancé, he called on Conway at Cambridge. "I just thought I would tell him what my ideas are and what I'm working on and see if he had any interesting comments." Fredkin's ideas attracted enough attention over the years to warrant a 12,000-word feature in the *Atlantic Monthly* in 1988, which quoted him as follows: "I find the supporting evidence for my beliefs in ten thousand different places. And to me it's just totally overwhelming. It's like there's an animal I want to find"—sometimes he likens it to Bigfoot, sometimes to a web-footed duck—"I've found his footprints. I've found his droppings. I've found the half-chewed food. I find pieces of his fur, and so on. In every case it fits one kind of animal, and it's not like any animal anyone's ever seen. People say, Where is this animal? I say, Well, he was here, he's about this big, this that and the other. And I know a thousand things about him. I don't have him in hand, but I know he's there. . . . What I see is so compelling that it can't be a creature of my imagination."

That's an illustration of how Fredkin can't quite get to the explanatory meat of his theory, which in some ways doesn't seem entirely crackpot. His theory of digital physics holds that information is more fundamental than matter and energy; that atoms, electrons, quarks, and everything ultimately are comprised of bits of information. But then he continues to conjecture that a single programming rule, "the cause and prime mover of everything," governs the bit-filled universe. The problem, as the *Atlantic Monthly* article noted, is that Fredkin's theory raises metaphysical questions that he can't answer, sending his theory into a spiral of infinite regress. If electrons are made of information, what is information made of? And furthermore, "Where is this computer that Fredkin keeps talking about? Is it in this universe, residing along some fifth or sixth dimension that renders it invisible? Is it in some meta-universe? The answer is the latter." Which also lands at the problem of infinite regress. It is a problem solved, in a sense, with the fable of the turtles. As recounted in Stephen Hawking's *A Brief History of Time*, it goes roughly like this: The Cambridge philosopher Bertrand Russell was in the middle of a public lecture on cosmology when an old lady interrupted. "Everything you've been telling us is rubbish," she said. "The world is actually a flat plate, supported by a giant elephant that is standing on the back of a tortoise." Russell gave a superior smile and asked: "What is the tortoise standing on?" The old lady replied: "You're very clever, young man, very clever. But it's turtles all the way down!"

When Fredkin visited Conway in Cambridge, things went similarly pear-shaped. He explained his ideas and hoped that Conway might have at least a few interesting comments. "He didn't," says Fredkin. "I talked to him about the game and such. And he didn't share any of my interests in cellular automata. I'm interested in it as a potential model for physical processes at the bottom, wherever the bottom is. What I mean is the most microscopic aspect of physics might be a cellular automaton process. It wouldn't be the Game of Life, certainly, but some other cellular automaton. He had no interest in what I was interested in. That was obvious to me right away. He was polite but in some sense dismissive."

Dismissive or not, Conway gave Fredkin's ideas some airtime in 1982, when he finally wrote up something on Life in *Winning Ways for Your Mathematical Plays* (with coauthors Elwyn Berlekamp and Richard Guy). In the chapter titled "What Is Life?" an epigraphic answer is provided by a reprimand from Mrs. Abraham Fraenkel, the wife of an Israeli mathematician: "Life's not always as simple as mathematics, Abraham!" With that sentiment in mind, the chapter ends with a nod to Fredkin:

> Analogies with real life processes are impossible to resist. If a primordial broth of amino acids is large enough, and there is sufficient time, self-replicating moving automata may result from transition rules built into the structure of matter and the laws of nature. There is even the possibility that space-time itself is granular, composed of discrete units, and that the universe, as Edward Fredkin of MIT and others have suggested, is a cellular automaton run by an enormous computer.

As Conway notes,

You could read or misread that we support it.

And even if he was unsupportive, Conway appreciates where Fredkin is coming from.

If you have a crazy idea and it works out, then suddenly you are the great genius. Einstein had a crazy idea and it worked out. Newton had a crazy idea and it was criticized as occultism. Most people who have crazy ideas just have crazy ideas. On the other hand, the obvious idea turns out not to be true. You know: obviously, the world is flat.

As the G4G9 weekend wound down, with Conway still inert on the settee, inside the Ritz ballroom programmer Tom Rokicki delivered his 10-minute news report on "Modern Life." The latest news was that the π calculator, which Conway predicted in 1970, had recently been discovered—a Life-form that physically prints the endless string of digits 3.14159265358979323846264338327950288419716939937510582097494445 ....

Rokicki also showed off the latest gadgetry for simulating Life with a program he'd designed called Golly, which churned out googols of generations and billions of cells. Screen-watching way back when at Cambridge, Conway had patiently waited for the PDP7 to generate maybe 10 generations per second, which is to say that Golly is to the PDP7 Life program as Excel is to an abacus. Although Conway passed on Rokicki's talk, the private screenings of Life on Bill Gosper's laptop continued, including a showing of the π calculator, with Neil Bickford, as well as 2 more incandescent kids, Julian and Corey Ziegler Hunts (all 3 of them Gosper's tutees). Gosper also flitted through Internet sites where Life-forms are collected with a philatelist's ardor. The "Stamp Collection," for example, is a collection of 650 oscillators. The "Life Status Page" documents all the known patterns and the known unknowns, color-coded by period. And on and on it goes. A few months after the Gathering, my e-mail inbox received several Google Alerts announcing yet another new Life-form. Slashdot reported: "First Self-Replicating Creature

Spawned in Conway's Game of Life." Usually, Rokicki's Golly Life simulator is downloaded 100 times a day; on that day, downloads reached nearly 2,000. And copious online comments debated the finer points of the term "self-replicating." As Gosper says, "One of the main things Conway's game has shown us is the intensity of the human instinct to engineer."

When he's in the mood, Conway can be flattered, or at least bemused, by the mania.

> I rather like this. It gives me a feeling that I was walking through life and I set off a disturbance and 40 years later still it's going on.

The disturbance reverberated like the proverbial flutter of a butterfly's wing, though Conway offers a less clichéd simile. Once his accident-prone friend Simon Norton entered a Cambridge coffee shop and, seeing Conway, marched over toting his massive backpack, knocking over a woman's coffee cup, toppling a man's chair . . .

> He left a trail of havoc and he was blissfully unaware. That's what happened with the Game of Life. It left a trail of havoc.
>
> I'm astonished actually that it all carries on. When it started there was a fantabulous amount of interest. . . . But we proved Life can do everything. So now every time they prove it can do something, YEAH, I KNEW THAT! I lost interest. When you've proved it can do everything, it reduces your interest when people produce a particular configuration. There is a configuration that can do any particular calculation you want. That's what we proved. And then somebody produces a configuration that does a particular calculation. Well, yawn. Well, except I don't actually feel like yawning. They are wonderful things that they produce.
>
> You know this old joke about the girl? "Will you sleep with me if I pay you one million dollars?" And she says yes. And then he says, "Will you sleep with me for one cent?" And she is, you know, very insulted—"What kind of girl do you think I am?" And he says, "We've settled what kind of girl you are, we're just arguing about the price."
>
> And here, we've settled what kind of girl Life is. She can compute anything. And now we're just arguing about the price. How big a configuration do we have to make to compute π? Or whatever.

And so, the tenets of Religion notwithstanding, Conway switched Life off. His later disdain was rooted in his sense of disappointment that the rules were not nearly simple *enough*.

> The Life game, although the rules are very simple, the action is not simple. It was too complicated. It was a pleasant failure. It didn't live up to the dream in the sense that it wasn't natural. You know, this 2 or 3 to survive, 3 to give birth is sort of rather arbitrary and not intellectually simple enough for me. And there is no reason why it should be those numbers rather than some other numbers. And for the dream, I would have liked it, when I found it, to be wonderful and obvious and unique. I suppose I've given up on that dream. Well, I haven't thought about it for a few years. Every time I do think about it, it's with a sort of wistfulness, you know? I'd like to get back into that. I wonder what wist is. When I'm wistful, what am I full of? Wist?

His contempt for Life seemed to be loosening, a melancholy nostalgia setting in.

> Maybe I should start thinking about the old *Jugendtraum* again. I've got nothing to do. I might produce something good. All it would take is one simple rule. And it would be nice to succeed. . . .
>
> I used to say, and I've probably said it to you the requisite number of times, that I have grown to hate Life, or I had grown to hate Life. I've overcome that hatred now. Just about. I still have some negative feelings. I learned to hate it and now I am slowly learning to not exactly love it again, but I realized that, you know, that's not quite true that I hate it. I'm proud of it. It's an interesting thing.

Hath hell frozen over? Not quite. Sometimes Conway seems to change his mind just to keep things interesting.

But his renewed respect for Life was, at least to my mind (remember, I'd been hanging out with Conway rather a lot), suspiciously in sync with the rare reappearance in 2013 of cicadas with a prime-number life cycle. Emerging every 17 years, as many as 1.5 million per acre, the Magicicada Brood II were due to visit parts of Connecticut, Maryland, North Carolina, New Jersey, New York, Pennsylvania, and Virginia.

Borrowing from the novelist Nathanael West, Bob Dylan wrote a song called "Day of the Locusts," referring to the emergence of a different brood of cicadas, in 1970, the year he accepted a Princeton honorary degree at the Princeton's open-air convocation ceremony as the insects "sang off in the distance." Since Conway's arrival in town, he had lived through 2 comings of the cicadas, and, as one would expect, he had along the way added some entomological expertise to his repertoire of tales. First of all, he provided a clarification: the imminent Brood II cicadas would not likely descend on these parts this year, since it was another 17-year brood, Brood X, that had made Princeton its home base.

The cicadas in Princeton came in 1800 and then every 17 years thereafter. Now, 11 17s is 187, so that means they came in 1987, which was very shortly after I came here. And I remember I sat there all afternoon watching one of these cicadas. It crawled up out of the ground onto a fence. And then it pulled itself out of its shell, which took about an hour. It was very hard. You know these eighteenth-century high boots that officers wore, and they had to have a servant help to get them off? Well, this cicada didn't have the requisite servant, and it was hellish hard to pull its legs out. It sat there gasping from the result of the effort for 20 minutes or something. And then it crawled into the sunlight, and its wings, which had been all crumpled, slowly uncrumpled. And then it flew off. I watched the whole sequence.

That was 1987, so the next time was 2004. And the next time will be 2021.

There is a reason why they choose these big prime numbers—big for a cicada to count. What happens is, there are quite a lot of predators, and maybe food as well, that have 2-year cycles. Now if you are a cicada and choose an even number and you happen to get into matching years with your predator, then you get wiped out, or if you get out of match with your food, you also get wiped out. So it's not a good idea to choose a multiple of 2, and similarly it's not such a good idea to choose a multiple of 3 or a multiple of 5—because there will be some other insect that can't count very high, and has settled on 3 or 5 as its period. And so that makes them choose primes somewhere in the teens.

So they are in this business of counting. How they actually count, I do not know. I have thought about it and read about it and nobody seems to have any idea. They have a signal that tells them which year to come up, which is this counting. But then there is also a signal that tells them whereabouts in the year to come up, and that is quite well understood. They are living under a tree, and they can detect the sap in your trees, which is a sort of proxy for the temperature. They all come out when it reaches a suitable temperature. So they are sort of ticking off the calendar, looking at their watch, so to speak, and they are doing it with a remarkably little brain.

And Conway was correct, of course, regarding Brood II versus Brood X. Regardless, the Institute for Advanced Study, where I was still ensconced, researching and writing, forwarded an e-mail warning that had been sent out to all the states that might be affected in various regions: "Sometime in April or May of this year, a swarm of insects called Brood II Cicadas will rise from the earth and fill the skies. . . ." It sounded like the end of days, but the bottom line was not to worry, the cicadas are "relatively harmless." Relatively harmless like Conway and his publish-and-be-damned threats. His bark is worse than his bite. He'd survived the Life inquisition.

That wasn't too torturous. Torture all the way down. You know the word "tortoise" is etymologically connected with "torture"? "Turtle" is similar. As you know, my second love after mathematics is etymology—I was just about to say women—etymology would be my third, in that case. Torsion, twisting, they [all] come from a Latin root or word. The tortoise is so called because its legs look twisted. And torture is derived from the same because one of the easiest ways to torture someone is to twist their arm, or their leg.

10.

SNIP, CLIP, PRUNE, LOP

Time is a game played beautifully by children.

—Heraclitus

"In the beginning, everything was void, and Conway began to create numbers"—his pride and joy, the surreal numbers. This Genesis takeoff comes not from Conway himself, but from a little book of fiction by Stanford computer scientist Don Knuth titled *Surreal Numbers: How Two Ex-Students Turned On to Pure Mathematics and Found Total Happiness*.

Knuth is better known for writing *The Art of Computer Programming*, his multivolume bible of fundamental algorithms, a labor of love that has consumed him for decades. He's also known for designing the TeX typesetting program, which has revolutionized scientific publishing. But in the early 1970s, Knuth dropped everything and redirected his energies toward writing a Conway-inspired novelette—shorter than a novel, longer than a short story, shorter than a novella, derived from the same Italian word, *novello*, meaning "new."

And to reel in the yo-yoing chronological collage, Conway's discovery of the surreal numbers came at around the same time as the Conway group and of the Game of Life. He had struck gold thrice in 1969.

> I usually round it up to 1970. That was my *annus mirabilis*. It really was a supremely productive period.

While zeroing in on the Game of Life, he'd also been fiddling with other sorts of games and noticing that they unexpectedly spat out, astonishingly enough, new numbers.

In keeping with tradition, Martin Gardner gave substantial column space to this latest brainchild. "Surreal numbers are an astonishing feat of legerdemain," he reported. And he offered a very general explanation: "An empty hat rests on a table made of a few axioms of standard set theory. Conway waves two simple rules in the air, then reaches into almost nothing and pulls out an infinitely rich tapestry of numbers. . . . Every real number is surrounded by a host of new numbers that lie closer to it than any other 'real' value does. The system is truly 'surreal.'"

The key to Conway's invention, again, was his desire for simplicity— simple rules, this time only 2. The rules dictate that a surreal number is the "simplest number" between numbers. "Simplest" has a uniquely precise definition, which we'll try to get at later. But the simplest number between 0 and 1 is $\frac{1}{2}$. So $\frac{1}{2}$ is a surreal number. More specifically, each surreal number is the simplest number between 2 sets of numbers that surround it to the left and to the right.

On the left there are the numbers
$$L = \{a, b, c, \ldots\}$$
On the right there are the numbers
$$R = \{d, e, f, \ldots\}$$
And the notation for a surreal number is written like this, with a line indicating where the surreal number falls:
$$\{a, b, c, \ldots \mid d, e, f, \ldots\}$$
Conway usually shortens it to
$$\{L \mid R\}$$
Fortuitously, the starting point of this number system is nothing. If each set L and R is empty, this defines 0.
$$\{\mid\} = 0$$

To wade in a bit further with the rules, Conway generalizes them as follows (while to seasoned veterans this generalization might seem so general as to be erroneous, Conway insists that it is accurate and adequate): If L and R are 2 sets of numbers, and no member of L is greater than or equal to ($\geq$) any member of R, then there is a number $\{L \mid R\}$ (which turns out to be the simplest number strictly between L and R). All numbers are created in this way.

N.B. There is a very specific definition of $\geq$ and that is touched upon in Appendix C on page 396.

Gardner contemplated "nothing" in his column and drew analogies to the abstract artist Ad Reinhardt's 5-by-5-foot canvases painted black, and composer John Cage's *4'33"*, a symphony of silence lasting 4 minutes and 33 seconds. Both arguably nothing, but something, these voids. From Conway's void emerged the surreals. As Knuth narrated in his novelette, "Conway said to the numbers, 'Be fruitful and multiply.'" Obediently, they did.

For their creator, these numbers just fell from the sky. Conway wasn't looking to create or discover new numbers. He was trying to analyze games such as Go, trying to classify the moves available to each player.

> I wasn't trying to analyze with a z, I was trying to analyse with an *s*—the word "lysis" means "cutting up," as in electrolysis, cutting up with electricity.

Conway was trying to cut up the games, classify the moves of each player, determine who was ahead and by how much. While doing this deconstructing, *analysing* the sum of mini games within the larger game, he happened upon the surreal numbers. Like an Escher optical illusion, say, a regular tessellation of birds morphing into fish, Conway easily enough beheld the game, and then he saw that it embedded or contained something else entirely, the numbers.

Conway's innovation amounted to a rather large increase in the num-ber of numbers. One might have assumed that all numbers were known, that the job of numerical classification was complete, especially with Cantor's ordinals spiraling off to infinity. But then Conway came along with his new scheme of numbers, encompassing all numbers, infinite and infinitesimal—of which Cantor's numbers, however improbably, were just a special case. Even Conway was incredulous. He couldn't believe it back then, and he can't quite believe it even now.

> What are numbers, really? I've been studying them for 50-odd years and I don't think I know!

As he likes to mention, when he discovered these new numbers, he was awestruck, he wandered around for weeks in a white-hot daze.

No, not really a daze. I don't think of it as a daze. With a daze you're lost, there is some fuzziness about a daze. I went round in a *daydream* for what I usually estimate as 6 weeks.

He also likes to compare the thrill of discovery to that felt by the Spanish conquistador Cortés, and sometimes for good measure he rattles off a few lines from Keats's sonnet "On First Looking into Chapman's Homer":

> *Then felt I like some watcher of the skies*
> *When a new planet swims into his ken;*
> *Or like stout Cortez when with eagle eyes*
> *He stared at the Pacific . . .*

Because I was sort of like this stout Cortés standing on the banks of the Pacific—he sees a world that nobody's seen before. Well, sorry, he saw a world that doubtless some American Indian tribes had seen before. But what I'm really meaning is that I don't think anybody had seen these surreal numbers before.

The surreals were a new world and a very big world, too. You could stop anywhere and pick up a new flower, as it were, and have a look. I walked around for weeks in the daydream thinking to myself, Isn't this a fabulous world, and you discovered it, John. There was always that in the back of my mind, some manner of self-congratulation.

In searching out more than the mythopoetics, such as dates and so forth, I discovered that Knuth was an invaluable source, nearly as knowledgeable about the discovery of surreals as the discoverer himself, and in some ways more so. This was due to the usual reasons, especially Conway's habit of putting off publishing his own results (he's a conqueror, not a colonist), but in this instance it was also due to the fact that at a certain point when the surreals were gestating in his brain, Conway realized he had everything backward. He decided he had to make a subtle but sweeping change to his 2 rules. He had to interchange Left and Right. And in order to prevent confusion he decided he had to purge all his original notes—100 or so scraps of paper scattered here, there, and everywhere. He dreaded the task. He couldn't do the changeover piecemeal, changing a note at a time here and there, because then he'd have some bits of paper dating from before the change and some bits of paper dating from after the change, with the same symbols meaning opposite things. Gradually he collected all the scraps of his theory. And then on a weekend he saw his opportunity to execute the mission. His wife, Eileen, was working in the garden at their home at 78 Blinco Grove, on the outskirts of Cambridge. She was digging out weeds and winter detritus and burning it in the incinerator. Conway set a garden chair next to the fiery drum, and with wafts of smoke getting in his eyes and a nice new notebook in hand, he revised and recopied theorems, definitions, all sorts of stuff, scrap by scrap, dropping the obsolete remnants into the flames as he went.

> It was like a doctor dealing with an epidemic—you must make sure to kill it all, that none of the infected stuff survives. Let there be no taint left behind!

In the end, the purification process took a couple hours, and the notes boiled down to 10 pages in the notebook. And with all evidence of the original immolated, the new record also was eventually lost.

Knuth, by contrast, has recorded his lifelong comings and goings in an online computerized diary, wherein resides evidence of every interaction he's ever had with Conway, backed up and cross-referenced with hard-copy archives in filing cabinets that fill an entire room of his house. "I'm at your service," he says, when I get him on the phone. "Don't feel too stressed by trying to compress." As it happened, Knuth that day was working on the latest volume of *The Art of Computer Programming*, volume 4 of 7, and writing a section about the Game of Life. "The kind of thing I'm doing in my book right now is a computer technique that's good for answering questions like, 'How many patterns in Life on a 10-by-10 board vanish in 1 step?' And the answer is 4 trillion something. I can compute it very fast. This afternoon I'll have it even faster."

This was tempting material, but I was calling about other matters. I needed all he had on the surreals. "I'm here by my computer where I have my diary. So let me see . . ." He typed "Conway" into his search engine, fearing it might pull too much. "Conway, oh boy. Wow." They first met in 1967 at a conference in Oxford, where Conway presented a theorem about knots using kids' toy necklaces made from "pop-it beads," taking them apart and putting them back together over the duration of the lecture. Knuth refined his search with some more typing. "Yeah. Here it is. 'Conway, germs of his theory of numbers and games, letter, March 1970.' I think I must have gotten the letter from Martin Gardner, a copy. Just a second, I'll check . . ."

Down went the phone, and his footsteps receded into the distance. Pause, silence. And then his footsteps returned. "Thanks for your patience. Yeah. Okay. This is in a bunch of things that Martin Gardner copied for me. I spent 2 weeks going through all of his files from his *Scientific American* columns, and then he Xeroxed for me some of the most important gems I found in there. It's dated—John didn't date the letter, but in Martin's handwriting it says 'March '70.'" This is the same 12-foot letter in which Conway revealed the Game of Life, along with all the other games he was playing around with at the time. Knuth perused the letter, looking for the surreals. "He goes into talking about Hackenbush. And then he says:

> *Very recently (over Christmas in fact) I've been working on unimpartial games where the moves available differ for the two players . . . draws are impossible . . . the complete theory is complicated, but there is a lot that can be done in particular cases.*

"And then he shows his notation. This is all the beginning of his beautiful theory . . ."

Knuth had first learned about the theory in February 1972, when he and Conway visited the University of Calgary for a conference. After Conway's talk, they had lunch in the cafeteria and Conway scribbled down the theory's key points on a napkin. "By the time we were done eating, the napkin was full," says Knuth.

Knuth's life that year was a blur as he prepared to leave on a sabbatical, working desperately on the overdue volume 3 of *The Art of Computer Programming*, and continuing to host weekly math salons at his new house, bought with royalties from volumes 1 and 2. Notices announcing the salons and the special guest speaker were tacked up on bulletin boards around Stanford. For 2 consecutive salons in April, the scheduling theorist and quasi-randomness expert Ron Graham gave a participatory introduction to juggling. Conway was in town for the spring semester that year, invited to Caltech on the coattails of his Conway Constellation. He was Knuth's special guest at the salon on May 8, drawing a full house. "I have the signatures of everybody who was there," says Knuth, among them combinatorialist Richard Stanley, graph theorist Vašek Chvátal, coding theorist David Forney, futurist and robotics expert Hans Moravec—50 people in total. Knuth recalls that Conway talked on "Puzzles and Games," including his theory of the surreals, stressing the games, not the numbers.

Conway can't marshal quite as much information about that day in May.

That was one part of one day of my life!

He agrees he would have been more likely to emphasize the games. The games are the more general creatures; the general theory of games yields the surreal numbers as 1 special case.

△ ▢ ◈ ◎ ◈

Ah, yes, the surreals. Plenty to get wrong there! First you have to know that it all began with a game called Nim. Have you met Nim yet?

We met Nim briefly with Conway's Lexicode Theorem at the Gathering for Gardner. In the grand scheme of game theory, Nim was the prototype for impartial games—a game being impartial when the legal moves are the same for both players. The theory of impartial games holds that every individual impartial game can be reduced to the game Nim, which in turn means that every individual impartial game is equivalent to that bizarrely behaving numberish object called a nimber. Having enamored himself with nimbers and impartial game theory, Conway's intellectual wanderlust next made him ponder what would happen with a more typical game, a game in which legal moves for each player are different, such as chess, tic-tac-toe, Go, and most other games. Beginning his investigations, he originally called these types of games "unimpartial."

That's a terrible word, "unimpartial." But the negative of "impartial" can't be "partial" for a mathematician, because "partial" means there is only part of it present. And using the other sense of "partiality," in which I am partial to something or other—you know, partial to women rather than men—that doesn't work either. So for a time I called them unimpartial games. And then I was discussing it with someone, I think it might have been Richard Guy, and we came up with "partizan"—and it's partizan as opposed to partisan. We deliberately chose the less common spelling. Mostly because "partisan" with an *s* reminded me of "Napisan." In England, a nappy is a diaper, and I had a fair number of babies, and this Napisan was some horrible stuff—well, it was great stuff actually, you put the dirty nappies after rinsing them a little bit into a big plastic bucket and then stuck some Napisan in it to clean them off. Anyway, "partisan" reminded me of Napisan, so I didn't really like it, and that's one reason why I chose the *z* spelling. But the word "partizan" has the right flavor, since it means you are taking sides. So a game in which the 2 players have different legal moves is a partizan game. And I had always intended to find out what the appropriate theory of adding partizan games was.

Serendipitously, during the surreals' period of gestation and invention circa 1970, the British Go champion, Jon Diamond, was then a Cambridge math undergraduate. He founded the Cambridge Go Society, fueling a steady run of Go games in the common room. Diamond, now president of the British Go Association, doesn't recall ever playing Conway. That's probably because Conway rarely if ever actually played the game. He lurked nearby, stared at the board, and wondered why the move Diamond or his pal just made was a good move or a bad move.

They would discuss it as they played, and kibitzers were sitting around saying, "Why'd you make that stupid move?" And it looked just the same as all the good moves to me. I never understood Go. But I did understand that near the end of the game it broke up into a sum of games—within the big game there were a few smaller games in various regions of the board. So that provided the spur for me to work out the theory of sums of partizan games.

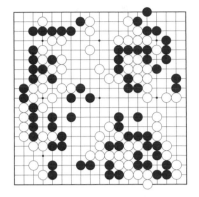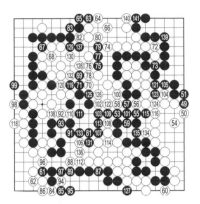

At left, an example of Go late in the game (after move 148) from the British Championship in 1974 played between Jon Diamond (White) and Paul Prescott. Conway noticed that games break into a set of smaller games. At right, the game as it played out to the end, with Black winning by 4.5 points.

This spur, as if one was necessary, encouraged ever more gaming. Conway always carried the necessary ammunition on his person, all the better to snare an unsuspecting opponent. And oddly enough in this pursuit he kept himself semi-organized with a leather games case well stocked with dice, checkers, a board, paper, pencils, maybe some rope, and always a few decks of cards. Card games and card tricks were his strong suit. He was still quite fond of his old professor Samoilovitch Besicovitch's fearsome card game; he taught it to students and once in a while managed a rematch with the old man himself, still always losing. Besicovitch had retired, and after spending several years touring around America he returned to Cambridge at the height of Conway's gaming. They ran into each other at a party for Cambridge's Russian community. Conway had a few ins, as it were, with the Russians, and occasionally went to Russian parties, where he met Stalin's daughter, Svetlana Alliluyeva, known to be a bit of a flake (her KGB nickname was "cuckoo bird," though when she defected to the United States, the CIA gave her an IQ test and her score was off the charts). But the point being that at the party Conway again played Besicovitch at his game.

> And, my god, I beat him! However, I wish I hadn't. He was so upset. And I only beat him, I think, because he was getting old and he didn't pay attention.

Mostly Conway played silly children's games—Dots and Boxes, Fox and Geese—and sometimes he played them with children, primarily his 4 young girls. And of course he also played games with his floating population of acolytes, often games they invented for his delectation. Colin Vout came up with the game COL and Simon Norton made up SNORT, both map-coloring games. Norton also produced Tribulations, and Mike Guy parried with Fibulations, both Nim-like games based on triangle numbers and Fibonacci numbers. Conway invented Sylver Coinage, whereby 2 players alternate in naming different positive integers, but they are disallowed from naming any number that is the sum of any previously named number, and the first player who names 1 is the loser. Conway also devised Traffic Jams, in which a fictitious country is represented by a triangular map and towns are represented by letters, all named after real towns in Wales—such as Aberystwyth, Oswestry, and . . . hmmm, how to even fit it on the page . . .

Llanfairpwllgwyngyllgogerychwyrndrobwllllantysiliogogogoch.

One suspects that Conway designed this game solely to provide himself with an opportunity to offhandedly pronounce

Llanfairpwllgwyngyllgogerychwyrndrobwllllantysiliogogogoch,

a word he saw stretched out on a sign at said town's railway station and on a sign at the town square; he observed that they differed slightly, having 57 and 58 letters. The pertinent question regarding this game is, What move should the first player make?

How to play Traffic Jams: 4 players/vehicles, starting at Aberystwyth, Dolgellau, Ffestiniog, and Merioneth, travel from town to town. A move is to slide your car along a 1-way street to the next town—until all players are stranded at the town of Conway, from which there is no escape (and actually, Conway is the English name for the Welsh town of Conwy). Once all vehicles are stranded at Conway, then the next player meant to move loses.

All these games provided raw data when Conway's surreal number theory was in development. The perfect guinea pigs, the 2 key players, were his eldest daughters, Susie and Rosie, then about 7 and 8 (Conway memorized his girls' birthdates by classifying them as "the 60-Fibs," since they were born in 1960 plus the Fibonacci numbers, i.e. 1960 + 2, 3, 5, 8 = 1962, 1963, 1965, 1968). He often asked Susie and Rosie to engage in a game called Domineering, played with dominoes on the chessboard. It is yet another game he invented. Or did he?

No. Yes. I'm not sure, to tell you the truth.

Conway did not invent Domineering, but he did invent an improvement on the name (previously it was called Crosscram). When his daughters played, he allowed them a mere 12 moves before he suspended play, leaving them waiting while he analysed the board.

 For an introductory analysis, see Appendix C on page 396.

As with Go, in studying the mini games within the bigger game of Domineering—each move, essentially, being a mini game—Conway noticed it was possible to assign values to the moves available to each player, or more technically speaking to the options available (the move is the road, the option is the destination). His analysis of games with students, professors, visitors, or by himself and barefoot on the common room floor, evolved from single games to compound games, with players playing lots of games at once—sometimes, say, a game of chess and a game of Go as well as a game of Domineering—and deciding 1 turn at a time in which game to make their move. He filled his usual landslides of foolscap analysing these games. Then, as he told a reporter from *Discover* magazine who came calling at Cambridge:

I had a fantastic surprise. I realized that there was an analogy between what I was writing down and the theory of real numbers. Then I looked at it and found it was much more than an analogy. It was the real numbers.

He wrote twin papers on this subject, "All Games Bright and Beautiful" and "All Numbers Great and Small."

You know the hymn, "All things bright and beautiful, All creatures great and small." But in the case of this theory, it's all games bright and beautiful that come first. And you winnow out the games that are equal to numbers. The games are logically prior to the numbers.

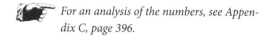 *For an analysis of the numbers, see Appendix C, page 396.*

One might wonder what Conway's colleagues thought of all this. Conway did, when moments of guilty self-doubt still intruded on his psyche. His work was done and he could do whatever he pleased without compunction, but still, he wondered. He was aware of a historian at Trinity Hall, a "tall, stooped, craggy-faced man," as described in the *Oxford Dictionary of National Biography*, who after receiving his life fellowship in 1911 spent much of his time walking around Cambridge with scissors, trimming hedges and the like, until his death in 1974. Frederick Arthur Simpson filled his days "snipping, clipping, pruning, lopping the leaves, the twigs, and the branches of the trees and bushes. He seemed omnipresent and could be pointed out with satisfaction to the wondering visitor as Snipper Simpson, the college eccentric. His rooms finally contained a glittering array of pruning instruments, from scissors to pole secateurs. His track round the courts and walks could often be traced by the litter of vegetation which he left behind him." Conway's gaming eccentricity wasn't quite so conspicuous, though his friend Richard Guy also wondered what other people might be thinking. Guy noted in an article he wrote on Conway titled "Mathematical Magus" that Erasmus Darwin advocated conducting damned fool experiments, "such as blowing a trumpet at a bed of tulips. To his more conventional colleagues, some of Conway's investigations of bizarre and exotic structures seemed just about as likely to lead to significant results. . . . By playing a myriad of often quite trivial games he gradually developed their theory to such an extent that it includes the most comprehensive theory of numbers that we now have."

It was only gradually that Conway became aware of what he'd accomplished. There wasn't any binge of work, there wasn't any tremendously complicated or difficult calculation, and there was no splashy *Eureka!* moment in the tub. It was more a slow-dawning awareness, over the course of a few days. First he found the games with the values like $\frac{1}{2}$ and $\frac{1}{4}$ and $\frac{3}{4}$. These numbers were familiar, and not just as fractions. They looked familiar from his foray into group theory. A similar collection of numbers belonged to a big group called $\mathbb{Z}_{2^\infty}$. This made Conway suspect that somehow he'd embedded this group into his theory.

> For those who know group theory, $\mathbb{Z}_{2^\infty}$ is a big group. It's the additive group of the integers, generated by 1, $\frac{1}{2}$, $\frac{1}{4}$, $\frac{1}{8}$, dot dot dot. Start with 1, 2, 3 and so on, and −1 and −2 and all those. And now, if you adjoin $\frac{1}{2}$ to that group, you've doubled it—it's the same group, just now you've got all the multiples of $\frac{1}{2}$ as well as all the multiples of 1. And if you adjoin the number $\frac{1}{4}$ to that, you've doubled it again, but it's still the same group. Now let's adjoin $\frac{1}{8}$ and $\frac{1}{16}$ and all the fractions $\frac{1}{2^n}$. That's the group. For those who don't know group theory, they won't be helped, but then there is no help for them, so to speak.

So the numbers falling out of the games initially looked like this particular collection of numbers Conway had seen before. But then the games started spitting out all the real numbers. For instance, there was a game that spat out the value $\sqrt{2}$, or 1.41421356237309504880168872 4209698078569671875376948073176679 ... In this game, the player Left is winning by $\sqrt{2}$ moves. And the bottom line was that there were all kinds of games with all kinds of values. As Conway mentioned to Gardner:

> In general, these compound games can be numbers, ambiguous numbers, infinitesimals or <u>horrid compounds</u> of everything under the sun.

Once the theory began to coalesce, Conway had another realization, this time quicker and more eclipsing. He decided to drop everything else and get the surreals theory down in some semblance of a book. This was 1970 still, spring had turned to summer and summer to early fall, with the Michaelmas term fast approaching. Conway binged, typing for 7 days straight from 8:30 A.M. until midnight. Why the rush? Because Conway's discovery of the surreals butted up against some bad timing, as he revealed in the prologue to the second edition of the book *On Numbers and Games* that eventually resulted:

> *Because ONAG, as the book is familiarly known, was getting in the way of writing Winning Ways. Now that both books are happily being republished by A. K. Peters, Onagers (a word that also means "Wild Asses"!) can be told just how it came about before they surrender themselves to pure pleasure (as "Onag" means in Hebrew!).*

Winning Ways for Your Mathematical Plays was another book on games, then in the works with Elwyn Berlekamp from the University of California, Berkeley, and Richard Guy. This book was meant to be about impartial games. Conway worried that if his new partizan game theory were included as well, then *Winning Ways* would be overwhelmed. So he binged and produced the *ONAG* manuscript. The only glitch was that when Conway confessed all this to his collaborators, Berlekamp got angry, thinking that by rights the surreals material ought to go in their *Winning Ways* book, and he sent Conway a letter threatening legal action. Berlekamp begs to differ—the legal invocations, he says, pertained to a separate but related dispute. But then Conway begs to differ in return. And onward we tumble through the surreal mineshaft of memory.

Between them, Berlekamp and Guy have known Conway for about a century, and together these 3 musketeers are largely responsible for pioneering the field of combinatorial game theory. To Conway's wild child, Berlekamp was and is the sensible adult: neatly dressed, well organized, solvent. He keeps a stack of index cards at the ready in his shirt pocket, itemizing subjects he wants to think about when spare moments arise. A coding and game theorist, he applied his expertise to the algorithmic study of commodity and financial futures. He's been hooked on games since age 6. At MIT he took up bridge and wrote his master's thesis on algorithms for solving double-dummy bridge problems. Working at Bell Labs, he wrote a technical report on Dots and Boxes, which was returned by the powers that be with a note questioning how this was pertinent to the "needs of the Bell system." Guy introduced him to Conway at a number theory conference in Oxford in 1969. They played hooky and spent 10 hours at a pub playing games. As Berlekamp recalls, neither of them could ever prevail at a game the other had invented, but each of them always had more games up his own sleeve that only the inventor could win. Guy was the man in the middle, the glue that held their collaboration together.

In talking about Conway, Berlekamp is forthcoming, if sensibly restrained. "I'm not sure how much dirt you want to include," he says. "And I'm not sure how much I should be reluctant to provide." Berlekamp is not reluctant to elaborate on Conway's irresponsibility. "If somebody sends him a paper to review, he enjoys making a public display of dropping it in the waste can with many people looking on, and saying, 'That will teach the editors not to bother me!'" (Conway here issues a denial.) In this regard, Berlekamp feels Conway shirks his duty as a citizen of the mathematical community. However, he allows that this transgression is mitigated by Conway's love for parlaying the joys of mathematics to his peers and the populace at large. He remembers Conway putting on a good show during a lecture at MIT's 1000-seat Kresge Auditorium. Fielding questions from the audience afterward, Conway hunted frantically for an unused transparency to illustrate an answer. Failing, he made do by licking a marked-up transparency clean. This display of reckless spontaneity won converts and spawned legends. But, as Berlekamp tells it, the spontaneity was calculated. Someone had spotted Conway practicing licking transparencies clean in advance (lies, all lies, says Conway). "This is a great Conwayism— enjoying being center of attention," says Berlekamp. "This whole thing was an act. He's like a magician. It's all part of the show." Though he adds: "Conway *is* a very good showman." There was also the incident at a fund-raiser hosted by William Randolph Hearst III, the heir to the publishing empire, who holds a Harvard degree in mathematics. For the party at Hearst's home, Conway was meant to be the star attraction, and he'd been persuaded with some difficulty to swap his coffee-stained T-shirt for a dress shirt and tie. Thankfully so, because when he arrived, everyone was wearing a tie. Everyone except Mr. Hearst. And as Berlekamp recalls, "John got up, took his tie off, stomped on it, cursed it, and said,

If Will isn't wearing a tie, neither am I!

For his part, Richard Guy defers to his written record on Conway, the main source being that "Mathematical Magus" article. Conway's Cambridge office, he noted therein, was the seminal disaster zone, littered everywhere with dead cups of coffee, unopened mail, and "an amazing assortment of bric-a-brac, which has overflowed most of the floor and all of the chairs, so that it is hard to take more than a pace or two into the room and impossible to sit down." His colleagues called it an ancient ruin worthy of an archaeologist, and they marveled at what ingenious artifacts were lost for all eternity beneath the debris. Guy observed, "He often fails to find the piece of paper with the important result that he discovered some days before, and which is recorded nowhere else. Even Conway came to see that this was not a desirable state of affairs, and he set to work designing and drawing plans for a device which might induce some order amongst the chaos. He was about to take his idea to someone to get it implemented, when he realized that just what he wanted was standing, empty, in the corner of his room. Conway had invented the filing cabinet!" On the upside, Guy cited Claude Shannon's remark that he would rather spend days discovering a theorem than hours searching it out in the library. "Conway carries the Shannon philosophy to its extreme, often forced by his lack of system to rediscover his own results. With each rebirth, however, the product becomes more complete, more refined, more polished, and more translucent."

Berlekamp and Guy both painted a picture of Conway as a workaholic. This certainly goes against Conway's carefully crafted persona. Nonetheless, as Guy noted: "Thomas Alva Edison said that genius is 1 percent inspiration and 99 percent perspiration. If Conway's genius is more than 1 percent inspiration, then it's because he adds up to more than 100 percent! He does thousands of calculations, looks at thousands of special cases, until he exposes the hidden pattern and divines the underlying structure." For Berlekamp, the biggest frustration with Conway is getting his attention. "When you happen to be in sync with his obsession, whatever he is currently focused on, then he will listen to you and collaboration is possible. But otherwise he's the most difficult collaborator I've ever worked with." Even when they were on the same page, Berlekamp found him challenging to work with, especially when Conway insisted on staying up all night to solve a problem. "I've stayed up all night with him on maybe a dozen occasions and never does it succeed in solving a problem. After a while I just say, 'Sorry, I'm going to bed.'" Conway made a habit of staying up all night at least once a week, and when he didn't, he tossed and turned in bed until his wife threw him out. "Maybe the way to say it is that he is very focused," concludes Berlekamp. "And that is part of the key to his success. Most of us don't have this kind of focus. Most of us, after beating our head against the wall, we move on to something else."

Focus, however, was not Conway's strength with women, another topic Berlekamp addresses without hesitation, again for the relevant effect it had on collaboration. "When his love life is on course he is much easier to deal with. But he's never terribly faithful," Berlekamp says, "and after a while they throw him out, and he's back to frantic mode again. This was the sporadic state, in the seventies, for a period of a few years, bouncing from one affair to the next." So much so that it ultimately led Berlekamp to rue the title of their book, *Winning Ways for Your Mathematical Plays*, which began to seem like a suggestive double entendre. "That was the whole point of the title, it was pitched that way, but we didn't realize it would have as biting an edge as it does. The behavior of one of the coauthors has impugned the title somewhat."

Berlekamp's overall verdict: "If he weren't so good I wouldn't tolerate him. He is certainly original." And Berlekamp surely benefited from Conway's originality. A formidably ranked amateur Go player, Berlekamp found endgame positions that posed interesting problems and mastered the solutions by deploying and developing Conway's partizan theory. He put these solutions to the test during a visit to the Japan Go Association headquarters in Tokyo. He had some difficulty attracting the attention of the professionals he wanted to play until he agreed to take a lesson. He then proceeded to beat his teacher in several successive games. He'll admit that he is indebted to Conway. "Very, very much so. We're all indebted to him."

When things came to blows over the surreals book, Conway lost sleep. His confession had indeed been ill received, and he stewed over a response to Berlekamp's discontent. And staying up late one night he got something down in a letter. He advised that if differences were irreconcilable, then his coauthors should remove his name from *Winning Ways*. Guy played the mediator and restored the peace. The trio carried on and continued to encounter minor upsets. Conway and Guy were prone to silliness, punning back and forth and wasting Berlekamp's time. He called them "a couple of goons." In the end and against all odds the book became a bestseller (the color printing and unusual typefaces increased the production costs so much that the advertising budget decreased to nothing). It was a self-help book, of sorts, on how to win at games. The authors spilled out a cornucopia of theories, along with many new games to match the theoretical purposes.

> We would invent a new game in the morning with the intention of it serving as an application of a theory. And then after half an hour's investigation, it would prove to be stupid. So we'd invent another game. There are 10 half hours in the working day, roughly speaking, so we invented 10 games a day. We'd analyse them and sift them, and let's say 1 in 10 of them was good enough to make the book.

They amassed a surfeit of games without names and names without games.

> This was the Marriage Problem. You see we would invent a new game, and if it was a success, there would then be the problem of giving it some catchy kind of name. We'd try out a name, and usually we wouldn't solve this naming problem. So the game might go in the file called "Games Without Names." And then Richard, being his usual precise, pernickety self, had another file called "Names Without Games." Any attempt to invent a new name for a game generated a whole lot of names none of which were quite right, but they were quite often good names. So they went in the "Names Without Games" file. Each of these lists grew. And we seldom managed to marry one from this file to one from that file.
>
> I remember the name without a game that was the best name without a game. It was called Don't Ring Us, We'll Ring You. We never got round to inventing that game, but the type of game is pretty clear: In this game there would be some thing or another that each player would draw on paper, and the aim is to draw a ring around your opponent. For a game like that, Don't Ring Us, We'll Ring You would be a lovely name. But we never actually found a game to fit it.

In contrast to the 15 years it took to complete *Winning Ways*, Conway apocryphally dubbed his ONAG book on surreal numbers, The book I wrote in a week! Then he drawered it, put the manuscript away for publication at a future date. In the interim, he asked his friends for advice on the manuscript, advice he noticed was nicely summarized by 2 lines in the prefatory poem to John Bunyan's *The Pilgrim's Progress*, "The Author's Apology for His Book":

> *Some said "John, print it"; others said, "Not so."*
> *Some said "It might do good"; others said, "No."*

In April 1973, Don Knuth stopped in at Cambridge for a visit. Conway pulled his manuscript from the drawer, and Knuth handed over the first draft of his novelette.

Knuth hadn't been able to shake the surreals since their meeting in Calgary roughly a year before. Now he was living in Norway, spending the 1972–73 academic year on sabbatical at the University of Oslo. In December, he recorded in his diary that he was "awake 4–7 a.m. thinking about Conway's numbers." On January 5, he was "off to hotel in hopes of writing a novelette based on Conway's numbers, a crazy idea. . . ." He locked himself into his hotel room in downtown Oslo, near where the playwright and "father of realism" Henrik Ibsen had lived, in hopes of channeling some of his brilliance. He worked for a week with no distractions, save for conjugal visits from his wife ("Because we always wondered what it would be like to have an affair in a hotel"). Knuth's manuscript approached completion on January 10—"My birthday (35 years). Jill came to the hotel again. We had Chinese dinner, saw *Butterflies Are Free*. Then I had to rewrite chapter 13, all done at 3:15 a.m. Glorious Day."

Knuth's *Surreal Numbers* is a love story in the form of a dialogue between Alice and Bill. They leave civilization to find themselves, set up camp at the edge of the Indian Ocean, and there discover a big black rock covered in ancient Hebrew graffiti.

A. I heard there hasn't been much archaeological digging around these parts. Maybe we've found another Rosetta Stone or something. What does it say? Can you make anything out?

B. Wait a minute, gimme a chance . . . Up here at the top right is where it starts, something like "In the beginning everything was void, and . . ."

A. Far out! That sounds like the first book of Moses, in the Bible. Wasn't he wandering around Arabia for forty years with his followers before going up to Israel? You don't suppose . . .

B. No, no, it goes on much different from the traditional account. Let's lug this thing back to our camp, I think I can work out a translation.

A. Bill, this is wild, just what you needed!

B. *Yeah, I did say I was dying for something to read, didn't I . . .*

Alice goes off to pick some fruit for supper, allowing Bill time alone to read and come up with a fairly literal translation of the graffiti:

In the beginning, everything was void, and J.H.W.H. Conway began to create numbers.

Conway said, "Let there be two rules which bring forth all numbers large and small.

"This shall be the first rule: Every number corresponds to two sets of previously created numbers, such that no member of the left set is greater than or equal to any member of the right set.

"And the second rule shall be this: One number is less than or equal to another number if and only if no member of the first number's left set is greater than or equal to the second number, and no member of the second number's right set is less than or equal to the first number."

And Conway examined these two rules he had made, and behold! They were very good.

In the Hebrew Bible, JHWH is short for Jehovah, or God, thus getting Knuth into a bit of trouble with orthodox Jews who complained he besmirched their deity. Even before the book was published he ran into a bit of trouble talking to Conway during their Cambridge visit. Knuth learned that with his first draft he had the rules slightly wrong; he needed a remedial lesson. With the second rule there was a subtle difference between "less than" and "not greater than or equal to." And after all, he'd reconstructed the rules from memory, and Conway had swapped the rules since they spoke. The rules reminded Knuth of the Latin motto of the United States, *E pluribus unum*—"Out of many, one." But for the surreals it was more like the reciprocal, *E duobus plurimis*—"Out of 2, many."

I also needed remedial lessons with the surreals. On a Sunday I found Conway not at the alcove but at the Whole Earth café, another of his regular haunts. He had just devoured a bag of chips, 2 pints of blueberries, and the Sunday *New York Times*, and he was now making use of the newspaper's margins for calculations. Before I got to my questions, we changed tables to find a quieter spot. He grabbed his cane, and I grabbed all the flotsam and his coat.

Check that my specs are in the right-hand pocket of that jacket, would you?

They were in the left-hand pocket.

Oh, actually, that's what I meant. It's not a very sensible thing to say the opposite.

Before I could capitalize on this serendiptious left-right segue and corral Conway toward questions on the surreals, he leapt onto his latest obsession.

Did I mention the Empire State Building? Let me show you the latest picture of the Empire State Building . . . Oh, I do hope I've got it. If I haven't, I'm so annoyed. Ah yes, here . . .

He unfurled several sheets of paper taped together along the short edge and filled with a veritable skyscraper of numerical columns and rows. This version was printed out "by machine," though he'd done it by hand the week prior. The structure arose from 2 self-generating series,

Table of generalized Fibonacci / Lucas sequences (numeric grid).

mark	index→	0	1	2	3	4	5	6	7	8

mark	L															
fi		1	0	1	1	2	3	5	8	13	21					
lu		3	-1	2	1	3	4	7	11	18	29	47				
fi		4	-2	2	0	2	2	4	6	10	16	26	42			
fi		6	-3	3	0	3	3	6	9	15	24	39	63			
fi		8	-4	4	0	4	4	8	12	20	32	52	84			
		12	-7	5	-2	3	1	4	5	9	14	23	37	60		
		17	-10	7	-3	4	1	5	6	11	17	28	45	73		
		9	-5	4	-1	3	2	5	7	12	19	31	50	81		
lu		14	-8	6	-2	4	2	6	8	14	22	36	58	94		
		19	-11	8	-3	5	2	7	9	16	25	41	66	107		
		11	-6	5	-1	4	3	7	10	17	27	44	71	115		
		16	-9	7	-2	5	3	8	11	19	30	49	79	128		
lu		21	-12	9	-3	6	3	9	12	21	33	54	87	141		
	33	-20	13	-7	6	-1	5	4	9	13	22	35	57	92		
	46	-28	18	-10	8	-2	6	4	10	14	24	38	62	100		
fi	25	-15	10	-5	5	0	5	5	10	15	25	40	65	105		
	38	-23	15	-8	7	-1	6	5	11	16	27	43	70	113		
	51	-31	20	-11	9	-2	7	5	12	17	29	46	75	121		
fi	30	-18	12	-6	6	0	6	6	12	18	30	48	78	126		
	43	-26	17	-9	8	-1	7	6	13	19	32	51	83	134		
	22	-13	9	-4	5	1	6	7	13	20	33	53	86	139		
fi	35	-21	14	-7	7	0	7	7	14	21	35	56	91	147		
	48	-29	19	-10	9	-1	8	7	15	22	37	59	96	155		
	27	-16	11	-5	6	1	7	8	15	23	38	61	99	160		
fi	40	-24	16	-8	8	0	8	8	16	24	40	64	104	168		
	53	-32	21	-11	10	-1	9	8	17	25	42	67	109	176		
	32	-19	13	-6	7	1	8	9	17	26	43	69	112	181		
fi	45	-27	18	-9	9	0	9	9	18	27	45	72	117	189		
	24	-14	10	-4	6	2	8	10	18	28	46	74	120	194		
	37	-22	15	-7	8	1	9	10	19	29	48	77	125	202		
fi	50	-30	20	-10	10	0	10	10	20	30	50	80	130	210		
	29	-17	12	-5	7	2	9	11	20	31	51	82	133	215		
	42	-25	17	-8	9	1	10	11	21	32	53	85	138	223		
fi	55	-33	22	-11	11	0	11	11	22	33	55	88	143	231		
	88	-54	34	-20	14	-6	8	2	10	12	22	34	56	90	146	
	122	-75	47	-28	19	-9	10	1	11	12	23	35	58	93	151	
	67	-41	26	-15	11	-4	7	3	10	13	23	36	59	95	154	
	101	-62	39	-23	16	-7	9	2	11	13	24	37	61	98	159	
	135	-83	52	-31	21	-10	11	1	12	13	25	38	63	101	164	
	80	-49	31	-18	13	-5	8	3	11	14	25	39	64	103	167	
	114	-70	44	-26	18	-8	10	2	12	14	26	40	66	106	172	
	59	-36	23	-13	10	-3	7	4	11	15	26	41	67	108	175	
	93	-57	36	-21	15	-6	9	3	12	15	27	42	69	111	180	
	127	-78	49	-29	20	-9	11	2	13	15	28	43	71	114	185	
lu	72	-44	28	-16	12	-4	8	4	12	16	28	44	72	116	188	
	106	-65	41	-24	17	-7	10	3	13	16	29	45	74	119	193	
	140	-86	54	-32	22	-10	12	2	14	16	30	46	76	122	198	
	85	-52	33	-19	14	-5	9	4	13	17	30	47	77	124	201	
	119	-73	46	-27	19	-8	11	3	14	17	31	48	79	127	206	
	64	-39	25	-14	11	-3	8	5	13	18	31	49	80	129	209	
	98	-60	38	-22	16	-6	10	4	14	18	32	50	82	132	214	
	132	-81	51	-30	21	-9	12	3	15	18	33	51	84	135	219	
	77	-47	30	-17	13	-4	9	5	14	19	33	52	85	137	222	
	111	-68	43	-25	18	-7	11	4	15	19	34	53	87	140	227	
	56	-34	22	-12	10	-2	8	6	14	20	34	54	88	142	230	
lu	90	-55	35	-20	15	-5	10	5	15	20	35	55	90	145	235	
	124	-76	48	-28	20	-8	12	4	16	20	36	56	92	148	240	
	69	-42	27	-15	12	-3	9	6	15	21	36	57	93	150	243	
	103	-63	40	-23	17	-6	11	5	16	21	37	58	95	153	248	
	137	-84	53	-31	22	-9	13	4	17	21	38	59	97	156	253	
	82	-50	32	-18	14	-4	10	6	16	22	38	60	98	158	256	
	116	-71	45	-26	19	-7	12	5	17	22	39	61	100	161	261	
	61	-37	24	-13	11	-2	9	7	16	23	39	62	101	163	264	
	95	-58	37	-21	16	-5	11	6	17	23	40	63	103	166	269	
	129	-79	50	-29	21	-8	13	5	18	23	41	64	105	169	274	
	74	-45	29	-16	13	-3	10	7	17	24	41	65	106	171	277	
lu	108	-66	42	-24	18	-6	12	6	18	24	42	66	108	174	282	
	142	-87	55	-32	23	-9	14	5	19	24	43	67	110	177	287	
	87	-53	34	-19	15	-4	11	7	18	25	43	68	111	179	290	
	121	-74	47	-27	20	-7	13	6	19	25	44	69	113	182	295	
	66	-40	26	-14	12	-2	10	8	18	26	44	70	114	184	298	
	100	-61	39	-22	17	-5	12	7	19	26	45	71	116	187	303	
	134	-82	52	-30	22	-8	14	6	20	26	46	72	118	190	308	
	79	-48	31	-17	14	-3	11	8	19	27	46	73	119	192	311	
	113	-69	44	-25	19	-6	13	7	20	27	47	74	121	195	316	
	58	-35	23	-12	11	-1	10	9	19	28	47	75	122	197	319	
	92	-56	36	-20	16	-4	12	8	20	28	48	76	124	200	324	
lu	126	-77	49	-28	21	-7	14	7	21	28	49	77	126	203	329	
	71	-43	28	-15	13	-2	11	9	20	29	49	78	127	205	332	
	105	-64	41	-23	18	-5	13	8	21	29	50	79	129	208	337	
	139	-85	54	-31	23	-8	15	7	22	29	51	80	131	211	342	
	84	-51	33	-18	15	-3	12	9	21	30	51	81	132	213	345	
	118	-72	46	-26	20	-6	14	8	22	30	52	82	134	216	350	
	63	-38	25	-13	12	-1	11	10	21	31	52	83	135	218	353	
	97	-59	38	-21	17	-4	13	9	22	31	53	84	137	221	358	
	131	-80	51	-29	22	-7	15	8	23	31	54	85	139	224	363	
	76	-46	30	-16	14	-2	12	10	22	32	54	86	140	226	366	
	110	-67	43	-24	19	-5	14	9	23	32	55	87	142	229	371	
lu	144	-88	56	-32	24	-8	16	8	24	32	56	88	144	232	376	
	232	-143	89	-54	35	-19	16	-3	13	10	23	33	56	89	145	234

the Fibonacci numbers and the Lucas numbers. Conway found it remarkable that the thirteenth-century Leonardo Fibonacci and the nineteenth-century François Lucas were meeting here via their numerical series, introduced by Conway but organically intertwining to form "FiFi blocks" and "LuLu blocks," marshaling themselves into an impressive likeness of New York's iconic art deco tower.*

> It's absolutely fascinating. But I will not attempt to explain it to you, because you won't find it as fascinating as it actually is.

It seemed mystically mathy, the number theory equivalent of sacred geometry, as I suggested with some trepidation.

> It is a little bit bizarre. But it's real stuff. It's genuine stuff. This is an amazing fact. This table is defined quite simply and it has all these astonishing properties. What you do is . . .

And then he caught himself, but only to retract his previous promise not to explain.

> Okay, so I will say something about it, with great reluctance. I can't help it. Since you insist. Start with any 2 numbers you like . . .

He went on at Homeric length. Eventually he succumbed to my desperately rude interruption and accepted a change of subject—to Knuth's interpretation of the surreal number rules as "Out of 2, many." Conway liked the allusion but offered an improvement.

> From *no* things comes a great multitude.

Indeed, in Knuth's novelette, Bill remarks, "Man, that empty set sure gets around! . . . But come to think of it, Conway's rules for numbers are like copulation, I mean, the left set meeting the right set. . . ." The key point is the profligacy. Again trying to find an improvement, to find the

---

* And oddly enough, the Empire State Building is located at a "Fibonacci intersection," at the corner of West 34th Street and 5th Avenue.

aphorisme juste, Conway magically reached into his bag of tricks and produced a copy of his book *On Numbers and Games*. He flipped the book open to its epigraph, from Edward FitzGerald's *Rubáiyát of Omar Khayyam*:

> *A Hair, they say, divides the False from True;*
> *Yes; and a single Alif were the clue,*
> *Could you but find it—to the Treasure-house,*
> *And peradventure to The Master too!*

That little verse is really astonishingly apposite, as you say. Because Alif is the first letter of the Arabic alphabet, and it's really the same as Aleph, which is the first letter of the Hebrew alphabet. And Cantor used Aleph for all the infinite numbers. So, you know, that's amazing.

a single line, they say
divides the false from true

And I wouldn't say I divide the False from True with the single line, but I do separate the Left options from the Right options. And that separation gives the clue—"A single Alif were the clue . . . to the Treasure-house." And you know, I found that treasure house. I opened that treasure house and found all these amazing numbers inside.

The big clue for Conway came when he discerned that he was following not only in Cantor's footsteps, but also in the footsteps of another German mathematician, Cantor's friend and teacher Richard Dedekind. He wasn't only generalizing Cantor's theory of the ordinals, he was generalizing Dedekind's theory of the reals as well; Cantor's and Dedekind's theories were special cases.

What we are talking about is very, very simple, elementary stuff.

In his monograph "What Are Numbers and What Should They Be?" Dedekind provided a foundation for the irrational reals, the nonterminating and nonrepeating decimals (the rational reals, integers and fractions, were already reasonably well understood). In doing so, he defined the irrationals to be "cuts" or "sections" of the rational numbers. For example, π is a cut somewhere between 3 and 4. But to get even closer, it is a cut between 3 and $3\frac{1}{2}$, and again to get closer it is a cut between 3.13 and 3.15—a numeric slice of pie, as it were, between the numbers on either side, with the fat edge of the wedge narrowing to an ever-smaller sliver.

$$3.14_{15\,9526530\cdots}$$

To get even closer, π is less than $3\frac{1}{7}$ and it's greater than $3\frac{10}{71}$. Dedekind generalized that argument: π is greater than some rationals and less than others; π creates a "cut" in the rational numbers. And this is how π would be written in Dedekind's notion, but you have to imagine there are infinitely many numbers in between each number, not just the numbers written:

$$\pi = \{\ldots -1, \ldots 0, \ldots 1, \ldots 2, \ldots 3, \ldots 3\,{}^{10}\!/_{71}, \ldots \,\Big|\, \ldots {}^{22}\!/_{7}, \ldots 3\,{}^{1}\!/_{2}, \ldots 4, \ldots 5, \ldots\}$$

So π cuts the rationals at that single line—the line divides the rationals that are less than π on the Left from the rationals that are greater than π on the Right. This was Dedekind's way of dividing the rationals into 2 chunks, 2 sets, L and R. Every rational number is either in L or it's in R, and everything in L is less than everything in R. That's called a Dedekind cut of the rationals—you are cutting the rationals into 2 parts, and the irrationals are what does the cutting, so to speak.

In investigating his games, and naming them with numbers, Conway noticed that what he was doing was rather like these Dedekind cuts. But he noticed that in naming the games, the games cut numbers into many, many, many *more* slices.

After a few weeks of playing around, I realized I didn't just merely have some of the rationals from the big group, the $\mathbb{Z}_{2^\infty}$ nonsense. I realized, Oh, it's not just *some* of the rational numbers, it *really is* the rational numbers. But then I realized, It's not just *all* the rational numbers, it's the irrational numbers as well, and then, Oh, it's not just all the rationals and irrationals, not just the real numbers, it's also things like Omega and so on. . . . The size of it took some time to realize, that some of its members were like the real numbers, and that there were very many more, the surreal numbers and so on. It took some time to sink in.

And (not to be too repetitive, although with this refrain Conway is emphatically repetitive), really to this day he still isn't over it. Part of the astonishment was that it all came from these avowedly silly children's games.

You don't expect serious grown-up people to take an interest in Dots and Boxes. It's a game that's always been played by kids. I take an interest in it because I keep on taking an interest in childish things. I've not put away the childish things, or whatever it says in the Bible somewhere. I still haven't. That's part of the astonishment. To discover that by studying childish things, you have a new idea that beats the grown-ups, so to speak, at their own game.

That's the reason why I found it and nobody else did. The type of people who would be inclined to study these things would automatically make the assumption that the games they were studying were finite. And I wouldn't because I knew a lot about infinite numbers, infinite sets. So I didn't make that assumption. The seed fell upon fertile ground, so to speak. I was also capable of thinking about it in a sort of cool logical way, thinking about it in a grown-up way, even though it was a childish subject.

You'd imagine that frivolous little games, if they are connected with numbers at all, would not produce very much. But in fact, when you work your way up to big frivolous games, and infinite frivolous games, they produce many more numbers than the usual kind. They give you a theory of numbers that is much simpler than the usual one. . . . And it is astounding. This is the thing I'm proudest of, as I've told you. The simplicity is the beauty of it. That's why I'm so proud of it. Because it pokes fun at people who do things in complicated ways.

Nobody else in the history of the world did this thing. I used to wonder how Cantor felt. He was the only person who did a similar sort of thing, and he did the greater thing, really, because he first extended the numbers that everybody had lived with for 2,000 years or more. He discovered the infinite ordinals. He must have had the same dreamy feelings, the perpetual daydream. Eventually he went nutty. He died in a lunatic asylum in

1918, in Halle. I made a journey there once, when I went to East Germany a year or so before the wall came down. And the place looked like a warehouse, and like everything in East Germany it looked decrepit.

I was curious about Conway's visit to East Germany, but aiming to stay on track, I instead asked why it was he magically happened to have on his person a copy of his book *On Numbers and Games*, other than to make his biographer's day.*

That's not why. I possibly hoped that if I took it to the coffee shop somebody might ask a question about it. It's a damn good book, though I say it myself. And it's nice to read the comments on the back: "*ONAG* is a unique and wonderful book, certainly one of the top mathematical creations of the twentieth century. Warning: It is essentially as addictive as the Internet, because you will think of fascinating new things to explore as you examine every page." Of course, it's a friend of mine who said it.

The friend being Don Knuth.

But it's sort of true. Nobody had this idea. And I didn't really have the idea in a way, it just forced itself on me. I had this idea of adding games, and from then on it was the fact, the facts—"Just the facts, Ma'am"—that forced themselves on my attention. It is actually true that there *are* games that behave like all these numbers. I didn't make them behave like that. They do.

It's this sense in which mathematics is about a world that is not quite the same as this real one outside the window, but it is just as obstinate. You can't make things do what you want them to. "Everything is what it is, and not another thing," said Leibniz. Which sounds like a trite thing to say. But, you know, everything is what it is and it's not one of the things that it isn't. In this world of games, there is a smaller world of numbers, and that world of numbers is pretty large.

The surreal numbers gave me that feeling, the power feeling, more than anything else—the feeling that knowledge is power, but in my case knowledge is LIKE power, that's the way I would put it.

---

* *On Numbers and Games* (with coauthor Richard Guy) is Conway's bestselling book ever, the book that is translated into 11 languages.

I wonder what people who actually make real things feel—architects, who produce some wonderful building, they ordered it to be. I didn't produce any wonderful building and I can't take a couple of friends or tourists and show them this is what I made. I can teach them, This is what I discovered, but it takes a certain amount of time.

And it comes back all the time to the nature of mathematical existence. And the fact that you can tell things are really there if they don't move when you push them. That's what I think is different about the artist who creates something. The artist could have made it twist a different way, or changed the second line of the poem or whatever it was. And I can't do that. But the very fact that I can't just boss these mathematical entities around is evidence that they really exist.

And I still haven't sort of solved that problem. "How the hell . . . ?" But there are plenty of problems that none of us have ever solved. Why are we here? We grow up, we stop asking these questions in the end, at least many of us do. I certainly do. It's not profitable to wonder why I am here. It doesn't get me anywhere. People produce answers involving God and this, that, and the other. But none of the answers ever really answer anything. We're just here. Get used to it. And we do get used to it. And the numbers are here, too, in a different way.

When we left the subject and parted ways, I escaped to the Internet. Waiting in my in-box was an e-mail from Simon Norton, with a message for Conway (Norton, like a number of Conway's friends and colleagues, had cottoned onto the biographer back channel communication route). Having recently spent time with Conway in Cambridge, Norton wanted to discuss some new results. I sent him Conway's cell phone number, and just out of curiosity, I asked to what these results pertained. To the surreal numbers, of course! Riffing off a talk he'd heard Conway give on the Lexicographic code, Norton had worked something out by analogy and produced a symmetric diagram that was reminiscent of a diagram he and Conway came up with while investigating group theory, and now he'd tried to apply the basic principles to the surreal numbers. "I wondered if there was any connection."

To get back to the land, to the games, Conway submits for consideration a game called Hackenbush. Sometimes Hackenbush is classified as a "Conway game" because this is another game Conway invented, among the many games he invented in creating a laboratory to test his theories (and, to correspond to the surreals notation { L | R }, he refers to the players of games as "Left" and "Right," or sometimes "Lefty" and "Rita"). As the name Hackenbush suggests, the game involves hacking away—snipping, clipping, pruning, lopping—at metaphorical bushes, and from this exercise in mathematical topiary the surreal numbers emerge.

With Hackenbush you have a picture like this, which we'll call the Hackenbush Homestead—there's a nice little house, with a rain barrel, a tree and flower here and there, and let's put a dog in . . .

You want it to be a childish picture. The ground is not part of the picture but it is a rule that everything's got to be connected to the ground. It's also a rule that each edge of the picture joins 2 spots or nodes, and this may be the same spot twice, producing a loop.

And then the game goes like this: Left chops a black edge, and Right chops a white edge. Get me? And then after each move, anything that's no longer connected to the ground falls away. The game ends when no edges remain to be chopped, and the player unable to move is the loser. This is an example of a sum of games—the game has 4 parts to it, the house, the tree, the flower and the dog, so it's the sum of 4 separate games.

Now let's take a look at how Hackenbush produces the surreal numbers. For this purpose we'll start with the game 0, a picture with just the ground:

—————————————————————————

We are thinking of the game in reverse now, if you understand me. Because when you are analysing a game, you always do it from the end of the game toward the beginning. And here, we're at the end of this game, since all the edges are rubbed off and nobody has a legal move. So the value is { | } = 0.

Then, from this stripped-down, pure-research version of the game, the numbers sprout with the "beanstalks," as Conway calls them, after the fairy tale.

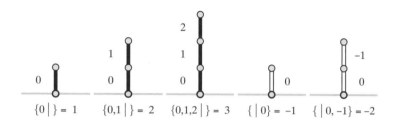

$$\{0 \,|\, \} = 1 \qquad \{0,1 \,|\, \} = 2 \qquad \{0,1,2 \,|\, \} = 3 \qquad \{ \,|\, 0\} = -1 \qquad \{ \,|\, 0,-1\} = -2$$

The numbers on either side of these beanstalks, gathered also beneath in the {L | R} sets, indicate the state of play, the moves or options available to the respective players if they chop that edge, and this scenario in turn produces, or equals, a surreal number, the numerical value of the game.

As a game's beanstalk grows taller, the numbers, too, might grow incrementally larger, or the numbers might decrease. Either way, the values emerge slowly as the beanstalks climb to the sky.

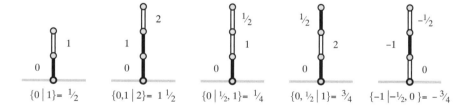

$$\{0 \,|\, 1\} = \tfrac{1}{2} \qquad \{0,1 \,|\, 2\} = 1\tfrac{1}{2} \qquad \{0 \,|\, \tfrac{1}{2}, 1\} = \tfrac{1}{4} \qquad \{0, \tfrac{1}{2} \,|\, 1\} = \tfrac{3}{4} \qquad \{-1 \,|\, -\tfrac{1}{2}, 0\} = -\tfrac{3}{4}$$

And if we allow infinite games, infinite numbers sometimes emerge, such as Cantor's Omega . . .

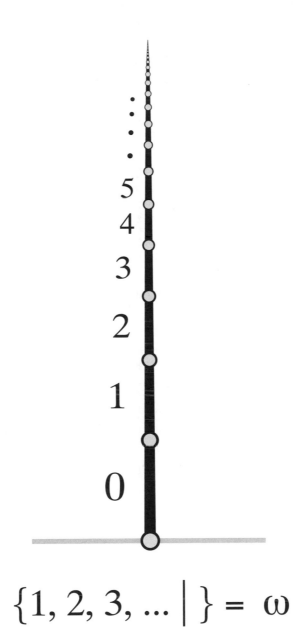

$\{1, 2, 3, \dots \mid \} = \omega$

Other times, an infinite game might wobble up and down, up and down, to reach only $\frac{2}{3}$.

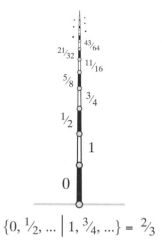

$$\{0, \tfrac{1}{2}, \ldots \mid 1, \tfrac{3}{4}, \ldots\} = \tfrac{2}{3}$$

Carrying on, other numbers emerge—numbers that normal people wouldn't recognize as numbers, and numbers that even Conway didn't recognize as numbers. These are the things he described to Gardner as horrid combinations of everything under the sun. These are the surreal numbers. For instance, Omega −1.

Omega −1 is the simplest number that is bigger than all the finite positive integers and less than Omega. It's an infinite black beanstalk Omega, with a length 1 white beanstalk on top. If it had 2 white edges at the top, then it's Omega −2. And if it had 3 white edges, then it's Omega −3.

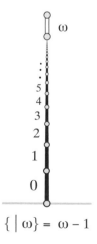

$$\{\;\mid \omega\} = \omega - 1$$

And then there is Omega divided by 2, which is the simplest infinite number bigger than all the finite numbers, but it is also infinitely less than Omega. It's an infinite black beanstalk, with an infinite white beanstalk on top of it. And it's nice to compare it to $\frac{1}{2}$, which consists of a length 1 black beanstalk, with a length 1 white beanstalk. $\frac{\text{Omega}}{2}$ is a sort of magnified version of $\frac{1}{2}$.

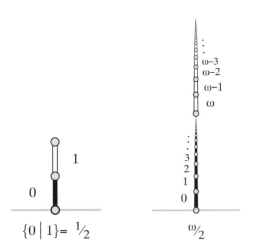

And the square root of Omega is an infinity of infinities of white beanstalks on top of 1 black infinite beanstalk.

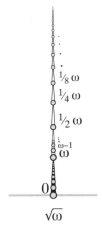

That's a sampling of how the surreals fall out of the game Hackenbush. Again, I couldn't help but wonder how Conway thought to invent such a thing. But this is just what he does, he invents games. Richard Guy named this game after the character Dr. Hugo Z. Hackenbush, played by Groucho Marx, in *A Day at the Races*. And the name "surreals," Conway is embarrassed to admit, is another name he did not invent. Naming credit goes to Knuth. Knuth came up with the name when he was casting about for a term that would suggest something in between the ordinal numbers. Because just as the real numbers fill in the gaps between the integers, the surreal numbers fill in the gaps between the reals. Conway had just been calling his new numbers "Numbers," with a capital *N*, because they were so simple, so fundamental.

> My idea was that if you put an adjective in front of "Numbers" it restricted them—whole numbers, rational numbers, real numbers, prime numbers, they are all just *some* of the numbers. And I was dealing with ALL numbers. So I thought there shouldn't be an adjective.
>
> That was a bad career move. Because you know the name "Numbers" doesn't give any way of saying that you are referring to this new kind of number. I might have been hoping that people would call them Conway numbers, but I don't think I really was.
>
> I'm very, very happy with Knuth's name. I'm really delighted with it, actually, because it seems exactly right. It gets the connection with the real numbers right—it says that they are over or above the real numbers, since *sur* is the same prefix as "super," just corrupted a bit or simplified by the French. And it's also got this connotation of being bizarre, which seems to fit.

So far we explored infinite surreals that get infinitely bigger and bigger. Their counterparts, their reciprocals, are the infinitesimals. Every real number, every little dot on the continuous number line, is surrounded by surreals, crushed in on either side to the point of claustrophobia by surreals that are closer to it than any other real. Dorothy L. Sayers argued that an infinity of angels could dance on the head of a pin, and the same could be said of surreals at any infinitesimally pinhead-sized sliver on the number line. For instance, how about 1 divided by Omega . . .

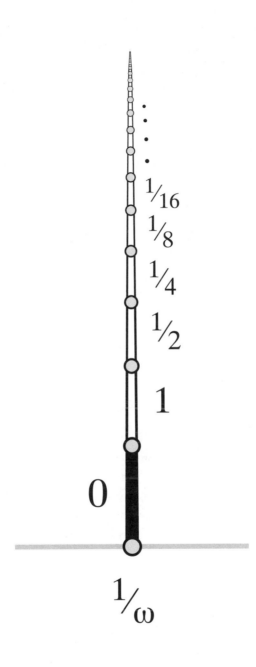

Or, how about π divided by Omega, or the cube root of Omega? Or Omega squared over Omega +1? I haven't the faintest idea how to work out the beanstalk for that. Well, I do, but we won't bother.

Instead we could take a look at the surreal number line, which is enormously big.

If you take out your magnifying glass and look between 0 and 1, then there's $\frac{1}{3}$ and $\frac{1}{2}$, and then here is $\frac{1}{Omega}$ and $\frac{2}{Omega}$, and so on.

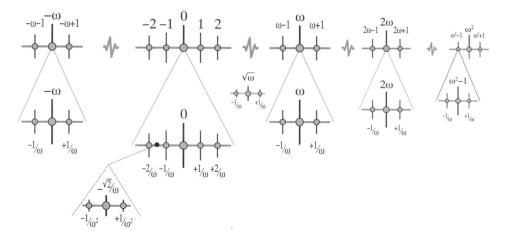

If you look between 0 and –1, WOOOSH, there you go again. Same thing happens out by Omega. WOOOSH, there's $\frac{1}{2}$ Omega, Omega × 2, and Omega². Wherever you look at the damn thing, it's worse. There's more of it. It's horrendously large. Wherever you magnify it, WOOOSH WOOOSH WOOOSH, you'll come out and you find an entire copy of the surreal line anywhere in it, all over the place. It's huge. It's almost impossible to convey how big it is.

It's a huge world. There is the square root of omega, and π times Omega, and π times Omega + 79, and so on. Many, many more. I can't tell you how many more there are. They are not just achieved by adding Omega and doing arithmetic. They are tremendously large and it takes some time to realize how big even the set of real numbers is.

When you're a little child you puzzle about the fact that the set of integers is infinite. And then you learn about fractions, and there seem to be vastly many more fractions than integers. But then there are irrational numbers, like $\sqrt{2}$ and π and the mathematical constant e, and they vastly outnumber the rational numbers. And then there are the ordinal numbers. AND THEN, there are the surreal numbers, which include all of the ordinal numbers and all the real numbers and a hell of a lot of other things besides. It's an absolutely huge collection of numbers. And it's the thing I'm proudest of, it really is.

And when I found these things I really did go round in a daydream for a long, long time. I must have looked pretty catatonic from the outside. I had to do some teaching, so I came out of it for an hour every now and then. But I do remember that most of my waking hours were taken up with thinking about it, not in any technical way, not proving any more theorems or anything, just contemplating it.

Gazing out at these numerical galaxies, he also detected more and more games. And just as there were more and more games, these games were more and more intangible. The games could not be adequately described with numbers, because they were not numbers that anybody, even Conway, knew how to express numerically. So in lieu of numbers, he resorted to his penchant for wordplay, christening these games with abstract names such as Star.

$$* = \{0|0\}$$

Star, the game, is very close to 0 and is often confused with 0 in a technical sense. It is less than every positive number and greater than every negative number, neither positive nor negative nor 0. For this reason, by Conway's reasoning, star is "fuzzy," like any star in the sky observed with the naked eye.

There is also the game Up—upward ever so slightly from 0.

$$\uparrow = \{0|*\}$$

Up is less than every positive number, but greater than zero. So it is less than 1, less than $\frac{1}{2}$, $\frac{1}{3}$, $\frac{1}{1000}$th, and $\frac{1}{1000000}$th, and even less than $\frac{1}{\text{Omega}}$ and $\frac{1}{\text{Omega}^2}$. In fact, it is less than every positive surreal number. It is positive, and less than every positive number, and that must imply that it is not a number itself, because it is equal to itself and greater than 0.

And then there is Down, greater than every negative number, yet less than 0.

$$\downarrow = \{*|0\}$$

Up and Down and Star are only just the beginning. There is Double-Up, Double-Up-Star, Up-Down-Second-Star, Semi-Up-Star, Semistar, and Superstar. Trying to get hold of these games and their infinitesimality in all directions feels like reaching for something ephemeral, like pinpointing the temporal dividing line between past and present, present and future. Or contemplating the outermost edge of the universe—ever-expanding and ever-receding, the universe's outermost reaches aren't an edge at all, it's more the horizon of an as yet undifferentiated origin. Like memory, and like happiness, the surreals are elusive. Although they furnished Conway with a good supply of bliss. And Martin Gardner delighted in the surreals' exotic nomenclature and all the theory's fanciful subtheories. Games were "Restive" and "Restless," "Extroverted" and "Introverted." Games were subject to a temperature theory complete with, as Gardner marveled, "thermographs on which hot positions are cooled by pouring cold water on them. . . . [Conway] has a Mach principle for the small world: the atomic weight of a short all-small game is at least 1 if and only if the game exceeds the remote stars! Conway's theorem 99 conveys some notion of the book's whimsical flavor. It tells us . . . that any short all-small game of atomic weight zero is dominated by some superstar." And, as Conway likes to point out, in his *ONAG* book, theorem 100 is the best and easiest theorem of all:

> This is the last theorem in this book.
> (The Proof is obvious.)

Gardner summed it up as "Vintage Conway: profound, pathbreaking, disturbing, original, dazzling, witty and splattered with outrageous Carrollian wordplay."

"Are these not trivial beginnings?" he asked. "Yes, but they provide a secure foundation on which Conway, by plugging newly created games back into his left-right scheme, carefully builds a vast and fantastic edifice."

⊿ ▢ ⬦ ⊛ ⊛

But an edifice of what? In his "All Numbers, Great and Small" paper, Conway concluded with a similar question:

Is the whole structure of any use?

"It is on the boundary between funny stuff and serious mathematics," said Hungarian-American mathematician Paul Halmos. "Conway realizes it won't be considered great, but he might still try to convince you that it is."

Quite to the contrary. Conway believes the surreals are great, and there's no "might" about it. If anything, he is keenly disappointed that the surreals haven't yet led to something greater. He had good reason to hope. And at one time he had good reason to believe. Based on his readings of Kurt Gödel's work, he thought the surreals might crack Cantor's Continuum Hypothesis—the hypothesis proposed by Cantor speculating on the possible sizes of infinite sets, stating that there is no infinity between the countable infinity of the integers and the uncountable infinity of the real numbers. Gödel and Paul Cohen collectively showed the hypothesis to be "probably unsolvable," at least according to the prevailing axioms of set theory, leaving the door ajar a sliver. When Cohen got his glorious result in 1963—the result Conway described as the work of an alien being—Gödel wrote Cohen a letter from his office at the Institute for Advanced Study in Princeton. "I think that in all essential respects you have given the best possible proof and this does not happen frequently," he said. "Reading your proof had a similarly pleasant effect on me as seeing a really good play."

Gödel and his wife, an exotic dancer, had fled Nazi Vienna and landed in Princeton in 1940. They planted plastic pink flamingos on their lawn and Gödel became good friends with Einstein, working on a theory of relativity that entailed a nonexpanding "rotating universe" wherein time travel was a physical reality. In various iterations, Gödel expounded at length on this idea:

[B]y making a round trip on a rocket ship in a sufficiently large circle, it is possible in these worlds to travel into any region of the past, present, and future, and back again, exactly as it is possible in other worlds to travel to distant parts of space.

This state of affairs seems to imply an absurdity. For it enables one, e.g., to travel into the near past of those places where he has himself lived. There he would find a person which would be himself at some earlier period of his life . . .

If only! A time travel research trip would have come in handy.

In addition to the relativity theory Gödel also did his part regarding the Continuum Hypothesis while at the Institute. And even after having proved the impossibility of a disproof, the issue with the infinities nagged him. In 1947, he published a paper, "What Is Cantor's Continuum Problem?" in the *American Mathematical Monthly*. He tried to provide an answer, first with some reinterpretive questions. "Cantor's continuum problem is simply the question: How many points are there on a straight line in Euclidean space? In other terms, the question is: How many different sets of integers exist?"

Conway had a vested interest in this subject dating back to his Ph.D. He read this and later papers by Gödel numerous times, before discovering the surreals and after (and fairly recently he spent a hefty sum on Gödel's multivolume collected works). What struck Conway during these readings was Gödel's assertion—the Surprising Assertion, as Conway calls it—that a solution to the Continuum Hypothesis might yet be possible, but *only* once the correct theory of infinitesimals had been found. Conway couldn't help but wonder . . . With the surreals, he believed that he had indeed found at least *a* correct theory of the infinitesimals (and he still believes so). He wouldn't go as far as to say it was *the* correct theory, at least not before eliciting Gödel's opinion on the subject. During a visit to Princeton in the 1970s, Conway got the chance to ask the great man himself.

He would never have been so daring as to simply ring Gödel and request an appointment. The meeting came about via their mutual friend Stanley Tennenbaum, a mathematician and logician. Tennenbaum was a dead ringer for actor Martin Landau, with piercing eyes that made people think he might be mad. For a time he lived alone in the woods in

New England, but he did the rounds through Montreal, Chicago, New York, and Princeton, the last being a regular pit stop for the purpose of talking to Gödel.

> Stan was a sort of pet or protégé of Gödel's. They had an almost son-to-father relationship. He had done various things in mathematical logic and he wrote lots of letters to Gödel, and Gödel responded. So he had the ins to Gödel, and he said, "If you like, I'll introduce you to God"—that's what he always called him. There was a thing: all the big people in mathematical logic had vaguely religious names. Gödel was known as God, Georg Kreisel was Christ, Alonzo Church was the Church, and then Errett Bishop came a good time later, and he was the Bishop. God, Church, Christ, and the Bishop, I think that's the set. So anyway, Tennenbaum offered: "Would you like to be introduced to God?" I said, "Yes, of course." You don't turn an invitation like that down.

Conway and Tennenbaum had met in Montreal, where Conway gave a talk on the surreals and Tennenbaum succumbed to their addictive pull. And then they met again some time later in Princeton, where Conway had been invited to give a talk to the undergraduate math club. The date is difficult to pinpoint. The year had to be less than 1978, when Gödel died, and greater than 1970, the year Conway found the surreals. Probably also less than 1976, after which Gödel was in very poor health and rarely left his home, and greater than or equal to 1972, when Conway spent the spring term at Caltech. Somewhere therein, Conway and Tennenbaum went to visit Gödel.

Over the decades, Gödel had continued to keep busy with the Continuum Hypothesis, exploring possible proofs. In 1970 he submitted a paper to the *Proceedings of the National Academy of Sciences* titled "Some Considerations Leading to the Probable Conclusion that the True Power of the Continuum is $\aleph_2$." Ultimately, he determined that this conclusion was wrong and withdrew the paper from circulation, blaming the mistake on his failing health. But still having his fingers in the pie, he might have been intrigued by a visit from Conway—who, when wanting to pull rank on the subject of infinity, especially when wanting to smother my niggling tautological questions, isn't shy about asserting his authority.

I'm the world expert! You can take my word for it!

Regarding Gödel, however, he might revise that to *a* world expert. And about that visit, the details are fuzzy, like Star. Never mind what year it was. Where did the meeting transpire? In Fuld Hall at teatime, or in Gödel's office just off the mathematics library? What was Gödel like? Was he wearing his round glasses? All my badgering made Conway, fellow of infinite jest that he is, laughingly wonder whether he'd met the great Gödel at all. But all joking aside. He had met him. And luckily, some proof, or at least something heading in that direction, is archived in the Institute for Advanced Study's Gödel Papers, within Gödel's files on Tennenbaum. Mostly the files were full of more personal matters. Tennenbaum applied for various academic positions in the 1970s and put Gödel down as a reference. His mentor obliged with the requests for "frank and searching" evaluations. "Tennenbaum has the rare gift of originality," Gödel said, also noting (if only in a draft) that he "does not get along well with people." Though Gödel added that he personally always found Tennenbaum very pleasant. Conway got along nicely with him as well. And in a file, labeled "discussion notes" for 1974, I came upon a sliver of the proof I was looking for amid Gödel's elegant mostly illegible handwriting (using the German secretarial shorthand Gabelsbergerschrift). In a list detailing his roving discussions with Tennenbaum, touching on everything from politics to mathematics—from Nixon, McGovern, hippies protesting the middle class, drug addicts, Vietnam, riots and the decay of U.S., to Cohen and Dedekind, Coxeter and modern geometry, Nash and games, Chomsky and the "linguistic aspect of math ed"—I found a single word that looked like "Conway," then an eminently legible "Game of Life." This goes some distance, at least, in confirming a date for Conway's visit. When pressed for details of the meeting, Conway digs around in his memory bank and supposes they talked about some generally logical things while he worked up the nerve to ask Gödel about his Surprising Assertion.

So I had, it can't have been much more than 10 minutes with him. Between 5 minutes and half an hour, because it didn't seem to go on very long. But it might have actually just been because I wanted more.

Anyway, whatever it was, I hesitantly asked him: Had he heard of the surreal numbers? And he had. And I asked him about the Surprising Assertion he'd made. I said to him that I thought I'd discovered the correct theory of infinitesimals. And he agreed. And I said, "Well, what about your idea that we would learn more about the Continuum Hypothesis?" And he said, "If I said that, I was wrong. Yes, you may very well have discovered the correct theory of infinitesimals, but it's not going to do anything for us." I wonder what exactly his words were. The words I remember are "I was wrong." And I do remember the feeling of disappointment.

And by the way that seemed right to me. I never understood what he meant by the Surprising Assertion, what was in his mind. I think it was probably just a passing idea that he had without any real support for it. But I'm happy to have met the great man, even if it was only for a short interval.

Those 10 minutes, give or take, count as 10 of the most interesting minutes of Conway's life—even if his theory of the infinites and the infinitesimals was still left bereft of greater application.

However, others still hold out hope. Don Knuth, for instance. Contemplating the relevance of surreal numbers, versus, say, real numbers, Knuth sees the scenario as analogous to the ancient Euclidean geometry that students memorize in school versus the more recent discovery of non-Euclidean geometry that Einstein showed pertains to our universe at large. "It's the same with surreal numbers," he says. "In school we learn how to calculate numbers with decimals and so on, and we sort of assume that nothing else is possible. But here is something even simpler than the real numbers, something that includes the real numbers and goes way, way beyond."

"Suppose surreal numbers had been invented first," he says, "and real numbers second—suppose it had gone the other way and we had all grown up learning surreal numbers. And then someone said, 'Well, yeah, but there is this special case of the numbers you can write in decimal notation and so on.' If everybody had known surreal numbers from childhood, then physicists would believe that surreal numbers were real and that the universe, the laws of physics, would be defined by surreal numbers—and they would assume that things that are true of the surreal numbers are true in quantum theory. This makes me realize how much a leap of faith it is even to believe that physics based on real numbers is real. Because there is no more reason to believe that all the things in our universe can be infinitely divisible according to real numbers than there is to believe in surreal numbers. It's just a matter of familiarity with a concept. So when people develop theories of chaos based on real numbers, there is no reason to think that this could actually be true of the real world. In the same way, it wasn't until Einstein came along that people realized that there could be curvature in space with non-Euclidean geometries or that maybe the universe is only finite."

That's where Knuth leaves the subject, philosophically speaking. Following up with more nuggets from his diary archive, he mentioned the time he and Conway climbed Mount Mansfield in Vermont, with Conway going barefoot. And he e-mailed me excerpts from a letter he wrote in 1980 when Sir Michael Atiyah solicited recommendations for potential fellows for the Royal Society. "I wrote: 'It is surely an honor for me to be asked to comment about two such nonoverlapping FRS candidates as [computer scientist] Tony Hoare and John Conway! I have unbounded admiration for each person, in disjoint ways.' Then I gave my recommendation for Tony Hoare, which I'd better keep private. Finally I turned to Our Hero: 'John Conway is the most creative mathematician I have ever met. I guess the reputed sign on the office door at Cambridge best describes him: "For number theory, see x; for algebra, see y; for analysis, see z; for anything else see Conway." But in fact he has made nontrivial contributions to number theory, algebra, and analysis, besides everything else. I think his revolutionary work 'On Numbers and Games' will prove in the long run to be a great contribution to mathematics; it will take some time before the remarkable consequences of such radical new directions are perceived just as his earlier work on regular languages is just now flowering in computer science and logic.'"

In short, Knuth's recommendation boils down to his oft-quoted dicta: "The best theory is motivated by practice, and the best practice is motivated by theory." The theory of surreal numbers is the best of the best as theories go, and Knuth and Conway (as well as others whom we will meet later) hold out hope that it will lead to an equally superlative practical application.

With that in mind, perhaps the concluding sentiment on the subject of the surreals, for now anyway, should go to Conway's poetic proxy, Edward FitzGerald and the *Rubáiyát of Omar Khayyám*:

> But leave the Wise to wrangle, and with me
> The Quarrel of the Universe let be:
> And, in some corner of the Hubbub couch'd,
> Make Game of that which makes as much of Thee.

11

DOTTO & COMPANY

You boil it in sawdust: you salt it in glue:
You condense it with locusts and tape:
Still keeping one principal object in view—
To preserve its symmetrical shape.

—LEWIS CARROLL

One day Conway and I were sitting in the computer room at the Princeton math department planning a trip to Japan's Kavli Institute for the Physics and Mathematics of the Universe. He'd been invited as the keynote speaker of a workshop on the Monster group—a rare sporadic group, an exquisitely symmetrical entity that lives in 196,883 dimensions.

Discovered in the early 1970s, the Monster continues to hold mathematicians in its thrall. They hunt it down at conferences and workshops worldwide. In the not so distant past there'd been Monster meetings at Müggelsee, a lake resort suburb of Berlin, and 2 back-to-back gatherings in Scotland, in Skye and Islay. And coming up was the workshop in Japan.

It would just be an ego trip. As far as I'm concerned, anyway.

That might be interpreted as lack of interest, but clearly an ego trip would be a trip Conway would want to take. We traveled separately to Tokyo and the morning after the 13-hour flight I sought out my subject with fingers crossed. I'd wondered, as had his wife, whether Conway would safely make the journey; whether he might not accidentally end up in Argentina. But there he sat at breakfast in the hotel dining room, holding forth, talking about himself, same as always. Except today he was talking at John McKay. McKay, with his white beard and rosy red cheeks, was pleased to see his old friend and immediately took a mothering interest. "You have to use your influence to get John to take his meds," he told me. "Otherwise he's going to die."

With cosmic equanimity, Conway got on with his day. He seemed to have traveled via VIP wormhole, depositing him halfway around the world entirely unfazed. His amanuensis, meanwhile, was flattened 1-dimensional by jet lag, drunk on GPS disorientation. Or maybe that was just the topic at hand. Mercurial and massive, the Monster is notoriously hard to wrap the brain around. I came to think of it as a very distant cousin of the icosahedron, n times removed, transformed and permuted through a labyrinth of intermarriage, incestuous liaisons with the dodecahedron, and other polytopal indiscretions. A tawdry analogue, but the Monster defies description. It is very difficult to understand.

Nobody does. We just think about it.

The lack of understanding is something Conway has contemplated since first encountering the Monster, and it's a state of affairs that doesn't change much year after year. At another Monster meeting, in 2004 in Edinburgh, Conway began his talk by demanding applause beforehand:

You'd better all applaud now, before I give the talk, because it's going to be a failure. I've given this talk in Princeton recently and it was a failure there. It was a failure again in Rutgers. But I believe in try, try, try again.

As predicted, in Edinburgh he failed again, losing the audience halfway through. McKay fell asleep and began snoring. Undaunted, over the next few days Conway spent his time trying to find a more cogent explanation, using pictures instead of notations and equations, and he convinced the conference organizers to let him try his talk again. By some reports, this time there were fewer glazed looks, and people certainly forgot their troubles in the evenings while Conway entertained with his folded origami jumping frogs, his tongue gymnastics, and his tricks with cards and pennies and birthdays. He managed to achieve some marginally clearer thinking about the Monster over the course of the

2-week gathering, yet any profound understanding remained unattainable. And he noted the same 5 years later, during his keynote at the Institute for the Physics and Mathematics of the Universe:

> This is something that perpetually intrigues me. There are these abstract objects that are as real as trees or cats, but we can only access them by thinking about them. One feels the Monster can't exist without a very real reason. But I don't have any idea what that reason is. Before I die, I really want to understand WHY the Monster exists. But I'm almost certain I won't.

△ ▢ ⬦ ⊗ ⬡

Dateline: Cambridge, 1973. The typical scene featuring Conway loitering in the common room had changed somewhat. Now he could be found crawling around the floor, as if under a hypnotist's spell. He had printed out more than 100 feet of fanfolded computer paper and arranged it in a 12-by-9-foot tiling on the floor of the common room. The tiling formed a "character table" of numbers, describing and defining the Monster group (named by Conway!).

Earlier that year 2 mathematicians, Bernd Fischer at Universität Bielefeld and Bob Griess at the University of Michigan, had separately predicted the existence of this new group. They did so in a manner similar to how physicists predicted the existence of the Higgs boson, the quantum of the Higgs field that pervades the ether and endows elementary particles with mass. Circumstantial evidence indicated something was there. And so just as physicists went hunting for the Higgs boson, mathematicians went hunting for the Monster—for information, confirmation, clues or crumbs, scat or spoor.

The Monster has been likened to the titular creature in Lewis Carroll's poem "The Hunting of the Snark." Carroll, when pressed, would say only that his snark was inadmissible and unimaginable—though he indicated courage is needed on a snark hunt, and that the best tools to wield in its capture were thimbles, care, forks, hope, or else to "charm it with smiles and soap." With the ragbag of groups that had been discovered during the Classification Project, mathematicians similarly used a ragbag of methods. Conway's initial method for the Monster involved a Hamann Manus R mechanical computer. It had levers and gears and looked like a souped-up old cash register, and his girls liked to play with it and take it apart. Later he resorted to his handheld HP-65 programmable calculator, and by the end of the year he had calculated the Monster's size, or its order, its number of symmetries. Fischer had laid the groundwork using what's called the Thompson order formula, indicating a maximum size and that the size could be expected to fall within a certain arithmetic progression. Conway programmed the calculator with these constraints, left it running overnight, and when he awoke the next morning there was his answer. He sent a postcard to Fischer with the news:

Dear Bernd, The order of the Monster is . . .

And then a very big number, approximately $8 \cdot 10^{53}$. Or, more precisely:

$$2^{46} \cdot 3^{20} \cdot 5^9 \cdot 7^6 \cdot 11^2 \cdot 13^3 \cdot 17 \cdot 19 \cdot 23 \cdot 29 \cdot 31 \cdot 41 \cdot 47 \cdot 59 \cdot 71$$
$$= 808,017,424,794,512,875,886,459,904,961,710,757,005,754,368,000,000,000$$

Roughly 808 sexdecillion. Again, not infinity by any means, but careening off in that direction. There's not much that can be done with such a large number, so Conway put it in that giant character table—a character table being a little like a legend of animal markings and droppings found in a field guide, a reference to be consulted while on the lookout.

When we used the character table for the Monster, we'd often want an entry that was in the middle of this massive table, and of course you can't see it if you stand carefully at the edge. So we'd sort of crawl in, 3 rows down, 7 columns across . . .

And the Monster was only part of Conway's latest and larger obsession at the time. Energized by finding the constellation of Conway groups, he'd already begun an ambitious collection of numbers pertaining to groups. With his penchant for knowing everything, he wanted to collect all the interesting properties of all the interesting groups, and he wanted to gather this sum total of knowledge in a comprehensive reference guide of some sort, a dictionary or a handbook—he ended up calling it *The ATLAS* (caps, as ever, are Conway's).

This organizational desire originated with those stimulating conversations with John Thompson. The discussions went on and on and on, though only on an intermittent basis, since Thompson usually split his time between Cambridge and Chicago, and since Conway, riding the coattails of his namesake group, had set out in 1972 for a term at the California Institute of Technology. He'd been invited by Marshall Hall, an eminent group theorist with a southern drawl and an impressive collection of ancient coins. The romantic in Conway spun this sojourn, his first stay of any length in America, into his California dream, another chance for a new beginning. And, as he likes to recall,

> It made for a total change.

All his girls, giddy with the excitement of catching trains and planes, made an ordeal of getting packed and out the door on New Year's Day. When the Conway family was almost on their way, the front door key disappeared. There were no duplicates; it was a very old house and a very old key. The Conways left the house unlocked for 8 months.

Due to bad weather, what was supposed to be a direct flight to Los Angeles took 36 hours, including a 14-hour layover in Oakland, the girls running around, the parents sleeping. Eventually they landed at LAX, got into a taxi, arrived at their rented house in Pasadena, tumbled into bed, and awoke to the Californian sun, intense and bright—not unlike the light in Norway, land of the midnight sun, where the rays beat down and reminded Conway (during a brief visit) of the sun in Camus' *L'Étranger*. The protagonist in *L'Étranger*, Monsieur Meursault, noted "the cymbals of sunlight crashing on my forehead," "inhuman and oppressive." The California sun did not oppress Conway.

> I had fantasies of living off the land. I'd walk down to the campus, and on the way there was a guy with a huge orange tree in his front garden. First time I went past I said, "Mind if I take an orange?" He said, "No, no, here—take a box." Fruit was dripping from the trees, falling to the ground and rotting, it was a great nuisance. So I used to fantasize about sleeping

outside, waking up, getting some figs off the tree that was sheltering me. It was rather nice. I must say, there is another aspect to it. You know, a clap of the hands and the dancing girls appear. I mean, it was just a fantasy, nonsense really.

For the first month, the family lived off the modest amount of money Conway had in his pocket. He worried it couldn't possibly last until payday. When payday arrived, he had money like the sun, 10 times the amount they'd lived off during the last month. Straightaway they bought a car, a Lincoln Continental, previously owned by a Catholic priest. It cost $800 and was as big as a tank, among the largest cars ever made. Not that Conway should have been driving. He's never had a driver's license. He drove in California, since Eileen was afraid of the car and the girls had to be driven to school. He also managed a road trip, to Sequoia National Park to see the big trees, but he was pulled over by the police on the way back. He purportedly pretended to be his grad student, Robert Curtis, who owned the necessary documents. Curtis had joined him in California and lived with the family on South Holliston Avenue.

He is very good on gossip, by the way. He'll tell you the sauce. Yes, he's the one. Curtis, unfortunately, can give you the dirt.

"Most of my recollections are not for public consumption," says Curtis. That year he was working on his Ph.D., partly on the Conway groups— particularly the biggest Conway group, called Co_0 or ".0" and nicknamed "dotto" (dotto involves, or contains, the Conway groups Co_1 and Co_2 and Co_3). And during the California stint he and Conway also laid preliminary plans for *The ATLAS*.

Curtis managed to tell a few tales that needn't be censored, or at least not too too much, such as the story about Conway's first driving lesson. He kangaroo-hopped down Colorado Boulevard. Once on the freeway he hit the brake instead of the gas, turned through 180 degrees, and ended up facing oncoming traffic, and then calmly turned the car around again and continued on his way. Curtis also recalled Conway's speaking engagements all over the United States. Almost weekly, either Curtis or Eileen would drop him off at the Hilton Hotel, where he caught the airport bus, and then they'd pick him up at the same spot outside the hotel a few days later. Curtis teased Conway that he never left the Hilton, that in reality he spent the time at the hotel, perhaps not alone, returning home under the pretense that he'd been to Boston, Chicago, Atlanta, talking up his big group.

Since Conway discovered his groups, reports of more sporadic groups had only continued: the Suzuki group, 2 more groups found by Janko, the McLaughlin group, and the Held group. What often happened in this enumerating of the simple groups was that someone precisely predicted a group, knowing certain properties about it but needing somebody else to prove its existence and do the construction—the honor of the name went to the person who did the bulk of the work, on whichever end of the equation. With his groups, Conway did almost all the work himself in that 12-hour blitz, investigating Leech's very loose prediction. At Caltech, he partook in this relay action again. On precisely the fourth of May, 1972, at 3 o'clock, Conway's host, Marshall Hall, received a telegram from the then unknown Arunas Rudvalis, a Lithuanian American mathematician at Michigan State University. The telegram contained a precise and detailed prediction for yet another group. Hall wanted to investigate, but he was due at a meeting of the Senate Committee on Mathematics Education. He handed the telegram over to Conway and Caltech's David Wales. They easily worked out a representation of the group in 28-dimensional space, but each of 2 arguments in favor of the representation led to a contradiction.

> We worked out Case A and Case B. We spent a few days on Case A and got a contradiction, and then spent a few days on Case B and got a contradiction. We had 2 arguments that led to a contradiction, and we trusted neither of them.

Attempting to break the stalemate, Conway got crafty. He found some stiff cardboard boxes and cut out 2 pieces roughly the size and shape of hand mirrors, for ease of holding and reading. He pasted the Case A contradiction and the Case B contradiction on the fronts and backs of each. They sat in Wales's office, staring at their hand mirrors, flipping back and forth, trying to find their error. The cases were composed only of about 6 lines each—the mistake should have been easy to find.

> We were absolutely sure that this group existed, because what Rudvalis said about it was very coherent. So we were sure we'd made a mistake. We each

held a hand mirror, and said, "Okay. Case A, line 3 looks fine, what can you see that might be wrong with line 4?" And then when we got to the end, we turned the hand mirrors over and said, "Okay, what's wrong on case B, then?" And we couldn't find a damn thing wrong with either of them. We turned them over every half hour or so and considered the other case and got a contradiction again. And then in the end, after wasting maybe a week on this, we decided to go ahead and examine the group another way, which didn't require deciding which of Case A or Case B it was, and carefully steered clear of the contradiction. But that was a lot harder, because if we had determined which case was right, that would have led to a lot of information about the group. Instead we were arguing in the dark. Eventually we managed to construct it. We wasted the first week of what turned out to be our month in this futile attempt to settle whether it was Case A or Case B.

When they had a construction that they believed worked, they sent it off for verification to computer programmer Chris Landauer, now at the Aerospace Corporation. Then all they could do was wait by the phone for the results.

I remember precisely, we were sitting in the house I rented, waiting for a telephone call from Chris. And then the telephone went. I said, "Ah, this will be Chris now." I looked up at the clock on the wall and the second hand was about 5 seconds to 4 o'clock. I watched it tick down 5, 4, 3, 2, 1, and I picked up the phone. I said, "Well, Chris?" He said: "Yes." And it was done. We worked on it from 3 o'clock on the fourth of May until 4 o'clock on the third of June. In other words, 1 month minus a day plus an hour, and we had finished it, we had constructed the Rudvalis group.

They walked into the department at Caltech, arriving just in time for tea. Conway and David Wales and everyone at tea that day raised paper cups bubbling to the brim with champagne. Then someone asked, "What about those contradictions you were agonizing over for a week?" They went back to Wales's office and dusted off the hand mirrors abandoned on the windowsill. Instantly they saw the error.

It was just bloody obvious that the mistake was on line 3 of Case A. I used to think of this as an example of how groups manage to do impossible things. This is the trouble with groups, they behave in astonishingly subtle ways that make them psychologically hard to grasp. And that's why it's so difficult to find them. You know, in *Through the Looking Glass*, the White Queen says something about doing 6 impossible things before breakfast. Well, groups are adept at doing impossible things before breakfast.

This makes Conway uneasy. He has the nagging worry there might be a lost sporadic group somewhere out there in the ocean of symmetry, a beguiling group behaving impossibly, persistently and deceptively putting up a contradiction and therefore deemed disproved, relegated to nonexistence by an investigator who lacked the necessary obsessive conviction. Conway's philosophy of study, which has served him well, is to always take his investigations several steps beyond what any reasonable human being would do. His collaborators and students have felt the sting of his critical admonishment in this regard when he berates them with:

No no no no no! You're being far too REASONABLE.

Conway's mum, aged 67, died of a heart attack on May 13, 1972, in the midst of that Rudvalis month. He didn't go back for the funeral. He hadn't been informed of her declining health until it was too late to make the trip back, as per her wishes—it wouldn't have been reasonable. Before heading home to Cambridge in August, he made a final visit to the Hilton Hotel, onward to the University of Colorado in Boulder for a conference on number theory. In the printed proceedings he gave notice of his changing coordinates:

California Institute of Technology Jan.–Aug. 1972
University of Cambridge Aug. 1972 → ∞

△ ▢ ◈ ⊗ ⬟

The Rudvalis group did impossible things to the order of

$$2^{14} \cdot 3^3 \cdot 5^3 \cdot 7 \cdot 13 \cdot 29$$
$$= 145,926,144,000$$
$$\approx 10^{11}$$

Then the next year, in 1973, came the Monster—predicted to exist by both Bernd Fischer and Bob Griess. It was impossible to the order of 808 sexdecillion. And at Cambridge this beastly group led to even more sporadic groups, including the Harrada-Norton group:

$$2^{14} \cdot 3^6 \cdot 5^6 \cdot 7 \cdot 11 \cdot 19$$
$$= 273{,}030{,}912{,}000{,}000$$
$$\approx 3 \cdot 10^{14}$$

And the Thompson group:

$$2^{15} \cdot 3^{10} \cdot 5^3 \cdot 7^2 \cdot 13 \cdot 19 \cdot 31$$
$$= 90{,}745{,}943{,}887{,}872{,}000$$
$$\approx 9 \cdot 10^{16}.$$

Conway fixed his sights on learning more about the Monster, which was still nothing but a will-o'-the-wisp prediction. He was also inching forward with his plan for a grand groups reference book, collecting all these interesting creatures and compiling all their interesting numbers. Before the time when such information was at everybody's fingertips on the Internet, *The ATLAS* was bound to become an indispensible research resource for group theorists (and to wit, Harvard's Benedict Gross later remarked that if the library were on fire, he would run into the flames and save *The ATLAS*).

With Robert Curtis's help, Conway applied for and received a 3-year grant from the British Department of Science and Industry Research. The grant paid Curtis's salary, and an exorbitant £82 went to Heffers bookshop, where Conway purchased a large guard book, a special expandable scrapbook with a leather cover, in which he pasted more and more pages for character tables—tables he and his team worked up themselves, tables they found by trawling published sources, and tables that arrived by mail once other mathematicians heard what they were up to. The guard book grew obese and occupied its own chair in the common room—a chair on wheels, all the more easily to be shot around the room for consultation, deliberation, and debate.

It was the type of book Mr. Audubon might have used for paintings of his birds. I remember the guard book particularly fondly—the good old guard book. And not just because its content was so valuable. I loved its name, "the guard book," because it implied both care and permanence. The title seems to say, "This is the book we guard. It's a safe place, something permanent and reliable in a shifting world."

After Curtis, next aboard *The ATLAS* enterprise was Simon Norton, followed by Richard Parker and Robert Wilson (the alphabetical order matches their chronological order in coming aboard). During the research trip Conway and I had taken to Cambridge, these sum chums gathered for enforced nostalgia sessions. Curtis, easygoing and urbane, spiffy in a black leather jacket, twirling his mustache; Norton, brilliant but odd, a rip in the crotch of his pants offset by his hundred-watt smile (great teeth for an Englishman); Wilson, neat and quiet with hidden depths, tenacious, skilled on the violin and viola; and the scrappy and outspoken Parker, said to have accumulated an unknown n-number of . . . Well, as Parker himself suggested: "I think some of the truth should be subtracted." And what a discrepant crew they were. But they all lamentingly agreed that times had changed. Group theory was no longer such a major part of mathematics; it had been taken over by the "bloody physicists," who now use group theory extensively and intensively, believing that symmetry is the key to the universe.

Back in the day, Curtis's office at the math department was christened "Atlantis," because it was mission control and because as the great big book grew, the office came in danger of sinking under its own weight, like the fabled island that sank into the ocean, according to Plato's *Timaeus*, "in a single day and night of misfortune." Conway's crew suffered many days and many nights, some more misfortunate than others, many at the pub, some in celebration of a good day's work. When a character table was converted into the proper format, or a precarious piece of information reached stability, convention dictated that it was formally said to be "Atlantified," printed on "Atlantic blue" paper and filed away, and then the authors went for some "Atlantic beer."

We didn't work very conscientiously. Every now and then we spent a day. We'd say, let's see what we learn about such and such a group. It's very

hard work intellectually, you understand. These are tremendously complicated and difficult calculations. And we were doing it all by hand, and by
head.

Every now and then the authors would fall back into backgammon
for a break, or they'd play another game. Or, to be more mathematically
correct, they would engage with a game, interface with it on a meta-
analytical level. "With a game, you shouldn't do anything as vulgar as
play it," said Norton. After a couple of weeks of games, Conway et al.
would realize that perhaps they should get back to *The ATLAS*. After a
week or so with *The ATLAS*, exhausted intellectually from the enormous
task of wrangling the groups, it was time again for a well-deserved break.
As Conway likes to say (borrowing words of wisdom he learned from a
graduate student), the day can be saved with 45 minutes of work. In this
case, work budgeted for 3 years consumed 15.

During the enforced nostalgia session, Norton, who through special
dispensation still maintains an office at Cambridge, ran off from our
gathering for a while and came back with a stack of the original folders
with the manuscript mock-ups for each group. When *The ATLAS* was
under way he was in the middle of his Ph.D. in group theory, with Conway as his de facto adviser. He was designated the project's trouble-
shooter, since he could not countenance contradictions; he could not
sleep if something was amiss; and so all the difficult problems were sent
to him with the unwavering conviction that they would instantaneously
be solved, all errors corrected. Norton was also known to speedily solve
the anagrams that flew around in the interest of wasting time—though
not altogether off subject from symmetry and groups, since anagrams
involve a rotation or permutation of letters to form a new word or
phrase. For instance, somebody'd asked, "What's an anagram for
'phoneboxes'?" And before anyone could even cock his head to ponder,
Norton declared: "Xenophobes!" The name of Miles Anthony Reid, a
research fellow in the department, turned out to be unusually fecund
source material, permuted by various people to "earthly dimension" and
"Lenin made history" (fitting because Reid spent time in Russia as a
student), and the winner for lewdity was, "I tried Nola's hymen."

I was quite fond of mine: If you miss off the Anthony you can get "slime ride," which I thought was quite nice. I remember also "Sir William Vallance Douglas Hodge," which gives: "Ah, a million vulgar cads will see God."

Pressing mathematical concerns intruded as well, causing further delays to *The ATLAS*. It was during this period that Conway refined his formula for figuring out the day of the week for any given date, producing his Doomsday algorithm. This began, as one might expect, during another of his visits with the funster Martin Gardner. Conway flew to New York and waited for Gardner to pick him up at the airport. And waited, and waited, and waited. Gardner did not turn up as planned.

> Initially I thought, Okay, he's going to turn up in 5 minutes. But I waited there a hell of a long time, probably an hour, I don't know. And I had started to think, Well, what happens if he doesn't turn up? I didn't have a phone number for him. And it wouldn't matter if I did because I didn't know how to work the American pay phone system—I'm still like this, you might notice. So the easiest thing to do was to just sit there and hope.

More than 2 hours late, Gardner came running in, waving madly from the far end of the arrivals terminal, apologetic and promising, "You'll forgive me as soon as you know what I've just discovered!" He'd been at the New York Public Library, where he found a note published in an 1887 issue of *Nature* magazine—"To Find the Day of the Week for Any Given Date," sent in by Lewis Carroll, who wrote: "Having hit upon the following method of mentally computing the day of the week for any given date, I send it you in the hope that it may interest some of your readers. I am not a rapid computer myself, and as I find my average time for doing any such question is about 20 seconds, I have little doubt that a rapid computer would not need 15." Gardner couldn't resist photocopying this choice find, but there was a long queue at the copying machine. He got in line. The line moved slowly. By the time it became apparent that he was bound to be late picking up Conway, he'd already invested 30 minutes, and he figured another 15 would suffice. He felt it was worth the wait, and he knew Conway would agree.

When they finally arrived at the house at 10 Euclid Avenue, Gardner went straight to his file cabinets and produced 20-odd articles about working out the day of the week for any given date. The Lewis Carroll rule, in his view, was the best yet. All the same, he turned to Conway and said, "John, you ought to work out an even simpler rule that I can tell my readers." So during the long winter's nights after the Gardners had toddled off to bed, Conway thought about how to work out the day of the week in a way he could explain to the average anyone on the street.

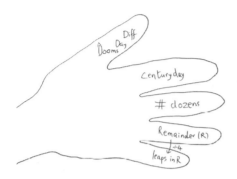

He was still thinking during the flight home, and back in the common room. When he hit upon a method he called it the Doomsday Rule. The algorithm requires only addition, subtraction, and memory. Conway devised a mnemonic method of sorts, whereby as you work through the algorithm you store all the necessary information on the fingers of your outstretched hand—outstretched so as to better bear the burden of the megabytes. And in order to remember a certain important piece of information about the date in question, Conway bares his teeth and bites into his thumb *really* hard.

Tooth marks must be showing! That way the thumb remembers. And whenever I lecture on this I go to someone in the front row and ask them to certify that they can see the tooth marks. It really does help. You can't get serious people to do it, because they think it is childish. But the point about doing it is that this whole business occupies quite a substantial part of your brain, and then you forget what the person said their birthday was. This way the thumb remembers how far the birthday was away from the nearest Doomsday, and your thumb is perfectly capable of remembering that for you.

Over the years Conway has taught the Doomsday Rule to 1000s upon 1000s—and on occasion as many as 600 or so at a time, all crammed together in a conference hall calculating each other's birthdays and biting their thumbs. And always endeavoring to be unreasonable, Conway was not satisfied with his easiest of algorithms. As soon as he designed the algorithm he started improving it. The main motivation was that he yet again wanted the rule to be as *simple* as possible, especially for the purposes of teaching. He and Richard Guy composed another mnemonic aid, a mathematical poem—doggerel, Conway calls it, and being doggerel it is easier to remember.

DOGGEREL DOOMSDAY RULE

Lesson One: Months

The last of Feb., or of Jan. will do

(Except that in Leap Years it's Jan. 32).

Then in even months use the month's own day,

And for odd ones add 4, or else take it away.*

*According to length or simply remember:

You only subtract for Septem. or November.

Lesson Two: Years

Now to work out your Doomsdays the orthodox way

Three things you should add to the century day:

Dozens, remainder, and fours in the latter,

(If you alter by sevens, of course it won't matter).

Lesson Three: Centuries

In Julian times, lackaday, lackaday,

Zero was Sunday, centuries went back a day,

But Gregorian four hundreds are always Tues.

And now centuries extra take us back twos.

Performing and teaching the rule ad nauseam, Conway noticed shortcuts and devised more mnemonic tricks to make the shortcuts more memorable. From iteration to iteration, the algorithm became easier to teach, easier to learn, easier to memorize, easier to execute, even for Conway. He noticed he got faster and faster at calculating the day of the week for any given date, and unlike Lewis Carroll he came to fancy himself a rapid computer. Then he came up with another *grand projet*: to halve his speed every 5 years.

Meanwhile, Penrose tiles also got in *The ATLAS*'s way. Discovered by Oxford physicist Sir Roger Penrose, Penrose tiles produce only nonperiodic tilings of the plane. Finding this collection of tiles had been a long-standing geometric puzzle, initially solved with a set of 20,462 tiles, later reduced to 104, then 92, then 6. Penrose's interest in tiling ran parallel to his interest in physics, and he went looking for something simpler than 6 tiles that produced complicated patterns and structures. "Because one sees that sort of thing in the universe," he says. "One hopes that the laws are ultimately simple." Conway took an interest when Penrose got the minimum number of tiles down to 2.

> And by the way, nobody knows that you can't get the number down to 1.
> Every now and then I've tried. But I haven't succeeded. Not yet.

Generally, Conway preferred to call the tiles "Penrose's puzzle pieces," and more specifically, he called the 2 most interesting pieces "kites" and "darts," or "dites" and "karts" when his tongue got tangled. He developed nomenclature for some of Penrose's discoveries, such as the phenomenon of "inflation" and "deflation" that proves the number of possible tilings with the pair of tiles is uncountable, and then Conway proceeded to conduct his own analysis and produce his own uncountability proof. In pursing his investigations, he usurped some of his wife Eileen's territory, covering the dining table with an infinite nuisance of tiles. He cut them out himself, causing his right hand to hurt with cramps for days. To Eileen's dismay, he studied the dining table mosaic for a year, relegating family meals to the kitchen and prohibiting dinner parties.

Conway took these investigations on the road in 1976, when he was due in September at Ohio's Miami University for the Fourth Annual Mathematics and Statistics Conference. The theme that year was recreational mathematics. Others on the program included Wolfgang Haken, who a month earlier had announced (with his colleague Kenneth Appel) a computer-assisted proof of the 4-color theorem, stating that no more than 4 colors are necessary to color a map in such a way that no 2 adjacent divisions of the map, be it into countries, provinces, cities, districts, or regions, would ever be the same. This was another mathematical object pulling at Conway's heart, and he would have preferred a proof by a human computer. Martin Gardner was also due to attend the conference, and en route to Ohio, Conway made another weeklong pit stop at 10 Euclid Avenue. Gardner was working up a column about the Penrose tiles—at long last, since he had been waiting for Penrose to secure the patent. Gardner pumped Conway for information, and Conway generated another large mosaic using Gardner's personal Roneo machine, a copier producing tiles in shades of mimeograph purple. He generated 20 or 30 pages of fairly large tiles, cutting them out and taping them together, and then he reduced this large canvas section by section on a more modern photocopier, recutting and retaping it all together to form a single page with an intricate tiling—artwork fit for the *Scientific American* cover accompanying Gardner's column in January 1977.

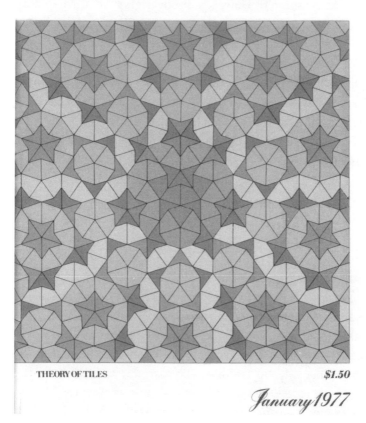

SCIENTIFIC AMERICAN

THEORY OF TILES $1.50

January 1977

Continuing with his fetish for nomenclature, Conway named several of the recurring patterns, such as the "cartwheel."

> Every point is in a cartwheel somewhere. If you jab your finger anywhere, on any point anywhere on the pattern, you are part of a cartwheel. The whole thing is overlapping cartwheels.

The spokes radiating out from the wheel he called "wormholes," consisting of "long bow ties" and "short bow ties." The 7 ways tiles assemble around a vertex he called "sun," "star," "jack," "queen," "king," "ace," and "deuce"—and these arrangements in turn force certain tiling patterns that directly and indirectly follow over the plane.

The plan was that after Gardner finished pumping Conway on the Penrose tiles, Conway would escort Gardner to Ohio. When Gardner came down to breakfast the morning of their departure he stopped short and said, "I can't do it. I'm not going." His fear of traveling, again getting the better of him. Conway arrived solo and delivered his talk about the surreal numbers (*On Numbers and Games* having recently been published). Then, because another speaker had canceled last minute, Conway was recruited for a fill-in talk, on "Penrose's Puzzle Pieces." "Conway was like a pied piper for students at that conference," recalls Doris Schattschneider, a tessellation expert from Moravian College. With the sun high in a clear blue sky, she found Conway lying on the campus lawn surrounded by students forming spokes of the cartwheel, all heads around his, everyone talking away. "To me, that's John That epitomizes his willingness, even eagerness, to interact on any level and communicate what he is doing."

Schattschneider also recalls—as does her friend Marjorie Senechal, a mathematician and historian of science at Smith College—attending another conference a few years later when Conway was still on his jag about Penrose tiles. "It was a delightful, insightful talk, and the audience was spellbound," says Senechal. During the coffee break she was milling about with Conway when someone neither of them knew approached and said, "Oh, Professor Conway! Roger Penrose is a genius!" Conway smiled politely.

> Yes, he's the gene, and I'm the -nius.

Penrose, when I interviewed him over lunch at Oxford, didn't seem at all miffed or competitive about Conway co-opting his tiles. "It was flattering," he says.

At yet another conference Senechal was sitting with Conway in the audience during a Penrose tiles talk, and as the speaker outlined the various and sundry theorems he'd proved, Conway muttered,

I already proved all that.

"Did you ever publish it?"* Senechal asked. No, he hadn't, naturally. "It reminds me of a passage in a biography of Peter the Great," recalls Senechal. "Peter traveled a lot, and insisted on going incognito. No announcements, no pronouncements, no royal trappings. Nevertheless, he was upset if he didn't receive the deference due to him. Says the biographer Peter Massie: 'The Tsar was the Tsar; the incognito would be respected, but everyone would know *who* was incognito.'"

Where shall we turn next in this kaleidoscope of inquiry?

Well, the Monster by this date was still traveling incognito. There was still no proof of its existence in those 196,883 dimensions. Conway's level of engagement as yet was to name the beast and to determine its order, its size, and number of the Monster's symmetries.

Then came another crazy tip from John McKay:

196,883 + 1 = 196,884

Elementary arithmetic, perhaps.

The year was 1978. McKay was at home in Montreal taking a moment away from group theory and poking around in papers on number theory.

---

* Sometimes other people, inspired by Conway's discoveries, published results for him. George Francis at the University of Illinois and freelance geometer and cosmologist Jeffrey Weeks, based in Canton, New York, started writing "The ZIP Proof" with Conway, but then for a number of reasons they "promoted John from the author list to the title," as Weeks recalls, and the paper was published as "Conway's ZIP Proof."

He came upon the number 196,884, a number of considerable significance in modular functions, far away on the other side of the mathematical universe from group theory. That this was a mere coincidence—196,884 being only 1 more than the Monster's 196,883 dimensions—seemed unlikely to McKay's suspicious mind. Bernd Fischer was then visiting in Montreal and just about to leave to visit John Thompson, then on sabbatical at Princeton's Institute for Advanced Study. McKay decided it couldn't hurt to share his suspicions with the god of groups. He sent a note via Fischer to Thompson, and when Thompson arrived back home in Cambridge he passed the tip along to Conway.

> He came back with this observation, which I always think of as the amazing fact that 196,883 is very nearly equal to 196,884.

Conway launched an investigation. Mucking around with *The ATLAS*, he had at hand mountains of data on the Monster. He didn't know the first thing about modular functions, a field that dated to the German mathematician Carl Gustav Jacob Jacobi's 1829 book *Fundamenta Nova* ("New Foundations" or "New Fundamental Facts" or "New Fundament"). Jacobi produced a new entity called the elliptic modular function, establishing a branch of mathematics still used today in complex analysis. Veering off course yet again, Conway and Parker and Wilson went on a wild-goose chase, trying to figure out this mysterious connection. David Benson, now at the University of Aberdeen, was in on it as well. He was a Ph.D. student of John Thompson's, but he fell in with Conway simply because while most professors resided in their offices, Conway, who never liked being called Professor, was always sitting around in the common room and was always willing to talk, no matter what his interlocutor's rank, status, or pedigree.

Norton wasn't part of these initial investigations. He was away. He had as a hobby traveling England's railway and bus routes. He toted around his collection of ticket stubs and timetables and exhibited them in impromptu show-and-tells. So, at the time he was off riding a rarely open British Rail line through the Pennines mountain range.

> For me, it was really lovely that Simon wasn't there. It was sort of a godsend. Because usually when there was some new discovery, Simon always

was the quickest at learning it. And he wasn't terribly good at explaining. He would explain the new thing to me, and then I would translate it to the acolytes around me so they could understand it. The information transfer was always from Simon. It was like that kids' game: Simon says clap your hands, Simon says cross your legs, Simon says all sorts of things. And if our Simon says something is true, then it was probably was true.

Simon has got a bottom of good sense. I don't know whether you know that quotation? This is from Boswell's *Life of Johnson*. There was a woman who was rather flighty, and Dr. Johnson said, "But she has a bottom of good sense." And everyone tittered. And Johnson said, "What's wrong? There is nothing funny about that. What I mean is she is *fundamentally* sound." They used to use the term "fundament" for the bottom in the eighteenth century. Anyway, Simon has a bottom of good sense. Although he's got various idiosyncrasies and is odd in various ways, he knows what's what.

While Norton was away, Conway combed the Monster's character table and discovered all sorts of seemingly coincidental connections between this new beast and the old modular functions. Another one was:

$$21{,}493{,}760 = 21{,}296{,}876 + 196{,}883 + 1$$

This confirmed an observation Thompson had made, noting that other coefficients of the elliptic modular function could also be expressed as sums of the Monster's various hyperdimensional properties. For instance, some of the dimensional representations of the Monster are:

$$a = 1$$
$$b = 196883$$
$$c = 21296876$$
$$d = 842609326$$

And these same numbers pop up in the modular function:

$$a \quad a+b \quad a+b+c \quad 2a+2b+c+d$$
$$\downarrow \quad \downarrow \quad \downarrow \quad \downarrow$$
$$\tfrac{1}{q} + 1968984\, q + 21493760\, q^2 + 864299970\, q^3 + \ldots$$

Numerology, plain and simple.

Yeah, yeah, yeah. Just sort of crazy stuff. This number is equal to that number, or this number is next to that number, and if you subtract one from the other, my god you get 196,884 again. The numbers were so large that you feel it can't be an accident. And then it turned out there were more and more and more of these numerical coincidences.

I remember in particular one of these numbers, 1010-something-or-other. I knew very little about these modular functions. But I worked out a series coming from the Monster group, and it contained the number 1010-something-or-other, and the fact that it had 1010 in it made it easy to remember, but dammit I've forgotten it, though I can look it up again. Anyway, I went down into our mathematics library in Cambridge and I got down Jacobi's *Fundamenta Nova Theoriae Functionum Ellpticarum*, written in Latin, one of the last books to be written in Latin. I opened the book and found the number and I got this feeling—you know the way the back of your neck gets prickles and goose bumps—it was a frightening, mysterious thing. The back of my neck went all tingly and I thought, My god, there Is something going on here.

When Simon came back, we had made a sizable amount of progress and he knew nothing about modular functions, which until 2 or 3 weeks ago we hadn't known anything about, either. And so he was acting the way we usually acted when he made his Delphic pronouncements, or "pronunciamentos" is perhaps the better word. So that was really rather nice.

Norton quickly caught up, and he and Conway wrote up the paper "Monstrous Moonshine" summarizing their findings, marshaling evidence to support the unexpected connection between these mathematical structures, and conjecturing that given the evidence, there should be something profound underpinning the Monster. The Leech lattice underpinned Conway's group in 24-dimensional space. Beneath the Mathieu group M_{24} lay the error-correcting Golay code. What underlay the Monster?

I arrived at the alcove armed with the "Monstrous Moonshine" paper (16 pages of conjecturing, with another 16 of numeric tables) in hopes of getting, if not an answer, at least some elaboration about what exactly he and Norton had accomplished.

I'm tempted to say nothing. The point in calling it Moonshine was because moonshine is illegally distilled liquor, and it seemed to me that this
was, in mathematical terms, an analogue of illegally distilled liquor—no
theorems, nothing was proved, we just conjured statements out of thin air
somehow. It was like the mysterious moonbeams lighting up dancing Irish
leprechauns. Because moonshine also means nonsense, ridiculous, airy-
fairy will-o'-the-wisp stuff that you don't quite believe. So it seemed an
appropriate title.

That paper was written in a hell of a hurry, by the way. It was a sort of
telegraphic communication. Because we wanted to get back to exploring.
It was a very exciting time. And it was written in a breathless style, and
the first line conveys the feeling: "A quick summary of the recent amazing
discoveries about the Fischer-Griess 'MONSTER' simple group . . ."

It's not like most mathematical papers because it doesn't have any theorems. It's all conjectures and numerical coincidences. They are just astonishing discoveries, all shattering. We were just making guesses and
distilling stuff from old and new sources and seeing that it was all the
same. And it started off a whole lot of stuff. You were at that meeting in
Japan, 30 years later or something, and it's still going on. And in a certain
sense, we still don't have a ghost of a clue about anything. Why are we
here? There's this question Stephen Hawking raised: Why does the universe go to all the bother of existing? I suppose we get used to the fact
that these great unanswerable questions are unanswerable. But this one
about the Monster doesn't seem as if it should be one of these great unanswerable questions.

Prototypes of the Rubik's Cube first hit Budapest toy shops in late 1977,
and via a circuitous route Conway got his hands on 1 of the first cubes
outside Hungary. Another object of his affections and procrastinations.

The cube came to be used as a prop in many an undergraduate group
theory course, since the set of moves to solve the cube is a group. Conway never used it in class, nor did its relevance to group theory explain
his interest cum obsession. His knowledge of group theory did not, in
his view, inform or influence how he solved the cube, or at least not very
much. His best time for curing the cube, for solving it, was 1 minute and
30 seconds, and he got it down to "Three Looks." He carefully inspected

the chaotic arrangement of squares before hiding the cube under a table or behind his back and twisting it around for a while; then he paused and examined the cube a second time, followed by more blind twisting; and then after the third look and some more secret twisting he victoriously held aloft a solved cube. And of course he developed an algorithm and a mnemonic. He worked his cube so hard that she fell apart. He stuck sticky tape inside, holding the cubelets loosely in place, but they often popped out of joint from their cubicles and he had to twist her gingerly, until she disintegrated for good.

This provided an added incentive to attend the next International Congress of Mathematicians, held in 1978 in Helsinki. Then aged 40, Conway wasn't likely to win the Fields Medal, but technically (due to the award's age limit) this would be his last shot. Not that this was at all on his mind. More important was that the cube was still available only in Hungary and there were bound to be Hungarians in Helsinki. Conway spent his time at the Congress running around asking

Do you know any Hungarians? I need another cube!

The Fields Medals went to Pierre Deligne, Charles Fefferman, Grigory Margulis, and Daniel Quillen. The Rubik's Cube went to Conway. He had all but given up, but shortly after the Congress, while he was walking along the quayside, a Frenchwoman approached. "You are Conway?" He flirtatiously agreed. She reached into her handbag and produced the object of his desire. "This is from Tamás Varga," she said, and walked away.

On another occasion entirely, a Frenchwoman approached and said, "You are Conway!" Again he agreed. She said, "Come with me!"—to a party.

I remember nothing more about her, or the party for that matter, other than I enjoyed it.

And these encounters remind Conway of yet another story involving a Frenchwoman, or perhaps it was a Frenchman, this time at the International Congress in Nice, France. Conway was at another party, a garden party with a pig roasting on a spit. There was a table of English speakers and a table of French speakers. The Frenchwoman, let's say, approached Conway's table and asked, gesturing to 2 spare chairs, "May we?"

Mais oui!

It is his proudest pun.

I've been trying to set it up again ever since.

12.

TRUTH BEAUTY, BEAUTY TRUTH

Symmetry is what we see at a glance.

—BLAISE PASCAL

The ATLAS continued to creep along. A popular Tuesday number theory seminar provided yet another distraction, attracting math students and professors alike, as well as an interloper named Reo Fortune, a Cambridge social anthropologist and the second of Margaret Mead's 3 husbands. Noticing the presence of this odd man out, some were given to wonder whether Dr. Fortune wasn't conducting a field study observing the oddball habits of mathematicians—just as in Papua New Guinea he and Mead had observed the cannibalistic behavior of the Mundugumor people and the male-female relations among the Mountain Arapesh. In the lectures Dr. Fortune daringly asked questions, and these "Fortunate questions," as they came to be known, conveyed a certain off-kilter knowledge of the subject, so he'd clearly done his research. During a session when Ian Cassels held forth, Dr. Fortune interrupted and asked: "But you can't square the circle, can you?" As it turned out, Dr. Fortune had no interest in the mathematicians. He was an amateur number theorist with bona fides, such as the namesake Fortunate numbers and Fortune's conjecture about primes.

The French anthropologist Claude Lévi-Strauss was known to have expressed a genuine investigative interest in mathematicians. His motive was to co-opt their tools in analyzing human behavior. He sought out advice from his fellow countryman, mathematician André Weil. Weil taught him the basics of group theory, which came to underpin Lévi-Strauss's book on kinship behavior, *The Mathematics of Man*, an investigation into who marries whom in Australian aborigine societies. How group theory, the mathematics of symmetry, plays out in tribal mating patterns might not seem immediately obvious. At root it's a combinatorial problem, and certain strictures apply, just as when combining the regular polygons to produce the Platonic solids only select couplings work.

Conway employs an entomologically inspired algorithm in explaining his own mating patterns. That he'd made a name for himself as a ladies' man, a Casanova even, many women can attest. I asked a prominent mathematician when she first met Conway. "I'm not sure," she says. "It goes back pretty far, well over 30 years ago. I can tell you he made a pass at me. He was very serious about bedding me. And I know of several women. Some said yes and several said no." Another respondent, without divulging whether she was ever the recipient of overtures herself, recalls first meeting Conway at a Cambridge Christmas party. He was in formal attire, but missing the bow tie, and he volunteered that it had been left behind in a lovely lady's room. Another respondent can't say she was the object of flirtation, though at a conference she witnessed Conway following another female mathematician into a hotel room. Even lately he's been known, sometimes in all seriousness and sometimes in all silliness, to propose marriage. To a recently divorced and like-minded group theorist, for example. And to me. I surprised him by solving one of the most frustrating puzzles he'd encountered, a chirally asymmetrical twist of metal bars called "the Menace" that can easily be connected but not so easily disconnected. He'd been carrying it around for a week and found nobody who could do the disconnection. He demonstrated for a while and then passed it my way.

Go to it. I'll be back in an hour.

I'd watched his hands and noticed what seemed like the pivotal loop-de-loop that liberated the bars, and then, ta-da, there they were, freed in a matter of minutes.

Dammit! You can't be confused. Well, it might take me a while to get rid of Diana, but will you marry me?

Diana, his third wife, had in fact already left him. He'd returned from a conference, followed by a love letter from a longtime on-again off-again dalliance. Since he never opens his own mail, Diana was the accidental recipient. Usually Conway tried to be more careful in this regard, keeping dalliances secret. Then again, "I was always pleased," notes Rob Curtis, of the times when Conway had a new woman. "Because he'd clean himself up. It was a dead giveaway." This is a lie, says Conway; he never cleans himself up, not even for a woman. But usually Conway at least attempts to keep things on the quiet, and he likes to keep things quiet forever thereafter. This I discovered upon presenting him with a bygone fling's name (provided to me by her son). He threatened to cease cooperating and cancel the Cambridge research trip if I pursued it. Though as one might expect he wasn't beneath manufacturing the odd rumor. He tells a story about himself and Andrew Ranicki, a mathematician now at the University of Edinburgh, who bills himself on his business card as a "Professor of Algebraic Surgery." Ranicki is noticeable for his bursting nest of curly white hair, and by Conway's telling he's also noticeable for his very loud and distinctive laugh.

> There was one other person at Cambridge who had a distinctive laugh, and that was Francis Crick. Francis Crick every now and then on Thursdays turned up to this interdisciplinary seminar at the statistics department, and what happened was you walked up to the department and you heard this laugh and you thought, It must be Thursday! And it would be if you heard that laugh. But Ranicki—he once said something which was vaguely insulting. It was only a joke, but I slapped his face. And he said, "I'll get you back for that sometime."

I wouldn't have bothered following up with Ranicki, but I happened to meet him at a math conference, and later by e-mail he elaborated. "What happened," he says, "was that I invited my rather formidable Aunt Gerda (my father's sister) to a feast at Trinity College, Cambridge, at which John was also a guest. I introduced them to each other saying: 'This is my great Aunt Gerda, and this is the great Conway.' It was slightly ironic, but hardly insulting! At any rate, Conway did slap my face . . ."

> And it was this wonderful thing that happened. There was later some social

occasion, and I was standing there chatting to various people, and Andrew strode into the room and said "Hello," and I turned around and he slapped my face really hard.

Ranicki aimed for the beard, to cushion the blow.

I knew what it was about, because he had threatened to slap my face on this previous occasion. We had a great time because my wife was there and she wanted to know why he slapped my face, expecting there must be some sort of reason. And neither of us would explain, because it was finished. But all the women were terribly intrigued by this. What was it? It was obviously some deep thing. I'd stolen his mistress or something, that's what they thought. Actually it wasn't anything. But it was much more interesting to let them wonder.

And it's best to be left wondering about Conway's tally of conquests; there's nothing to be gained in attempting to name all the names. Yet a question does arise: How, pray tell, does an unkempt nerdy mathematician get so lucky?

I don't know that it's a matter of luck, really. I studied the beasts carefully over a large number of years. Though it didn't help me much with the ones I married, I must say.

Conway's first wife knew her husband possessed 2 interests in life: math and sex. She often sat for hours listening to him talk math, and she put up with his throwing chairs around in frustration when she failed to follow along. "I was sympathetic but I didn't understand," she says. "I once suddenly had an insight with something connected to infinity, and John said with tears in his eyes, 'That's the most sensible thing you have ever said.' I wished I understood it better. I knew he lived for math. Math was his life and one respected that." Of math and sex, Eileen could supply only the latter.

By the late 1970s, the marriage was falling apart. The 40-something Conway left Eileen and coupled up with 30-something Larissa Queen, a Russian Ph.D. student in mathematics at Cambridge. She was about 7 years his junior, married twice before, with a young son.

But back to Conway's mating algorithm, which he borrowed from Jean-Henri Fabre, a reclusive nineteenth-century entomologist who taught in Corsica and Avignon. Hailed by Darwin as "the Homer of Insects," Fabre chronicled their lives and instincts with observations made mostly from his backyard, and he published a 10-volume treatise, *Souvenirs Entomologiques*. Until he lost it, Conway cherished his copy of *Insect Adventures*, the shorter version of the same work, translated and retold for youngsters.

> It's very interesting because he discusses insect behavior, and it's all just sort of mechanical and programmed, roughly speaking—behavior is governed by algorithms that require no memory.

Conway's staple story demonstrating his mating algorithm he titles "Wasp Logic," drawn from Fabre's discussions of the sand wasp.

> So this particular wasp, the female, stings a fly, wraps it in something like spiderweb except it's waspweb, if you understand me. And then the wasp digs a hole in the sand, puts the fly down there, lays her eggs in it, and then covers it up and flies away, having done her part for the continuance of the species.
>
> Fabre did this very clever experiment—it's one of a number of things he did along the same general line. When the wasp was busy filling in the hole after burying the fly, he put another ready-wrapped fly at the side. Then the wasp finished filling in the hole, turned aside, and saw the fly. And the program says, "If you see a fly resting on the sand, dig a hole." So the wasp dug a hole again, uncovering the fly that was already buried there. And the program says, "If you see a fly at the bottom of the hole, fill the hole in." So it filled the hole. Turned aside. Saw the fly. And so on.
>
> There is no memory in the algorithm. Even though only a minute has passed since the wasp buried the fly, it has no memory whatsoever of having done so. It just operates. And you see the point is, it's only a pretty small brain in there. You can't afford clever things like memory.

Conway's behavior with women is often characterized by a similar algorithmic amnesia.

Which is the sort of behavior that's gotten me into trouble over my lifetime: "If you see a pretty woman, marry it.'"

Perhaps the problem isn't the marrying per se.

Yeah. It's not the marrying. But I wanted the story to be repeatable.

Repeatable it was. He repeated it often. During the Cambridge research trip he repeated it for his sum chums over beer at the Champion
of the Thames pub. And he repeated it while visiting his sister Joan,
which is what prompted her to blurt out: "Australian lady!"

Which Australian lady?

"Weren't you one of her gentleman friends at one time? I'm trying to
think of her name . . ."
Silence. Then Conway's daughters chimed in, trying to help. "Fay Wel-
don, was it?" asked Annie. "Well known," offered Joan. "Germaine . . .?"
queried Rosie. She had it on the tip of her tongue. And then all of them in
unison: "Germaine Greer!!!"
Germaine Greer, author of *The Female Eunuch*, the 1970 international bestseller calling for the dismantling of the nuclear family and
rampant sexual freedom for women. Greer, described by *Life* magazine
as the "saucy feminist that even men like," is an alumnus of Newnham
College at Cambridge, where she received her doctorate in 1968.
Sitting there in his sister's cozy parlor, Conway exhaled an exasper-
ated mumble.

Oh god. Did I tell you that? Yes. Okay.

Thereupon he returned to his KenKen.

Once back in Princeton, I tracked down Greer's literary agent and
FedExed a letter on Institute letterhead—embossed with the official seal
depicting 2 women, the naked Truth holding a mirror with her friend
Beauty beside, a coupling that alludes to those famous lines by John

Keats: "'Beauty is Truth, Truth Beauty,—that is all Ye know on earth, and all ye need to know.'" After some pestering, Greer acknowledged my request for an interview but said she didn't have time. And Conway had no further comment. He wasn't about to dignify this latest of his sister's nonsense stories with a response. As far as I could discern, it would all seem to hinge on the context and meaning of that "that."

*Did I tell you **that**?*

And that "that" reminded me, if orthogonally, of something Eileen once said to her husband when she heard him talking with his fellow mathematicians about the math she didn't understand. "You're so affected," she said of the prissy way they pretentiously picked apart sentences. As Conway recalls:

> It was this business that I characterize as, "There was a *happy crowd of people* at the races yesterday" versus "There was a *crowd of happy people* at the races yesterday"—which do you mean? You know, in ordinary English they are the same thing. But if you say, "That's a large set of numbers" or "That's a set of large numbers" they mean 2 different things, and you have to ask, which do you mean? You have to be more careful about applying adjectives.
>
> I've often said that when you're speaking mathematical English, grammar is more important than it is in ordinary English, and people are usually surprised by that. And the reason is that in ordinary English you get hints from the context. You can't mean a happy crowd, because a crowd can't be happy. You mean a crowd of happy people.
>
> With mathematical statements you don't usually get information from the context, so you just have to ask, "Do you mean a large set of numbers, or a set of large numbers?" And when Eileen heard the way we were talking like this she said afterward, "Oh, you were being so affected and prissy, pretending it makes a difference." But it does make a difference! Mathematicians can't be careless. Logically the 2 statements are very different. One possible meaning is true, one possible meaning is false.

With distractions female and mathematical, *The ATLAS* made surreal slivers of progress. Conway became particularly fond of the Lyons group, which did impossible things to the order of:

$$2^8 \cdot 3^7 \cdot 5^6 \cdot 7 \cdot 11 \cdot 31 \cdot 37 \cdot 67$$
$$= 51{,}765{,}179{,}004{,}000{,}000$$
$$\approx 5 \cdot 10^{16}$$

Oh, let me tell you about Lyons!

First, some context, and another of Conway's twice-told tales. He and his second wife Larissa had moved into Stephen Hawking's old house at 6 Little St. Mary's Lane. Here Conway executed what he's been known to brag about to reporters deadpan as his most brilliant invention. There was a light switch awkwardly located behind the kitchen door. Upon going into the room, one had to partially close the door in order to reach around and turn on the light. Conway taped a matchbox to the back of the door in such a way that when the door opened, the matchbox hit the light switch and turned on the light. When Conway and Larissa invited their landlords, Stephen and his wife Jane, over for tea, Larissa went straight for the kitchen with Jane to show off her mastermind husband. Jane, having suffered the inconvenience of that light switch, exclaimed at the engineering. "Oh, come here, Stephen," she said. "Look at this ingenious thing. Now even you can switch on the light." They switched the light off and closed the door and Hawking came along in his wheelchair and banged the chair through the doorway (his standard way of opening doors). On went the light. Hawking started laughing, and then he started to cough, and cough and cough, a choking cough that had Conway seriously worried. But then Jane patted his back and the coughing fit passed.

I hadn't killed the famous cosmologist after all. And that was a great relief.

Conway has many fond memories of the house at Little St. Mary's Lane. His daughter Annie, whose school was nearby, would stop round for lunch and once found her father and Larissa reciting not poetry, but π. Larissa had asked her husband for the value of π beyond the few digits she knew, and then they decided that both of them should know more. Conway had memorized it as a teenager. His first job was up on scaffolding in a biscuit factory scrubbing the black ceiling, but since the ceiling never looked any cleaner for the scrubbing, he lay atop the scaffolding memorizing π instead, attaining 707 digits. Now the newlyweds decided to memorize 1,000 digits. Conway transcribed the string of numbers onto a poster and hung it on the living room wall opposite the sofa, and there they sat, staring at the poster, closing their eyes and reciting in 5-digit phrases. "I could never do that," said Annie. Her dad disagreed.

> Yes, you can. Anyone can. You can remember 50 digits before you go back to school.

And after school Annie returned with a friend, wanting 50 more. Conway and Larissa, at their 1,000-digit peak with π, strolled the banks of the River Cam, trading off at 20-digit intervals. Larissa was doing her Ph.D. on the Baby Monster, a subgroup of the Monster, which put potentially more sophisticated conversations about group theory out-of-bounds. Next the happy couple memorized the orders of all 26 sporadic groups. And this brings us back to the Lyons group.

> One day we were crossing King's Parade in Cambridge and I recited this 17-digit number—51,765,179,004,000,000—which is the order of the Lyons group. And then Larissa shouted, quite loudly: "LYONS!" Everybody on the street turned and looked, as if to say: Where! *Where* are the lions?

In the Classification Project's hunt for sporadic groups, there were now 2 remaining groups proving particularly hard cases: J_4 and the Monster. Both were predicted to exist but not yet constructed. Although Conway hadn't given up on the Monster, he went through a phase where he turned his attention exclusively to J_4. Meanwhile, back in the States, Bob Griess was newly married and newly impassioned. In the fall of 1979 he arrived for a sabbatical year at the Institute for Advanced Study. Holed up in the building that formerly housed John von Neumann's Electronic Computer Project, he set his mind to the Monster's construction. Other than some rest during Thanksgiving and Christmas Day, he worked nonstop. Every now and then the Institute's *éminence grise*, physicist Freeman Dyson, encountered him in the lunch line and asked how he was doing. By mid-January, following several tedious checks, Griess was confident he had the construction. He still had to put it all together in a publishable paper, but he sent out an informal announcement. Conway and crew were hard on the trail of J_4 when they got word. At first they were disappointed, since in a sense Griess's success meant they had lost the race. They took consolation in the fact that, when they corralled J_4, as was sure to happen soon, that would make them the last people in the world to construct a simple group.

Superficially, Conway and Griess's brute-force methods were similar in that Conway was again staying up all night long—it saved rebooting the brain. He pulled 20 or so all-nighters in search of J_4, with an interlude in Santa Cruz for a conference that addressed the imminent end of the Classification Project. When he returned to Cambridge he was struck down with a virulent flu. And then the critical idea for finding J_4, involving many hours of computer time, hit him while crossing the road, this time inducing no deleterious chain reactions with garbage trucks, which was remarkable because it was becoming apparent that Conway was no longer operating maximally.

"I must tell you about the coffee and the Conway error," says Richard Parker. "It's the key to understanding that chap." They'd been up all night working on J_4. They sat down at the backgammon table for a restorative game. "Conway went off and made a coffee, and then three quarters of the way back he spilled some on the floor. Then he stopped and poured some more on the floor. By which time I had completely lost control of myself and I yelled at him, 'Why did you pour coffee on the floor?' About half an hour later he admitted it. He wished there was less coffee on the floor, and then he made a Conway Error. A Conway Error is an error of sign, you confuse more with less, plus with minus—he's known to do that when lecturing; he confuses plus with minus. So here he did the same thing. He wished there was *less* coffee on the floor but instead he poured *more* coffee on the floor."

Errors also infested *The ATLAS* at an alarming rate, despite Simon Norton's troubleshooting. The authors kept an error book, and they noticed that the error discovery rate increased from 1 error per week to 1 error per day as they neared the manuscript deadline. The guard book by now was not only obese but bloated, and when the binding reached 6 inches deep it burst. Conway sewed the book back together with a curved bodkin and a pair of pliers, using some fake leather from a decrepit common room chair. So all the errors were due to the general precariousness of the book's existence, and procedural glitches, as much as intellectual short circuits. Some errors were caused by the scissors-and-glue assembly process, such as the minus sign that was inadvertently "guillotined off." The most egregious error occurred when Conway, Parker, and Norton congregated to finalize J_4's page. Pecking away at his orange typewriter, Conway probed Norton's brain for a relatively trivial piece of information. Norton delivered his usual quantumly quick answer. Conway typed in the requested data and then let out a gasp. Simon Norton had made an error. Thereupon Conway declared:

That is the beginning of the end!

By the early 1980s, the Classification Project was complete, or very nearly so. It was the largest collaborative mathematical effort in history. Internationally, hundreds of mathematicians systematically eliminated or confirmed groups, submitting tens of thousands of pages that amassed into a theorem and a proof. The project leader, Rutgers's Daniel Gorenstein, called it "The Thirty Years' War." He declared the war over in 1983, though revisions and a second-generation proof and a computer-check with a proof assistant carried on for another 3 decades. All the while, Conway considered himself an outsider to the enterprise, though he certainly got in on a good piece of the action. And from the sidelines, in an article in the *Mathematical Intelligencer*, he gave his verdict:

I was asked some time ago, about the question whether it was likely that all the finite simple groups were now known, whether I was an optimist or a pessimist? I replied that I was a pessimist, but still hopeful, and was delighted to find that this answer was misinterpreted in exactly the way I had maliciously desired!

Among those who are engaged in the great cooperative attempt to classify all the finite simple groups, "optimism" usually describes the belief that there are no more such groups to be found, since new groups appear as obstacles in the path of progress. My own view is that simple groups are beautiful things, and I'd like to see more of them, but am reluctantly coming around to the view that there are likely no more to be seen.

And now with the classification done, did anything remain for all those group theorists to do?

Yes! Lots! Understand it all, for one thing.

The Monster, especially. During a panel on large proofs at the Royal Society in London, a mathematician remarked, "Nothing good came of the Classification Project!" Sir Michael Atiyah, disagreed. "Not nothing," he said. "Only the Monster." But the Monster was still being coy. Griess's construction seemed only to have increased the intrigue, providing a partial illumination, revealing ever more eddies and undertows to ensnare mathematicians and scientists alike. When I got Griess on the phone, for the most part he agreed. He says there are still questions about the Monster, about its internal structure and its role in mathematics, that he would certainly like to see answered. The big question, he says, about the sporadic groups in general and the Monster in particular, is how they'll find their place in science. A hint of an answer came in 1982, shortly after he published his long-awaited paper detailing the construction that proved the Monster's existence. The paper ran to 102 pages, under the title "The Friendly Giant" (he hoped this new name would stick; it didn't).

Griess sent Freeman Dyson an advance copy of the paper. A few days after receiving it in his mailbox, Dyson addressed a typically distinguished group of scholars gathered at the Institute for a colloquium, but he spoke on the atypical subject of "Unfashionable Pursuits." In his talk he proposed that the Monster might be the answer to one of the great questions in physics. "The problems which we face as guardians of scientific progress," he said, "are how to recognize the fruitful unfashionable idea, and how to support it. To begin with, we may look around at the world of mathematics and see whether we can identify unfashionable ideas which might later emerge as essential building blocks for the physics of the twenty-first century." He surveyed the history of science, alighting eventually upon the Classification Project and the Monster and the "magnificent zoo of new sporadic groups." He asked, "What has all this to do with physics?"

Probably nothing. Probably the sporadic groups are merely a pleasant backwater in the history of mathematics, an odd little episode far from the mainstream of progress. We have never seen the slightest hint that the symmetries of the physical universe are in any way connected with the symmetries of the sporadic groups. So far as we know, the physical universe would look and function just as it does whether or not the sporadic groups existed. But we should not be too sure that there is no connection. Absence of evidence is not the same thing as evidence of absence. Stranger things have happened in the history of physics than the unexpected appearance of sporadic groups. We should always be prepared for surprises. I have to confess to you that I have a sneaking hope, a hope unsupported by any facts or any evidence, that sometime in the twenty-first century physicists will stumble upon the Monster group, built in some unsuspected way into the structure of the universe. This is of course only a wild speculation, almost certainly wrong.

In January 1983, John and Larissa welcomed into the world their son Alex, and that November the couple married at the Cambridge registry office. Conway has been known to leave a child alone in the house sleeping soundly in bed while he goes to the coffee shop and gets on with his day, forgetting that his duty was to bring along said progeny to the coffee shop where it would be fetched by its mother. With Conway and Larissa, at least once a similar scene played out. Conway sauntered into the common room, trailed by a supplicant, and fielded an urgent greeting from his wife: "*Where's* the baby?!"

DUNNO.

Conway knew from Larissa's tone that she knew full well where the baby was. He was making a game of it, making a game out of the mundane daily details. The Baby Monster, as Alex became known around the department, soon got in on the fun. As a toddler he learned to perform like his father. He stood on a chair at the blackboard, wildly scribbling and intermittently turning to address his audience: "Blah blah blah blah blah blah blah, blah blah blah blah blah. Blah, blah blah blah blah blah.

Blah, blah blah. Blah blah blah blah. Blah blah blah blah blah. Blah blah. Blah blah blah. Blah, blah blah blah."

With the Baby Monster and Alex Ryba, 1984.

The ATLAS, now under way for more than a decade, got short shrift yet again when Conway decided to go back to the Monster. He'd been reading Griess's 102-page paper. He was tempted to try for a simpler construction. Attending a summer conference in Durham with Larissa, he'd agreed to be the spouse, to truly take care of the baby and let his wife attend the talks. He wheeled Alex's pram around outside the auditorium, and as he went back and forth he tinkered with the Monster. By the end of the conference he had a new construction.

"Once John starts thinking, he doesn't stop," Larissa once said. "Not that it prevents him from doing other things like bathing the baby. When I get home, he'll just say, 'Well, I bathed the baby and proved this or that.'" But then as per usual he summarily dropped his Monster construction, he didn't write up the paper, and then he resumed with *The ATLAS*—or perhaps he first took a break with some backgammon, since Simon Norton had introduced the concept of the "long game" in which players go around and around and around the board for hours, never bearing off. A year later, Conway asked his wife what she wanted for her birthday. "I want you to write that damn paper!" It took 27 pages to Griess's 102, and it bore the dedication "To One Who Will Understand." This was a reference to a story in P. G. Wodehouse's collection aptly titled *Heart of a Goof*. The protagonist, aspiring novelist Rodney Spelvin, used the same dedication to cover all his many girlfriends. Larissa was in on the joke, since beneath the dedication Conway added her birthday, the very day he put his Monster in the mailbox.

For his crowning contribution to the Monster, he gave series of lectures. He worked it into the Part III course he gave each year; whereas most professors taught the same material year in year out, Conway shared whatever was on his mind. That year it was the sporadic simple groups, and a good number of the classes he devoted to the Monster, fitting together pieces of the puzzle with his stylishly sloppy technique. He strode up to the chalkboard on the first day, ceremoniously broke the chalk, scattered pieces at the ready along the ledge, and in a speedy blur peeled onto the blackboard a rat-a-tat stream of 54 digits that equaled the Monster group's order. During a subsequent class he discovered a mistake in that number. He smudged out the error with his fist and inserted the correction. By the end of the lectures his audience reemerged into the light of reality typically awed by his virtuoso display. The next day, however, the hangover rendered things a bit cloudy, and students yet again had to wait a very long time for the promised lecture notes that might help them reconstruct the course of events. A young mathematical physicist ran into him on King's Parade and asked for an ETA. Conway acknowledged that the notes might nearly exist. His inquisitor asked, "May I have a copy?"

You can if you come and help me do the photocopying.

In the midst of all the Monster madness, Conway advanced through the ranks at Cambridge. In 1981, the Royal Society installed him as a Fellow. "Not before time," commented department head Ian Cassels. Conway went around translating the FRS initials, telling people he was now officially

Filthy Rotten Swine!

To put it mildly, he was an original character among a demographic still largely populated by gray men closeted away in their colleges and living within a system that was only gradually transitioning away from its overtly stuffy heritage. He was the sort of person in whom colleagues could confide. They didn't worry what they said to him or how they said it, whereas with some professors one walked on eggshells. He was also ever willing to do a star turn at the math faculty's annual outreach courses for schoolteachers. The chair of the organizing committee, mathematical physicist Peter Goddard (later the director at Princeton's Institute of Advanced Study who invited me to visit), had merely to ask, and without hesitation Conway enthusiastically agreed. Goddard would double-check with Mrs. Conway to avoid any double bookings, and on the appointed day he'd assign a detail to keep track of Conway's whereabouts from 2 o'clock onward, and then at 4 o'clock take him by the elbow and lead him to the lecture room, where he would stride in, break the chalk, and commence his performance. "He was always intellectually outstanding," recalls Goddard, "effortlessly fun and accessible and entertaining, completely world-class—what more could you want?" True, one might have to go to considerable lengths to get Conway *to* the venue, but by comparison he was low-maintenance—some Cambridge mathematicians in similar scenarios could be ruthlessly demanding and impolite.

In 1983 Conway became a full professor, with his Ph.D. students numbering 10. In addition to *The ATLAS* coauthors Rob Curtis, Rob Wilson, and (ostensibly) Simon Norton, he most notably acquired Richard Borcherds, now of Berkeley. Borcherds was self-diagnosed as weird, and he recognized in himself some of the symptoms of Asperger's. Conway, by Borcherds's own reckoning, rescued him. No one else would take him on as a Ph.D. student. Frank Adams was thought to be the perfect fit, but he wouldn't accept Borcherds owing to an anomaly in his application.

> I'm not altogether sure what happened, but here's what I gathered. There was a form he had to fill in, and his friends got ahold of it and filled in silly answers. Like where it said, "Sex: Male or Female," they added a third option, "Yes, please!" Frank Adams was rather serious, and I asked him what happened, and I suggested Richard wasn't responsible and tried to smooth things over. He said, "Well, if you saw it, it was absolutely disgusting." I asked him, "Can you give me some example?" "No, I can't, I really can't."

Conway was one of the few mathematicians Borcherds had known about before arriving at Cambridge. As a high school student he'd read all Gardner's columns. "He walked up to me in the library," Borcherds recalls, "and asked if I wanted to work with him. He'd heard I was trying to find a Ph.D. supervisor and was having some trouble. I was a bit strange in those days and he seemed prepared to cope with slightly odd Ph.D. students. I was bad at interacting with people, although by mathematicians' standards I wasn't that unusual. People end up in math because they don't have social skills to do anything else. There are plenty of mathematicians who have perfectly good social skills and could fit in, could pass, wouldn't look out of place in the outside world. But math does have a somewhat higher proportion than normal of people who are slightly odd. There is more tolerance for eccentricity. It may be people behave oddly because there is a tolerance, and that if they all worked for merchant banks they would all wear suits and behave normally."

Borcherds didn't take part in the Conway social scene, all the pubbing and gaming. Though they were not without common interests. He once walked into the common room and found Conway and Larissa sitting on the sofa with Parker, all of them looking perplexed about something Monstrous that they'd been teasing out for weeks.

> Borcherds came by and asked us, "What are you doing?" And we told him. A month or more later, we were all sitting there when he came by and asked again, "What are you doing?" Same thing! He said, "Oh, didn't I tell you? I solved that." That was the first time I realized he was really good.

Borcherds had no expectations about what a good adviser would or should do, and Conway met those expectations.

> He was too bright. He never needed me.

He spent a lot of time hiding from Conway. The problem he tackled for his thesis, a messy problem pertaining to the Leech lattice and other lattices, was a problem Conway told him not to touch. Even with minimal interaction, Borcherds accumulated the usual fund of Conway anecdotes. "Once in the photocopier room Conway came in and took his sandals off and stapled them together with a stapler and wandered off again." And, he recalls, "There was a funny incident in a lecture. He couldn't decide between 2 possible topics. He said, 'All right, we'll toss a coin.' And the coin actually managed to end up on its edge."

By 1984, *The ATLAS* at long last approached its end. When a group reached completeness, it was awarded and stamped in red with the "Conway Seal of Grudging Approval." The paste-ups went to computer services for printing on the Diabolo printer, which lived up to its name, devilishly inserting more errors. The authors agreed to deliver the manuscript in "fascicules" of 25 pages at a time. Every month, a man from Oxford University Press visited, and the day before the visit the Atlantis crew spread out the 25 pages around the room's perimeter, a page per chair. They left them out overnight with signs warning: "Do Not Disturb!" When the pressman arrived the next day they did a processional walkabout, dictating special instructions for replicating this behemoth. With that fascicule sent on its way, the sum chums went about finalizing the next fascicule for the next month's visit, repeating this marathon over and over for almost a year.

With the final proofs sent there was great relief that it was all over.

But no, it wasn't. They had not written the introduction. As the authors later recounted in the book accompanying the tenth anniversary celebrations, the introduction "had to be substantial in order to explain all our notation, but it was always intended to be . . . a kind of introduction to simple groups in general. The resulting tour-de-force was almost entirely the work of Conway, but perhaps the rest of us had the more difficult task—of persuading him to do it!" They goaded him by offering to write the introduction themselves, knowing full well that the prospect of such mediocrity would incite Conway to action. In his remarks, Conway absolved the authors of their errors by borrowing a disclaimer from the first edition of the *Encyclopaedia Britannica* in 1771: "With regard to errors in general, whether falling under the denomination of mental, typographical, or accidental, we are conscious of being able to point to a greater number than any critic whatever. Men who are acquainted with the innumerable difficulties attending the execution of a work of such an extensive nature will make proper allowances. . . ." And this big book of groups bore resemblance to an encyclopedia in another way as well.

I called it scholarship. Us mathematicians, we are usually a bit down on scholarship. We do research, stuff that's new. I'm not putting scholarship down in any way, but that's not the sort of stuff we do—we mathematicians find something that nobody's ever found before, rather than organizing old material. But *The ATLAS* was scholarship. It was taking a whole lot of information and organizing it and presenting it in a way that people would find easy to absorb. And my god, it took 15 years. But it was 15 years mostly occupied with playing backgammon.

Published in 1985, *The ATLAS* was truly an amazing accomplishment, perhaps the most important book in group theory. It dominated the Cambridge math department's annual report that year; the report said nothing but "*The ATLAS* has finally appeared." Conway has not forgotten the concluding collective sentiment:

Thank god, it's excreted!

To which Richard Parker added: "After 15 years of constipation." Which Simon Norton corrected: "I think 'pregnancy' is a better metaphor."

When I sought out Conway for further elucidation on *The ATLAS*, he was in his own world, as usual—as his friend the geometrical sculptor Marc Pelletier astutely notes, "Conway has one toe in the third dimension, and where the rest of him is at any given time is anybody's guess." Before Conway pulled himself together, back to the coordinates of 3-dimensional reality that would allow him to properly register who was standing there before him, he gave me a welcoming greeting that was slightly askew.

Hello, Love.

Cognitive dissonance ringing in my ears, I could be confident at least of still being in his good books. But really, he explains, it's just the Liverpool in him—everyone calls everyone "Love" in Liverpool. I told him what was on my list for that day: a Q&A on *The ATLAS*.

Yes, but can I answer your questions? I don't know.

HN = F_{5+}

	ind	1A	2A	2B	3A	3B	4A	4B	4C	5A	5B	5C	D*	5E	6A	6B	6C	7A	8A	8B	9A	10A	10B	10C	10D	E*	10F	10G	H*	11A	12A	12B	12C	14A	15A	15B	C*	19A	B**	20A	B*	20C	20D	E*	
	:	@	@	@	@	@	@	@	@	@	@	@	@	@	@	@	@	@	@	@	@	@	@	@	@	@	@	@	@	@	@	@	@	@	@	@	@	@	@	@	@	@	@	@	
		2730	1774	36	544	29	15	5	3	630	500			2	1							2	1																						
		30912000000	08000	86400	320	160	360	760	840	000	000	15000	15000	500	440	576	360	420	80	64	27	000	200	800	600	600	100	100	100	22	72	48	12	28	180	30	30	19	19	80	80	40	20	20	
		p power	A	A	A	A	B	A	B	A	A	A	A	A	AA	AB	BB	A	B	A	B	BA	AA	BB	DB	CB	EA	EB	EB	A	AB	BA	CC	AA	AA	DB	CB	A	A	CA	CA	BB	EC	DC	
		p' part	A	A	A	A	A	A	A	A	A	A	A	A	AA	AB	BB	A	A	A	A	BA	AA	BB	CB	DB	EA	EB	EB	A	AB	AA	BC	AA	AA	CB	DB	A	A	BA	BA	AB	CC	DC	
χ_{1}	+	1	1	1	1	1	1	1	1	1	1	1	1	1	1	1	1	1	1	1	1	1	1	1	1	1	1	1	1	1	1	1	1	1	1	1	1	1	1	1	1	1	1	1	χ_{1}
χ_{2}	+	133	21	5	7	-2	5	1	-3	-7	8	5b5+3	*	3	3	-1	2	0	-1	1	1	-4	1	0	b5+3	*	1	r5	-r5	1	1	-1	0	0	2	-b5	*	0	0	0	0	1	*	b5	χ_{2}
χ_{3}	+	133	21	5	7	-2	5	1	-3	-7	8	*	5b5+3	3	3	-1	2	0	-1	1	1	-4	1	0	*	b5+3	1	-r5	r5	1	1	-1	0	0	2	*	-b5	0	0	0	0	1	b5	*	χ_{3}
χ_{4}	+	760	56	-8	22	4	8	0	0	20	10	-10	-10	5	2	-2	4	4	0	0	1	6	-4	2	2	2	1	-3	-3	1	0	2	0	0	2	-1	-1	0	0	-2	-2	0	0	0	χ_{4}
χ_{5}	+	3344	176	16	41	-4	16	8	0	14	-31	4	4	9	5	1	4	5	0	0	2	1	6	1	-4	-4	1	1	1	0	-1	1	0	1	-4	1	1	0	0	1	1	-2	0	0	χ_{5}
χ_{6}	+	8778	154	-54	21	3	10	-10	2	28	28	5b5+18	*	3	1	-3	3	0	0	-2	0	4	4	-4	5b5+6	*	-1	1	1	0	-1	1	-1	0	1	-b5	*	0	0	0	0	0	b5	*	χ_{6}
χ_{7}	+	8778	154	-54	21	3	10	-10	2	28	28	*	5b5+18	3	1	-3	3	0	0	-2	0	4	4	-4	*	5b5+6	-1	1	1	0	-1	1	-1	0	1	*	-b5	0	0	0	0	0	*	b5	χ_{7}
χ_{8}	+	8910	286	78	27	0	14	10	6	20	35	15	15	5	7	3	0	-1	0	2	0	11	-4	3	3	3	1	3	3	0	1	-1	0	-1	2	0	0	-1	-1	-1	-1	0	1	1	χ_{8}
χ_{9}	+	9405	77	61	36	9	-3	9	-11	55	30	5	5	5	-4	4	1	4	-1	1	0	2	7	6	1	1	-3	1	1	0	0	0	1	0	1	-1	-1	0	0	2	2	-1	-1	-1	χ_{9}
χ_{10}	+	16929	385	33	27	0	17	1	9	29	54	-21	-21	4	7	3	0	-4	1	1	0	10	5	-2	3	3	0	-2	-2	0	1	-1	0	0	2	0	0	0	0	2	2	1	-1	-1	χ_{10}
χ_{11}	+	35112	616	40	84	12	24	0	0	-28	-13	10r5-8	-10r5-8	7	4	4	4	0	0	0	0	-9	-4	-5	-2r5	2r5	1	r5	-r5	0	0	0	0	0	-1	*	b5	0	0	-1	-1	0	0	0	χ_{11}
χ_{12}	+	35112	616	40	84	12	24	0	0	-28	-13	-10r5-8	10r5-8	7	4	4	4	0	0	0	0	-9	-4	-5	2r5	-2r5	1	-r5	r5	0	0	0	0	0	-1	b5	*	0	0	-1	-1	0	0	0	χ_{12}
χ_{13}	+	65835	539	-85	63	-18	11	-1	3	-105	85	25b5+15	*	5	-1	-1	2	0	1	-1	0	-11	-1	5	b5+3	*	-1	r5	-r5	0	-1	-1	0	0	3	b5	*	0	0	1	1	-1	*	-b5	χ_{13}
χ_{14}	+	65835	539	-85	63	-18	11	-1	3	-105	85	*	25b5+15	5	-1	-1	2	0	1	-1	0	-11	-1	5	*	b5+3	-1	-r5	r5	0	-1	-1	0	0	3	*	b5	0	0	1	1	-1	-b5	*	χ_{14}
χ_{15}	o	69255	-153	135	0	0	-9	-9	15	45	5	0	0	10	0	0	0	-3	-1	-1	0	-3	-3	5	0	0	2	0	0	-1	0	0	0	1	0	0	0	0	0	1	1	1	0	0	χ_{15}
χ_{16}	o	69255	-153	135	0	0	-9	-9	15	45	5	0	0	10	0	0	0	-3	-1	-1	0	-3	-3	5	0	0	2	0	0	-1	0	0	0	1	0	0	0	0	0	1	1	1	0	0	χ_{16}
χ_{17}	+	214016	1408	0	104	40	0	16	0	161	16	-24	-24	6	4	8	0	5	4	0	-1	8	-7	0	0	0	-8	0	0	0	-8	0	0	1	-1	0	0	0	0	0	0	1	0	0	χ_{17}
χ_{18}	+	267520	1408	256	148	4	0	0	0	120	20	20	20	-5	4	4	4	1	0	0	-2	8	8	-4	-4	-4	3	1	1	0	0	0	0	1	3	-1	-1	0	0	0	0	0	0	0	χ_{18}
χ_{19}	+	270864	880	-240	189	0	16	-8	0	134	-11	24	24	4	-11	-3	0	6	0	0	0	5	-10	5	0	0	0	0	0	0	1	1	0	-2	-1	0	0	0	0	1	1	2	0	0	χ_{19}
χ_{20}	+	365750	2310	310	35	35	6	10	-10	0	125	0	0	0	15	-5	-5	0	0	2	-1	-15	0	5	0	0	0	0	0	0	1	3	-1	0	0	0	0	0	0	1	1	0	0	0	χ_{20}
χ_{21}	+	374528	0	-256	56	38	0	0	0	-112	28	-10r5+8	10r5+8	-2	0	8	2	0	0	0	-1	0	0	4	-2r5+4	2r5+4	0	2b5	*	0	0	0	0	0	-4	*	-b5	0	0	0	0	0	0	0	χ_{21}
χ_{22}	+	374528	0	-256	56	38	0	0	0	-112	28	10r5+8	-10r5+8	-2	0	8	2	0	0	0	-1	0	0	4	2r5+4	-2r5+4	0	*	2b5	0	0	0	0	0	-4	-b5	*	0	0	0	0	0	0	0	χ_{22}
χ_{23}	+	406296	2904	24	162	0	40	0	0	-84	-204	6	6	11	5	-6	0	-5	0	0	0	4	4	4	-6	-6	-1	-1	-1	0	0	-2	0	-1	-3	0	0	0	0	0	0	0	0	0	χ_{23}
χ_{24}	+	653125	1925	325	-41	-5	5	21	5	125	0	0	0	0	-1	7	-5	4	1	-3	1	0	5	0	0	0	0	0	0	0	3	-1	-1	0	-1	0	0	0	0	0	0	1	0	0	χ_{24}
χ_{25}	o	656250	-1750	250	105	15	10	-10	10	0	0	0	0	0	5	1	-5	0	0	-2	0	0	0	0	0	0	0	0	0	1	-1	1	1	0	0	0	0	b19	**	0	0	0	0	0	χ_{25}
χ_{26}	o	656250	-1750	250	105	15	10	-10	10	0	0	0	0	0	5	1	-5	0	0	-2	0	0	0	0	0	0	0	0	0	1	-1	1	1	0	0	0	0	**	b19	0	0	0	0	0	χ_{26}
χ_{27}	+	718200	2520	120	0	-27	24	0	-8	0	75	-25b5	*	0	0	0	-3	0	0	0	0	-5	0	-5	-5b5	*	0	0	0	-1	0	0	1	0	0	-b5	*	0	0	-1	-1	0	b5	*	χ_{27}
χ_{28}	+	718200	2520	120	0	-27	24	0	-8	0	75	*	-25b5	0	0	0	-3	0	0	0	0	-5	0	-5	*	-5b5	0	0	0	-1	0	0	1	0	0	*	-b5	0	0	-1	-1	0	*	b5	χ_{28}
χ_{29}	+	1053360	1232	-592	63	36	-16	8	0	210	235	10	10	10	-1	-1	-4	0	0	0	0	7	2	3	-2	-2	2	-2	-2	0	-1	-1	0	0	3	1	1	0	0	-1	-1	-2	0	0	χ_{29}
χ_{30}	+	1066527	2079	-225	0	0	15	-9	-9	-63	152	30b5-3	*	-3	0	0	0	0	-1	-1	0	4	9	0	-3r5	3r5	-1	-r5	r5	0	0	0	0	0	0	0	0	0	0	0	0	1	1	1	χ_{30}
χ_{31}	+	1066527	2079	-225	0	0	15	-9	-9	-63	152	*	30b5-3	-3	0	0	0	0	-1	-1	0	4	9	0	3r5	-3r5	-1	r5	-r5	0	0	0	0	0	0	0	0	0	0	0	0	1	1	1	χ_{31}
χ_{32}	+	1185030	1078	390	189	0	-26	10	30	-280	155	0	0	10	-11	-3	0	0	0	2	0	3	8	-5	0	0	-2	0	0	0	1	1	0	0	-1	0	0	0	0	-1	-1	0	0	0	χ_{32}
χ_{33}	+	1354320	2288	336	-27	9	16	8	0	70	-55	-30	-30	-5	-7	-3	0	-5	0	0	0	13	-2	1	6	6	3	1	1	0	-1	1	0	-1	-2	0	0	0	0	1	1	-2	0	0	χ_{33}
χ_{34}	+	1361920	1792	0	112	40	0	32	0	-70	-80	0	0	-10	-8	0	0	0	0	0	1	-8	2	0	0	0	2	0	0	-1	-4	0	0	0	2	0	0	0	0	0	0	2	0	0	χ_{34}
χ_{35}	o	1361920	-1792	0	112	40	0	0	0	-70	-80	0	0	-10	8	0	0	0	0	0	1	8	-2	0	0	0	-2	0	0	-1	0	0	0	0	2	0	0	0	0	0	0	0	0	0	χ_{35}
χ_{36}	o	1361920	-1792	0	112	40	0	0	0	-70	-80	0	0	-10	8	0	0	0	0	0	1	8	-2	0	0	0	-2	0	0	-1	0	0	0	0	2	0	0	0	0	0	0	0	0	0	χ_{36}
χ_{37}	+	1575936	3200	0	216	0	0	-16	0	91	-64	-24	-24	-4	-4	0	0	5	-4	0	0	0	-5	0	0	0	0	0	0	-1	2	0	0	1	1	0	0	0	0	0	0	-1	0	0	χ_{37}
χ_{38}	+	1625184	-1056	96	162	0	-32	0	0	204	-66	-6	-6	-1	6	-6	0	1	0	0	0	-6	4	6	6	6	-1	1	1	0	0	-2	0	1	-3	0	0	0	0	-2	-2	0	0	0	χ_{38}
χ_{39}	+	2031480	1848	120	-162	0	8	0	0	120	-270	0	0	10	-6	6	0	-4	0	0	0	-2	8	10	0	0	-2	0	0	0	0	2	0	0	3	0	0	0	0	-2	-2	0	0	0	χ_{39}
χ_{40}	+	2375000	-1000	600	-190	80	40	0	0	0	0	0	0	0	-10	-6	0	5	0	0	-1	0	0	0	0	0	0	0	0	1	0	-2	0	1	0	0	0	0	0	0	0	0	0	0	χ_{40}
χ_{41}	+	2407680	-1408	256	36	36	0	0	0	280	180	-20	-20	5	-4	4	4	-5	0	0	0	-8	-8	-4	-4	-4	-3	1	1	0	0	0	0	-1	1	1	1	0	0	0	0	0	0	0	χ_{41}
χ_{42}	+	2661120	0	768	0	-54	0	0	0	0	120	10	10	-20	0	0	6	0	0	0	0	0	0	8	-2	-2	0	-2	-2	0	0	0	0	0	0	1	1	-1	-1	0	0	0	0	0	χ_{42}
χ_{43}	+	2784375	3375	375	-189	0	-25	-1	15	-125	0	0	0	0	11	3	0	6	-1	-1	0	0	-5	0	0	0	0	0	0	0	-1	-1	0	-2	1	0	0	1	1	0	0	-1	0	0	χ_{43}
χ_{44}	+	2985984	4608	0	0	0	0	0	0	-36	-16	24	24	-6	0	0	0	-6	0	0	0	8	-12	0	0	0	-2	0	0	1	0	0	0	2	0	0	0	1	1	0	0	0	0	0	χ_{44}
χ_{45}	+	3200000	-3200	0	104	-40	0	16	0	125	0	0	0	0	4	0	0	-1	-4	0	-1	0	5	0	0	0	0	0	0	1	-2	0	0	-1	-1	0	0	1	1	0	0	1	0	0	χ_{45}
χ_{46}	+	3424256	0	0	-64	8	0	0	0	176	256	16	16	-4	0	0	0	-4	0	0	2	0	0	0	0	0	0	0	0	0	0	0	0	0	-4	-2	-2	0	0	0	0	0	0	0	χ_{46}
χ_{47}	+	3878280	-2520	648	0	0	-24	0	-24	0	-95	15	15	20	0	0	0	0	0	0	0	5	0	-7	3	3	0	-2	-2	-1	0	0	0	0	0	0	0	0	0	1	1	0	1	1	χ_{47}
χ_{48}	+	4156250	-1750	-550	-175	5	10	30	10	0	0	0	0	0	5	-7	5	0	0	-2	-1	0	0	0	0	0	0	0	0	-1	3	1	1	0	0	0	0	0	0	0	0	0	0	0	χ_{48}
χ_{49}	+	4561920	-1408	0	216	0	0	-16	0	55	-80	0	0	-10	-4	0	0	-1	4	0	0	-8	7	0	0	0	2	0	0	0	2	0	0	-1	1	0	0	1	1	0	0	-1	0	0	χ_{49}
χ_{50}	+	4809375	175	-225	-216	0	15	-29	15	125	0	0	0	0	4	0	0	4	1	3	0	0	5	0	0	0	0	0	0	-1	-2	0	0	0	-1	0	0	0	0	0	0	1	0	0	χ_{50}
χ_{51}	+	5103000	2520	-360	0	0	-24	0	0	0	-125	0	0	0	0	0	0	0	0	0	0	-5	0	-5	0	0	0	0	0	1	0	0	0	0	0	0	0	-1	-1	2r5+1	-2r5+1	0	0	0	χ_{51}
χ_{52}	+	5103000	2520	-360	0	0	-24	0	0	0	-125	0	0	0	0	0	0	0	0	0	0	-5	0	-5	0	0	0	0	0	1	0	0	0	0	0	0	0	-1	-1	-2r5+1	2r5+1	0	0	0	χ_{52}
χ_{53}	+	5332635	-693	27	0	0	-21	-9	-21	-315	135	-15	-15	10	0	0	0	0	1	-1	0	7	-3	7	-3	-3	2	2	2	0	0	0	0	0	0	0	0	0	0	-1	-1	1	-1	-1	χ_{53}
χ_{54}	+	5878125	-4675	-275	36	-45	45	9	5	-125	0	0	0	0	-4	4	-5	1	-1	1	0	0	-5	0	0	0	0	0	0	0	0	0	-1	1	1	0	0	0	0	0	0	-1	0	0	χ_{54}

What do you do with *The ATLAS*? What do you see when you look at the character tables?

> Eh. Ha. Heh. Yes, I just can't easily convey to you what happens. Let's go get *The ATLAS* and see if that helps.

We went into the common room, making a sharp left toward a massive carved-oak credenza, his treasure chest of prized possessions, unlocked but at least safe from some horrible fate in his office dump. He swung out the bottom left door and pulled open a wide, shallow slip of a drawer, such a perfect home for the book that it seemed custom-made to serve that very purpose. Back in the alcove, he plunked into his armchair and opened the red cover at a random spot (see page 260)—

> Here it is, *The ATLAS*, a book full of numbers. It's hard to explain what character tables are. They tell you numerical facts about the groups; they are the most compendious way to convey information about groups. But *The ATLAS* is not about numbers. It's about beautifully symmetrical things.
>   You won't understand any of this, so let's turn past it. When we were first working on *The ATLAS*, we didn't quite appreciate it. So you won't. I think it's best to get away from explaining with numbers. I use numbers reluctantly. It's the only way I can work out the beautiful things about these groups. I would do something else, draw pictures if I could—but I can't draw beautifully symmetric things in 7-dimensional spaces, or in case of the Monster, in 196,883-dimensional space. Even better, I would make the objects if I could; I would do it visually somehow, but I can't, so I do it with numbers. Numbers don't frighten me, which they do other people. They don't leave me cold, either. For me, numbers are a substitute for touch, feel, sight, everything else. With high-dimensional space, I can't touch it, can't feel it, can't see it. I can calculate it, but the calculation isn't the point. The numbers are a set of instructions. A set of instructions isn't beautiful, but that's what the numbers are, a set of instructions point by point.

And as with Chuck Close's pointillist paintings, it's not the dots that matter so much as the overall effect. Turning past that random page we'd started on, leafing backward through more pages of numbers, we arrived at the beginning.

What do we say here in the introduction . . . ? "The theory of groups is the theory of the different possible kinds of symmetry, and as such finds applications throughout mathematics and the sciences whenever symmetrical objects or theories are being discussed."

The ATLAS tells us the basic ways things can be symmetrical. One way is the rotation group of the icosahedron, A5. It's on the first page. Up at the top it gives the order of the icosahedral group, which is 60—these are the 60 true symmetries, the rotational symmetries you can actually achieve by moving the icosahedron. A little bit further down it says that the number of all the symmetries, rotational plus reflections, say, is 60 times 2, which is 120.

Looking at the icosahedron from different vantage points we can see some of these different symmetries. If we look at the icosahedron face on, as we might be most accustomed to seeing it . . .

. . . and if we imagine someone putting axes through the 10 pairs of faces, then rotating this object around in 60 different ways, the object will look exactly the same. For each face we can turn it 3 different ways, and there are 20 faces, so 3 x 20 = 60.

Or we could look at the icosahedron from a different angle, with an edge facing out . . .

Again let's count only the rotations. For each edge we can rotate it 2 ways, and there are 30 edges, and 2 × 30 gives us 60 again.

Then if we look at the icosahedron with a vertex pointing directly at us . . .

. . . there are 5 rotations ×12 vertices, which gives us 60 symmetries AGAIN.

In a way, this is the same thing that happens with the Escher picture that I call Angels and Devils. If you look at the object one way you see a big overall symmetry, and if you look at it another way you see another symmetry, a subset of the larger overall symmetry. That's why I liken these objects to Christmas tree ornaments. Because you look and see a starry object, and then it turns slightly as it hangs on the tree, and—oh, damn, that perspective is gone.

Lots of things have the same symmetries. The symmetries of these objects, the symmetry group, turn out to be more fundamental, more essential, than the objects themselves. And so the symmetries can be applied to other objects. What you do, in fact, in group theory is you ignore the object that you are taking the symmetries of, because roughly speaking there are simply too many objects around. There's the icosahedron and the great icosahedron and the stellated icosahedron. And there's the dodecahedron, the great dodecahedron, the stellated dodecahedron, the great stellated dodecahedron.

The icosahedron's analogue in 4 dimensions, with 600 faces, is called the 600-cell, or sometimes I call it the polytetrahedron, because all the cells are tetrahedrons. It's also got same the symmetry group as the analogue of the dodecahedron, the 120-cell, or polydodecahedron.

Eventually we landed on the Monster.

The 4-dimensional icosahedron has 120 vertices, and the Monster is the symmetry group of some clever object in 24 dimensions that has something like 10^{20} vertices—somewhere in these pages we would find this nice 21-digit integer. The Monster is near the end of the book. The character table is 194 columns by 194 rows, so there are 194 different types of symmetries, and the total number of symmetries is this long 54-digit number:

808,017,424,794,512,875,886,459,904,961,710,757,005,754,368,000,000,000.

And we'll see some numbers we recognize here. After a row of ones, which is a trivial representation, it tells us the smallest nontrivial place the Monster lives in is 196,883 dimensions. And then there is another representation in 21,296,876 dimensions, and so on, until down at the bottom left the largest representation is this 27-digit-number-dimensional space, 258823477531055064045234375—don't bother putting commas. The standard thing with very big numbers is to put a space every 5 because then you can count the number of digits easily, in which case it would be: 25 88234 77531 05506 40452 34375. Anyhow, you probably don't want to look at these objects in so many dimensions. But some of us do.

These things are so beautiful. It's such a pity that people can't see them. It's such a pity that I can't really see them. I mean, it's a kind of beauty that exists in the abstract, but we poor mortals will never see it. We can just get vague glimmerings.*

Anyway, I think it's a dead end, trying to explain this stuff, really. If you look at *The ATLAS* you don't see any beautiful things. So where are the beautiful things? If you attempt to describe it, it doesn't quite work. It's a funny thing, the way we mathematicians apprehend these beautiful things. Simply put, the character table of a group is the most informative way of studying a group like the Monster group. It's hard to understand. And you really won't get to understand it.

Do you understand it?

Sorry?

Do you understand?

Well, I mean, I know all the theorems. But there's still something that to me is unknown, unknowable. It's rather peculiar. Most grad students would say they understand group theory. I'm a professional nonunderstander, in the sense that I'm still marveling at it. Especially with the Monster, and I keep saying that it makes me sad that I'll probably never understand it.

The way to describe what we do is aesthetics. We talk about beauty and a proof being "beautiful." Nobody says a table of numbers is beautiful. But there is the sheer intellectual joy of seeing what kind of symmetry there is. That's what this search for the simple groups was all about. Really it all goes back to Plato and the Platonic solids, a few hundred years B.C.,

---

* For a vague glimmering, see the endpapers showing the lowly 248-dimensional group E_8.

and then to Euclid, and Leonardo da Vinci, who illustrated Luca Pacioli's book about the golden ratio and the magical number 1.6180339. . . . Symmetry has been a continuing theme in—I don't know, I've got to say something pompous: It has been a continuing theme in human intellectual development since the beginning of time.

As far as the aesthetics of symmetry are concerned, the Monster is a very nice looking thing. It's a symmetrical object the likes of which you have never seen before, and will never see again. In fact, I have never seen it and I will never see it, at all. But it's intriguing that it is THERE. It's like Everest and Mallory's famous saying. Why did he climb Everest? "Because it's there." Mallory died on Everest and they found his body in some expedition; it was still there, frozen, up on the mountain, and they left it there. Yes, well, I'm not going to die on Everest. I might die on the slopes of the Monster somehow. It won't be quite so painful, I hope.

Free of *The ATLAS*, Conway and his coauthors finally did feel considerable relief, but also considerable pain. By the end, $\frac{4}{5}$ of them had developed gout from all those years procrastinating at the pub. Conway and Rob Curtis took some pleasure in learning about their discomfort. The pain from gout can be so bad that the sufferer can't even tolerate the weight of a sheet on a gout-ridden toe. Benjamin Franklin suffered gout so severely that he spent much of his days in a large shoe-shaped bathtub, continually refreshed with piping hot water, and there he sat conducting his Founding Father affairs. They also learned the derivation of phrases they could use to describe their anguish.

There is the phrase "exquisite pain." "Exquisite" has to do with the Inquisition—as the Inquisition is screwing things out of you, you suffer exquisite pain. But the other thing is that King Henry II of France "enjoyed" a particularly painful death. And you know, in mathematics, you say something "enjoys" a certain property, which seems a peculiar usage. Originally this "enjoy" meant you have the joy of something. As well, you can enjoy rights of something; one person could own the property, but another person could enjoy the fishing rights. After a time in legal usage, you could enjoy responsibilities as well as rights. Then it sort of progressed until the most extreme example found in the OED is to "enjoy a painful death." What happened is

King Henry was out jousting with his aristocratic friends, and his opponent's lance split into 2, and the 2 parts went into his eyes. He enjoyed this death, which lasted for 10 days or 2 weeks or something. It took him quite some time to die. This is the most enjoyable death I've heard of.

Later in 1985, Conway accepted an invitation for a talk at Princeton. There was nothing special in being invited. But after his talk, Eli Stein, chair of the math department, said: "I want to talk to you about your future." He offered him a job. Conway immediately barked out his answer.

YES!

"Don't say yes so fast!" Stein suggested. "Maybe you want to take some time to think about it?"

Conway recalls the transaction as the opposite:

NO!

And Stein said, "Don't say no so quickly!"

In either case, Conway accepted a visiting professorship for the 1986–87 academic year.

"You'll never come back," Parker told him. And as he left Cambridge, Mike Guy ran after Conway's taxi waving a piece of paper with the solution to their latest problem. Some people were surprised Conway hadn't arranged to take Simon Norton along, in the right-hand-man equivalent of a spousal appointment. "I had a period of bereavement after he left," said Norton. He floundered and lost his Cambridge lectureship. Conway had been his mentor, his intellectual soul mate, his sole collaborator, for 17 years. "I got to a stage that I couldn't work without him. I couldn't do any work for a very, very long time."

Conway had intended to go back. When Princeton offered him a full-time position in April 1987, he and Larissa agonized over the decision. Tales abound of England's mathematical pope Sir Michael Atiyah organizing a letter-writing campaign and himself visiting Conway at Princeton, lobbying for his return. Conway contemplated flipping a coin. Although Larissa was all in favor of the move, she vetoed the coin toss on the grounds that both institutions would be offended. She told her husband to find a real reason. He didn't like the pace of American life, but Princeton was a quiet, pretty little place, "a wondrous little spot, a quaint and ceremonious village of puny demigods on stilts," as Einstein called it. A good fraction of Princeton's university architecture was Cambridge copycat, on the inflated scale of 1.5. The salary was also bigger. And by then Conway had 5 children and, for all financial intents and purposes, 2 wives to support. In the end, he jumped ship.

> Like a rat, I left a sinking ship. And by sinking I don't mean group theory; I mean the Cambridge math department. Curtis had left, Wilson went after me. Thompson took a 50-50 position in Florida. Frank Adams was found dead with his car wrapped around a tree. The net effect was that the quality of Cambridge math department was decreasing quite a lot.

It wasn't the state of the math department or Larissa's influence or the money that proved the deciding factor. It was the realization that he'd been in Cambridge for 3 decades.

> The thing that clinched it was realizing, If you say no to this offer, you'll be doing for the next 30 years what you did for the last 30 years. The prospect of being stuck in the same place for 60 years, that was a depressing thought.

For Princeton, it was a coup. The communications office sent out a glossy press release and the university president, Bill Bowen, in announcing the hire praised Conway into hyperspace. He was a "multifaceted phenomenon . . . one of the most eminent mathematicians of the century." And he was about to undergo an inversion—that is to say, mathematically speaking, his life was about to be turned inside out and upside down.

Act III

13.

MORTALITY FLASH

I can't go back to yesterday, because I was a different person then.
—LEWIS CARROLL

On an average Sunday morning in the early 1990s, Conway arrived at the Princeton math department, as on any other day. Except Sunday being Sunday, the door was locked. And Conway, being Conway, didn't have a key. But the man does know his own mind. He'd run into this problem before and devised a fail-safe solution. At Fine Hall's back door waited a piece of wire, carefully camouflaged in a garden of gravel. Conway swooped down like a pelican dive-bombing a fish, snapped up the wire, jimmied it into the lock, and popped the latch. Presto, he'd burgled his way into work.

Approaching the third-floor common room, engulfed by the Sunday quiet, he gradually came within earshot of an all-too-familiar

tap-TAP
tap-TAP
tap-TAP
tap-TAP
tap-TAP
tap-TAP
tap-TAP
tap-TAP
tap-TAP
tap-TAP

This was the sound of another nerd's nightmare in the making, embodied in the flesh by Stephen D. Miller, a 19-year-old smarty-pants Ph.D. student. Sunday was Miller's day in the computer room, where he trained his brain to beat Conway at calculating Doomsday.

Since inventing the Doomsday Rule after that visit with Martin Gardner in 1972, Conway had entertained many (and annoyed some) with his persistent peremptory demand,

GIMME A DATE!

And in the intervening years his passion for calculating Doomsday had not waned. He'd kept with the plan to double his speed every 5 years, 1977, 1982, 1987, 1992 . . . Crossing the pond decisively at the end of 1987, accepting a full-time Princeton professorship, did nothing to put him off course. He opted for an office down the corridor from the common room, among the graduate students' offices, rather than cloistering himself away in Fine Hall's tower with the other faculty. There in the thick of it he performed for anyone who'd give him a date. And if anyone showed sufficient interest, he happily taught them his turbo-charged method.

> Why did I want to be fast? It's impressive. It's a nice party trick. I don't know that it ever got me any girls, but it's the sort of thing that might've done occasionally with the right girl, a certain type of girl.

He persuaded a female graduate student to write a computer program to help him get faster—Conway called the program "GAD," the acronym for his persistent demand. Presented with a date such as 2/10/1879, Conway would smack 1 for Monday (in this case), 2 for Tuesday, 3 for Wednesday, and so on, followed quickly by a "carriage return," otherwise known as the Enter key. In addition to filling his office with his trademark mess and ostensibly "working" on this and that, GAD is how the newly minted and eminently titled John von Neumann Distinguished Professor in Applied and Computational Mathematics spent a good fraction of his time: smacking out the numbers 1 to 7 on his computer.

Word traveled. He attracted the attention of the *New York Times*. And

From a shoot with photojournalist Dith Pran (subject of the Academy Award-winning film
The Killing Fields), New York Times, *1993.*

although the reporter couldn't resist mentioning his idiosyncrasies—
"he is oblivious to the routines and customs of ordinary life. He recently
bought a pair of shoes, after wearing only sandals, even in winter, since
1969. Three weeks ago, he went to the barber for the first time in 30
years"—of course the profile opened with his Doomsday shtick: "Dr.
John H. Conway sits down at his computer and gets ready to log on. But
before the computer allows him to begin work, it quickly spews out 10
randomly selected dates from the past and the future, dates like
3/15/2005 or 4/29/1803. Dr. Conway has to mentally calculate what day
of the week each would be before his computer lets him open a file and
get to work. It is a game he has rigged up to play with himself." His record was then 15.92 seconds to calculate all 10 dates, roughly 1.5 seconds per. He was on track with his doubling goal, since when he started
it took him about 30 seconds per date, and he informed the reporter that
he was the fastest person in the world.

Then Steve Miller came along. Conway treated the competition with
Miller as a way to ward off aging. He'd always avoided mirrors, never
much liking his appearance, and as the years clicked onward he also
avoided catching sight of his mug in shop windows. This was all part of

deceiving himself into believing he was still only 5 years older than his students. It was getting to the point, however, where he wasn't so easily fooled. The poet-mathematician Gian-Carlo Rota once recalled his awareness of always being the youngest person in the room, and then suddenly being the oldest, with no time in between. The same mortality flashes were starting to visit Conway.

> You are young, and then you are old. And here, I'm always surrounded by brilliant young mathematicians. How do you keep your end up?

Keeping up with the young'uns was the gist of Conway's new nerd's nightmare: A hunchbacked centenarian, looking a wreck, he arrives at the common room with his walker and tips like a felled tree into a chair. "Who's the old geezer?" the grad student Bob asks his friend Alice. "I think that's what's-his-name, John Horton Conway. You know, the guy who invented that Life game." They go on about their conversation. Conway sits there impassive, wearing his Mona Lisa face, eyes still smiling beneath the wrinkles, waiting for an opportunity to pounce. Finally, in the course of the students' conversation they happen to mention a date. "When were you born, again?" asks Bob. "April 1, 2015," says Alice.

> And quick as a flash I work it out: "THAT WAS A WEDNESDAY!" And they say, "Oh, there *is* someone in there." It's my insurance policy against old age. This decrepit old guy snaps off a date.

Right then, fantasizing about his prowess in decrepitude, Conway was still sitting in the common room on the first day of the Free Will Theorem lectures. He had been doing all his fretting about the size of his audience, about the little old lady question, and about what his friend and colleague Joe Kohn was going to say in the introduction. He needn't have worried. The house was packed, the little old lady wasn't in attendance, and Kohn, who had teasingly threatened to introduce Conway as "the greatest genius since Aristotle," kept things slightly more modest in the moment. "Conway has a tremendous range of admirers and enthusiasts," he said, "and among them was the late Gian-Carlo Rota, who wrote very positively about John" (it was at least partially upon Rota's recommendation that Princeton hired Conway—Kohn had asked of Rota, "Who's the best combinatorialist?" and Rota said, "John Conway, but you'll never get him"). Kohn went on in his introduction to quote a review Rota wrote of *Sphere Packings, Lattices and Groups*, aka *SPLAG*, the book Conway wrote with Neil Sloane, "just to give you a flavor of the kind of enthusiasm he elicits: 'This is the best survey of the best work in one of the best fields of combinatorics, written by the best people. It will make the best reading by the best students interested in the best mathematics that is now going on.' So, here is John Conway."

Conway looked both pleased and embarrassed and began.

> Well, it's rather frightening to have to live up to that billing, but it was rather frightening before, anyway. I'll just try to forget what Joe said. Yes, well, you know, what am I trying to say? It's one of the surest signs of senility in a scientist—or a mathematician, for that matter—when after having made a reputation in one subject, he somehow feels he can make a contribution to something else. And the diagnosis is clinched when the patient, or whatever you want to call him, persists in this belief even after having been informed that it's one of the surest signs of senility.

With that Conway was off and running. He unfurled his simple statement of the Free Will Theorem: If experimenters have free will, then elementary particles possess free will as well, which probably explains why humans have free will in the first place. This was followed by his overview of the theorem's foundational axioms—the Spin axiom, the Twin axiom, and the Fin axiom. Though he lectured on these axioms at length, we'll delve into them now courtesy of a private tutorial, with Conway in the edifying alcove.

> The 3 axioms are not at all contentious. The first 2 axioms are predicted by quantum mechanics. And, you know, every prediction of quantum mechanics has proved to be true. So you are on a losing bet if you disbelieve them. The third axiom, confirmed by Albert Einstein's special relativity theory, also proved to be remarkably accurate.

And all the axioms have been verified experimentally in some form, the third axiom only recently, in 2013. It is also important to note, as

Conway and Simon Kochen take care to point out, that what they've done with the Free Will Theorem is not entirely novel. In building upon the axioms, the Free Will Theorem refines earlier work by Kochen with Ernst Specker in 1965. Kochen and Specker proved a theorem and applied it to show that a class of "hidden variables" can't exist. A hidden variable being a factor—like mass, velocity, spin, or charge, but an as yet unknown factor—that explains the mysteries of quantum mechanics.

Quantum mechanics, essentially, is a mathematical machine, a tool that provides predictions about the behavior of subatomic particles, predictions in the form of probabilities. Where it falls short is in providing definite values. Take, for instance, a lump of radium. Quantum mechanics specifies its half-life, the period of time in which $\frac{1}{2}$ of it will decay. It cannot specify when any individual atom will decay. The decay seems to occur spontaneously, without reason. And much of quantum mechanics's predictive power is similarly probabilistically impulsive. Some physicists were rather dismayed by the thought of a probabilistic world, Einstein among them. In 1935, working away at the Institute, Einstein and fellow physicists Boris Podolsky and Nathan Rosen produced their shocking "EPR paradox," purporting to show that a quantum-mechanical description of physical reality cannot be complete—shocking enough that the *New York Times* ran the headline EINSTEIN ATTACKS QUANTUM THEORY; SCIENTIST AND TWO COLLEAGUES FIND IT IS NOT "COMPLETE" EVEN THOUGH "CORRECT." Quantum mechanics—a theory for which Einstein was considered a grandfather of sorts—gave predictions that he described as "spooky action at a distance." Physicists conjectured that maybe there was something hidden away inside a particle that explained the imprecisions, something like a hidden alarm clock that triggered the radium atom's decay. As with Isaac Newton's classical mechanics, hidden variable theory suggests that if we only knew every possible factor and force affecting the world and all its particles, then we would be able to predict their predetermined paths and describe a universe governed by laws of cause and effect, rather than by chance.

The Free Will Theorem is the latest in a long line of arguments *against* hidden variable theory (incidentally, von Neumann was the first person to attempt a proof that hidden variables can't exist). The Free Will Theorem implies that physics cannot be explained by adding hidden variables. There are no hidden variables. Instead, quantum mechanics is explained by . . . who knows what. Conway and Kochen suggest that we simply must accept the indeterminacy of quantum mechanics as an ineluctable part of the structure of the universe.

Employing the Twin, Spin, and Fin axioms about the physical world, Conway and Kochen prove their theorem, which, to reiterate, states that if a human being has free will—say, a scientist doing an experiment—then so do elementary particles. Only a little free will is needed on the scientist's part, enough to make basic decisions in performing the experiment Conway and Kochen had in mind. In the experiment, a scientist sends a "spin 1 particle" through a machine called an electrical Stern-Gerlach apparatus that can be oriented in 33 directions. The experimenter needs free will merely to choose which buttons to press on any given trial in choosing the directions to test. Once the experimenter chooses 3 perpendicular directions and sends the particle through the machine, the particle responds with a 0 or 1 to each direction.

> We can prove that the particle's answer is not determined ahead of time. So each is a free-will decision—if the experimenter has free will, so do the particles. The Spin axiom states that the particle's responses must be 011, 101, or 110—the answer always consists of 2 1s and only 1 0. The question is—and this is the thing that in the end turns out to be a free-will decision—which is the 0?

Kochen and Specker, as a consequence of their work in 1965, proved that it is impossible for the particle to have decided ahead of time a fixed answer for each direction. Kochen and Conway then strengthened this theorem, with characteristic cleverness, by taking a different philosophical tack and by using basic geometry.

> Think of a ball of wool with 33 knitting needles running through it in certain cleverly chosen directions. And you're trying to make some of the needles black and some of them white in such a way that whenever 3 of them are perpendicular, there are 2 black, corresponding to the 1s, and 1 white, corresponding to the 0. The reason the particle's response cannot depend only on the direction is that this purely geometric puzzle turns out to have no solution. You simply can't do it.

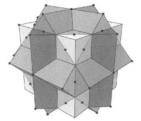

The 3 cubes shaded gray (above) are obtained by rotating the white cube 45° about the 3-coordinate axes. The dots—representing 33 knitting needles—show where the symmetry axes of the compound of 3 cubes intersect the white cube.

Escher used the compound of 3 cubes in his "Waterfall" that defies the laws of physics.

Is it possible, however, that the particle's answers are influenced not only by 1 direction, but by the combination of 3 directions? Here, Conway and Kochen apply the Twin axiom, which asserts that you can produce 2 twinned or entangled particles and separate them as far as you like, say 1 particle on Earth and another on Mars, and if you ask them about the same 3 directions, in any order—i.e. asking them by sending them through that electrical Stern-Gerlach apparatus—then you'll get the same 3 answers. But maybe the way the particle answers is influenced by previous questions? To prove that the previous answers can't influence the next, Conway and Kochen had to eliminate any suspicion that those twinned particles are somehow communicating their answers to each other. That's where the Fin axiom comes in, stipulating that information cannot be transmitted faster than the speed of light; it has a "finite" bound. So the Fin axiom prevents the twinned particles from conspiring, sharing their response—as with Conway and his imaginary twin brother playing Twenty Questions—because they do not have enough time, and the experimenter's spontaneous free-will choice means that she can make up her mind about which 3 directions to measure only at the last moment. Conway and Kochen used these well-established, uncontentious axioms to prune down the possible influences on the particle that could account for its unpredictable behavior. They use similar arguments to eliminate other potential influences. And with that, the Free Will Theorem really is QED.

> We proved it using very little, those 3 axioms. We know they are true because they are consequences of quantum mechanics and relativity theory, the best-tested scientific theories of all time, and moreover they say things that it's good to believe—for example, that physics is Lorentz invariant, this being a kind of symmetry that generalizes Galilean invariance. Galileo said that physics was the same on land as on a steadily moving ship, while Einstein used the example of a train. Incidentally I've just been reading Galileo's *Starry Messenger* . . .

The only outstanding uncertainty, then, is whether free will exists in the first place.

> It is impossible to prove that we have free will. But everybody tends to believe it. There is no evidence that the world is deterministic. Absolutely no evidence. The world has not been deterministic since the 1920s, when physicists noticed that quantum mechanics wasn't deterministic.

And that's about where Conway left it in the first lecture. He had crossed the Rubicon, 1 hour and 7,267 words later—that tally according to the Princeton University Press transcription, which, nearing the end, went as follows:

> So what am I trying to say? Physicists have believed in a certain sense in the result that we're proving for a long time. It's no surprise. "I knew all that," they say . . .

That was exactly physicist Sir Roger Penrose's response when I asked his opinion. Of the Free Will Theorem he says: "What's new? There is a nice piece of mathematics hiding behind it, which is certainly up John's alley. This kind of thing John is a whiz at, obviously. I think it is something worth doing, worth getting to the bottom of. It may end up somewhere interesting, but it hasn't quite got there yet."

To all the "I knew all that already" responses, Conway countered and concluded with the following:

> What they didn't know was that it can be deduced in this very precise,
> logical fashion from so little information. And moreover, information that
> is not at all contentious. These 3 axioms we use, they're routine, they're
> accepted. They follow from quantum mechanics and relativity. There's
> nothing dubious about them, and that's all we need, to sort of . . . well,
> I'm repeating myself. I'll stop!

With the first lecture in the bag, Conway, for the moment, anyway, was fretting no more. He shared a moment of jolly celebration with Kochen and walked home patting himself on the back.

> I've still got it. I worry about it. This is what I used to do all the time. I sort
> of wonder how long I can go on being interesting. . . . Now I'm going to
> luxuriate in the bath.

That was all the lollygagging he allowed himself. Next morning, thanks to his hidden alarm clock, he was up and out the door by 6:55 A.M., arriving at the Small World coffee shop to bask in the adulation of his coffee mates who'd attended the lecture—among them Cathy Smith, a hypnotherapist; Janice Hall, a trend forecaster; and 2 Princeton professors, economist Avi Dixit and Hal Feiveson, a nuclear energy and nuclear arms control research scientist. When Conway walked in that morning, Janice presented him with an article from the morning newspaper, "Oozing Through Texas Soil, a Team of Amoebas Billions Strong," about the world's largest known colony of clonal amoebas, and she read it aloud from the page. "Scientists found the vast and sticky empire stretching 40 feet across, consisting of billions of genetically identical single-celled individuals, oozing along in the muck of a cow pasture outside Houston. . . . Scientists say the discovery is much more than a mere curiosity, because the colony consists of what are known as social amoebas. Only an apparent oxymoron, social amoebas are able to gather in organized groups and behave cooperatively, some even committing suicide to help fellow amoebas reproduce."

"If that's not evidence of free will," Janice concluded, "I don't know what is!"

Conway set that aside and turned to questions coming his way about how the lecture went.

VERY well! I can be conceited again. I've got my groove back. I wondered if I was really capable of giving the blockbuster talk anymore. I wondered if I still had it. So last night was tremendously reassuring. My ego needs to be fed!

And yet, back to the fretting, he confessed lingering qualms.

Remember my remarks about senility. Knowing about it myself, that I'm getting on, and that I'm not quite capable of self-evaluating, leads me to wonder sometimes: Did we *really* get it right?

14.
OPTIONAL PROBABILITY FIELDS

Whatever is not forbidden is permitted.
—Friedrich Schiller

Hanging around the halls of the Princeton math department, surveying professors, students, secretaries, I set about measuring Conway's third act, as an expat in America. In a sense he'd been the quintessential Cambridge character, Cambridge being a place that cultivates and accommodates a wide spectrum of eccentrics, ranging from the painfully shy lifelong bachelor coddled by centuries-old customs and traditions to, at the other extreme, Conway, the flamboyant playboy, the beloved flagship oddball. His Cambridge colleagues, surprised and disappointed by his departure, wondered how he'd fare among the Yanks. As it turned out, his flamboyance put him on firm footing in America. He fit in nicely and attracted more media attention than might normally be allotted a man of numbers.

Another reporter from *Discover* magazine came calling and in answering her question about mathematicians' styles he said:

Mine glitters. I like things that shine somehow or look nice, sort of trashy. I have taste, but I don't exercise it very frequently. So I'm just as likely to be doing something that's not worth doing as something that is.

And in ruefully explaining to a *New York Times* reporter why he allegedly offered a $10,000 prize from his own pocket for a solution to a problem he presented during a symposium at AT&T Bell Labs, he said:

I love my subject, and I was trying to awaken some interest in it. . . . I give a fair number of lectures of this kind, and I've offered sums of money for various mathematical problems before, but nobody had ever claimed any.

He bathed in all this limelight, eager to woo the masses. "Conway is a seducer, *the* seducer," says his Princeton colleague Peter Sarnak—speaking exclusively of Conway's skills as a teacher, of course.

In time, Conway became the department's prize attraction, as ever holding forth in the common room. There he engaged Sarnak in a viciously aggressive (if ostensibly playful) competition with a spinning toy called a Levitron, but when Sarnak proved the superior levitator Conway banned the Levitron from the premises. He was trotted out every fall and charged with the task of delivering the welcoming lecture to math undergraduates and persuading them to stick with math as their major. In no small part, his powers of persuasion resided in grandstanding. At Princeton he was known to write on walls and chairs, to move classes outside and chalk the sidewalks, and to deliver town-and-gown tours on "How to Stare at a Brick Wall," marveling at the various constructions and patterns of brickwork that make up the various "bonds." He liked the challenge of taking the most boring subjects and rendering them interesting. Brick walls expanded his range on the subject of symmetry, since they are a practical manifestation of tiling the Euclidean plane.

And nobody looks at these damn things!

A video-taped record of his "How to Stare at a Brick Wall" tour began with Conway at the chalkboard in his office, doing his pacing strut, flipping his hair, which had recently been cut into a bob and sculpted forward at a slick angle to meet his Amish overgrowth of beard. The first stop on the tour, conveniently enough, was his office wall.

The commonest stuff you see—Muck! Filth!—is just running bond. The really lovely traditional bond is Flemish bond; every row is alternate headers and stretchers. That's really lovely stuff. There is some absolutely gorgeous stuff over there that is $\frac{1}{3}$ Flemish. . . . Well, let us journey into the real world.

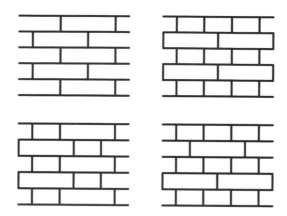

Clockwise from top left: running bond, English bond, Dutch bond, and Flemish.

He motioned out the window, dashed out the door, and descended into the stairwell.

The 2 really gorgeous ones that we'll see quite soon are the McCosh Health Center and a few buildings around it which are $\frac{1}{5}$ header and $\frac{2}{10}$ Flemish. ABsolutely GORGeous—ummh!

He sounded like a dandy fondling a new silk scarf. The meandrous campus paths take him to Palmer Hall ($\frac{1}{3}$ Flemish), Old Fine Hall (Dutch bond), the yellow houses on the either side of Nassau Hall (both with irregular "weirdo walls"). As Conway luck would have it, he happens upon stacks of bricks and a cement mixer churning away, the makings of Marx Hall (English bond). He ventures onto Nassau Street to the historic Bainbridge House (narrow American bond), Woolworth's (straight American), the swank restaurant Lahiere's ($\frac{1}{7}$ Flemish), Kinko's (rowlock running bond), and a pedestrian crosswalk (ditto the rowlock).

Isn't it fantastic? There are so many brick walls around. The world has now been alerted!

When it's all over, 2 hours later, Conway walked away from the camera without so much as a good-bye. A ways down the block he stopped, removed his sandals, and continued on his way.

For his more staid classroom lectures he flipped tables upside down and overturned conventions, lecturing with an elementary $1 + 1 = 2$ approach, though still conveying advanced concepts and claiming he could teach no other way. During an interview in a student publication, the *Princeton Eclectic*, an admiring reporter noted, "You're renowned for your energetic and slightly crazy teaching style. . . . Where does your teaching style come from?"

Deep inside.

Some might just call it crazy, plain and simple.

But with respect to teaching, it's not just for the sake of being crazy. It really does help people think. I mean one of the tricks I do, which I only started really when I came to Princeton, is shouting. There was this time when I was conducting this geometry course, and the kids always forgot one particular point, which was that the gyration point was not on a mirror. So one time I said, "A GYRATION POINT IS NOT ON A MIRROR"—I shouted it like all hell. And every now and then we'd organize shouting competitions with the whole class: "The gyration point is a point . . . that is NOT on a mirror!" Everybody would shout it. Actually once I shouted so loud that my trousers split. I sort of jumped up into the air at the shout. I jumped up like a . . . I don't know, like a cartoon figure so to speak. Legs apart and everything and this great ripping sound . . .

So, the reporter asked, these techniques help induce understanding?

Well, I don't know. Sometimes they just wake people up.

Other techniques included blowing his nose into his origami creations (that jumping frog, maybe) and wiping off the blackboard with his tongue (variations on a theme).

Not long after he settled in Princeton, Conway thought he'd made a terrible mistake. He was being treated with kid gloves, not put to optimal use. His first course on the roster was something uselessly abstract like

"Development of Mathematical Concepts." It bored him to tears, and his students too, he figured. Then he was slated to give a graduate course on the Monster. This seemed more promising. However, when he arrived at the classroom on the first day his audience included a few of the hotshot math professors on faculty, in addition to a half-dozen students (the standard size of a Princeton grad seminar ranging from 4 to 10 takers). To make matters worse, some of those hotshots were Fields medalists. Feigning nonintimidation, Conway got started with his signature 1 + 1 = 2 approach. But every now and then from the Fields hotshots he heard a condescending chuckle. He took things up a notch. He continued on this more formal path for weeks, since the hotshots stuck around. His resentment grew, as did his misery. He had to get out of this predicament, either cancel the class or get rid of the hotshots. When the course resumed after Christmas, he announced a return to his babyish ways— methods, he suggested, that some members of the audience mightn't be able to stomach. The hotshots politely persevered for a time as Conway galootishly got on with it, dumbing things down as low as he could go, and eventually he was rid of them. Victorious, he now had license to continue with his elementary style forever more, sometimes with no higher educational purpose.

One of many manifestations of this method was a number theory lecture delivered according to the rules of the "One Bit Word Game."

> When you play it, you can say just words that have 1 bit in them, not 2 or 3 or 4 or 5 or 6 . . .

> Bit as in . . . ?

> Those bits that words are made of.

> You mean you can only say words composed of 1 syllable?

> BANG! BANG! BANG! You said 3 words I may not say, but yes. We used to play it in the place I lived. And we would go to a shop to have tea, or cakes, or tea and cakes, things like that. And if the girl who served us found what went on, we all lost.

Delivering a number theory class in 1-bit words was a challenge, to say the least, especially due to the frequency of the 2-bit word "number," which Conway rendered as:

Those things you count with—you know, 1, 2, 3, 4, 5, 6, or more . . .

Even outside the classroom the simpleton approach prevailed, causing him at times to get up the nose of the establishment. When in 1998 Harold Shapiro became president of the university, he convened faculty dinner parties at which the guests, seated around the table, were asked to say a few words about themselves. Conway found this a crass exercise. When his turn came he recited a poem about elves and goblins that he'd memorized in elementary school. As he told yet another reporter who came calling:

Well, I wasn't invited to a dinner party again.* But I don't worry about that; I guess it looks as if I have an irresponsible attitude. However, to do good work in math, you have to be somewhat irresponsible. I only started doing real mathematics after I found the Conway group. I got a much-needed ego boost—obviously I don't need one anymore. Anyhow, after I made my name, I could do what I like, even if it was totally trivial. When I want to play backgammon instead of doing math, I play backgammon. If the people at Princeton don't feel that they're getting their money's worth out of me, that's their problem. They bought me!

Eli Stein, chair of the department, was immensely proud of the purchase. Whether Princeton still considered Conway a good buy after the fact was not Conway's concern, though sometimes he wondered why

---

* Nevertheless, in 1998 Conway persuaded Shapiro that Princeton should bid on the Archimedes palimpsest up for auction at Christie's in New York. Conway envisioned how lovely it would be to handle the 800-year-old recycled manuscript—containing a number of Archimedes's works existing nowhere else, and the best source of the diagrams Archimedes drew in the sand at Syracuse, despite having been scraped and washed and repurposed into a prayer book by a thirteenth-century priest. Conway fantasized about hosting a conference celebrating the acquisition and holding forth on all things Archimedean. The university put in a bid of $1.2 million, but the palimpsest sold for $2.2 million, going to a private American collector who deposited it at the Walters Art Museum in Baltimore for conservation and study.

Princeton bought him in the first place. Groups were a possibility. He was known foremost for his namesake groups and his work on group theory with *The ATLAS*, and since Princeton had no group theorists to speak of, maybe he was acquired to fill that void. The surreal numbers were another possibility. Conway always suspected that the late Martin Kruskal, chair of Princeton's program in applied mathematics, had a hand in his hiring. Kruskal, a mathematician and physicist who made groundbreaking contributions in astrophysics, nuclear fusion, and fluid dynamics, believed the application of the surreal numbers to physics would be his next big contribution. He was the most fervent devotee of the surreal numbers, almost to the point of obsession, and he was a big fan of their creator as well. "I almost revere him for what he's done, and for his tremendous insight," Kruskal once said. "He understands quicker than anybody."

Kruskal devoted the last 30 years of his career to figuring out how the surreal numbers, the largest collection of infinite numbers, might help physicists wrestle with the bugaboos thwarting quantum field theory— and by extension thwarting quantum field theory's ultimate elaboration in the coveted unified universal theory of everything. The surreals held promise, Kruskal thought, in nailing down precise meanings for some series, asymptotic series, that so far only give approximations. When physicists query the universe with what seem like perfectly sensible questions, the answers explode back with preposterously infinite divergences—functions that asymptotically veer off the graph, leaving scientists who are conversant only with normal numbers helpless and hopeless to cope. Not so if they knew the surreals, argued Kruskal. Simply put, he believed them to be superior numbers. "Surreals are in every logical, mathematical, and aesthetic sense better," he said.

There were holes in this thinking, to be sure. Gaps in the surreal number line rendered impossible the all-important process of integration, a process that solves the simplest differential equations—differential equations being the stuff of physics itself, the lingo in which laws of nature are expressed. "I'm working to fix it," Kruskal told those who came asking, sometimes Conway. And every now and then Kruskal cornered Conway in a classroom for a few hours and gave him a progress report. For Conway's part, more often than not when he talks about his colleague's crusade he punts on the details and changes the topic to Kruskal's alluring theory of the "soliton," a term Kruskal invented to describe a wave that rolls along with a continuing crest, infinitely unbroken.

> Did I tell you the famous story about a guy from the nineteenth century whose name was John Scott Russell? Riding along the banks of a canal, he sees a wave moving along at really quite a substantial lick. So he spurs his horse into a gallop and he keeps up with it for a mile or 2. And this wave kept its shape and just moved smartly along the canal, or the river or whatever it was. . . . This kind of wave is now called a soliton. Under certain circumstances, which really have to do with the depth of the water and the confinement, this particular type of wave can be astonishingly stable. And you could even have another different wave, say a smaller wave, and the 2 waves come toward each other and go through each other and they bypass each other and emerge unscathed. This is to do with physics, in a way to do with quantum mechanics and stuff. You have the question of whether a particle can be a wave, or a wave can be a particle—one of these great questions that it is so hard to understand. And one way of achieving some resolution of this paradox is Kruskal's concept of soliton.

Conway talked up the soliton. Kruskal talked up the surreals, at length, like his wave that wouldn't stop. Once Kruskal introduced Conway at a conference with such exuberance that the introduction ate up half of Conway's allotted time—not a form of flattery Conway appreciated. And while Conway did appreciate Kruskal's devotion to applying the surreals, he rebuffed Kruskal's efforts to recruit him for the cause. Conway owed Kruskal, that was true, and he desperately wanted him to succeed, but he let him go it alone.

> You know, we had a fundamental disagreement. I used to tell him every now and then that I thought he was going the wrong way about it. You see, what drove me when I was investigating the surreal numbers was the wonderful simplicity I observed in the theory. It was very, very simple, and everything was the simplest thing it could possibly be. And that made it very elegant.

Kruskal wasn't concerned with that notion of simplicity. He was trying to just find out what was true, forget whether it's simple or not. But for me simplicity was a very useful guiding principle. If it wasn't simple, maybe it's the wrong direction, that's what I thought. I thought he was attacking it the wrong way around. I said to him once, "If you throw away all this complicated stuff and proceed looking for simplicity, then if you succeed you'll succeed very easily, and if you don't succeed, well, it's just the same."

Of course, I haven't succeeded because I've never tried. And possibly the reason I've never tried is because I'm afraid of trying because it's possible that it wouldn't work. Kruskal spent 30 years trying to do his thing, and it didn't work, either. It's very sad. He made some progress, but really he got nowhere. And I think it's unfortunate. I wish he had got somewhere.[*]

Despite the media spotlight, a chairman's pride, and Kruskal's fervor, these first years at Princeton caused Conway some heart searching. With characteristic bravado he'd shrugged off the hotshots' snickering, but in truth he found it upsetting. And then there was Reaganomics and Star Wars, which he could no longer ignore by saying, That's *their* problem!

He and Larissa had put down roots, bought a big house on the wooded and winding Prospect Drive, and welcomed another baby boy, Oliver, born in 1988—the year Microsoft released Windows 2.1 and MIT released the first computer worm via the Internet. But all the while Conway wondered whether he'd made the wrong decision in leaving Cambridge.

What saved him was Bill Thurston, then at Princeton and a pioneer in

---

[*] The Harvard professor Jacob Lurie, who in 2014 won the $3 million Breakthrough Prize in Mathematics, is another surreals fan—or was. As an 18-year-old math whiz from Bethesda, Maryland, he won the $40,000 Westinghouse Science Talent Search prize in 1996 with a project on the computability of surreal numbers. He tried to explain what he'd done to a "mathematical illiterate" reporter—"I wanted to see to what extent surreal numbers could be manipulated by computers, answering questions like, Can you get computers to add surreal numbers, things like that, and I found it could be done." But their Q&A ended on more general terms. "Q: How long have you been working on this? A: It's not clear when I started or when I finished, but at least for now, I'm finished. All the questions that have yet to be answered are too hard."

A pattern displaying a "wallpaper group."

the field of topology (while geometry measures fixed distances, topology allows shapes and solids to shrink, stretch, or twist, but no cutting or pasting is allowed). Thurston, as it happened, had been one of the Fields hotshots sitting in on Conway's class. He won the prize in 1982 for his Geometrization Conjecture—reintroducing geometry and distance to topology and conjecturing that all possible 3-dimensional spaces can be made from 8 types of geometric pieces, which, as Thurston liked to say, is like fitting everybody in the world with 8 outfits.

By the time I'd worked my way up to the late 1980s in Conway's chronology, Thurston was facing an early death from a recently diagnosed advanced melanoma. I was advised to call him as soon as possible. If an interview was an intrusion, he made it a life-affirming one. He'd spent a lot of time talking to Conway in the Princeton common room, he recalled, and it didn't take long before they landed on the subject of plane crystallographic groups, or wallpaper groups as they are often called, since these 17 groups describe repeating patterns sometimes found on wallpaper. Thurston and Conway were both fond of this subject, but they approached it from different angles. Conway approached it as a geometer, with a group theory and symmetry slant, and he'd developed a notation to explain how the patterns repeat. Thurston approached it more from a topological perspective, with a concept he'd invented called an orbifold—something with many folds, and folded such that each orbit becomes a point. As Thurston and Conway both tell it, Thurston tended to go on a soapbox about his orbifolds, and he was eager to convey it to Conway. But before he could get going, Conway cut him off—

I said, "Oh, I have a nice notation for the crystallographic groups, let me tell you about it." And Thurston said, "No, first you must let me tell you my ideas." And I said, "Why should you go first?" And he said, "Well, give me 10 minutes." And I said, "No, I'll give you 5." I gave him his 5 minutes. And after he had his 5 minutes, I didn't want to tell him my ideas and I became the keenest advocate of his ideas. He had never enshrined his ideas in a notation, which I must say was rather stupid of him.

When I talked to Thurston, he said his soapboxing with the orbifolds typically did not leave such a favorable impression, or much impression at all, and he said he was grateful when Conway took it up and found a notation that worked and invented catchy terminology—Conway *adores* naming and renaming things, and renaming things that even he named, or renamed, again and again and again (though all of his children's names seem to have remained fixed).* "That's part of his magic," says Thurston. "He thinks a lot about how people will understand something, he thinks a lot about ways to communicate with people, to surprise and impress, not to keep them mystified, but to make them wake up and take note."

Thurston was also known for his opinions on mathematics education. In his view, students did not benefit from the first-year linear algebra hurdle and the 10 varieties of calculus thereafter. An egalitarian-minded Quaker, at Princeton he created a new kind of math course, a course that would appeal to math and poetry majors alike. He named it "Geometry and the Imagination," inspired by the book of the same name published in 1932 by the universalist mathematician David Hilbert. (Hilbert, upon hearing that a student had dropped math to study poetry, said, "Good! He did not have enough imagination to become a mathematician.") To publicize the new course, Thurston and his co-organizer Peter Doyle,

---

* This is the sort of thing that got in the way of publishing Conway's "ZIP Proof" thus promoting Conway from the author list to title: "Conway's ZIP Proof." Recalls Jeff Weeks (and co-author George Francis agrees): "John was pretty busy during that period, so we didn't hear a lot from him. But the suggestions we did get from John became a bit awkward: from our point of view, it felt as if he wanted to bend the exposition to accommodate various plays-on-words that he had devised, and, more seriously, it seemed that John's endless series of ideas for adding and changing things might prevent the article from ever being completed at all."

then Thurston's postdoc student and now a professor at Dartmouth, placed ads in the university's student newspaper, the *Daily Princetonian*. Thurston stressed that this "creative mathematics" would still involve serious hard work, but curiosity-driven fun would be paramount; usually in mathematics there was too much delayed gratification. They expected 20 or so takers. When the course drew 92 students—the kind of number usually reserved for the no-brainer gut courses—they roped in the new man Conway, the perfect addition to their sideways, subversive effort. Together, the Thurston-Doyle-Conway trio designed a course tackling the most intractable of mathematics problems: How to teach.

For starters, the professors made a ritual of entering the classroom en masse, sometimes with great pomp and circumstance, sometimes carrying a flag, sometimes wearing bicycle helmets, often pulling a red kiddy wagon heaped with polyhedra, mirrors, flashlights, and fresh produce from the grocery store. In Thurston, Conway found a true soul mate, because both men loved lecturing with vegetables (Thurston was a goody-goody vegetarian and christened all the computers in Fine Hall with vegetative names). In contemplating the curvature of surfaces, for instance, Thurston and Conway might lead the class in peeling potatoes—peeling a single strip around the potato's equator and laying the strip flat on the blackboard in order to measure the angle by which the peel fell short of closing a full circle, or the angle by which it exceeded. This, they explained, measured the Gaussian curvature, the total curvature, for the region of the potato enclosed by the peel. To the same end, Thurston liked to get the class cutting up lettuce, cabbage, and kale. Conway, meanwhile, not a vegetarian, preferred using as a prop his protuberant stomach. In this display of curvature he turned down the lights, laid himself on a table before the class, lifted up his T-shirt revealing his magnificence, and planted the back end of a shining flashlight on his belly button. Tracing the flashlight around his stomach's circumference, he advised the students to watch the path the light beam traveled on the ceiling and to imagine how the light's path might differ were it traversing flatter terrain.

Another exercise explained the bicycle helmets. Prior to class the teachers found large rolls of paper, tore off strips that were 6 feet by 20 feet at least, and borrowed some bicycles. They painted the tires of each a different color, and then starting from some small distance away, rode a bike across a strip of paper. In class, the students were presented with this artwork and asked, regarding each set of tracks, "Which way did the bicycle go?"

The first step is identifying which track was made by the back wheel and which by the front. There are many ways to do it, but the easiest is to realize that the front wheel's track always has more pronounced curvature, initiating turns this way and that, and then pulling the back wheel along on a smoother path.

Determining the direction of travel then involves taking a tangent line to the back wheel's track (the bold track in the diagram above) and marking where it intersects the front wheel's track, producing tangent line segments.

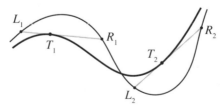

When considering the tracks and the direction of the bike's travel, these tangent segments should equal the length of the bicycle as measured between the centers of the front and back wheels. Measuring the tracks in one direction, the tangent line segments will be of equal or constant length, while in the other direction the tangent line segments will be of different lengths. So in determining the direction of travel, the teachers advised students to weigh the hypothesis that a bicycle of constant length went one direction against the hypothesis that a bicycle of variable length went the other way (moving to the left, $T_1L_1 \neq T_2L_2$, but moving to the right, $T_1R_1 = T_2R_2$, therefore the bike was traveling to the right).

A certain set of tracks, however, stumped the students. For that set Peter Doyle had pedaled up the sheet of paper and then back again, but on a unicycle.

All in all, the course was a big exercise in imagining, drawing heavily on symmetry and geometry. "Geometry is the user-friendly interface of math," as Thurston liked to say. The modus operandi was to expose the students to a barrage of activities that would change the way they saw and thought about things, mathematical things at least. Usually, as Conway commented to a reporter, teaching geometry from a textbook is like taking a dog for a walk around the block:

> *You take the student out in the yard and let him do his thing, then you bring him back in.*

"Geometry and the Imagination," by comparison, let students loose to romp and run free.

> *You have to let them exercise.*

Or, according to the student Graham Burnett, then a junior history major and now a Princeton professor in the history and philosophy of science: "The professors didn't tell you things. They led you to the brink of discovery and left you hanging there to make the discovery yourself." For the independent project Burnett constructed a set of photograms depicting the geometrical transformations underlying cartographic projections. While the math was "patty-cake," says Burnett, he recalls that Conway was politely impressed. Although he also remembers that Conway's focus was elsewhere—on a 16-year-old savant, Bernie Freidin, then a high school sophomore who constructed dozens of paper models of crystalline tessellations that divided 3-dimensional space into 2 infinite and indistinguishable manifolds. "The 2 children clearly clicked," says Burnett, "rotating countless wacky paper forms in front of the window and using up a lot of Scotch tape." As reported in Freidin's high school newspaper, he used 50 rolls of tape and nearly 120 square feet of card stock, transforming 15,000 polygons into what he called Semiregular Hyperbolic Isotropic Tilings, aka SHIT.

Burnett didn't quite know what to make of Conway, and he'd seen it all at Princeton, including a spectral John Nash working away in the recesses of Fine Hall's basement. But wearing his science historian hat, probing the psychology of genius, he offers an assessment. "Conway felt like a lunatic, to be honest," he says. "He was fundamentally elsewhere, at least as I saw it. Inaccessible. But not because he wasn't 'there.' On the contrary, he had a lot of enthusiasm, even something akin to spring-in-the-step affection for everyone. And yet the enthusiasm and the affection—in fact, his whole mode of reaching toward other humans—appeared to be achieved exclusively through what felt like a giant prosthetic carapace of mathematical knowledge and mathematical appetite. That's what he could reach toward you with. And this was unusual. It left me with a genuinely disconcerting feeling that I've known really on only one other occasion, with another person I think deserves to be called a genius. It is the feeling that one has fallen under the attention of a very animated and apparently good-willed god-monster-being, who really wants to connect, but whose capacity to do so is entirely mediated by this huge and very powerful and just-barely-controlled exoskeleton. He's in there, you can tell. And he's probably friendly. He seems friendly. But what you're actually dealing with—what is looming up over you, swinging its arms around like a dervish—is this gigantic, unwieldy, and frankly sort of menacing animatronic erudition/cognition. And he/it is reaching toward you. Clearly, the only way you are going to be able to interact—and it doesn't look like you have much choice, because he seems to be very excited to see you—is through the giant articulations of the strange prosthetic machine. If you are going to hug him, you are going to hug that. . . . Plenty of very learned people are sort of 'trapped' in their tremendous learning. But most of them—the ones who are really trapped—do not give a shit about reaching out. [With Conway] there is a real buoyant exuberant appetite for connection, it's just that it works in a way that is really not normal, it's not normally the way you see somebody reaching out toward you."

This might seem to contradict the Conway we've come to know, with his simple $1 + 1 = 2$ approach that speaks to the masses. But Conway can turn it on or off; he can go high or low. He's got his high-mathematical-mastery-inaccessible-exoskeleton mode, and to be sure when he's in that mode he's hard to reach. He can also come down to earth with treats for mere mortals. Conway and the 16-year-old were communing way up there where the air is thin. When I reach back to Conway's unwieldy reaching out, it's with an instrument too blunt and too cumbersome, which forces the conversation down to a more breathable level. "The problem is with us, not with them," as Burnett says. "You can't give him what he wants. He needs to be hugged, and you and I are not equipped to do that—we don't know what the hell to do. That's what was so interesting about watching him with the kid. Because the kid, the kid was a prodigy. He could reach back. It was normal. They were hugging each other. It was working."

Conway deemed "Geometry and the Imagination" a success for the following reason, as he does with any teaching:

> Marx is nowadays not regarded as a very great philosopher. But his ideas are still useful. And in particular he said something that applies to teaching. It was something to the effect that "the secrets to success in life are honesty and sincerity. If you can fake those, then you've got it made."
>
> And I think that is terribly important in teaching. I would stick enthusiasm in with honesty and sincerity—enthusiasm is very important in teaching. You don't *have* to fake it. If you actually have it, that's the best thing. But if not, you better fake it. So you know, I've been teaching such-and-such a subject for 50 years—my god, half a century. And so it's difficult sometimes to pretend not to be a bit bored with it, when I am actually quite a lot bored with it. How do I do it? Fake it. I'm really serious that if you can fake it you've got it made.
>
> By the way, it was Groucho Marx who said that, not Karl. Groucho has a lot of lessons to teach us. "I won't belong to any club that will have me as a member," that's another one.

Conway and the team mustered enough enthusiasm to teach the course twice at Princeton before Thurston accepted a job as director of Berkeley's Mathematical Sciences Research Institute—known as MSRI and pronounced "misery" until Thurston got there and changed the pronunciation to "emissary," in hopes that it might make a good base camp for furthering his mission to revolutionize teaching. In advance of Thurston's departure, the team took their show on the road for a 2-week summer course for high school teachers, held at the University of Minneapolis's now defunct Center for Geometry. "The course work was extremely difficult," reported the *Minneapolis Star Tribune.* "The atmosphere was Barnum & Bailey." As Conway commented:

At Princeton we call it a circus.

He also disclosed some of the teachers' dirty laundry.

We fight like hell.

The fighting actually turned out to be as essential to the course as geometry or imagination. The teachers had their daily morning fight, a last-minute planning meeting of sorts, before the 10:30 A.M. class. The meeting usually left them still at odds and they often bought themselves some time by pushing the barefoot Conway, wearing a polyhedron as a hat, into the classroom to pontificate extemporaneously for 10 minutes. This became a regular stopgap segment known as "Fantastic Facts." The fights were usually between Conway and Thurston, both bigwigs with big ideas and egos to match. Thurston was set on getting his way, and he'd been up since dawn thinking about the class. He always had an idea of which proof was absolutely and unequivocally the best proof to teach; more often than not it was one of his own. And even to Conway, Thurston seemed close to invincible.

Sometimes the disagreements would be left unresolved, but even then the content and the dynamic of disagreements, as they played out in front of the class, often proved instructive. The teachers interrupted and contradicted one another with abandon. And the plan had been for the course to be "team taught," everyone teaching everything in tandem. Sometimes this evolved unexpectedly. "A number of times," recalls Rutgers' Jane Gilman, who became the team's fourth teacher, "after I finished explaining some point or concept to the class, I would back away from the front of the class and notice that 1 or even 2 of my colleagues had been drawing pictures and diagrams on the blackboard to illustrate my point or they had improvised an illustration behind me using some of the props from the wagon." After a number of these episodes, a student came into the Geometry Room—stocked with Legos, Tinkertoys, Constructo-Straws, string, mirrors, deflated soccer balls, the makings of papier-mâché, a sewing machine—and informed his teachers that he did not feel he was being team taught so much as he was being gang taught. And even the gang method was executed with varying degrees of harmony. As the *Star Tribune* reported: "John Conway jumped to his feet and rushed to the blackboard, marker in hand, to draw an orbifold. He was forced back to his seat by a verbal barrage from his colleagues, who told him to sit down and shut up. Conway's artistic skills are considerable and his enthusiasm unbridled, so when a colleague mentioned a tetrahedron, a symmetry pattern or anything else geometric, it was a siren call for the English mathematician, tugging him almost magically toward the board. He sat down, but it was clearly hard for him to remain in his chair."

Perhaps the most conclusive story comes from Peter Doyle. He remembers Gilman at the chalkboard going on and on about the generalities of something to do with measuring lengths in the hyperbolic metric. Doyle found her long explanation frustrating. He felt it was high time the specific formula be stated explicitly. He shouted out to the class: "For 5 bucks, I'll tell you the formula!" Then Thurston offered: "I'll tell you for free." To which Conway countered:

I'll pay you to listen!

It would not have been the first time.

Conway not infrequently offered payment—payment he could ill afford—for treasures outside his grasp, and likely beyond most everyone's grasp, he assumed, meaning it was unlikely he'd ever have to pay up. A particularly infamous instance again landed him in the *New York Times* in 1988 under the headline INTELLECTUAL DUEL: BRASH CHALLENGE, SWIFT RESPONSE.

Conway had been passing insomniac nights counting out numeric sequences, cousins of the familiar Fibonacci sequence 0, 1, 1, 2, 3, 5, 8,

13 . . . One night, a particularly interesting variation marched into his brain. Who knows exactly *how* the sequence made its entrance, but the procession went like this: 1, 1, 2, 2, 3, 4, 4, 4, 5, 6, 7, 7 . . .

As he told the *New York Times*:

> *I used to invent sequences every night in hopes of finding something in-teresting. This sequence was the only one I found.*

And as he told me:

> The procedure for calculating the next number is this: You take the value of the last number in the series, 7 in this case, and use that value to select 2 numbers within the sequence that will be added together to produce the next number in the sequence. You obtain the first of these 2 numbers by counting backward 7 steps from the last number—if you go back 7 places from the last 7 you land on 3. And then you get the second number by counting forward 7 steps from the beginning of the sequence—go 7 places from 1 and you land on 4. So the next number in the sequence is 3 + 4, which gives us another 7 . . .
>
> 1, 1, 2, 2, 3, 4, 4, 4, 5, 6, 7, 7, 7 . . .
>
> And on it goes from there. The counting measure is again a 7, the last number. Going backward 7 places we get 4, and if counting forward 7 places we get 4 again, 4 + 4 = 8, so the sequence now progresses to
>
> 1, 1, 2, 2, 3, 4, 4, 4, 5, 6, 7, 7, 7, 8 . . .

What struck Conway about this sequence was that the last number never increases over the second-to-last number by more than 1. He also noticed that when he divided any number in the series by the value of its position in the sequence—3 divided by 5, or 6 divided by 10—the result was always in the vicinity of $\frac{1}{2}$. Sometimes it was somewhat greater than $\frac{1}{2}$, sometimes it was equal to $\frac{1}{2}$, sometimes it was somewhat less, and the further along in the series one went the closer and more consistently it tended toward $\frac{1}{2}$. Having made this observation, Conway next wanted proof of the convergence toward $\frac{1}{2}$. He succeeded, he proved it—with the help of his wife Larissa—but it was hard work. And it left him unsatisfied that he knew everything worth knowing about the sequence. He wondered about the outermost number, the "magic point" in the series beyond which the ratio of the number to its position is always within $\frac{1}{20}$ or .05 of $\frac{1}{2}$—that is, always within the range of 0.45 to 0.55. This seemed much more difficult than the convergence proof, and Conway had all but surrendered, concluding the sequence was too chaotic and unpredictable and the solution out of reach. Around that time he was scheduled to give a lecture at AT&T Bell Labs in Murray Hill, New Jersey, where he was still spending a lot of time working with Neil Sloane. He made this quandary the centerpiece of his talk, titled "Some Crazy Sequences," and in the midst of it he posed a 2-pronged challenge to his audience of 500 or so accomplished mathematicians and scientists. From his own pocket Conway offered a prize of $100 to anyone who could solve the relatively easy problem of determining the rate at which the sequence converged to $\frac{1}{2}$. And to anyone who calculated and proved the magic number he would happily shell out a prize of 10 times that amount. Conway was being paid $1,500 to deliver this talk, so no matter what, he'd come out ahead. Regardless, he loved his subject, he wanted to incite interest, and claimants to these challenges rarely surfaced. Especially given the crazy nature of the sequence as he'd observed it, Conway assumed nobody would come up with a solution.

He received a long letter containing a proof 2 weeks later. It was from Colin Mallows, then an AT&T statistician, who viewed the main challenge of his discipline to make it seem less like sorcery. "I can't resist a challenge like that," he explained to the *New York Times* reporter. "Even if the money hadn't been attached to it I'd have had a go at it. Within two or three days of Conway's talk, just messing around on the backs of envelopes, I found what looked like a general rule for the thing." He employed a Cray supercomputer to analyze the sequence and search for clues, looking for hidden structure within the foothills and humps of data that climbed the printouts. Mallows identified strikingly regular patterns throughout the series without doing the plodding step-by-step calculations Conway used, homing in on the convergence point at the 1,489th number in the sequence. "It was great fun," Mallows said. "I consider this a victory for the techniques of data analysis."

Conway checked the proof, acknowledged Mallows's victory, and reported back to Sloane that he was about to write a check for $1,000. Sloane then drew it to his attention that the prize he'd offered was *actually* $10,000. Conway couldn't believe it. He'd offered $100 for the first puzzle, and 10 times that amount for the second, or so he thought. The symposium proceedings had been recorded, so Sloane checked the tape, and there it was. Conway had gotten confused. What he'd said out loud was $100 for the easy problem and $10,000 for the hard problem (as with many a mathematician, basic arithmetic is not his strong suit). He honored his erroneous word. He mailed off the check with the briefest of notes:

Dear Colin: Well, here you are. It seems I made a fool of myself (or was I already one?) Enjoy it, & don't boast too much.

Upon receiving the letter, Mallows already knew of Conway's slip. He called him and offered not to cash the check. Conway tried (not all that hard) to persuade Mallows to go ahead, but they agreed the $10,000 offer was a mistake, and Conway issued a $1,000 check as a replacement. Mallows framed the first check and cashed the second. Conway then discovered that Mallows had made a trivial mistake in his proof—easily fixed, yet a mistake nonetheless. This closed the matter to Conway's satisfaction.

Then Douglas Hofstadter entered the scene. "I was totally flabbergasted," he recalls, "to see an article in the *New York Times* about a nested recursion—not exactly your everyday newspaper fare!"

I'd gotten in touch with Hofstadter, a professor of cognition and computer science at Indiana University, because I knew he and Conway shared a passion for triangle geometry. "I don't know when he caught fire concerning the subject, but I recall very clearly that I myself got obsessed with it in the early 1990s," says Hofstadter, who, like Conway, has long planned to publish a book on triangle geometry. *The Triangle Book* has been in Conway's head since he was a teenager, and a good chunk of it he composed almost half a century later with the help of a high school math teacher, Steve Sigur, from Atlanta, Georgia. Then Sigur died at age 52 from brain cancer, with the manuscript locked in his laptop and Conway without a copy. Sigur's brother dug the file out of the machine, and then Conway, with some help from his publisher's tech department, reclaimed the manuscript and went about finding a new coauthor. Once completed, *The Triangle Book*, according to a clause in the contract at Conway's insistence, will be produced in the shape of a scalene triangle. And naturally, he'll include his "undisputedly simplest proof" of Morley's theorem. Says Hofstadter, "Have you looked at his proof of Morley's theorem? I think that's something that shows his genius really beautifully. He takes a theorem that people had always considered to be difficult and shows *really* what's at the crux of it. His proof dispels the complexity and reduces it to what it's *really* all about. And it's quite stunning in that regard. He saw to the core of it, and nobody else had."

"Probably most people would say, 'Who cares, it's not important, it's a trifle, a curiosity,'" Hofstadter continues. "But I don't feel that way. I think that there are some things in mathematics that are absolutely stunning and beautiful and Morley's theorem is one of them. It's so unexpected and so out of the blue. It seemed so difficult and so strange, its proof seemed counterintuitive—it never, you could never quite grasp, even after seeing a proof, what, where did it come from? And then all of a sudden Conway just peered deep down into it and saw what it *really* is. And I think that's a great contribution. . . . I think that's a wonderful gift that he has. Unlike most mathematicians whose heads are always above the clouds, his head is at ground level, on numbers and shapes, Cayley diagrams, pictorial things, things that are very concrete. Other mathematicians are involved in infinite dimensional representations of hierarchical abstractions that nobody can possibly understand, you can't even think about them. Whereas he is thinking about things that are so concrete. And yet he winds up with profound ideas, and I think that makes him so different from your run-of-the-mill high-quality mathematician. And when I say run-of-the-mill I mean great geniuses like Andrew Wiles. I don't think Andrew Wiles would touch triangle geometry with a 10-foot pole. Conway really is an iconoclast, off in his own territory."

The common territory between Conway and Hofstadter also included that crazy sequence. Hofstadter, in his 1980 Pulitzer Prize–winning book *Gödel, Escher, Bach*, discussed the idea of "meta-Fibonacci" sequences and nested recursion. What exactly is recursion? "The concept is very general. Stories inside stories, movies inside movies, paintings inside paintings. Russian dolls inside Russian dolls." Or a sequence of numbers defined from within, the next term defined by previous. Hofstadter looked closely at a sequence of numbers he called the Q-numbers, or the Q-function (a function being a formula or algorithm whereby numerical input generates numerical output). With the Q-numbers, the next term is obtained by adding 2 earlier terms, but both of the earlier terms are obtained by counting backward from the last term. With the following sequence, he took the last two terms, 10 and 9 . . .

1, 1, 2, 3, 3, 4, 5, 5, 6, 6, 6, 8, 8, 8, 10, 9, 10 . . .

and counted back 9 and 10 positions, landing on 6 and 5, making the next number in the sequence 11. Conway, with the insomniac sequence, had been pondering something very similar. When Hofstadter read the piece in the newspaper, he thought Conway had serendipitously tweaked his Q-function. Then Hofstadter went to his files and found that some years prior he had also discovered this *same* function. He sent off excited letters to Mallows and Conway, Conway's running to 5 pages. "Let me close this letter," he wrote, "by telling you that there is very great interest here in both the Math Department and the Computer Science Department in having you as a colloquium speaker. In addition, I have some funds at my disposal that I might be able to contribute. Altogether, I am sure we would be able to offer a very generous honorarium— enough, most likely, to make up for your loss to Mallows!" And, he added, on a more intimate note: "Knowing of your incredible creativity, I personally would be most interested in a talk that focused on how you think your mind works, in inventing mathematical ideas, in discovering mathematical facts, and in deciding on what is mathematically interesting and elegant. I think your mathematical style and mine are probably somewhat similar—playful, empirical, attracted by quirkiness and chaos hidden in orderly structures, fascinated by simple, easily grasped structures, and so on. I think it would be truly interesting to have some interchange, whether in private or in public, on that particular (and quite rare) style of mathematizing. Would you be interested? I certainly hope so."

Hofstadter's letter to Mallows led to an exploratory back-and-forth. The 5-pager to Conway led to zilch. "To my disappointment (even shock), Conway never acknowledged my letter at all." They never connected for that creative mind meld. "I admire him greatly as a mathematician and a creative spirit, and even as a kindred spirit, in the sense that we have had overlapping interests," says Hofstadter. "I have huge admiration for Conway, but frustration with him at a personal level. He's never been unkind to me . . . he's just been sort of oblivious. Like, 'Oh yeah, there's that Hofstadter fellow, yeah, he'll be a good audience to talk to.' I'm just a receptacle." Hofstadter recalls once visiting Princeton to give a talk, followed by a dinner in his honor at Lahiere's restaurant, to which a small group was invited, including Conway. "Luckily he arrived late," says Hofstadter. "Because for the first half hour I had a pleasant conversation with everybody around the table. But the moment Conway arrived the conversation became completely Conway-o-centric. He just dominated the table. I'm not saying he's not interesting . . ."

And as for the sequence, as Hofstadter recalls, "that Conway made so famous (for rather silly reasons), [it] is now known as the 'Hofstadter-Conway-Mallows sequence,' or sometimes just the 'Hofstadter-Conway sequence' or 'Conway-Hofstadter sequence.'" Or, according to the On-line Encyclopedia of Integer Sequences, it's known as the "Hofstadter-Conway $10,000 sequence"—sequence "A004001" just in case you want to look it up while passing insomniac nights.

In April 1992, Conway was elected a Fellow of the American Academy of Arts and Sciences, together with Princeton writer Joyce Carol Oates and mathematician Robert MacPherson, then at MIT (now at Princeton's Institute for Advanced Study). MacPherson recalls that at the ceremony Conway accepted his honor wearing what appeared to be green running shorts. The citation listed Conway as both a mathematician and an educator, though by his own appraisal he was now more the latter than the former—a realization that can be first traced to a session with a reporter from *The Sciences*. In casting a glance around Conway's office, the reporter inquired about 7 long sheets of paper with larger-than-life-size footprints. Conway started explaining that they represented the different types of symmetry in 2 dimensions:

> *One day, I was walking along, trying to think of an example of translation linked with reflection. All of a sudden, I realized that walking was just*

*what I was looking for! I xeroxed my feet and made up these pictures.
Each one represented a type of symmetry. And each symmetry has a polyhedron associated with it.*

Whereupon he sank with a "pensive thump" down into his chair.

I'm not really doing mathematics right now.

And then he stared contemplatively at the ceiling.

*I guess you can say that I'm expanding it. Instead of trying to prove new
theorems, I'm trying to fill in the holes that other people have left behind.
I want to have a better understanding of what we already know. I want a
more visual, more intuitive feel for math . . .*

And then he stopped short, a little stunned.

I guess you can say that I've almost ceased being a mathematician.

The realization is reminiscent of G. H. Hardy's classic acknowledg-
ment of his waning intellectual prowess in the essay *A Mathematician's
Apology*—described by C. P. Snow as "a passionate lament for creative
powers that used to be and that will never come again." Conway perhaps
wasn't quite ready to throw in the towel, but he happily embraced his
main role as teacher. He is always game to teach. As he likes to say:

*If it sits down, I'll teach it. If it stands up, I will continue to teach it. But if
it runs away, I maybe won't be able to catch up.*

He taught not only in Fine Hall classrooms. He taught on *Math Chat*,
a live call-in TV show produced by Princeton students, dispensing the
following piece of advice for sustaining one's mathematical curiosity:

Preferably, stay being 4 years old all your life.

He taught at public lectures and private parties. During a math department party at Peter Sarnak's house, Conway pulled out his best parlor

trick and performed it all night in the kitchen. Mostly for women. The come-on, still attempted now and then, Conway relishes recounting:

> "I can make U.S. pennies land the way you want for the rest of your life!"
>
> The setup, the patter, is crucially important. It goes like this: "You see, there's recently been this quantum mechanical effect discovered called optional probability fields. However, it's a little bit difficult to manage. I've learned how to switch on a probability field. Unfortunately I haven't learned how to switch it off. But if you like, I can show you. You can choose which way you want U.S. pennies to come up—heads or tails. And if you come into the kitchen with me, especially if you are a lovely young lady, I'll do it. But you must promise not to tell anybody but me which way you choose, heads or tails."
>
> And then somebody comes into the kitchen. And we do a certain experiment. And when they go back to the party they give their reports: "9 times out of 10 I got my result! It's a fantastic thing!"

Martin Gardner taught Conway the first part of this trick. How to make U.S. pennies almost always land heads: stand the coin on its edge on a table and knock the table gently from underneath, knocking the coin over. With that method, more than 95 percent come up heads. The second part of the trick, how to make pennies mostly come down tails, Conway happened upon when he was idly spinning coins on a kitchen table with a friend. He spun 4 of them and they all came down tails. He might have dismissed this had he not known the heads trick, which made him wonder whether there might be more to it. So he kept spinning the pennies on the table and found that above 75 percent landed tails. Since the probability wasn't quite as good with tails, Conway usually has to give the pennies 20 spins to allow, say, 16 tails to present themselves. And for this reason, he engineered his patter to dissuade people from picking tails, to steer them instead toward heads. For example:

> "You must be really sure that you don't mind if U.S. pennies come the way you choose from now on . . ." Do they really want them to come tails? I sort of suggest heads is perhaps more agreeable: "And keep in mind I can't change it. It's no use coming to me in a few years' time and

telling me how your husband has left you and so on. I REALLY CAN'T SWITCH IT OFF!"

"He was the center of the party," recalls Sarnak. Conway is his own party, and he's always at the center.

In June 1993, Princeton's Andrew Wiles announced that he'd proved Fermat's last theorem. Journalists descended from Brazil, Japan, Switzerland, everywhere. The Princeton University communications department noted during the onslaught that Wiles was attracting more media attention than a number of other notable events on campus in recent years—including Brooke Shields's graduation and the awarding of an honorary degree to President George H. W. Bush. Conway was the perfect person to play gatekeeper to the press.

"Before I talked to Wiles, I had to talk to Conway," recalls John Horgan, who was reporting for *Scientific American*. "I got to the Princeton math department, asked where Conway was, and someone pointed out his office. I entered the doorway and was astonished at how messy it was. The floor was covered in garbage, paper, food wrappings, etc., and it was actually kind of smelly, and lots of weird stuff, paper polyhedra and so forth, was hanging from the ceiling. And there was this guy . . . crack of his ass showing above his jeans, before a computer, and without turning around he yelled out, WHAT'S YOUR BIRTHDAY?!"

Conway took calls from reporters on the Batphone in the common room. Students picked up as well—one answered a few ho-hum questions, hung up the phone, and announced, "That was *People* magazine." They were compiling the list of "The 25 Most Intriguing People of 1993," among them Princess Diana, Yasser Arafat, Lorena Bobbitt, Michael Jordan, Jerry Seinfeld, Lyle Lovett, and Bill Clinton. Wiles's mini-profile reported, "Mathematicians were amazed and elated by an electronic message zapped through Internet, the worldwide computer network: 'F.L.T. proved by Wiles.' . . . How did he feel about his achievement? Said Wiles: 'There is a sense of loss, actually.'" Generally Wiles was reluctant to talk,* but answer-

---

* Wiles did not speak that October at "Fermat Fest"—which sold out all 1,000 seats and left 200 people turned away at the door—put on by Berkeley's MSRI and hosted by the

ing the big "Why?" question for CNN, he said: "It's like climbing Mount Everest—we do it because it's there." Exactly 2 months later Wiles was back on the mountain after experts found a bug in his proof. When the media circled back, naturally Wiles was even more reticent, and Conway offered some advice—surely the only time he advocated the merits of obfuscation.

> I advised Andrew to shut it up in the following way, which he did. I said, "What you should do is, rather than say nothing"—which had been his method—"say something involving some highbrow technical terms. Say you have it under control, and say the problem involves gobbledy gobbledy gook. And then all these reporters will go round asking mathematicians what gobbledy gobbledy gook is, rather than asking, 'Do you think it's likely that he'll be able to correct the bug?'" And so he took that advice, and sure enough, if you get the papers from around this time, they are all asking what gobbledy gobbledy gook was. And that stopped the conversation from being about whether he'd be able to cure it.
>
> Everybody here was very nice and sympathetic. We sort of asked each other, "Was Andrew smiling when you saw him this morning? What did he look like?" It was like Kremlinology in the old days, like these experts or Kremlinologists who worked out what was going on in Soviet Union politics by observing who was standing between Brezhnev and Andropov at the latest May Day celebrations—there was no information, really.

Wiles didn't give much information away for about a year. Then again, he never gives much away. One evening I found myself sitting across from him at a formal dinner celebrating the Institute's eightieth anniversary. Conway was the only thing we had in common to explain such a seating plan—it was meant by the savvy party planners to be a research opportunity. When I asked him about Conway, Wiles wouldn't say much, other than "Ask him about his tongue."

Exploratorium in San Francisco. Lecturers included Robert Osserman and Lenore Blum on background, Ken Ribet and Karl Rubin on details (since their contributions played a role in the proof), and Conway summed it all up with what was described as "his own inimitable narrative."

⬧ ▢ ◈ ◉ ◈

Tongue tricks and Doomsday and optional probability pennies notwith-standing, Conway still wrestled with the "slough of despond."

"He's just an ordinary human man, you understand," Kruskal once said, "and he has his foibles, no doubt, but he awes me." Says Doyle: "There's that Robert Frost line: 'We love the things we love for what they are.' People's good qualities and bad qualities are cut from the same cloth." And as Conway himself once said:

I guess I'm a Sybarite. I like beauty, and I like to eat and drink . . . I used to anyway. My heart attack changed that somewhat.

By the time of Conway's first heart attack in 1992, he and Larissa had separated. He tried fidelity. He lived like a monk, for a time. He wanted to save the marriage, but his efforts came across as calculated, contrived to produce the impression that he wanted to save the marriage when really he couldn't be trusted and surely he didn't want to be married at all. This is all from Conway's perspective. Larissa declined to discuss her ex-husband. I spoke to her briefly by telephone and we arranged to meet for an interview. She followed up with a voice mail canceling. Certainly, there wasn't much narrative value in probing the breakdown of a marriage. Per Tolstoy, all unhappy families are unhappy in their own way. Per Chekhov, the same holds true for individuals. And while there was no point in a Kitty Kelley-style treatment and digging up dirt, I had been looking forward to talking to Larissa, the mathematician wife on her mathematician husband, who together produced 2 mathematicians in their sons Alex and Oliver. Possessed of some wishful or even magical thinking, I went for the interview anyway at the appointed time and place, in case she turned up. She did not.

Conway's heart attack followed a talk he gave at Temple University in Philadelphia. He was running to catch the train back to Princeton. He felt funny, sat down, missed the train, and caught the next one. He didn't realize exactly what had happened until that weekend with his boys. Alex jumped on his back and wanted his dad to piggyback him around. Conway couldn't do it. Something was wrong. He was gruff with the kids. He called Larissa. He went to the hospital.

Several weeks later, well on the road to recovery, he felt fantastic. He'd lost a lot of weight. He remembers having a hyper-giddy fit in the presence of the late Dimpy Pathria, a visiting research fellow with whom he had been coteaching a class. He was bubbling and bouncing around, even more than usual, whereas doctor's orders were to take it easy, to rest and lie down whenever possible. Pathria tried to get him to calm down, be serious, and focus on the business of catching up.

But when he calmed down, he went down too far.

> I got very depressed after this heart attack, and that was very understandable, because I damn nearly died. I realized life is finite and all that.

About a year later, in the spring of 1993, he landed in the hospital again. Another heart attack, his friends Simon Kochen and Joe Kohn told those who needed to know.

> They didn't exactly lie. Metaphorically it was true.

When his Doomsday competitor Steve Miller visited, Conway told him the truth:

> I tried to commit suicide and I damn nearly succeeded.

Miller assumed Conway meant he'd been cheating on his diet. Then he realized Conway was speaking literally. He had saved up his sleeping pills, and during lunch at the Nassau Inn with Larissa (and the lawyers, according to Conway's version of events), he ate the sleeping pills like an entrée. After this stunt he walked to his doctor's office, a block away on Witherspoon Street, and Dr. Seed got him to the hospital. From Miller's vantage point Conway's suicide attempt didn't make any sense, since by all outward appearances nothing was wrong. "I was devastated when I found out what happened," says Miller, now a professor at Rutgers and vice chair of the math department. "It was terrible to know that he wasn't happy, because he made so many people happy. . . . He made me so happy."

Even Conway, to some extent, didn't know what was *so* wrong. Loneliness, the acrimony with Larissa, the alienation from his children, the alimony and the lawyers that left him broke. Scientists and mathematicians often regard money with contempt, and Conway had always pushed this to the *n*th degree. He didn't know what his house was worth when he bought it—$30,000 or $300,000—nor the value when it had to be sold. All the dead checks in his unopened mail, all the professional travels paid from his own pocket since he couldn't be bothered to file expense reports. Now he felt the consequences acutely, living off a few dollars a day. The combined psychological effect did him in. He wanted out. "It was a complicated situation," says Miller, "but he conquered it. It was pretty clear he wanted to live. He's a smart enough guy that he managed not to kill himself."

Conway doesn't think of it as the time he *attempted* suicide; he thinks of it as the time he *committed* suicide. He came that close. He doesn't recall what happened after he reached Dr. Seed's office. At the hospital they brought him back, and once he came to he was deliriously happy to find himself alive, never mind the black tube running through his mouth into his stomach, pumping in a toxin-absorbing carbon solution and making him want to gag for more than 24 hours straight. After 4 days of suicide watch, with a nurse keeping guard at his bedside, Conway next confronted the problem of how to orchestrate reentry into society. He asked himself,

What would Conway do here?

This is when he inaugurated his "Let it all hang out" policy. He confronted this personal predicament the same way he would any public appearance: grab the largest amount of attention possible. In order to execute a key component of his plan, he asked a favor of his friend Neil Sloane.

Sloane had always been up at the very top of my To Call list, right beside Martin Gardner. As I went down my list, asking for interviews, some of Conway's dearest friends and closest collaborators hemmed and hawed and eventually refused to participate. Sloane instantaneously put his system preferences on mute—he knew Conway too well and didn't want to be faced with the anxiety-inducing possibility of revealing too much. A number of Conway's people only reluctantly submitted to off-the-record interviews, hesitant to expose him to the scrutiny of a stranger, someone outside the mathematics family. Inside the bubble, people understand him, love and appreciate him, warts and all. Like anyone, he's comprised of contradictions. He's high-maintenance, he's generous. He's emotional, he's impassive. He's a sweetheart, he's an asshole.

Sloane had seen his friend through thick and thin, and he was instrumental in Conway's revival plan. First off, Conway had sent a group e-mail to close colleagues and friends, a suicide note of the "post-attempted" genre, a philosophical commentary on what he was grappling with. He sent a letter to the chairman of the department, and to the dean of the university. He wanted everyone to know. But then there was the question of how to deal with everyone else in Princeton who were no doubt talking. This is where Sloane came in. An avid outdoorsman and rock climber, Sloane owned a T-shirt Conway needed to borrow. A souvenir from climbing a steep California summit graded 5.13 on a scale that topped out at 5.15, the T-shirt shouted **SUICIDE** in big bold letters, with the little tiny word ʀᴏᴄᴋ beneath.

> I thought to myself, What's the correct way to handle this? This is the problem: you've just attempted suicide, you've been in hospital for a week, having your stomach pumped and all that, how do you come back and get past it? And so I turned up in this T-shirt, which was a nice way of saying, "I couldn't care less if you talk about it . . . . Don't feel you have to go into a corner and whisper to each other." You know, I mean everybody in this damn town knows me, and I didn't like the feeling that they were saying things behind my back. I wore it for 2 or 3 days until it got too sweaty. I always like to do things with a bit of splash. It shocked a few people. They made me go across the road to a counseling service—awfully tedious—and I turned up in this T-shirt saying "SUICIDE" and the counselor took on a rather pained expression.

For fortification day to day, he carried in his pocket a talisman, a copy of Rota's "best best best, best best best" review of the *SPLAG* book, which Conway had written out in black pen with the "bests" in red. And another *SPLAG* review, by electrical engineer and information theorist G. David Forney, also always cheered him up immensely: "There is nothing else like it, and as an intellectual accomplishment it is breathtaking." Sloane was also vital to Conway's resurrection in another way. He made

Conway promise not to attempt suicide again for at least 1 year, since it would take at least that long to finish the next tranche of papers they had flowing through the pipeline. Based on previous published papers, compiled in *SPLAG*, they had received U.S. Patent No. 4,507,648, "Decoding Techniques for Multi-Dimensional Codes," applying their sphere-packing work in coding theory, figuring out how to most efficiently send signals across telephone and fiber optic lines and the like. It all comes down to a geometric problem, since the signals must be packed as tightly as possible, yet not too closely, because if they overlap the signals get confused. And after years of peppering him with the odd question, this is the only topic that got Sloane engaged, by e-mail: "It is known from the fundamental work on information theory of Claude Shannon that it is more efficient to use coding schemes that are based on configurations of points in high-dimensional space. One of the drawbacks is the complexity of the encoding and decoding. JHC and I wrote a series of papers showing how this could be done quite easily (in certain cases)." The "Conway-Sloane decoding method" is also cited in patents assigned to Ericsson Inc., as well as "The United States of America as represented by the Director of the National Security Agency." So Conway was an important part of a practically productive enterprise—despite his best intentions, he had done something useful! And because of Sloane's bargain

Steve Miller took this photo of Conway's hexagonal close-packing of tennis balls (about 1,400 tennis balls, a few years' worth of cast-offs from Simon Kochen).

with Conway, his promise to see through these investigations, Sloane helped keep him alive in the immediate aftermath of the suicide attempt, when he might have been vulnerable to slipping back into depression.

Prozac also helped get Conway functional, but he found it intellectually deadening. It killed his creativity. So he went off it cold turkey. Dr. Seed persuaded him at least to carry the pills on his person at all times, in case he felt himself dipping down. Conway noticed the curve of his mental health followed a sine wave, with a delirium-to-depression peak-to-peak cycle that was excited exponentially, the amplitude growing bigger and bigger. He could almost predict where he would be from one day to the next. Dr. Seed was worried about the manic episodes as much as the depressions. Flying high on neurotransmitters run amok, one can get strange ideas, such as, "I wonder what it would be like to jump off this building and fly home." Conway hadn't contemplated Fine Hall's rooftop, but he was interested in the oddly mesmerizing intellectual equivalent.

> Whatever it was, I was interested in exploring it.

The intellectual cliff jumping manifested in what might be called etymological ecstasy. Every word spoken lit up Conway's brain with hypertext. He did an experiment with Kochen whereby he had his friend stop him at any point in a conversation and ask him for the etymology of the last word used. Even in humdrum exchanges, his brain played a constant riff exploring alternate choices for every word and phrase.

> I was actually conscious that my mind was looking at this word, looking at that word, looking at the other word, and then picking this one. All the time there was this branching, all the possibilities for words and phrases, and 3 or 4 sentences presenting themselves as options. Usually the branches that you don't select you're not aware of. On this occasion the cap is taken off and you become aware of what the brain is doing to keep you going. Which very strange. If you think about what must be happening when you have a conversation with somebody, the words are being selected before you say them, and there are alternatives for each theme, for each word. The selector mechanism is doing this all the time and you are unconscious of it, and the selector mechanism must be very

quick. Look, I just said, "The selector mechanism must be very quick." I could have said "exceedingly speedy." In this manic state I was aware of all the possibilities all at once.

The intellectual cliff jumping also manifested itself with his GIMME A DATE! madness, which peaked in the year after Conway's suicide attempt.

It was while watching Conway do his thing in the common room that Steve Miller became smitten with the Doomsday algorithm. "It's so beautiful you would never think there was any easy way to predict it. It's something that once you see it, you get the feeling that it must have secretly existed for all eternity, and Conway was just the one to dig it up. It's so beautiful it doesn't seem that it's something that came out of a human's mind." Miller was convinced he would never be able to learn it himself. "But Conway is such an amazing teacher that it was one of the most magical educational experiences of my life. Maybe the best. Within a half hour he taught me something that I never imagined I could possibly do. It was sort of like telling someone you can control a 747 flying in the sky with your mind, just by concentrating really hard. You wouldn't think you could do it, and then all of a sudden you are flying spaceships just by looking at them. That's the power of his teaching skills. He can really get you doing things you never imagined you could do, and quickly."

For Conway it also served as a good barometer of his brain.

I actually found myself studying the brain. There were several interesting things that happened. My time was $1\frac{1}{2}$ seconds for a single date. And $1\frac{1}{2}$ seconds is a pretty good time. You have to think fantastically quickly to do it. I used this an as exercise if I had 9 o'clock lectures, to warm up for class. I would come in a little bit beforehand, sleepy and everything, and I would just do this a few times and it, you know . . .

Snap go his fingers.

... it got me thinking, FAST.

And there was this one occasion, very, very funny. My best time was off by about 2 seconds from what it usually was. My record time then for

10 dates might have been 15.02 seconds. But this time when I came in I couldn't do better than 17 seconds or something. I just couldn't get to what I'd been routinely getting the day before. Then I learned the reason a day later. I came down with a horrible head cold. This was a wonderful diagnostic device, a tremendously sensitive indicator of my health, and it detected I was ill, some time before I noticed any other symptoms. I got the information a day earlier. Not very nice information: you might feel fine today but tomorrow you will feel awful.

At first, Miller did 10 dates in 45 seconds. After a few weeks of practicing, he and Conway were racing, both steadily getting faster and faster. Trying to beat each other's records, Conway and Miller practiced hours on end, easily totting up 1,000 dates per day. Improvements were hard won. The GAD program read out their times to 2 decimal points, and knocking off $\frac{1}{5}$ of a second—from 13.64, say, to 13.62—was tremendously difficult. Conway taught Miller everything he knew about thinking quickly, the most basic tip being to empty one's brain completely. Gradually they both whittled down their times.

After about 6 months, Miller got his best time down to 10.66. Not much later Conway gave up—maybe he could best the 10.66, get it down to 10.64, but then Miller would just best him back. Miller's brain was youthfully plump and as perfect as it would ever be. Conway's brain by then had suffered at least 2 decades of shrinkage, the fatty myelin insulation withering away, slowing the transmission of signals across the synapses and decreasing reflex speed. So Conway surrendered to Miller and gave up the punishing GAD regime. He moved on to factorizing big numbers and constantly demanding,

GIMME A NUMBER!
The great lightning calculators of the nineteenth century stayed away from factorization because it was too damned hard. So I thought, Okay, let's try that.

If factorizing *truly* big numbers got too easy, a lot of things in society would fail. The e-security and e-commerce systems of banks and governments and private companies depend upon the difficulty of factorizing—a numerical padlock, of sorts—and these systems would disintegrate if anyone discovered a fast algorithm for factorizing very large integers, like 1,000-digit numbers. Conway wasn't factorizing numbers anywhere near this large. But give him a 4-digit number, any number up to 10,000—say, 3,421—and he'll give you the factors, and as an added bonus the closest prime.

> 3,421. That's 11 times 311. That was an easy one—and 3,413, I think that's prime, and 3,433.

Every now and then, even after surrendering to Miller, Conway still dabbled with GAD on the computer, and then there was the time when he came back at it with seemingly superhuman powers. During a manic intellectual cliff-jumping escapade, he wondered what his time would be. He was almost too scared to try. He sat down at the computer and ripped off 10 dates in an astonishing 9.62 seconds.

> I didn't try again. My heart was pumping away like mad. I got this enormous amount of adrenaline, I actually felt liquids pouring into my brain. Maybe that wasn't true, but that's what it felt like. I felt like I could actually detect the various juices that get your brain ready to do things. And it was scary as all hell. But it was interesting, taking the lid off and seeing how the brain works.

These meta-moments he rather enjoyed, so much so that he didn't want to come out of the mania. He fancied the idea of delivering a lecture, "On My Present Mental State." He mentioned this to his doctor. "For God's sake, don't," said Dr. Seed. "Don't be such a fool." He didn't. But he wishes he had.

> I would like to hear that lecture, to hear my description of what was happening while it was happening. I thought it was intensely interesting. I still do. You know, it was weird. Because as well as being amazingly interesting, it was frightening. I didn't have much sense of control.
>
> You wake up in the dark, in the pilot seat of a plane, no window, and your task is to bring the plane down safely. You don't know how to fly the plane. You try this throttle, WOOooo. Everything I did during the manic

phase was highly exaggerated. I had to learn to keep the plane on an even keel. I landed. I don't know how I landed. But I came out of this damn thing. And WOOooo, that was it.

I look back on it with some affection but also with some fear. I would love to get back into the manic state again. Very much. Really, I would. I would be scared of it. But I would love to get back, if there was a guarantee I could get out.

15.
LUSTRATION

I was taught that the way of progress was neither swift nor easy.
—Marie Curie

In his cocksure way, Conway has always liked to boast about his ability to walk into a lecture room at a moment's notice, give a talk on any random subject, and hold his audience rapt. After his suicide attempt, he lost his mojo. More insomniac than ever, he managed 1 or 2 hours of sleep a night, maximum 4. He always kept a few books by his bedside to help him pass these nights—a detective story, something by Agatha Christie; a scientific book; a big historical tome; and a biography or autobiography, say Casanova's 6-volume *History of My Life*. His daytime performance suffered, however, and during a games conference in Berkeley in July 1994, he gave a really rotten showing.

> It was a disaster. On the other hand, a talk that I think was a disaster other people often think was quite reasonable. I'm so much better at giving talks than other people that . . . well, never mind. But it really is the case. The prevailing standard in mathematics is just god-awful. But anyway, I gave my talk and it wasn't much good, that's all you need to know.

The next day there was a no-show, and the conference chair, Richard Guy, then working with Conway on *The Book of Numbers*, asked his coauthor to fill in. Conway gave his usual knee-jerk response in the affirmative. But given the recent disaster he immediately had second thoughts. He asked Guy when this talk was scheduled. "Now!" Walking the short distance to the front of the lecture room, Conway did his typical impromptu preparation and decided it would be a good idea to pull out his golden oldie, "The Lexicode Theorem—Or Is It?" This talk went over less disastrously, in Conway's estimation; it might even have been something of a success. As the audience milled around afterward, gradually making their way out of the room, a bottleneck formed at the exit and Conway ended up behind the door waiting to leave. As he stood there unseen by the people filing out, he heard the Canadian mathematician Aiden Bruen give his assessment: "That's more like the Conway we know and love."

> That told me 2 wonderful things: That my impression of the first talk was right—I had an objective opinion, someone else thought the first talk was a disaster too, which I needed to know because I needed to know that my impressions were in accordance with reality. And then it told me that the second talk was, in fact, really more like the Conway we know and love.

The next month, in August, Conway was due to deliver a plenary address at the International Congress of Mathematicians in Zurich. His resurrection in Berkeley made him worry less than he might have about this honor, but still he worried, and he made it known he was worrying. His girlfriend, for example, knew very well the extent of his worrying They'd met when a summer workshop for high school teachers convened at the Princeton math department and he infiltrated the gathering, hijacked the itinerary, and marched the group outdoors, seducing them, this woman literally, with sweet nothings about how to stare at a brick wall. They arrived in Zurich during the middle of a heat wave, with temperatures reaching 95 degrees and no air-conditioning at the Congress venue. Conway's was the second-to-last talk on the last day, the hour before Andrew Wiles's much-anticipated progress report on the Fermat bug.

Conway's invited talk committed him to speak on a specific subject; in retrospect he titles it "A Boring Talk," describing recent advancements in sphere packing, lattices, and codes. He'd given numerous talks on sphere packing, and sometimes he lightened the mood by mocking the usual way mathematicians employ the overhead projector, covering their transparency's content with a piece of paper that they slowly move down, revealing their exposition line by line by line. Conway covered his slide with 4 sheets of paper overlapping length- and width-wise, leaving only a tiny square window visible at the center, and therein a point representing sphere packing in 0 dimensions. Then he expanded his viewfinder of sorts slowly outward, revealing a narrow horizontal band of space representing 1 dimension, then expanding further for a representation of 2 dimensions, and enlarging further to represent 3 dimensions, and then blowing it all up to reveal a hyperdimensional packing of spheres. A couple of hours before his Zurich talk, he launched another anti-boredom intervention when he happened upon a new way to energize the sphere-packing lecture, which he intended to truncate, and then in a bit of a dirty cheat he planned to segue to "The Lexicode Theorem"—remounting his golden oldie, despite the fact that it had little to do with the sphere-packing subject he'd been assigned.

When he arrived at the lecture hall it was packed full with 3,000 mathematicians. He figured they were all there to hear Wiles and wanted to make sure they got a seat. And all of them were sweating into near stupor owing to the saunalike conditions. It was particularly odd, then, that when Conway stepped onto the dais he was wearing a utility jacket. Behind him, the overhead projector announced the lecture title, "Sphere Packing, Lattices, and Codes." He grabbed a marker, scrawling an addendum to the title: "AND GREED"—since the Lexicode is defined by a "greedy algorithm" (an algorithm that instructs you always to "take" the first item possible—e.g. aa before ab, or 001012 before 001103).

He began with some modest throat clearing.

Here I am winging it at an International Congress.

And then he got on with it.

Nobody knows how to fill our ordinary 3-dimensional space as densely as possible with identical spheres. It is supposed that the best way is to pack the balls in rows and layers, in the way I'll show you now . . .[*]

---

[*] The Kepler Conjecture stated that the densest sphere packing in 3-dimensional Euclidean space was a pyramid-shaped packing (a cubic or hexagonal close packing), which was proved true in 1998 by Thomas Hales.

He pulled from his coat pocket a crumpled piece of something that popped alive in his hand to form a blue foam ball the size of a cantaloupe. That took care of sphere packing in 0-dimensional space, where there is only a single point in the space and the sphere is hardly meaningful at all. Then he reached into various other pockets and produced a few more spheres, red, green, blue, purple, yellow, which he arranged on the table as a 1-dimensional sphere packing, a hypothetically infinite line. More balls emerged from more pockets and he configured a triangular grid of spheres illustrating 2-dimensional space, and then more and more balls still emerged from more pockets, accumulating into a 3-dimensional stacking.

This nonsense took somewhere between 5 and 10 minutes. It was all a wonderful coincidence really. We'd walked to the conference hall and on the way was a toy store. There was a basket of these squashy polystyrene balls. And I thought, Hey, I'm supposed to be talking about sphere packing—those might be useful! You could squeeze them down to almost nothing. So I went in and bought the entire stock, which was 14 of them. I distinctly remember 14.

Having thus covered the talk's requisite sphere-packing content, Conway stripped off his coat, flung it to the floor, and carried on with the Lexicode Theorem

I said, "Now I'm going to change topic slightly, and some of you won't quite see the connection with sphere packing before the end of the talk." Well, what I didn't say was that some of them wouldn't see the connection with sphere packing after the talk.

Ever the smooth talker, at the end of his talk, Conway quickly and effortlessly tied it all together with a bow.

How are lexicographic codes related to sphere packings? The answer is, they ARE sphere packings!

Because lexicographic codes, although generated playfully in that parallel universe of addition (or slightly more precisely, in a funny non-

Euclidean kind of space), also turn out to be an effective way of producing error-correcting codes. Computer memory, like human memory, can get corrupted, by cosmic rays for instance. Having error-correcting codes, codes that are preprogrammed to correct their code words with a lexicographic auto-spellcheck of sorts, is another way of efficiently making codes more fault-tolerant.

Having tied off these loose ends, Conway then concluded by sending the 14 balls flying into the audience. And to demonstrate just how pleased he was, he got down on his back on the floor and did his dance of glee, rolled around waggling his arms and legs and laughing. Frivolous nonsense, but it earned Conway a spot in the hearts of even his most serious colleagues. He has since met 2 people who caught the balls and saved them. The New Zealand mathematician Marston Conder's sits on his mantelpiece, a precious relic, and Germany's Dierk Schleicher keeps his purple ball in his Conway shrine (as Conway calls it). The Russian mathematician Vladimir Arnold was also impressed, and he mentioned Conway in his report on the Congress published in the *Mathematical Intelligencer*. The headline asked: "Will Mathematics Survive?" That is, will it survive its self-cultivated image of elitist inaccessibility, "perpetuated by Druids recruiting acolytes in the mathematical schools by Zombie-like mental subjection?" Conway, Arnold felt, was one indication it might. "Eccentric as it was, Conway's was one of the most understandable talks in the Congress," said Arnold, who took pleasure in recounting the antics play by play. "The trouble is the progressive conversion of congresses," he continued, "into Reputation Fairs: speakers are trying to show what great scientists they are more than to impart something to the audience, and they think their purpose is served by incomprehensible lectures. . . . Most talks at the Congress were like sermons. The lecturers plainly didn't expect that listeners would understand anything. Sometimes they went so far as to state obviously false theorems to the respectfully silent auditorium. The sermon mood was so pervasive that most of the introducers didn't even ask for questions at the end. And when some old-fashioned professors did urge people to ask questions, very few listeners overcame the fear of exposing their ignorance sufficiently to do so." Conway at the Congress was an antidote to all that. And, the Congress cured him.

I bounced back to my usual hyper self. I regard that as my coming back to life. It felt so damn good. And then also the girlfriend helped. . . . Having a girlfriend does wonders for you, if you happen to be the type who likes girlfriends.

At the next International Congress, in Berlin in the summer of 1998, Conway's former Ph.D. student Richard Borcherds received the Fields Medal for his proof of the Monstrous Moonshine conjecture. As noted in the citation:

> This conjecture was formulated at the end of the '70s by the British mathematicians John Conway and Simon Norton and presents two mathematical structures in such an unexpected relationship that the experts gave it the name "Moonshine." In 1989, Borcherds was able to cast some more light on the mathematical background of this topic and to produce a proof for the conjecture. . . . In his proof, Borcherds uses many ideas of string theory—a surprisingly fruitful way of making theoretical physics useful for mathematical theory. Although still the subject of dispute among physicists, strings offer a way of explaining many of the puzzles surrounding the origins of the universe.

Conway did not attend the Berlin Congress, despite the fact that Borcherds's prizewinning work evolved from Conway DNA. "More or less every paper I've written can be traced back to an idea Conway had about a certain 26-dimensional lattice," says Borcherds. "It is a rather obscure paper that very few people know about. But without the idea in that paper, almost nothing I've done would have worked."

Well, it's nice to know he thinks that. I never taught Borcherds anything. I really didn't. He's obviously read some of my papers.

To deliver the laudation at the Congress, Borcherds had invited not Conway, as might have been expected, but the mathematical physicist Peter Goddard, in part because Goddard's "no-ghost theorem" (together with Charles Thorn) had been put to critical use in the proof. The ceremony was grandiose, with string quartets and dignitaries in dinner jackets. Even the mathematicians on the program were done up in suits, Goddard and Borcherds among them (though Borcherds always maintained his suit was "Ursula's suit," passing it off as his wife's, not wanting to admit ownership himself). Goddard began with formal and effusive praise of Borcherds's achievement, and then moved onto the technical details. "Since I'm going to get down to work, you'll excuse me if I become a mathematician," he said, taking off his jacket and tie to applause. "Displaying penetrating insight, formidable technique, and brilliant originality," he continued, "Richard Borcherds has used the beautiful properties of some exceptional structures to motivate new algebraic theories of great power with profound connections with other areas of mathematics and physics. He has used them to establish outstanding conjectures and to find new deep results in classical areas of mathematics. This is surely just the beginning of what we have to learn from what he has created."

The juxtaposition therein of new algebraic theories with classical mathematics gets at the crux of why Borcherds chose Goddard over Conway for the laudation. Borcherds correctly anticipated that his approach to proving the Moonshine conjectures would be a mismatch with his adviser. And Conway, over the years, has not hidden his lack of enthusiasm. I witnessed this firsthand when I sat in on his lecture to a Princeton group theory seminar. As Conway wrapped up the lecture he tied together all the groups under discussion by drawing an image of a mountain range, with 4 nested mountains.

I don't know what the point is of tying them all together. I suppose it helps to understand. If you can't understand something, you can at least relate it to something else you don't understand. That's how Borcherds got his Fields Medal. He didn't understand the Monster, but he related it to everything else in the world.

Thereupon he concluded,

That's it. I give up.

He grabbed his copy of *The ATLAS* and disappeared out the door of the classroom. "He ends class like that sometimes," said Boris Alexeev, a graduate student. "He just runs away." And facing Borcherds's proof, Conway similarly flees, although he was pleased for Borcherds himself.

It's rather nice to have a student who got the Fields Medal. It's the next best thing to getting the Fields Medal yourself.* He got it notionally for proving these Moonshine conjectures. He proved them in the sense that he sort of verified them. They haven't really been proved. That's still a slightly contentious thing. I prefer to call it verification. Strictly speaking and legally speaking, a verification is a proof. But it's got a different feeling to it. A proof should really give you some explanation why it's true.

When I mention all this to Borcherds, he laughs and doesn't seem to take offense. "I always got the impression that he was never entirely happy with the proof that I came up with," he says. "My impression was he had fairly definite ideas about how the Moonshine conjectures ought to be proved and what they should be related to. And my proof doesn't fit into his ideas of how it should have been done."

"For example, one part of Conway and Norton's conjecture says that various functions should be genus 0," he continues. "That means there

---

* This happened again in 2014, when Princeton professor Manjul Bhargava won the Fields for (in part) proving Conway's 15 Conjecture and 290 Conjecture, having to do with quadratic forms and the geometry of numbers. Conway himself had proved the 15 Conjecture, thus transforming it into the 15 Theorem, and then Bhargava reproved and improved it. Bhargava also did the much harder job of proving the 290 Theorem. Since Conway rarely looks at official teaching documents such as the roster of his Ph.D. students, for a time he believed Bhargava was his student, but in fact he belonged to Andrew Wiles.

should be a genus 0 Riemann surface lying around somewhere—in other words, there should be a sphere. And in the proof of the Moonshine conjectures there are no spheres anywhere in sight. The proof was very algebraic, and I think Conway was hoping to have a more geometric proof. You probably know this famous quote by Hermann Weyl about the difference between geometry and algebra, one being from God and one being from the devil"—the angel of geometry and the devil of algebra, fighting for the soul of all mathematical domains. "Conway was fond of messing around with geometrical diagrams. He'd draw little patterns of triangles and hope to get a representation for the Monster out of these."

"It's well known that the first proof of anything is always somewhat clumsy," Borcherds adds. "There were definitely some rather clumsy parts. But then so far nobody has really come up with anything better." This gets to the heart of Conway's discontent. He worries that with the word on the street being "the deal is done," future mathematicians won't take up the cause. For a while he had Boris Alexeev working on the Monster for his Ph.D. dissertation, though Conway was scared he might ruin him in the process.

> I was reluctant to take him on because my record with graduate students has not been stellar. I vaguely tried to dissuade him, but in the end I decided he was brilliant enough to survive having me as a teacher.

Alexeev eventually moved on to pursue a medley of subjects for his Ph.D., with the Monster only making a brief appearance at the end, and he's since left pure mathematics for a job at a Berkeley finance firm although he is seriously considering a return to academia. So for Conway, there are still plenty of reasons to ask, with the dogged persistence of a 4-year-old, "Why? Why? Why?"

The Moonshine conjectures postulated that given the mathematical evidence, there should be an object (or a series of spaces) on which the Monster enacts its symmetries. There was an early near proof by computer, a numerical verification, but it was unsatisfying to everyone. Then a number of mathematicians and physicists picked up the problem of finding an explicit (albeit abstract) object that explained the Monster's properties. Some of these efforts were covert operations fueling competition among colleagues, not always without collateral damage—and most of these efforts were wrong or abandoned. Borcherds's proof drew upon advances by a trio of mathematicians, Yale's Igor Frenkel, Rutgers's James Lepowsky, and Lund University's Arne Meurman. They constructed a "conformal field theory" whose symmetry group is the Monster. This arguably bestowed the Monster with its raison d'être, but it did not prove the Moonshine conjectures. Their conformal field theory construction used vertex operator algebras, a tool in string theory, and I found their book, *Vertex Operator Algebras and the Monster*, at the Institute library. The checkout card bore the name "Witten"—the Institute's own Edward Witten, the so-called "pope of strings" and the "Einstein of our day"—a warning sign if ever there was one that hazardous reading lay ahead. When the book found its way into Conway's hands, he proceeded with caution, and in the end he decided it would be better to find an alternate route, because even when granted a private tutorial by the authors he simply didn't get it.

It seemed terribly complicated. They use all sorts of complicated ideas coming from physics that I don't understand. I basically have no hope of reading it or understanding it. For me it's too complicated. And I don't just mean it's too complicated for me to understand. It's too complicated to be the explanation for the Monster.

Which leads him back to his mantra:

I still say that the one thing I want to do before I die is understand WHY the Monster exists.

Conway may have missed his chance when he left Cambridge. Cambridge had its cabal of group theorists, the "groupies," all working on some variant of the Monster and Moonshine, Borcherds among them. When Conway came to Princeton there were no group theorists, which was a moot point at the time, because having just finished *The ATLAS*, he was sick of group theory anyway.

I didn't want to ever see a group again for quite some time. I always knew that I would want get back to it later. It's like Saint Augustine's prayer: "God make me chaste, but not yet." I knew I would like to do group theory again, but I'd just had enough for the time being.

He has gotten back to it since, every now and then. He'd still like to discover what he considers the equivalent of the Leech lattice for the Monster. The dodecahedron is the object underlying a particular Coxeter group, and the Leech lattice is the object underlying the Conway group. What is the entity underpinning the Monster group? For Conway, the conformal field theory doesn't cut it as the raison d'être, and neither does Borcherds's proof. Borcherds reinterpreted and refined the Frenkel-Lepowsky-Meurman construction and proved the Moonshine conjectures by setting the Monster in a larger context, that of a sort of string theory, with a wider symmetry, and in doing so he invented a new sub-branch of mathematics. As Goddard puts it, "By setting the Moonshine results in this more general context he showed *why* they are true (*pace* Conway)."

Conway truly hopes there is still another answer to his WHY. He doesn't expect the answers to be trivial. And indeed, the complexities are only increasing. In recent years there has been a Moonshine revival, not in connection with the Monster group but this time in connection with the Mathieu subgroups—so it's Mathieu Moonshine, where similar mysterious numerological coincidences are popping up and inspiring a resurgence of interest. Even so, Conway still expects the answers to be simple. He is committed to the moral imperative of simplicity, whereas currently all the explanations are hard. Borcherds's proof, for Conway, is hard. And its algebraic nature strips the Monster of its fetching individuality, its exceptional beauty and sporadic personality—attributes Conway finds alluring and irresistible.

Goddard once approached Conway about an idea he thought he might appreciate. Of the 26 sporadic simple groups, some had been found to be the symmetries of codes, some the symmetries of lattices, and others the symmetries of conformal field theories. Codes, lattices, and conformal field theories are, in a sense, all different versions of the same thing, with some clever twists—complementary objects of escalating sophistication. So a question arises: Can one find all of the 26 sporadic groups in this way? Is there a uniform structure of some sort that would allow for a unified understanding? "So I went to Conway and said, 'What do you think of the idea that somehow there should be some way of constructing a whole set of things that would produce all the sporadic simple groups and would enable you to have a more uniform understanding?'" Goddard has not forgotten his response:

That is an absolutely disgraceful idea!

He seemed horrified and offended, as if Goddard had proposed dragooning some of his most beloved and eccentric friends, putting them in uniforms, as it were, and subjecting them to a military drill. "He was almost emotional about it," Goddard recalls. "And what I managed to understand was that in his view any uniform understanding would destroy the individuality of these objects. This is a sort of division in mathematical thinking," he says, "a tension between the particular and the general. Most mathematicians would say, 'Great, we can understand all these things in a uniform way—it all fits together. All these complications, all the clever twistings, are things that you don't really need to do. It was marvelous to see them done, but now we understand things uniformly.' This is something that Conway finds repugnant. He wants to understand them all as being some baroque combination of interrelating objects."

Conway, for his part, doesn't remember his "disgraceful" comment.

Okay, if Goddard remembers it like that, he remembers it like that. If he believes I said that, that's fine. But I can't really believe I said that, because it's counter to what I've always thought. So maybe you could put in a rebuttal . . .

I love the simple groups, I would love to see them explained, and I would love it if the explanation were uniform. When I discovered my group, it brought the total number of sporadic groups to 14, and 12 of them were involved in my group. That looked like an approach to unifying, and I was delighted with that—of course I was partly delighted because it was my group that did it. And then Bernd Fischer discovered his group, F_{24}, and I remember getting off a train in Germany where he lived,

Bielefeld I think; he was coming to meet me, and I shook my fist at him, a friendly fist as a sort of joke, because his group was a million times bigger than mine. And then came the Monster. That's the reason I want to know what the Monster is all about, because it's the next best thing to unifying them all. But it doesn't succeed.

Conway's purported disgust might have been more specific than general. Which is to say that unification, executed specifically with something so complicated as the conformal field, wasn't to his taste, and it would be unpalatable to think that that might be the only answer. Another truth lost to history. Although Conway admits the gist of Goddard's impression is well founded. Conway loves mathematics' bizarre, baroque ornamental entities.

It's true, I like interesting individual things.

He falls for the individuals, and he lingers over them with a certain self-indulgence. He prefers the individual and exotic to the generic and the generalized. He likes the special argument, whereas others prefer the general argument. The former is like putting a jigsaw puzzle together one piece at a time, and the latter is like taking the whole picture and cutting it up into jigsaw pieces. Says Goddard, "In other hands, his way of doing it, which is called case splitting, is often messy and inelegant. Conway raises it to a very high art. When he does it, it's like watching a world-class juggler. But the problem is, if you try to carry some oranges upstairs and you see someone do it by juggling, it doesn't really help you, because you can't juggle."

It also leaves Conway disappointed and dissatisfied with what is so far known of the Monster and Moonshine. Although this view is not shared by all, neither is it unique to Conway. At Monster and Moonshine conferences, symposia, and workshops that continue to convene annually, scientists—mathematicians and physicists alike—pine for greater clarity. One tome, *Moonshine Beyond the Monster*, collecting the latest research, asked: "So, has Monstrous Moonshine been explained? According to most of the fathers of the subject, it hasn't. They consider [the explanations so far] too complicated to be God-given. The progress, though impressive, has broadened, not lessened, the fundamental mystery. . . . Explaining away a mystery is a little like grasping a bar of soap in a bathtub, or quenching a child's curiosity. Only extreme measures like pulling the plug, or growing up, ever really work." Conway ascribes to neither of those measures. Time and time again he keeps questioning.

WHY is there a Monster? I don't know, I have no idea. I would love to know, before I die. I doubt if I will. It's rather sad. I would like to be able to SEE the Monster, in some sense.

He keeps trying, returning to the subject periodically.

Every now and then I take it out and polish it and think about it a bit more. Have I used the word "lustrum" in your presence? Well, "lustrum" is an English word meaning a period of 5 years. And I've seen it used twice in English books. One is in Benjamin Disraeli's novel *Sybil*, where it says of a young man that he had not yet finished his fifth lustrum, as a way of saying he was not yet 25. And then I saw it again in a detective novel by A. E. W. Mason, *The Prisoner in the Opal*. And then some years ago the word "lustration" appeared in Czech politics—anybody who had collaborated with the previous regime had to undergo a probationary period of 5 years before they were rehabilitated, and that was called a "lustration."

Well, I have these lustral ideas. Once a lustrum, roughly, I take out the Monster and try to think about it. And roughly every time I do that I have some success, or a bright idea. And I call those lustral ideas. Because the word "lustrum" has something to do with brightness as well. It is connected with luster. In Roman times, apparently, every lustrum you underwent some sort of period of intense spring cleaning, you polished everything up. So I have these lustral ideas about the Monster.

He knows any real success on this front is likely to take many more lustra than he has left. That doesn't keep him from reciting his mantra:

I still don't understand why the Monster exists. That's THE thing I want to understand before I die. It seems unlikely that I shall now. I've not totally given up hope, but . . .

16.
TAKE IT AS AXIOMATIC

Two things are infinite: the universe and human stupidity;
and I'm not sure about the universe.

—Albert Einstein

When I first met Conway at the Canada/USA Mathcamp in July 2003, he was 65 going on 16. The camp that summer was held at the University of Puget Sound and the Mathcampers shared the grounds with a cheerleading camp. The male-to-female ratio for the former was 5:1, for the latter 1:25. And while the socks-with-sandals Mathcampers might well have been conducting one of those no-soap bacteria-rich hygiene experiments, the cheerleaders blow-dried and beribboned their hair every day at 6:00 A.M., applied and reapplied moisturizer to their head-to-toe perfect tans, and bounded around campus wearing pom-pommed flip-flops and very short shorts (which eventually gave way to perfectly creased miniskirts). One might think it difficult for the young mathematicians to concentrate with cheerleaders swarming the fields outside their classrooms and high-kicking to a megaphoned "1 and 2, up, 3 and 4, and 5 and 6, and 7 and 8." In the event, they barely seemed to notice, let alone lust after their neighbors.

Mathcamp is a haven where mathematically minded kids get their feet wet, not in pools and lakes (*maybe* on their day off), but rather in the universal ocean that is research mathematics. Every summer Conway gives over 2 weeks to talk math with kids—spending a week at Mathcamp with teenagers 15 to 18, and a week at MathPath with 11-to-14-year-olds. This setting puts Conway in heaven, pretty much, and the same can be said for the campers. "We basically do whatever we want every day," said Mathieu Guay-Paquet, then 18, a helix-haired camper from Montreal. "There's a lot of freedom and no curfew, because if we had to go to bed at a certain time, that might interrupt some important mathematical ideas." All classes at camp are optional, and the campers have total freedom to decide how they spend their time. Not surprisingly, they choose to spend a good amount of time in the classes, which might include sessions on algebraic curves, calculus without calculus, p-adic numbers, the mathematics of juggling, vector fields, basic cryptography, complex analysis, hard-core problem solving, multilinear algebra, big numbers, paradoxes of probability, geometric crochet, and the John Conway Hour with his subject NTBA (Not To Be Announced).

By the time I arrived, it was Conway's last day and a triple-header: first a Conway lecture at 9:00 A.M. (on a Saturday; no sleeping in), second a Conway games challenge at noon, and then his closing act in the evening. It was also coming up on the final week of camp, and over the past 5 weeks the campers had been staying up later and later, for the all-nighter bridge tournament, the 50-hour puzzle hunt, the last-minute yearbook edits, or simply to do more math—"Meet here at midnight Tuesday," read a sign posted on the notice board, under the heading, "Math Until We Die."

Conway, although young at heart and head, was by then beginning to look like his friend Archimedes, as portly as ever but increasingly bearded and increasingly gray. Still, with his regular rotation of T-shirts and yesterday's shorts he camouflaged well among the campers. In this company, however, he is a wizard and a saint, the living embodiment of math for math's sake. Application is not the point, he tells the kids—

> Beautiful intellectualizing, that is the satisfaction. The intellectual life of society should allow some people to do interesting things.

I had sought Conway out for an interview about his hero Donald Coxeter. I got what I wanted, and I was surprised by what I got in addition. He treated my recording device like a confessional. He told me about his divorce from Larissa and how he missed their boys. He told me about his heart attack and his suicide attempt. He told me about his third wife, Diana, 28 years his junior, whom he'd met at the coffee shop and married at the registrar's office after a 5-year courtship. During one of their early dates, at a university function, Conway got into an argument over words with the last person you would want to pick a word fight with, the linguist Noam Chomsky. Diana was both embarrassed and impressed. She worked in public relations but soon discovered she had a knack for numbers and switched to accounting. By that summer at Mathcamp, they had a toddler, Gareth, then nearly 2. It was hard to know what to make of Conway's confessional orgy. I later learned he unburdened himself with other reporters as well, and he still sometimes prefaces a math talk with more than a passing reference to his suicide attempt. He blocks out life, the quagmiric muddle of the personal and interpersonal, until he can't stop the raw unresolvedness of it all from rushing back into the breach. And then that's that. He's purged it for the moment and he continues on his way.

The chatter among the campers, waiting for Conway's morning lecture, had it that he'd be performing his notorious tangle trick, as he did the year before, and surely in prior years as well. This is another of his golden oldies. Stragglers trickled into the lecture room, from the cafeteria or straight from bed, and while he waited for the audience to settle he opened up the floor to requests for his closer that evening. One camper raised his hand and asked for the Game of Life.

All right. And another suggestion?

Another hand, another Game of Life. A third camper suggested Game of Life again. It seemed they had his number.

I've got a better idea.

He turned to the blackboard and scrawled his chosen topic: "How to Beat Children at Their Own Games." That settled, he pulled a jump rope out of his shorts pocket and another rope from a plastic bag and proceeded as expected with his tangle trick, also known as "Rational Tangles" or "Square Dancing"—a tangle being a piece of "knottiness" with 4 ends coming out. He warned anyone who saw the trick last year to keep their big mouths shut. "It'll be a lot of fun anyway," said Mat.

To begin, Conway selected 4 volunteers and arranged them in a square. He produced 2 ropes and gave each volunteer an end of rope such that the ropes formed the square's top and bottom edges, or back and front edges from the audience's viewpoint. He then jerked the rope out of the hand of a distracted volunteer, startling her but making the point that it's important to pay attention and hold those ropes tightly, since a dropped rope is a disaster. From there he shouted explanations of his square-dancing calls. "Twist 'em up!" meant the camper in the back right corner of the square should lift up her rope, allowing her counterpart in the front right corner to duck underneath and become the back right corner (the dancers on the right switch positions). "Turn 'em 'round" meant the campers should each rotate a single position clockwise. "Display" meant show the tangle to the audience—the back ropes lift, the front ropes lower. And then the experiment began:

Twist 'em up!
Twist again!
Twist!
Turn 'em 'round!
Twist!
Turn!

The square dancers moved hesitantly, waylaid by giggles and uncertainty. Another volunteer, the appointed arithmetician, recorded the moves on the blackboard: $0, 1, 2, 3, -\frac{1}{3}, \frac{2}{3}, \frac{3}{2} \ldots$ This was a discovery of Conway's dating to his teenage foray into knot theory: tangles behave like fractions. Starting at 0, for each "Twist" in the ropes add 1, and for each "Turn" take the negative reciprocal. Soon the ropes are in a fine clumpy mess of a tangle, with a sum total of $\frac{31}{43}$. Conway covered up the knottiness with a plastic bag and made the dreaded order:

Now, have a go at getting it back to 0.

He expected his volunteers, with directions from the audience, to untangle themselves. Blind. No looking at the tangle.

Come on now, away you go!

They are not entirely blind, because if the arithmetician's record on the blackboard is correct, it will act as a map and allow the square danc-ers to retrace their steps and reverse-engineer the tangle. After about 20 minutes of this rewound square dancing, consensus had it that the tan-gle should be back at 0.

> Well, I'm not so sure. I have a horrible feeling someone twisted when they should have turned.

Not to mention that the plastic bag was now ingrown with the tangle. Conway knelt to solve this problem. He chewed into the bag, tearing it off piece by piece with his teeth. With the bag gone, the ropes still looked a mess. Fingers crossed, Conway instructed the square dancers to give the ropes a good yank and "Display!" The tangle dissolved, to hoots of joy from the audience. Then Conway told them that when he was a stu-dent, enumerating 1,000 knots or so, he got to know knots like personal friends. Tie any knot in a rope and he knows which knot it is, and whether it's the same knot he encountered last week or last month. There is a certain knot problem, however, that has gone unresolved.

> I've been struggling with this problem about knots all my life: how to de-scribe a knot to someone over the telephone. Now, keep in mind, the per-son on the other end of the line is probably a nerd, just like you . . .

Over the next while, I saw quite a bit of Conway. I sought him out in Princeton for further interviews about Donald Coxeter, and he vetted my Coxeter manuscript, making sure his hero got something close to his due, making sure I didn't get caught up romanticizing the complexities.

> It's a mistake to assume that what mathematicians do is esoteric, deep, and difficult. All the great discoveries are very simple. Like Coxeter's and Einstein's.

After Conway's ego had gotten the better of him and he agreed to this biography, I saw more of him still. Hanging around at the Institute year in and year out, cornering him in the alcove, more than once I was dis-turbed by an annual ritual that unfolded on the 3rd month and the 14th day—Einstein's birthday, by the way—at 1:59:26 P.M. precisely.

"5 ... 4 ... 3 ... 2 ... 1 ..." went the official countdown in the common room. And everyone screamed "Happy Pi Day!" Across town, the Institute served pie instead of cookies at tea, and MIT is known to mail out their acceptance letters on this very special day. At Berkeley a man was spotted with π shaved into his beard. The first official Pi Day celebration took place at San Francisco's Exploratorium in 1988, and it has since been recognized with a resolution by the U.S. House of Representatives. The celebrations are not always formally concerned with commemorating how the mathematical constant pops up in physics and biology, architecture and engineering, astronomy and statistics; and not so much concerned with the fact that if mathematicians were able to find a pattern among its infinite digits, humanity would certainly be the wiser. Pi Day is more about pure and simple fun. It is also a good example of Conway's gift for spontaneous combustion. When Conway turns on, sparks fly.

The Princeton party began with a contest Conway knew well: Who could recite the most digits of π? Working from memory, Conway served as de facto adjudicator, augmenting the speed-reading skills of student judges who followed along with multipage π printouts. The first contestant managed no more than 20 digits. The next contestant blanked after 91, the last few numerical groupings issued with increasing interrogative uncertainty: ... 4825342117? ... 0679821?? Adam Hesterberg, then an undergraduate (now a grad student at MIT), fired off the π-recitation equivalent of "Flight of the Bumblebee," an allegro staccato 140 digits that had spectators finger-snapping and foot-tapping to his automaton tempo—until, in a moment of distraction, he paused. "He's calculating!" hollered a heckler. Wearing a MANIC SAGES T-shirt from Mathcamp, he then shrugged and gave up. "I've lost my place," he said. This was a disappointment. His personal best is 243.

With the 5 competitors done, the president of the math club attempted to inveigle Conway's participation, having heard rumors of his prowess. "Professor Conway . . .?"

No, no. I'm sorry, I haven't been practicing. I always mean to, but I forget.

That made Adam the winner. After he received his prize, a binary clock, next came the pie-eating contest. Contestants were allotted 3 minutes and 14 seconds to devour as much of a pie as possible, utensils optional. This time Conway was tempted to take part. As usual, he hadn't eaten lunch. Then again, pie was not on his diet. He declined.

I suspect it would be the cause of my death.

The contestants took their seats, took their marks, and dug in. To everyone's dismay, they employed their plastic spoons. Grumbles from the audience declared it miserable to watch, the most pathetic, lackluster, shameful showing in Pi Day history. Then, with nary a minute left on the stopwatch, Conway lost his self-control. He inched forth from the back of the crowd, surveyed the selection of more than 3 dozen pies, sextuplets of apple, pecan, blueberry, peach, cherry, a very bouffant lemon meringue. He chose pumpkin, gingerly peeled back its foil plate from beneath, opened and angled his hairy mouth for the best approach, and took a monster bite. Then another, and another and another. He chomped his way around the pie's circumference. "He's going to eat it all!" "He's going to win!" And he did. Catching his breath, he rubbed his stomach and accepted his binary clock. "That was ridiculous," commented a student.

Why, thank you!

Gareth won the Princeton Pi Day recitation contest in 2011, deliberately stopping at digit 315.

⟁ ⬭ ⬗ ⊛ ⬢

A few years into this enterprise I called Conway on his cell phone to make plans for another research trip. Lucky day, he picked up, and I greeted him with a seemingly innocuous "How are you?" He boomed back:

> ALIVE! Thank you.
>
> I always say that. I'm afraid I got into that habit after my suicide attempt. I was so happy to come back. It's meant to sound positive and hopeful rather than depressing, but I realize it probably sounds the wrong way.

Making plans with Conway can be challenging. He's dead easy to triangulate when he is somewhere between common room, home, and coffee shop. It's harder when together you have to catch a plane or a train. It seems impossible that he'll remember the deviation from the norm, that he'll bring the necessary mental forces to bear—that he'll allow those mental forces to be diverted—to get himself to the train station, say, on time. Miraculously, more often than not it works out. But there are exceptions. He's been known to stand up audiences of 1000s. Once when he was introduced at the Canadian Mathematical Society meeting in Victoria, British Columbia, he was nowhere in sight for a few long, tense minutes, until he appeared at the auditorium entrance and strode down the aisle carrying a nightstand from his hotel room on his shoulder, which he deposited beside the lectern and made no further use of. In San Diego, at a Joint Mathematics Meeting of the Mathematical Association of America and the American Mathematics Society—a gathering of practically all the mathematicians in the country—Conway failed to appear at all. He was snug in his alcove in Princeton. His friend Simon Kochen happened by and said, "Aren't you supposed to be in San Diego?"

> And do you know what I said? I said, "That's next week." And Si said, "No, it was yesterday."

However, when we made a date to travel to Poughkeepsie, he turned up on time for the train. We maneuvered our way through Grand Central

Station, Conway clutching a plastic shopping bag filled with his *New York Times*, blank pages for mathematical doodling, and a custom-made cubic puzzle. We were on our way for a day trip to visit a mathematician at the Hudson River Psychiatric Center. Conway had never met George Odom, a 60-something amateur geometer of considerable repute. Odom had made at least 5 startlingly elegant geometric discoveries pertaining to the golden ratio, a ratio that quantifies the pleasing proportions of certain shapes, usually rectangular. Odom's discoveries are remarkable because they relate the golden ratio to the cube. And over 3 decades of correspondence with 2 professional mathematicians—Coxeter and Father Magnus Wenninger, a Minnesota-based Benedictine monk who, over his 95 years, has constructed metaphorical millions of multicolored polyhedral models—Odom published his discoveries and made his reputation. Conway was drawn to Odom's work because his golden ratio discoveries provided a construction for the pentagon, which Conway in turn used in devising a new construction for the dodecahedron that was much simpler than Euclid's. And so the pair of them, Odom and Conway, sat down at an oblong conference table in the library, lined with shelves of psychiatric journals. Conway began the conversation with some flattery.

I've known your name a long time.

Odom, meanwhile, dressed in cargo shorts, black sneakers, white knee-high sport socks, and a paint-smeared T-shirt (he considers himself primarily an artist), was unaware of Conway's status. "I came here to get away from people," he said, somewhat apologetically. He recalled making a promising start to his art career in the 1960s, exhibiting his fiber optic light machines at a gallery next to Tiffany in New York. The Met and MoMA were favorably impressed and wanted to see more of his work. But Odom let his momentum lapse. He survived "a rather dramatic" suicide attempt with an overdose of Sominex, and for more than 3 decades had been "solipsistically sealed" at the psychiatric center. "In this place there is an absolute minimum of small talk and polite conversation," he said. "I've had 30 years here totally alone to do exactly what I want to. Wherever you go you have to deal with people. And they are a distraction, people. I wanted to be alone.

"You're a mathematician at Princeton University?" he asked. "Well, you won't be much interested in me. I'm just a dilettantish dandy. I'm not a real mathematician. I dabble in mathematics, in philosophy and psychology and Bible interpretation." He said his golden ratio discoveries, which came to him during daydreams, were "in spite of myself, not because of myself.

"I've always felt the primacy of the cube," he continued. "Not just because there are so many cubes around us—rectilinears, parallels, and right angles—but the Bible says the City of God at the end of history is an enormous cube coming down out of heaven. And the 666 that you've heard about in the Bible are the 6 tetrahedron edges, the 6 octahedron vertices, and the 6 cube faces—the old Platonic atoms all pulled apart, and the edges, vertices, and faces, like Humpty Dumpty, unable to get back together again; a fragmented view of reality, rather than the 7-12 unity of the cube itself."

Conway looked on, arms folded on his belly, skeptical but intrigued. How unusual: Conway was *listening*.

"And the cube is the 7-12 unity because it has 12 foundations in the Bible," Odom continued—"12 edges for the 12 apostles, the 12 tribes of Israel, the 12 months of the year. It has 7 axes of symmetry for the 7 days of creation, the 7 days of the week, the 7 early churches. And it has 9 planes of symmetry, for the 9 hours of the crucifixion. So it's full of biblical meaning."

"When I was very young, growing up," he went on, "I used to salvage cardboard boxes from dumps and wrap them in colored crepe paper. I thought the box was so beautiful. I just admired the box for its simplicity and symmetry."*

Finally addressing the origins of his golden ratio theorems, Odom

* Odom's thoughts on symmetry amused and intrigued Conway, who was then putting the finishing touches on *The Symmetries of Things,* a "year-zero" manifesto, as described by his co-author Chaim Goodman-Strauss, about a subject that Conway loves dearly. The book was published in 2008, with a third co-author, Heidi Burgiel from Bridgewater State University. The reviewer Branko Grünbaum, something of a symmetry expert, criticized the book for the Conwaynian habit of renaming things—for example, the common term "glide reflections" was renamed "miracles," and "translation" became "wonder." Asked Grünbaum: "Do they really expect that these cute terms will be generally accepted?" Conway's requested rebuttal is to wonder whether the reviewer really read the book, because those terms define different things.

said he was drawn to geometry after seeing a 1960s exhibition of Buckminster Fuller's models. "That's when I was struck by the beauty of mathematics. It was more than alphanumeric utilitarian scribbling. It was beautiful things that you could see and touch."

Conway pulled from his paper bag the folding puzzle: 2 cubes comprised of smaller cubes in red and blue, hinged together. The trick was to fold the pair of cubes so that they displayed identical red-blue patterns on all faces. Conway said he could do it in about $\frac{1}{2}$ a second, though he noted that the puzzle took him 20 years of thinking to invent. "You should manufacture it and get it into classrooms," Odom suggested, refusing to take a try. He changed the subject to a patent he holds on a variation of tic-tac-toe. "*Hollywood Squares* should be paying me royalties," he said. "I won't go into it, but if you ever want to play tic-tac-toe, a better way to play it is with all X's or all O's. There is less chance of a stalemate."

When do you get a point?

"When you make a row; the last X to make the row gets the point for the row."

And if you make several rows at once?

"You get multiple points."

Conway grabbed a pen and sketched on a piece of paper his version of a similar game, magic squares, only played on a hexagonal grid and with numbers instead of X's and O's. Odom shook his head. "I don't like numbers," he said dismissively.

You don't like numbers?

"I don't trust them one little bit. I think they're negative differentiators." Conway let that pass, and Odom gladly went on to expound about the geometric properties of a compound of 10 cubes, which he discovered, and then about his discovery of interwoven triangles that he claimed could make a self-supporting structure for a building. "Geometry is the dynamic," he said.

I *love* geometry.

"I was drawn to mathematics because of its beauty," Odom said. To which Conway replied,

So was I.

Conway still maintains an enviable travel itinerary, usually to destinations farther flung than Poughkeepsie. He's been back to England countless times. Once, en route to Birmingham, he got off the train and as it pulled away he saw through the window his luggage, containing his passport, traveling onward without him. By the time he got it back, his return to the United States had been postponed by 2 weeks. On another conference trip he arrived home without his house keys, having stashed them for safety in the best secret spot in his short-term furnished apartment: in the cardboard box containing the iron. He's holding a rain check for Brazil, and he recently accepted an honorary degree in Romania. "I told him he must go," says his third ex-wife, Diana. "Dracula lives there!"

Thrice he's wintered in New Zealand, and he's hit all the major cities in Australia, as well as Hobart, Tasmania. He went to Rome for the Festival of Mathematics and to Milan for something or other. And Switzerland, and Portugal. And Mexico for groups, as well as Mayagüez, Puerto Rico. And he added to his roster the new International Mathematics Summer School for high school students and undergraduates, which has taken him to Bremen, Germany, and Lyons, France—for the France flight he refused the offer of a first-class ticket, since he didn't want to get stuck sitting beside someone prattling on about their latest business deal.

Back for another summer at the Canada/USA Mathcamp, this time in Maine, Conway was somewhat dismayed to learn that a certain number of campers attended his class and no others. These are the Conway worshippers, as he sometimes calls them.

It's nice to be, what's the word, apotheosized. I get a bit sick of it sometimes. But still.

The campers seem impressed by his versatility. For instance, the 15 topics he offers as candidates in the vote for the Conway Hour (this time game theory came first, surreals second, and the Free Will Theorem third). "I think he is the closest thing the world has to a polymath," said Sachi Hashimoto, 17. And then she confessed: "The first time you see surreal numbers, you break, you just break; your brain cracks open."

Not all campers, however, are "Conway lovers," as he othertimes calls them. There have been those rare times that he can't for the life of him find anyone willing play Dots and Boxes. And certain campers—notably those whose parents are celebrated mathematicians—have little patience for his accostations of GIMME A DATE! and his unprepared, impromptu talks, which can go off the rails quite spectacularly. Such was the case with a class on the surreals. He didn't have any overheads prepared, so he drew the setup for a basic game of Hackenbush using Magic Marker on a desktop, then asked for 2 volunteers to play.

Silence.

Come on!

Silence.

If there are no players, this lecture is over.

No one wanted to play a game with Conway.

Okay, I'm leaving. 'BYE! COWARDS!

The class seemed unsure what to do after he stormed out. They did nothing. Then Itai Bar-Natan, 19, a camper who had long ago read *On Numbers and Games*, Conway's rather advanced book on the subject of surreals, took over at the front of the class. "I'm not quite prepared for this," he said, reveling in the role, "but I will continue the lecture." Conway fumed in the hallway. He was truly upset. The class sent out a few representatives, pleading for his return. They came back empty-handed. Eventually, he poked his head in the door.

I'll come back if you can prove $\frac{1}{2} + \frac{1}{2} = 1$.

More typically, Conway suffers the opposite problem, with more opponents volunteering for games than he can handle. The year I first met him at Mathcamp, the bulletin board in the lounge announced Saturday's Conway challenge in the cafeteria at lunch. As advertised, he was willing to play anyone 10 games of Dots and Boxes, and if any opponent got a single game off him they'd be declared the winner. The campers were seeking comfort in numbers, soliciting support for a Dots and Boxes team on the bulletin board: "We've studied, we've trained . . . now we're ready to challenge Conway to a game of Dots and Boxes! Come watch us play (and probably lose)." The math campers are nothing if not self-deprecating. The bulletin board also announced the choices for the camp T-shirts, which included MATH: BECAUSE WHEN YOU CAN'T GET LAID, YOU MIGHT AS WELL BE GOOD AT SOMETHING and NOTHING COMES BETWEEN ME AND MY MATHCAMP. The winner in the end was IN MATHEMATICS, EXISTENCE IS FREEDOM FROM CONTRADICTION.

The campers on the Dots and Boxes team had been practicing for days with Conway's book *Winning Ways for Your Mathematical Plays*. They were outraged to discover that Conway himself had borrowed a copy of his book from the camp office for a refresher. The camp director intervened, and Conway promised to memorize only 1 page.

> I hope that's enough to beat the kiddies. I haven't played the game seriously in ages.

The kids figured the only way they could beat Conway was to force him to play their entire team in a simultaneous display, and he agreed. He circled his dozen opponents seated at the long lunch table, making his first move with each challenger and continuing around and around the circuit. It wasn't long before some conceded defeat. As the competition thinned, the crowd thickened, everyone egging on the campers. A brazen competitor balanced a spoon on his nose while he played. "I'm trying to psych him out," he said. And it worked.

> Wait a minute. What's happened here? You seem to have won!

In the end, Conway lost not a single game but 3, an all-time record in Mathcamp history—only once before had a camper beaten him. This rare turn of events made Conway's final lecture that evening a riotocracy of ironic excitement. He had, after all, earlier the same day chosen to deliver another of his golden oldie talks, "How to Beat Children at Their Own Games," on the theory behind Dots and Boxes. So now Conway had to open with a footnote:

> You appreciate, of course, that even if you succeeded in beating me at Dots and Boxes, you didn't really. It was just that I made a mistake.

And he closed with a couple homilies to guide their mathematical futures:

✱ Take it as axiomatic that you are stupid. If you think you have proved something, think again. Find the holes in your own proofs.[*]

✱ If you have indeed discovered something, but then discover that someone else discovered it before you, consider yourself in good company, and mark your progress. If you find something already discovered 2,000 years ago, then 200, then 20, at least you are improving. And then, if you're lucky, next maybe you'll discover something new.

Afterward, campers trailed Conway back to the lounge, where he plopped himself into a sofa. He accepted a final challenger for Dots and Boxes and simultaneously embarked on a game of Philosopher's Football with Mat. Nearly 2 hours later, approaching midnight, he'd regained some Dots and Boxes dignity. The camper looking on at Conway's left had conked out and was sound asleep with his head drooped on the arm of the sofa. The match of Philosopher's Football, meanwhile, was taking forever.

> You're giving me a sweaty game. Who have you been playing with?

---

[*] This is contrasted by the tongue-in-cheek Princeton Axiom that I once heard Conway mutter at Mathcamp and then retract just as quickly: "Take it as axiomatic that people outside this room are stupid"—"this room" being any intellectually specialized environment, such as the Princeton common room or the Mathcamp lounge.

"No one," Mat said, "since you taught me how to play last year."

Curses! I might cry about that move.

Overconfidently, Conway had given himself a handicap, ultimately making Mat victorious and himself delightedly disconsolate.

I wish I wasn't going home tomorrow. We really should play again.

That fall, in November 2003, Conway suffered another heart attack and underwent triple bypass surgery. And chattering away after the surgery with his cardiologist, Dr. Anderson, Conway collected a few tales to add to his repertoire.

Afterward my doctor said something that made me feel really funny. He said, "Your heart is particularly smooth. When I was holding it in my hand . . ." This made me feel, *ewwwwuuuuh*: this guy held my heart in his hands.

Initially Conway had been slated for a quadruple bypass, but when Dr. Anderson opened him up he found 1 of the arteries was in fine shape. The other 3 he replaced with a 9-inch piece of the saphenous vein from Conway's leg.

The effect of this piece being taken out is that this leg swells up every now and again; that vein must have been doing something. Before the surgery I never really realized which way I crossed my legs, which I should have done because I've done some research on this stuff. Have I told you about this? Fold your arms. Go on, do it now! Now fold them the other way. Have you done it? Doesn't it feel weird? Everyone has made their own decision about this sort of stuff. Everyone has worked out which leg they cross over the other one. And the fact that he took the vein out of this left leg was wrong for me because it interacted nastily with how I cross my legs. He should have asked me first which way I crossed my legs. It's a damn nuisance now, crossing the wrong leg over. I meant to write Dr. Anderson a letter about it. . . .

Wanting to get this new nugget of Conway's genius clear, crossing over as he was into medical science, I tried to clarify: He crossed the left leg over the right, or right over left?

> Ha! You know the story about asking the centipede how it walked? Well, it was unable to walk after somebody asked it. You are roughly doing that to me now. I remember looking at an octopus once. It was so funny. I stopped and looked at this octopus, and my god, that octopus looked back, twirling 3 or 4 legs at once. Creatures of that sort, I think they really must be quite clever, to have all those limbs operating independently.

17.
HUMPTY DUMPTY'S PREROGATIVE

What is mind? No matter. What is matter? Never mind.
—LADY FRANCES RUSSELL *(Bertrand's grandmother)*

And this brings us up to the prevailing present. Conway had made it through the first of his free will lectures, he'd bathed in congratulations at the coffee shop (and dodged questions about the communal amoeba colony), and all the while he wondered, as much to himself as aloud . . .

Did we *really* get it right?

During the following weeks, doling out 1 lecture per week, Conway loitered as usual in the common room and found himself in the middle of a war zone. The annual springtime ritual of Assassin had broken out in the math department. Graduate students, each assigned a target, wielded candy-colored water guns, set bounties, and placed bets. They darted around squirting walls as often as their targets and diving recklessly for safe zones, the stairwells and the alcoves and the presence of any professor. And so it was partially in the interest of self-preservation that another 19-year-old smarty-pants grad student, Jacob Tsimerman, had been spending lots of time with Conway, alternately playing Phutball and debating the merits and demerits of the Free Will Theorem. Tsimerman thought the theorem was deep and fun and puzzling, if not particularly philosophically assertive. To Conway's contention that there was no evidence for determinism, Tsimerman was shocked. As for the theorem's reliance on quantum mechanics, he said, "I feel it's not fair to use quantum mechanics because it's not understandable."

It doesn't have to be fair.

"You were mentioning the second viewing of the universe," said Tsimerman, trying a different tack. "What about the time reversibility?"

I will answer with the same: WHAT ABOUT time reversibility? I don't see cats walking backward. Have you seen raindrops falling upward? . . . You are trying to use time reversibility to say the future is as determined as the past.

Thinking this through, Tsimerman pensively shook his right foot. Then the shaking stopped. "Pardon me for a second," he said. "Kevin is about to take my gun." His gun had been stolen 3 times already; this time he'd left it lying out on a coffee table across the way. And so with a James Bondian leap-dive-and-roll, he catapulted over a neighboring cluster of sofas and chairs, knocking over a glass of water and sending some Phutball stones scuttling across the floor, and just as quickly he leapt back and resumed his seat with Conway, having retrieved his translucent pink water gun. "Yes, about quantum mechanics . . ."

Tsimerman made better progress with Phutball. Before playing Conway, Tsimerman was well-known as an abysmally bad Phutball player. "Jacob! Are you losing?" asked a passerby. "Losing, yet again?" asked another. John Nash sauntered by in a spiffy spring suit and glanced over to see what was what. Playing Conway, Tsimerman had quickly improved. Within days he mastered the tactical skills and became a formidable opponent for his professor. "This is arguably the greatest triumph of this man," he said. "And I don't mean that condescendingly. It's a great game." After some tsk-tsking from Conway followed by a "pfwooooah!" from Tsimerman, the youngster enthusiastically conceded another defeat. "Your game, Professor!" Then he accepted a rematch, even though yet another game was bound to make him late for his seminar due to start in 2 minutes. And so they started playing again . . .

I'm not very good at this game, even though I invented it.

That's some uncharacteristic modesty from Conway, and he went on to say that he considered Tsimerman a superior player. "Thank you! You really think so?"

I don't *think* so. I just *said* so.

Blushing and distracted with the semi-praise, Tsimerman suffered a setback. A few tackles later and it was Conway facing serious trouble, yet he cautioned,

Reports of my death have been greatly exaggerated!

This time he was indeed beaten at his own game, and the victorious Tsimerman sprinted off to class.

But he's now 15 minutes late. That's my real aim in getting them to play these games, to ensure they don't do well in math, to destroy all these formerly promising mathematicians.

On the day of the second Free Will lecture, Conway was back in full fret about the size of the audience. Kochen meanwhile was pondering whether it was advisable to play "Freewill" by the band Rush as the audience arrived. "It's not trivial," he told Conway. "We can be sued." He'd given a CD to the techie to load onto the laptop, but when the duo arrived at the hall that night, the webcast live-streaming had already begun, so on account of the legal worries they couldn't play the song after all. And it didn't really matter, anyway, because the techie hadn't even arrived with the laptop—loading "Freewill" had apparently crashed the machine. Eventually, everything ready, Conway stood before his audience. Again it was a full house, with people reclining in the aisles as if lying back on a hillside, hands folded behind their head, ready for a contemplative evening.

This time there is going to be some content, as we mathematicians say.
Last time was all airy-fairy.

As the lectures progressed, Conway continued with his fretting while Kochen worried about how they should try to avoid repeating previous glitches, but this wasn't such a concern for Conway.

I'm not concerned about the past.

"No, okay," said Kochen. "But I *am* concerned about how the past affects the future." Kochen also worried that Conway was doing the lectures too much on the fly. And sure enough, in the third lecture, which was meant to address the Fin axiom in depth, Conway motored through, ran out of material, and galloped onward. By the fourth lecture, ahead of schedule, he'd reached his detailed explanation of the proof.

Yes, we've reached a comfy stage with the audience now. Nobody is sitting in the aisles anymore. Quite a good thing. That means I've frightened a lot of people off with last week's lecture. Well, I'm going to frighten a lot of you off with this week's lecture, because this is the—I've decided to bring forward the proof. The proof was going to be in next week's lecture, but the last lecture seemed to have doubled and the lecture that was to have been this week was done in a few minutes at the end of last week's. And so anyway, I'm more nervous about this lecture than I've been about any of the others. I always believe in letting it all hang out. I'm quivering inside.

He made it to the end, albeit with some circumlocutions and disruptions, such as the telemarketer who called on his cell phone. Then there were the questions. "There's no use listening to these questions afterward," a Princeton University Press editor sitting next to me said. "Sometimes I think it's just a pissing contest, who can say the most unintelligible thing. They're all talking gibberish." Conway fended off an audience member's request for an extra lecture in the form of a debate, and again headed out into the night with a sense of relief.

I'm on a local high. I'm not sure how long it will last. But that's the worst of it over. The theorem is proved. Nothing can hurt me now. Nothing can kill me now.

The following morning at the coffee shop, quietly contented with the world, with the universe, and with himself, he wore one of his favorite T-shirts, decorated with a cartoon by Sidney Harris:

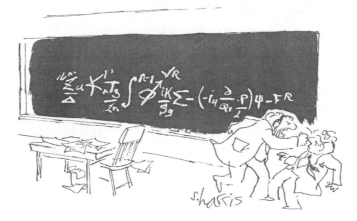

"YOU WANT PROOF? I'LL GIVE YOU PROOF!"

On the morning of the grand finale lecture, President Barack Obama gave a talk at the National Academy of Sciences, reiterating his campaign commitment to "restore science to its rightful place." He urged scientists to take action themselves, to move out of the laboratory, as it were, and engage the citizenry. Conway was doing his part. Now that he was in the homestretch, his worrying had abated. He'd moved on to worrying about his walking, which seemed to be getting worse from day to day. I asked him whether the partial loss of control over his limbs due to the stroke amounted to a loss of free will on some level. He tried not to think about it, he said.

> There is a cathartic effect of doing mathematics. You can forget the world more easily.

Practically speaking, this is an application for mathematics that Conway readily appreciates. Math allows him to escape worldly maladies, sometimes even physical ailments, like the time he was due to give a talk at the Swedish Academy of Sciences in Stockholm and he developed a vicious toothache the night before. It was almost the worst pain he'd ever experienced, second only to the gout, and it kept him awake and in agony all night long. The next morning he stepped up to the lectern, his tooth still throbbing. And then as soon as he began the lecture:

GONE! It's the analgesic power of thinking hard.

When he suffered the stroke, however, he couldn't power think his way out of the longterm effects entirely. Quickly enough he'd become ambidextrous with his writing and mobile with a cane, yet the long-term reality was daunting. He contemplated the immediate options head-on. To be depressed, or not to be depressed. He decided not to be. But he has regrets.

I was struck down with this awful thing and it changed my life, utterly. It was 20 seconds that aged me by 20 years. And I feel such a fool. Had I paid attention to my diet it wouldn't have happened. The road not taken was not taken at my folly. I feel old now; I never felt old before the stroke. It's a permanent intimation of mortality. Every day I think about death. With these lectures, I want to get the message out before I die; I want to get this damn stuff out. I want people to recognize the truth of it about the world. And not in 100 years' time. I want to see them recognize it.

Talk among the graduate students about the Free Will Theorem for the most part focused on how their professors had managed to infuriate 2 departments at once—trespassing on physicists' territory in such a way as to make philosophers' hair stand on end. By the last lecture, things were getting a little hairy between Conway and Kochen. Conway was not at all sure what he was going to say.

It'll come to me.

"I'm worried you won't have anything to say," said Kochen. "You don't want the lectures to just sputter out."

What's wrong with sputtering out?

The concluding message in the last lecture was this: The Free Will Theorem disproves determinism. It refutes the possibility that the particle's behavior in the Stern-Gerlach machine is predetermined; the particle's behavior cannot be a function of the past. The Free Will Theorem also disproves—and this, as Conway and Kochen always take pains to point out, is the more subtle point—that the particles' behaviors, the quantum correlations, are not explained by randomness. This is the "Randomness Doesn't Cut It" argument.

> There's a third alternative, what we call "free," or maybe technically we'll use a slightly different word, partly free or semi-free. The free decisions taken by particles cannot be explained by random numbers. This is something that's different from both randomness and determinateness. Far from regarding randomness as the opposite of determinism, we regard them as both in the same scale pan, roughly speaking, and the opposite of both is free.

So the opposite of "deterministic" is not "random." To put it another way, indeterminism and randomness are not one and the same, as is sometimes thought to be the case. To clarify and illustrate how randomness doesn't cut it, Conway made use of yet another game. Much the way he made use of Twenty Questions to show how the particles' behaviors were not deterministic, now he made use of trusty old backgammon.

> So you see, there's a certain confusion in people's minds between—how can I say it?—between nondeterministic and random. People think that if a theory isn't deterministic, it must be because God is playing dice with the universe, in Einstein's famous phrase.
>
> Well, I like playing backgammon. The only thing you need to know about backgammon is that it's a game that involves dice. Normally when you play backgammon against one opponent, you throw the dice, and that determines what your legal moves are. Now I'm going to tell you what happens in backgammon tournaments. You have, say, 50 tables and at each table there's 2 people waiting to play. So the tournament director will throw the dice and say, "The first throw is a 2 and a 4." And then the player to start at each table must make a move that's legal given that 2 and 4 were thrown. Of course, from table to table, all the starting players

make different moves because they all have different ideas about what's a good move for 2 and 4. And then the tournament director says the next throw is a double 6, and so on. The idea here is that each table gets the same throws. So when the winner of the tournament prevails, the other people can't say that he did it by good luck, because 49 other people had the same luck. And that's that.

Backgammon is a game that involves randomness, but it is not entirely random. The point about that is it doesn't make any difference if the dice are thrown just as they are needed during the tournament, or if they are thrown in the past. So if the tournament director sits up in his hotel room, with some witness no doubt, the previous night, and throws the dice lots and lots of times, and records them somewhere, then it doesn't change things. He could still say, "The first throw is a 2 and a 4," or he should say, "The first throw *was* a 2 and a 4." But that doesn't affect the system at all.

We proved this Free Will Theorem that says the way the universe works cannot be explained if you suppose that what a particle does is a function of past history. Well, it follows from that, and from the backgammon argument, that you can't explain the way the universe works if the behavior of a particle is a function of its past history PLUS random numbers. Because you can suppose that random numbers are past history.

Suppose, for instance, that God is throwing dice, as Einstein didn't want to believe. God says, "The first throw, or the current throw, is a 2 and a 4." And then every particle in the universe instantly hears this deep-voiced "2 and 4" and behaves accordingly. Well, God could sit up in his hotel room before the universe started, and throw the dice a lot of times, and that still doesn't explain the behavior of the particle. Adding in randomness doesn't help because rather than throwing the dice as needed, one could imagine that they were thrown beforehand—that in fact, there's this big table of random numbers and God's just reading those off, or the particles can perhaps read it directly without needing a God. But in any case, it doesn't affect the validity of any potential explanation of the universe. Because now, all throws are in the past. And so the particle's behavior is determined by its past, and the past includes all those random numbers.

The basic argument is you can treat random numbers as if they were past history. The inexplicable behavior of the particles can't be explained by suggesting it is a function of randomness in the world.

So somehow we have managed to produce a situation where it's conceivable that God does not play dice with the universe. If the Free Will Theorem is true—WHICH IT IS! IT'S A THEOREM AND WE PROVED IT'S TRUE!—then God does not play dice with the universe and the opposite of determinism isn't randomness. It's a new property, freedom, or something.

Freedom in this sense is a particular kind of freedom exhibited by elementary particles. How does "free" differ from "random"? Well, random choices can be made in advance, but free choices cannot.

I don't understand it. I actually think we are the first people to realize there IS a difference. We don't understand the difference between randomness and free will, but we know there is a difference. It reminds me of Euclid's *Elements*. The first few pages of definitions don't seem to be based on anything. So in order to proceed and get into it, you have to "swallow the worm," I call it, at the very beginning.

Conway admitted toward the end of the final lecture that the concepts were dizzyingly ineluctable.

Ineluctable: literally it means you can't struggle out of it. . . . So what am I trying to do? I'm trying to, in this famous phrase of Wittgenstein's, I'm trying to whistle around something that I can't actually talk about very precisely. It's that we sort of expect subtle concepts to be hard to define and we should appreciate that, almost as a positive virtue, as a sign of deepness.

Conway and Kochen were struggling with it all in real time during the lectures, and they still are struggling, nearly 10 years beyond the formative 10 years that produced the theorem in the first place. They named August 19 Free Will Day, and still almost daily they turn over ideas trying to elude the ineluctability and figure out what's going on with those particles. Once I caught them talking about the continuum of existence spanning a stone to a magnet to a human being.

> A magnet is the closest purely physics object to being alive. As a kid, I was fascinated with the way 2 magnets repelling each other was even stronger than attracting each other, and when they repel each other they are pushing against you. That's a macroscopic object that shows these quantum effects in a very strong way.

"Lots and lots of macroscopic effects are due to quantum results," said Kochen. "Why should a stone not fly apart or do other strange things? These effects are due to quantum mechanics. You can't explain them classically." They were toying with ideas and trying to refine and tighten their argument before they put it down in stone, as it were, in the book for Princeton University Press, and before they responded further to some of their critics.

They'd already faced their most vocal critics, those being critical on ideological grounds, during a series of discussions in Kochen's office. A regular participant was Roderich Tumulka from Rutgers. "I am critical of the Free Will Theorem," he tells me by e-mail. "I got the sense that John regards it as his most important contribution to science, and I feel sorry for him that the achievement he is most proud of is fundamentally flawed. The Free Will Theorem is a mathematically correct theorem, but John and Simon give it an incorrect physical interpretation. In fact, they are deluding themselves about the significance of their result." Stephen Adler, a physicist at the Institute for Advanced Study, was similarly critical but perhaps a bit more receptive. "The theorem is correct," he confirms. "They are good mathematicians, so when they prove something, they do it right." However, Adler believes there may be some other physics underlying quantum mechanics and relativity that unifies both, which makes the Free Will Theorem's reliance on the Spin, Twin, and Fin axioms fundamentally problematic. Philip Anderson, a Nobel laureate in Princeton's department of physics, was more optimistic in his comments around the time of lectures to the *Daily Princetonian*. "The theorem may cause people to rethink some things that they've basically known all along. It may cause me to rethink some things that I've basically known all along."

Hans Halvorson, a Princeton philosopher specializing quantum theory, also commented critically for the *Daily Princetonian* story. But when I got in touch with Halvorson years later, he said that he regretted his criticism, since it underplayed the significance of the result. It's a profound result, he says, and it started an important new discussion, especially among philosophers and philosophically minded physicists. And as he's said on record more recently, introducing a book titled *Deep Beauty*: "Conway and Kochen's argument exemplifies the method of applying mathematical argument to the task of gaining new conceptual insight—in this case, insight about the logical connection between certain statistical predictions (which are in fact made by quantum mechanics) and traditional metaphysical hypotheses (freedom of the will). If their argument is successful, then Conway and Kochen have provided us with insight that transcends the bounds of our current mathematical framework, hence insight that will endure through the vicissitudes of scientific progress or revolutions."

In fulfilling the philosopher's role as punctilious conceptual critic and word police, in his initial comment to the newspaper, Halvorson was more nitpicky: "In fact, what it seems is that [Conway and Kochen] proved indeterminism—that the future is not fixed by the past. There are good arguments that free will and indeterminism don't have a lot to do with one another. There are old arguments going back to Immanuel Kant that you can have free will in a completely deterministic world. It's called compatibilism.

On this point, Conway is ready with a rebuttal.

Compatibilism in my view is silly. Sorry, I shouldn't just say straight off that it's silly. Compatibilism is an old viewpoint from previous centuries when philosophers were talking about free will. They were accustomed to physical theory being deterministic. And then there's the question: How can we have free will in this deterministic universe? Well, they sat and thought for ages and ages and ages and read books on philosophy and God knows what and they came up with compatibilism, which was a tremendous wrenching effect to reconcile 2 things which seemed incompatible. And they said they are compatible after all.

But nobody would *ever* have come up with compatibilism if they thought, as turns out to be the case, that science wasn't deterministic. The whole business of compatibilism was to reconcile what science told you at the time, centuries ago down to 1 century ago: Science appeared to be totally deterministic, and how can we reconcile that with free will, which is not deterministic?

So compatibilism, I see it as out of date, really. It's doing something that doesn't need to be done. However, compatibilism hasn't gone out of date, certainly, as far as the philosophers are concerned. Lots of them are still very keen on it. How can I say it? If you do anything that seems impossible, you're quite proud when you appear to have succeeded. And so really the philosophers don't want to give up this notion of compatibilism because it seems so damned clever. But my view is it's really nonsense. And it's not necessary. So whether it actually is nonsense or not doesn't matter.

Another critic was their loyal adjutant Joe Kohn. "If a particle has will, it would be free," he said, "but do particles have will? If you were saying the laws of physics can't be deterministic, nobody would blink an eye. But 'free will' carries a certain emotional meaning. 'Will'—that's where I want to debate it. I don't know if particles have will, do they?"

Well, where there is a will, there is a way.

To this kind of quibble over the anthropomorphic terminology, Conway wielded what he calls the Humpty Dumpty prerogative, first put forth by the humanlike egg while arguing with Alice about semantics and pragmatics in *Through the Looking Glass*: "'When I use a word,' Humpty Dumpty said, in a rather scornful tone, 'it means just what I choose it to mean, neither more nor less.'" And when Conway uses the word "free" and says, "If humans have free will, so do the particles," he is not implying that the particles are capable of decision making; he means the particles act in a free way that is not a predetermined function of the past or a function of randomness. In tightening their argument, he and Kochen were considering alternative terminology. They considered "free action" or "spontaneous action." "That sounds like it's going back from free will," said Kochen, "but the word *sponte* means 'will' in Latin, or 'one's own accord'. It's actually the same word. You don't object to the word 'spontaneous', do you?"

No. Except that it's not provocative enough.

Kochen agreed. And when it came right down to it, Conway wasn't all that worried.

> I expected this. I deliberately and tendentiously and provocatively used the term "free will" for the particles, for the very good reason that the theorem itself shows it to be the same property that has always been called "free will" for people. I think that's a good thing to do, to tell people they are the same. People don't like the idea, and they never have, of equating a human property with a nonhuman one. However, I think it would be silly to have our theorem say that if people have free will, then particles have indeterminacy.

"There is no essential difference," said Kochen. "We're not talking about free will as a moral decision, about good and evil, or whether or not you should divorce your wife. If the experimenter's choice is to be called free will, I don't see why free will can't be used for the same property of the particle."

> The world is a wonderful, willful place. Where does free will come from? Well, we're made of particles. So probably, somehow, our own free will is derived from that of the particles we're made of. The theorem renders it extremely plausible that somewhere in our brains there is a way of distilling the willfulness of the universe. We obtain our free will, I believe, from the willfulness we have proved is all over the world.

Somewhere in our brains—Conway wiggled his fingers over command central when he made that suggestion. But where does the brain fit in with free will? If our free will is derived from the free will of all our constituent particles, our neurons especially, how might that work, exactly, in the brain?

> The brain is well adapted to reason about the world. . . . We didn't use complex variables to avoid predators. But the problems of survival are very complex. A cat catches mice. A giraffe runs fast. I think what's happened

to the brain is this: Mathematics gets a free ride on this problem-solving machine. We've acquired this thinking ability. And we now apply it in these esoteric ways. We are parasites, we mathematicians, on the proper function of the brain.

"Speak for yourself," said Kochen. "It isn't just that we have 5 senses. There is the sixth sense of thinking." And the thinking, the decision making, the free-willfulness that seems to emerge from our brains is a product of that spontaneous action of the elementary particles. "It's a kind of indeterminism that may be used in the brain," ventured Kochen. "We're not neurobiologists," he said, though he has a friend who is a neurobiologist and previously a quantum physicist, so Kochen knows that neurobiologists disbelieve the notion of the so-called "quantum brain." The temporal and spatial factors in brain function are too big for the magical and spooky and entangling "quantum coherence" effects to work. It's roughly the same scenario as a quantum computer. Theoretically, we know quantum computers will be better, faster computers; practically speaking, these computers are as yet impossible to build in a way that sustains quantum coherence. "It's hard to keep this going in a computer," said Kochen, "so why should it happen in the brain?"

You believe it does happen in the brain to some extent?

"I believe it's possible for it to happen in the brain. Penrose believes that too, and he actually gets together with biologists and tries to give models and so on. I think that's probably premature, simply because we don't know enough about the brain. We're at the beginning of this exploration of the brain, and they can only do experiments at certain time and space limits. It doesn't mean that the brain can't use these effects. I think in theory it's possible. Evolution, if anything, is always opportunistic. It uses whatever it can. And quantum effects are everywhere. So it's hard to believe that evolution won't use these effects if it can."

In May 2010, I started looking into flights for our trip to visit Martin Gardner. Conway was excited to go. He hadn't seen Gardner in years, more than a decade maybe. Gardner had said any time was good, but when I called to confirm the date, there was no answer. The next day a Google Alert announced "RIP Martin Gardner."

I called Conway and told him the news.

Oh my god.

He went silent for about a second, apparently executing the Control-Alt-Repress command in his brain, because he did a 180 and immediately changed the subject to *The Triangle Book*. Then he mentioned that at that moment he was sitting on the doorstep of his apartment, waiting for Tanya Khovanova, who was in town organizing the Institute for Advanced Study's Program for Women and Mathematics, a weeklong mentoring session for undergraduate and graduate students. She was coming by to pick him up since she'd recruited Conway to give a talk.

So wait a minute. He died yesterday, you say?
My. I'll tell Tanya. She'll be upset, too.

That fall, in December, we were off on another trip. I'd booked Conway for an assessment with neuroscientist Sandra Witelson at McMaster University in Hamilton, Ontario. Witelson is best known for a 1999 study published in the *Lancet*, "The Exceptional Brain of Albert Einstein," revealing unique anatomical features of Einstein's brain that had been overlooked by other neuroscientists. She is also known for her brain bank. She has 125 cognitively normal brains in her collection, and her work with Einstein got her interested in cognitively exceptional brains. She studied Donald Coxeter's brain pre- and postmortem, and she asked Coxeter for recommendations on further specimens. "Talk to John Horton Conway," he said. Witelson got in touch with Diana, who is responsible for a good portion of her husband's executive functionings. Plans with Witelson stalled when Diana tired of her husband's emotional absenteeism and infidelity. She sat him down in a lecture room at the department and told him she was leaving. Given the near-suicidal fallout after his breakup from Larissa, Diana was quite concerned about how he would react. His immediate response was one she never anticipated:

Oh god. Now who's going to deal with Larissa?

"I think John is the most selfish, childlike person I have ever met," Diana says. "One of the reasons I find that so intolerable is that I know damn well he can be human if he cares enough to bother. John really *is* capable of stepping up when circumstances are dire. I don't know how 'personal' the book will be, but if you'd like I'll tell you about the (rarely seen) caretaking side of John. I saw it exactly 3 times."

The first was when she was ill with pneumonia and couldn't get out of bed. "Not only did he bring the doctor to our house (unheard of), but he attempted to do the washing. I instructed him about the washer, then the dryer, et cetera. A while later he came up the stairs with a basket of clothes covered in powder. He couldn't figure out why. He had put the powder in the washer as instructed, and never turned it on. When he went back to check, the clothes were dry, of course, so he assumed he had completed the entire process even though he had no recollection." The second was after their first son was stillborn. "John was a gatekeeper, letting people in when he thought I could manage it, taking care of everything around the house." The third was after Gareth was born, when Diana suffered postpartum depression. He insisted she get outside and sit on a bench in the sun. "He took care of me *and* the newborn Gareth 100 percent. I could not even function for a couple of weeks. His daughter Rosie came over from England, and between them, mom and baby were cared for."

She hastens to add: "John is the most interesting person I have ever met. Unfortunately, as a result, I've now set the bar rather high so I'm not sure I'll ever couple up again."

Not long after their separation (which ultimately proved very amicable), Conway suffered his stroke. And a short while later, one summer at Mathcamp, he suffered a second, smaller stroke—smaller at least in that it didn't strike him down, but over a day or two it inflicted a gradual diminishment of his left peripheral vision that had him tripping over everything. So it wasn't until several years after Witelson's initial inquiry that the premortem testing she wanted to do on Conway seemed logistically feasible. I was happy to be the go-between. It was bound to be good fodder. When I called Conway to finalize details of the trip, he'd composed a footnote for his usual answer to "How are you?"

> ALIVE! But overshadowed by this *memento mori* that you've got me into—*memento mori*, a reminder that I must die.

He got another reminder when Dover expressed interest in reissuing his first book, *Regular Algebra and Finite Machines.*

> When Dover asked if they could reprint it I had mixed feelings. And I had mixed feelings because the authors Dover usually reprints are dead.

The new edition was also a tricky business logistically, since Conway did not possess a copy of his book (long story). He advised Dover it was available for $799 on the Internet.

But back to the business of the neuroscientist studying his brain.

> Before when this business came up I was taking a rationalist attitude. I just thought, When I die, I'm dead. I don't give a damn about bits of my body after I'm dead. Chop off my arms and legs and head—go ahead. But now I'm basically thinking of it as if I'm going to Toronto to have my brain taken out, that's what I was telling my class yesterday. Once I get there I'll be interested in the study, and to hear about her work on Einstein's brain and Coxeter's brain, and to hear the odd anecdote.

As I waited for Conway at the Toronto airport, Chris Noth, Mr. Big from *Sex and the City,* strode through the arrivals gate in all his glory. Conway came along soon after, not such a sight for sore eyes, and not at all his usual Archimedean self. The day before he'd been to the barber, where he was brutally shorn (it happens roughly once a year). Now he looked like a septuagenarian Dennis the Menace who'd just paid a visit to a science center and kept his hand for a few seconds too long on the hair-raising Van de Graaff static electricity generator.

The next day, sitting in Witelson's office in the company of an Einstein action figure and all sorts of brain paraphernalia, Conway began to collect the anecdotes. Witelson, with her bouffant black hair, talked about how she came into possession of Einstein's brain. The Princeton pathologist Thomas Harvey, who performed the autopsy on Einstein in 1955, took the brain home and decades later drove it to Hamilton, where he deposited a sample in Witelson's brain bank, including pieces of the pa-

rietal lobe, the area of the brain responsible for visual and spatial reasoning. Conway had vaguely followed the saga of Einstein's brain and
remembered there was a groove that was deeper or out of the ordinary
somehow. "It wasn't deeper," said Witelson. "It was in a different place.
We looked at all the atlases of the human brain that are available, and we
couldn't find 1 brain with that variation. So his anatomy was unique, but
I say 'unique' in a very precise sense."

Witelson carried on with a synopsis of her investigations thus far. "I
can tell you this because there is nothing you can do to fudge your results, so you don't have to be a naive or blind subject. In Einstein's brain
we found a 15 percent expansion of the parietal lobe, in addition to the
groove being in a different place, and one was the consequence of the
other. In Coxeter we didn't find the groove in a different place. His overall anatomy was very typical. But his parietal lobes were expanded. And
of course I think that the kind of mathematics he did was a very visual
type of math. He thought in images, images, images."

Continuing, she pulled out an old book, Jacques Hadamard's *An
Essay on the Psychology of Invention in the Mathematical Field*, published
in 1945. Hadamard explored 2 kinds of mathematical thinking: "the
logical," formulaic and algebraic reasoning, and "the intuitive," visual
and geometric reasoning. The categories were based on the responses he
received from a questionnaire, included in the book as Appendix I, "An
Inquiry into the Working Methods of Mathematicians." Query 30 read:
"It would be very helpful for the purpose of psychological investigation
to know what internal mental images, what kind of 'internal word'
mathematicians make use of; whether they are motor, auditory, visual,
or mixed, depending on the subject which they are studying."

Witelson asked, "Do you know this book?" Conway did. "I have to
admit that what I really like," she said, "is Appendix II: 'A Testimonial
from Professor Einstein.' And here are the sentences from Einstein's response that many people refer to: 'The words or the language, as they
are written or spoken, do not seem to play any role in my mechanism
of thought. The psychical entities which seem to serve as elements in
thought are certain signs and more or less clear images which can be
'voluntarily' reproduced and recombined.' The idea, as he said here and
in many other places, is that when he is trying to think about things, he
is not putting it into words, but thinking in terms of images and pic-

tures, like his famous statement about 'riding on a beam of light.'"

Conway agreed that Einstein seemed a very visual type. And with Witelson's prompting he reflected on his own visual methods—his 4-dimensional helmet, his sticking out extra arms and legs in various directions, all his eccentric attempts at envisioning higher-dimensional space. "I have people asking me," Witelson said, "whether Einstein's brain got to be the way it is because he did so much physics. And of course I think it is the other way around. I think he did so much physics because his brain had a certain anatomy."

> I am sort of rather opposed to that view. How can I say it? I'm anti-elitist, though I have taught in elitist universities all my life. I tend to believe that anybody could do, roughly speaking, what I can do. I think it's pretty easy. And I often teach people who don't think they can do such and such, and they can in the end. Now, on the other hand, it's a very common opinion that special gifts come at birth or something. And all I can say is that I don't really want to believe it.

"Why not? Could everyone be a Mozart?"

> I believe that everybody, almost everybody, could do mathematics pretty damn well. And I think that there is a danger in thinking you have to be gifted at birth in order to be good at something. I think that is a terribly limiting . . .

"It's not a question so much of belief," said Witelson. "Clearly there are variations in ability. The differences can be qualified."

> But they are not so great as people think. That's what I really do honestly believe. I'm trying to say that I believe that given the right education, the right upbringing, anybody could be pretty good at everything.

Getting back to the specimen at hand, Witelson described what she was after with the neuropsychological assessments and the functional MRI. "With imaging, one can look at the anatomy of the brain, the microscopic anatomy of the brain, just through a picture. So what I'm hoping is that the tests we've been designing for you will get at different types of mathematics, and we will be able to see different parts of your brain lighting up when you are thinking in different ways. We want to see which part of your brain is particularly active when you are thinking some of your great mathematical thoughts."

> Yeah. Well, you know, I'm not sure that I can have great mathematical thoughts to order. I can have lesser thoughts.

"That'll do."

> I do these mathematical tricks—the day-of-the-week trick. Very few good mathematicians do this sort of thing. Von Neumann did, and he was one of the best mathematicians of the century. Gauss did it a long time ago. But mathematicians in general don't do these calculational tricks. They think it is rather beneath them. My colleagues in Princeton think it's rather beneath them. They don't think anything is beneath me.

Subjected to the standard arsenal of neuropsych tests over the following days, Conway got a bit bruised up—at least his ego did.

> They've been putting me through a battery of tests, and I feel pretty battered.

The team of postdoctoral students in charge of the tests also, by the end of it, had taken a beating, from Conway. They'd pulled all-nighters, assembling the relevant tests from the extant literature—the same tests administered to other people as part of other studies—that would capture basic mathematical thinking in the fMRI, dissecting Conway's brain into 32 2-millimeter slices. And they had designed a test especially for Conway, whereby they would get images of his brain as he did his trick of rapidly calculating the sum of squares that would add up to any number given. The first day went reasonably well, though Conway hadn't slept much the night prior, which he thought accounted for his mild irritability. He criticized the fMRI tests, which he found flawed in content and methodology. During a geometrical test, he questioned the skills of the artist responsible for the images on the screen.

That's not a square! That's a rectangle! . . . And I suppose *that's* intended
to be a circle?

Another test flashed a spatial grouping of geometrical figures for 200
milliseconds, then showed what might or might not have been a partial
grouping of the exact same arrangement. Conway was instructed to pull
a forefinger trigger to indicate yes, it was the exact same arrangement, or
a thumb trigger indicating no, it was different. He had 2 seconds to make
his response before the next grouping came flashing into view.

There is no time for any reflection!

"That is the point," explained Chris Scott, the postdoc in charge.
"We're not trying to measure the higher ability to count and process and
actively manipulate the information that you are holding in memory.
We want you to passively respond to the information. We want to see
the difference in brain activity between when you are doing really well
and when you're not."
Conway was unconvinced.

I'm just going to fail all over the place. I can't do this, I'm sure I can't. I
have a feeling that this is going to be totally useless for you.
   If I try to make a response as often as I can, then what will happen is
I'll make a lot more wrong responses. Suppose I only respond $\frac{1}{2}$ the time
and get 'em right, compared to responding all the time and getting $\frac{2}{3}$
wrong?

"It will be very difficult, but that's the point. The thing is, we didn't
want to risk it being too easy. Because if it doesn't tax you, we don't learn
anything."

But you're not so concerned about it being too difficult. If it's too difficult
you also get no information.

"We actually do," Scott explained. "We can compare the activation
in particular areas of the brain with performance levels and difficulty
levels. Although we are interested in your actual responses, we are

most interested in what your brain is doing while you are thinking about these responses. What your brain is doing in there, preparing your responses, is the most important thing—that is the functional MRI data."

And my brain is just expressing horror.

But it relented. Conway took off his shoes and his belt, emptied his pockets of his crumpled bills, his phone, his wallet, his debris, and allowed himself to be rolled into the machine. Afterward, that night at a special dinner in his honor, hosted by another of the principal investigators, neuroscientist Sandra Black from Toronto's Sunnybrook Heath Sciences Centre, Conway was in a state over the answers he knew he'd gotten wrong. "It's not that you get the answers correct," Dr. Black tried to reassure him, "it's that the brain is stimulated."

But what's preventing me from just thinking of sexual fantasies when I'm in the machine?

These notions of sabotage became a concern again when the second round of fMRI tests began the next morning. The task set for him that day involved his agility with the sum of squares—a number would flash on the screen, and he was to pull the forefinger trigger when he had worked out the squares that would sum to that number.

Oh, you're not listening to my answers, then?

"This task is all in your head," Scott said.

Well, then, I can do anything I like, can't I? . . . I find this rather distressing, that you're not listening. There is no incentive to get it right.

He needs his audience.

You're asking me to do something, which is to think REALLY hard, and get it right et cetera, and you're not even listening. It's bloody insulting.
    I think frankly it makes this test more or less useless. I need a sufficient

incentive to think hard. 'Cause, you know, it's almost sweat producing. It's certainly adrenaline producing, if I'm trying to do these things quickly.

You're asking me to think very hard, and it doesn't matter if I think really hard. You may think it matters to you, but I mean if you're not listening . . .

"But we are listening, to your brain."

Yeah, yeah yeah yeah yeah. But you might just pick up the parts of the brain that indicate noise. And anyway, I don't think I could possibly summon up the intensity that I would normally apply to the sum of squares. So you would not get the parts of the brain that you want.

This went on for some time. The investigators apologized, and Conway apologized, and at first he again seemed to be relenting.

I don't mind going through with this charade. But I will be strongly tempted to say anything.

But he did mind. And he changed his mind. He refused to do the custom-designed sum of squares test. He agreed to do a standard calculus test with integrals, a test that allowed the investigators to check whether his answers were right or wrong. And he agreed to the scheduled hour of structural imaging, producing a 3-dimensional picture of every nook and cranny of his brain. Dr. Black showed him the pictures afterward, pointing out the damage caused by his strokes and the areas vulnerable to future strokes—good incentive, she hoped, for Conway to take care of himself.

In the end, even with the hiccups, the tests produced lots of data, structural and functional—and Conway properly impressed Dr. Witelson when he aced a visual reasoning test that involved reforming a flat sheet of paper to copy a 3-dimensional rectilinear sculpture (she'd never seen anyone do it successfully). None of the scientific results can be made public, since they haven't yet been published. But already, the fMRI tests have proved 1 thing for certain: Conway can be bloody-minded, if not without simultaneous remorse. Even in the moment, he confessed that he felt guilty about getting so upset. He was sorry he couldn't bring himself to do the sum of squares test. He wanted everyone to remain friends. Still, as we left, he was hardly waving the white flag. Instead he had a parting salvo for the unsuspecting research assistant, who, not having been privy to his meltdown, innocently asked, "What do you hope we found in your brain?"

> I couldn't care less! I know who I am. I know what I can do. I have a healthy ego and this won't put a dent in it.

I followed up with Witelson a few years later. By this point I was wondering, mostly in jest, whether a brain's memory bank could perhaps be usurped by an over-domineering math bank, as it were; whether Conway's insatiable mathematical appetite maybe had the anatomical side effect of causing the parietal lobe, math's usual headquarters, to invade the memory's frontal lobes in search of more space, more neurons and synapses, to do all its cogitations. Witelson's first reaction was no, though she seemed intrigued and said she'd think about it.

And she hadn't forgotten the foofaraw over the tests. "It didn't really matter if he got the right answer," she says. "It was more about the process he was thinking through. But what John pointed out, which is a good point, is that his brain would be doing different things if he got the right answer or the wrong answer."

However, what really struck her and stayed with her about Conway was something else entirely. "The thing that I found about Conway is—and it sounds so sort of juvenile to say this—but his eyes were so electric, so magnetic. You know how they talk about Einstein's eyes being so bright? With Conway, you're just drawn to him, even when other people are surrounding him. His eyes are like sponges, darting around, pulling everything in."

EPILOGUE

When the hurly-burly's done
When the battle's lost and won.

—William Shakespeare

Were Conway not so long-winded, this biography might have wrapped up some time ago. And while the volume of primary source material doesn't dictate the length of a book, Conway's talent for chattering on guaranteed his biography would be something more than a jumped-up character sketch—he's hard to turn off, and he's difficult to condense. Whenever I followed up on a fact-checking question, for instance, he could never bring himself to answer concisely. Rather, he'd pause for a second or 2, rummage around in his repertoire of tales, and then launch into the relevant

Did I ever tell you about . . . ?

So on a gloomy winter's day, 6 years after the start of the project, I sought him out with the express purpose of finding THE END. Whatever he said that day, more or less, would comprise our conclusion, or at least point in that direction. As usual, when I sat down in the alcove he was tinkering away with something or other, but he deftly segued to worrying about his lost passport, his soon-to-expire temporary replacement green card, and his general state of entropy, bits and pieces falling off him.

My wrist aches . . . and a drowsy numbness pains my spirit. That's Keats.
But he says, "my heart aches," not "my wrist."

375

His good leg was also giving him trouble. Being an iatrophobe, he wasn't about to seek help.

I do really suffer from iatrophobia, because I don't go to the doctor until I'm nearly dying from whatever it is.

He'd recently retired, taking a golden handshake buyout from the university and receiving in the mail a letter in fancy calligraphy announcing his new status as John von Neumann Professor Emeritus. He regretted retiring, but he was hardly having trouble keeping busy. From all points of the compass, supplicants arrived at his alcove seeking consultations and collaborations. The inventor of KenKen, Japanese educator Tetsuya Miyamoto, stopped in at Princeton for the Pi Day celebrations and said he wanted to meet Conway. They shook hands and talked KenKen—in Japanese it means "wisdom squared," and it demonstrates Tetsuya's educational philosophy, "the art of teaching without teaching." Then there were the Oakes twins, Ryan and Trevor, artists known for their drawings that "employ split focus and a curved easel to render illusionistic space in 3 dimensions on a 2-dimensional surface"—their work has been touted as "one of the most original breakthroughs in the rendering of visual space since the Renaissance." They visited for a day accompanied by their Boswell, writer Lawrence Weschler, all of them seeking Conway's mathy interpretation in preparation for an exhibit at MoMath, the National Museum of Mathematics in New York.

There was also a spate of people volunteering for coauthorship on papers and books, the result being that the retired Conway was "working" harder than ever, and the *Mathematical Intelligencer*, noticing this spurt of productivity, made him a casual columnist. Princeton student Edgar von Ottenritter arrived irregularly, aiming to reconstruct and publish the tetraflexagon theory Conway had devised during his student days at Cambridge. Conway had misheard Ottenritter's name as Nottenritten, so he joked about how the student had got "nuttin' written" yet. More regularly, nearly every Monday, Conway expected Derek Smith, one of his Ph.D. students from the 1990s, now at Lafayette College; they were working on revisions for a new edition of their 2003 book, *On Quaternions and Octonions*. Every Friday produced Alex Ryba, who in a sense has become Conway's right-hand man. Formerly at

Cambridge and now at Queens College in New York, Ryba had a slew of projects in the works with Conway: Finishing *The Triangle Book*, starting a book about the Monster, as well as a book that grew out of a number of papers they'd written on Pascal's theorem, about a mysterious hexagon, the Hexagrammum Mysticum.

Another nail in the coffin of my reputation!

And more nails were just waiting to be driven, such as their paper on magic squares, advancing a subject that hasn't seen any advancements in 320 years, since Frenicle de Bessy's classification of the 880 possible magic squares of order 4, published in 1693—a distant ancestor of Sudoko, a magic square is grid filled with numbers that add up to the same number, the "magic constant," in every direction of rows and columns and main diagonals.

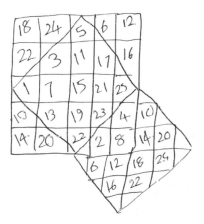

A magic square of order 5 constructed by the "odd diamond" method (the numbers in the center diamond are odd).

They also wanted to write up their further findings based on Conway's continuing love affair with Fibonacci; they'd already finished a paper for the *Mathematical Gazette* on "Fibonometry," introducing a rule that converts trigonometric identities into numerical identities involving Fibonacci numbers.

And then there was Conway's paper "On Unsettleable Arithmetical Problems."

It makes simple but extravagant claims that are true but neither provable nor disprovable. What makes it so strange as a mathematical paper is that usually mathematical papers contain some variation on proof.

Still, this paper was refereed and published. And, it should be noted, the paper would not have been written at all without the assistance of another fan, Dierk Schleicher, of Jacobs University in Bremen, Germany—which recently awarded Conway with the latest of his innumerable honorary doctorates (he certainly can't enumerate them). In the abstract, Conway laid out his intentions:

It has long been known that there are arithmetic statements that are true but not provable, but it is usually thought that they must necessarily be complicated. In this paper, I shall argue that these wild beasts may be just around the corner.

He built his argument around a simple assertion about the 3n + 1 problem:

Do you know this 3n + 1 problem? Let me remind you:
Start with any number, say 7, and if it's even you halve it, and if it's odd you multiply by 3 and add 1. So 7 multiplied by 3 plus 1 is 22, and 22 you can halve, and the rules say you always halve if you can, so you get 11. That you can't halve so you multiply by 3 and add 1 getting 34, then halving to 17, and that goes up to 52, 26, 13, 3 13s plus 1 is 40, 20, 10, 5, 16, 8, 4, 2, 1, 4, 2, 1, 4, 2, 1. That's what happens to every number that anybody's ever tried: it always gets to 1. No matter what number you start, it always get to 1.
That was conjectured in 1940, maybe a few years earlier, by Lothar Collatz, whose name I've only ever heard in that connection. And the claim that most people find outrageous, which I make in this paper, is that it's really quite likely that the Collatz conjecture is true—more likely than not, and I think very much more likely than not—but also, that there is no proof of it. And I don't mean just that nobody has found a proof. I mean that there is no proof. A proof doesn't exist even in an abstract sense. So if you are searching for a proof, you won't find it, matie. It's like searching for an elephant in the common room. There aren't any.
I'm deliberately causing a bit of a splash, or trying to. In mathematical

papers you are supposed to back up assertions with proofs. I don't give proofs. And I say there aren't proofs. Anyway, people find it a rather radical assertion. A colleague of my friend Alex [Ryba], his response was, "Ah, so Conway has finally gone off his rocker." My response to that is, "I haven't *finally* gone off my rocker, I went off my rocker years ago." But the more sincere thing is to say that since 1931, with Gödel's Incompleteness Theorems, people who have asserted this haven't necessarily gone off their rockers. Although Gödel did, later in life, come to think of it. And I don't mind saying it myself, maybe I'm off my rocker. But I've got a serious purpose in doing this: to remind people that mathematics is not defined by axioms. For those for whom set theory is the basis of mathematics, this is shocking. But my view is we are trying to find the truth, and there are other ways of finding the truth than proofs. And this is unsettling to mathematicians.

Is it actually true that for every positive integer, if you do this 3n + 1 game, it gets to 1? Most of us feel it's either true or false. It's false if and only if there is some integer that doesn't get to 1. That seems a good enough notion of truth.

Truth in mathematics is a funny business. It's not up for argument in the same way that truth is for—well, for instance, with the statement about no elephants in that room. A statement that refers to the real world, let's suppose I say there are no cats in that room—or no cockroaches, that would be a little more risky. Maybe you could find the left leg of a cockroach and a little portion of the abdomen, or the entire abdomen and two back legs, or maybe you can find a bit of the thorax as well. When does it become true? What I'm trying to point out is that in the real world, you have this graduation from truth to falsehood. And in our mathematical world we imagine that is not true—there, I've used "true"—we imagine that that is not the case, that that's not in accordance with the facts.

But the facts are rather funny because they are about things we can't quite see, numbers and so on. There's always some worm, some bug, that stops you getting a clear picture. Either you can't see the entire cockroach, or you're talking about numbers, which you can't see. We think they exist. But it's funny, you pay for the extra precision by having to resign yourself to abstract entities. And where are they, numbers?

On another attempt at a concluding visit—a last visit among a collection of last visits—I persuaded Conway to take me down the hall to his office to see if we might try (again) to find his Ph.D. thesis. When we reached his office, not only was the door unlocked, it was wide open, and the interior looked as though it had been hit by a tornado. A 4-foot shard of tree bark lay splayed across the sofa, the underside containing a caption in Conway's script: "This very piece of bark was shot 250 feet off a tree that was struck by lightning."

Tiptoeing around the office, he used his cane to clear his path, including a film reel with the return address "Groovy Geometry Institute." The storm that had created this most recent havoc was Hurricane Gareth. The fire marshal had declared the office a hazard, what with all the paper polyhedral models hanging from the ceiling, to say nothing of the swirling construction of 292 pencils warming on the radiator. Gareth took care of the problem, knocking the models down like piñatas, stomping them flat, and lobbing them into the trash. Then for good measure he spun a web of sticky tape around the room.

> Curses! How on earth do you think we can possibly find anything in this mess?

We couldn't. Mission aborted. We went back to the alcove.

Still larking about plying his trade at every invitation, Conway had recently returned from another Gathering for Martin Gardner in Atlanta, where he'd spent most of his time at the back of the Ritz ballroom. He'd nodded off during a talk on "RetroLife." For the most part he was kept on his toes because the formal theme of this Gathering—the first time there was ever a theme—was none other than himself. He was feted and roasted at every opportunity. One speaker tried to make something of his initials, "J.H.C.," which also match Jesus H. Christ. Sporting his SCHRÖDINGER'S CAT IS DEAD T-shirt, Conway prefaced his own talk on magic squares (an obsession of late) by acknowledging the honor:

> I've never been a theme before, and I meant to do some research on how I should conduct myself, because I wouldn't want to engage in any *un-themely* behavior.

In the months ahead, Conway also had on his calendar a talk about magic squares for a conference featuring the German artist, mathematician, and magic-squares fan Albrecht Dürer at the Metropolitan Museum of Art in New York (Dürer depicted a magic square with magic constant 34 in his 1514 engraving *Melancholia*). And being the grand old man of artificial life that he is, Conway was on the roster as a keynote speaker at ALIFE 14, the annual international conference on the synthesis and simulation of living systems, also in New York, where he planned to begin his address by proclaiming,

I HATE LIFE!

Then there was his upcoming TED talk—TEDx Stuyvesant High School with the theme "What Makes You, You?" And he'd all but accepted an invitation for a talk at Auburn University in Alabama, where the organizer beseeched him with "If you come, everyone will!" In the end he went to Auburn, demonstrating with his talk that he still hadn't learned his lesson about offering money for problems. However, in proposing "Five $1,000 Problems," he thought his money was surely safe this time, though in a way, he also hoped not:

I'd love it if it turned out not to be safe with the first problem, to tell you the truth. That's the Thrackle Problem, and I really want it solved. I came up with it when I was a teenager, shortly after my dad finally got the car he'd been waiting for, for 7 years—in those days, after the war, you couldn't just buy a car, you had to go on a waiting list. So he finally got his Vauxhall, or whatever it was, and to celebrate we went on a family trip to Scotland.

We drove along a lonely road and to the right side there were rows and rows of trees, and every now and then you could see water between the trees, a Scottish loch of some sort. And then when we stopped for lunch a grizzled old Scottish fisherman walked by and said something like, "My line is all thrackled." You could tell just by looking at it what he meant, it was a hell of a mess. And from that I came up with the name, the "Thrackle Problem."

A thrackle is a messy doodle of lines with distinguished points, called spots, and the question is, "Can you have more paths than spots?" A path is any line between spots that does not cross itself and does not pass through another spot. It's related to knot theory but it's also topological. People have conjectured that you can't have more paths, but I believe there is a thrackle out there with more paths than spots, it's just maybe too complicated to be found.

That's 1 of 2 problems that have been with me since I was 14 years old. The second one I called the Dead Fly Problem. The wallpaper in my bedroom when I was a boy was covered in dark green flowers, and at dusk they looked like dead flies. I stared at the wallpaper and tried to find the largest convex region I could that didn't contain a dead fly. So that's was another $1,000 problem, and the question is, "Suppose every region of area 1 has a fly in the interior, can the arrangement of flies have only finite density?"

He'd also relatively recently been to Marseille, for a conference on groups. During the overnight flight across the Atlantic, he willed himself to stay awake so he could rememorize the periodic table. He had done this before, long ago, but he hadn't done it very well, and this time he was determined to fix his method. He invented a mnemonic, reciting it and the corresponding elements for the entire flight. He continued this exercise at the conference, managing a few recitations (silently, to himself) during each talk. By the time he returned home he knew exactly which elements were which—beginning at neutronium with atomic number 0, and then going all the way up to copernicium, the element with atomic number 112. Just mentioning this, he decided he was due for some practice.

Neutronium, helium, lithium, beryllium, boron, carbon, nitrogen, oxygen, fluorine, neon . . .

Those first 10 he knows too well to need the mnemonic, but from there he leans on his mental prosthetic.

Nab Molly, touch Ruth, in Rhoda's pad, you aging cad—that's niobium molybdenum, technetium ruthenium, rhodium palladium, and Ag for silver, and Cd for cadmium . . .

Once he gets going, it's hard to make him stop.

Caesar, bare in lace, praised nudity—cesium, barium, lanthanum, cerium, praseodymium, neodymium—promenading through some of Europe—promethium, samarium, europium . . .

Gadding terribly dyspeptically through the whole Earth to Thule—gadolinium, terbium, dysprosium, holmium, erbium, thulium . . .

Why be Lucy and have to worry, oh sir, about the pot of gold—ytterbium, lutetium, actinium, halfnium, tantalum, and W and Re for tungsten and rhenium, osmium, iridium, platinum, gold . . .

Let's hug 'til the pub by the pole at the roundabout—that's Hg for mercury, thallium, and Pb for lead, bismuth, polonium, astatine, radon . . .

And so on.

I like knowing things. It's my aim to know everything. And you know, I'm progressing, slowly.

Speaking of knowing things, and pots of gold, for his first year of retirement Conway accepted a lucrative 1-year position as the Daniel Gorenstein Distinguished Visiting Professor at the City University of New York's Queens College. The professorship is named after the Classification Project's great Gorenstein and is awarded only sporadically, when there's a suitably glorious candidate. "Of course," says Ryba, who recommended Conway, "all he had to do was apply and it was his." As a result Conway was living in New York 3 days a week, teaching Tuesday and Thursday, and on Wednesdays reprising the John Conway Hour, which often went into overtime.

Before he retired, but brooding about the prospect, Conway had vague hopes that a permanent plum position might materialize that would solve all his financial worries. One invitation in particular got him fantasizing about the possibilities. He'd been invited to deliver the monthly math colloquium at Renaissance Technologies, aka RenTec, the $23 billion hedge fund started by Jim Simons, a mathematician who had a career in academia (winning a top geometry prize and leading the math department at Stony Brook University) before moving on to apply mathematical models to the financial markets. The invitation arrived via Conway's former student Jade Vinson, now a RenTec research scientist, and Vinson organized the logistics of the visit, including door-to-door limo service from Princeton to Long Island, nearly a 3-hour trip. Vinson also suggested that Conway was welcome to bring a guest, student, colleague, or girlfriend. Conway brought me, ostensibly because at the time he was between girlfriends (after his stroke he briefly dated a nurse he met in the hospital; his current companion, whom he met at the coffee shop, wears Hermès-esque scarves and picks him up for dinner in her Mercedes sedan).

We arrived at RenTec on the appointed day and took a seat in the lobby. Vinson soon presented himself as the perfect host. "May I have a seat?"

Shouldn't you kneel?

As a graduate student Vinson had found the first "holyhedron." He explained for my benefit that a holyhedron, a concept devised by Conway, is a polyhedron with each face possessing a polygonal hole. Conway had proposed that such an entity would exist, offering a prize of $10,000 divided by the number of faces—fortunately, Vinson's holyhedron had 78,585,627. That bit of mathematics out of the way, Conway came out with the most relevant question.

What kind of mathematics goes on here?

"We can't really talk about that," said Vinson. RenTec utilizes top-secret mathematical analysis to execute automated digital trades in infinitesimally small slivers of seconds. Since it was nearing lunchtime, we moved on to discuss RenTec's computerized lunch delivery system. After lunch, Conway met with Jim Simons, who was tanned and sockless in his loafers—as tanned as his beautiful vintage hardback leather briefcase, which stood open and at attention on his desk. Both then 70, the 2 mathematicians discussed their imminent retirements. Simons was back working on mathematics again after 30 years. "It's supposed to provide rest and relaxation, but it's driving me crazy. Understand me?"

Totally.

Conway gave Simons a run-through of the Free Will Theorem, and then it was time for his talk. The subject was Conway's choice, though Vinson had advised that some of his fellow researchers had expressed an interest in hearing about surreal numbers. Escorted to the auditorium, Conway started planning—he'd come unprepared, naturally. Looking around the room for some objects to play a surreals game, he settled on a plate, an empty pop can, and a box of tissues. Afterward he was wined and dined, then he slid into the limo and arrived home well past midnight, having earned a $5,000 honorarium.

Not long after the RenTec gig, Conway delivered the prestigious Simons Lecture Series at MIT, 3 talks in total and equally lucrative. It was all these Simons intersections that had him fantasizing about a retirement pot of gold. Simons is the founder of Math for America, he's a benefactor of MoMath, and he is perhaps the most generous private funder of the sciences in America (estimates reach $1 billion and counting), including his support for the Institute for Advanced Study, not to mention his own Simons Center for Geometry and Physics at Stony Brook University. Simons didn't offer Conway a job. Though no matter.

> You know, now I actually feel quite rich! I have no idea if I am. But it's how I feel.

And the Simons intersections continued. The Simons Foundation website launched a "Science Lives" project, documenting the history of mathematics with video interviews and written profiles of "the giants of 20th-century mathematics and science." I was contracted to write a number of profiles, including Conway's. Reading over the 6-hour transcript of his video interview (by filmmaker George Csicsery), I recognized every story almost word for word. Until I came to a lengthy stretch given over to a topic on which I'd never before heard him pontificate. Here he was giving a 3,000-word riff on, of all things, rainbows:

> *You know, when you have a raindrop falling in the sky, if a ray of sunlight enters it and bounces once, that's the first rainbow. If it bounces twice, that gives the second rainbow. If it bounces 3 times, it's the third, and so*

on. I read about this a long time ago, at the age of, I don't know, I was a
teenager probably, in a book called Teach Yourself Meteorology, *and it*
said the third and fourth rainbows are occasionally seen, but the fifth
never.

Conway eventually came across another, more modern book. He couldn't remember the title, but he remembered he was upset to read therein the crazy untruth that even the third and fourth rainbows are never seen.

They would be seen if people knew what to look for!

For a more reliable and extensive primer on the subject he recommended *The Rainbow: From Myth to Mathematics*, by Carl B. Boyer: "The rainbow has had hosts of admirers—more, perhaps, than any other natural phenomenon can boast—but it has had few biographers." And in rushes Conway. The first rainbow, he'll tell you, occurs when a ray of sunlight enters a raindrop, refracts and reflects, and leaves the raindrop at an angle of 41 degrees from the path it was traveling when it entered. This is the most vivid rainbow, the classical bow, a slice of a full circle with most of the circle out of view. It's red on the outside and blue inside, and it's the easiest rainbow to see. The second rainbow is slightly bigger and it has a broader bow, since it occurs when a ray bounces twice and leaves the raindrop at 53 degrees. The colors are slightly less vivid, and reversed, blue uppermost on the bow and red beneath. And here, again, Conway has a mnemonic to help remember which is which among the rainbows:

If the number is odd, the sun sees red.
If the number is divisible by 2, the sun sees blue.

With the first 2 rainbows, it's key to remember that the sun is outside the bow, so to speak, whereas with the third and fourth rainbows, the sun is on the interior. The first clue that you might be witnessing the third or fourth rainbows is that the arcs are much, much bigger and the colors much more diffuse, usually so faint as to be barely visible at all. The angles at which the light rays bounce for the third and fourth rainbows are almost identical, both with a radius of 70-something degrees, so if you catch a glimmering of them at all, the third and the fourth will be difficult to tell apart. Hence it's all the more important to have Conway's mnemonic in mind, and then when you see the rainbow to quickly notice which color, red or blue, is at the top of the arc.

Conway claims to have seen all 4 rainbows. For the first 2, he has no noteworthy tales to tell, besides the fact that he saw plenty in rainy England, and a multitude of double rainbows, the first and second rainbows together back to back, during his insomniac sunrise mornings when visiting Hobart, Tasmania. The third and the fourth rainbows, however, are apparently part of his repertoire of tales.

> I saw the fourth rainbow from this very alcove, and it was very funny. I couldn't see the sun, but I saw a horizontal piece of rainbow, a straight stretch of rainbow coloring, and I thought this was some defect in the glass. So I got up and moved along the corridor to another alcove. And it was still there; the glass in this window appeared to have the same defect, so I thought it was from the same batch of glass. But you know, when I stood up, it moved in the way that it would if it weren't a defect in the glass. But I wasn't sure. So I went outside and there it was in the sky: a horizontal patch of straight-line rainbow. And then I met 2 people who can confirm my story. My first witness was Derek, who was my grad student at the time, and the second was John Nash, who didn't seem very interested. But Derek and I came inside and borrowed a journal from the library and worked out what it must be: part of the fourth rainbow.

> The third rainbow I saw later when I was on my way to Lisbon. I was sitting in a left-hand window seat, and the plane was flying toward the sun as we landed at the airport—it must have been hell for the pilot. We went through some cloud as we were approaching and very briefly I saw a left parenthesis of rainbow out of my window. People on the right-hand seat might have seen the right parenthesis. By this time, since I'd seen the fourth, I knew it was important to notice which color was on the outside. I sort of thought to myself, That's another rainbow; I must remember which side is red and which side is blue. I had about 5 seconds to observe it, because we came through the cloud and it was gone.

Conway can go much deeper on rainbows, especially historically. In

A.D. 200, Alexander of Aphrodisias observed and explained why the space between double rainbows is so dark, an area thusly called Alexander's dark band. And it was Descartes who finally properly explained the refraction of the light rays in raindrops (the explanations in school textbooks were always slightly wrong). Newton then wiped the floor with the problem, as Conway says, providing a formula for telling exactly what the appropriate angle was for the nth rainbow.

> And then, people managed to forget it. Richard Dawkins wrote a book before he wrote *The God Delusion* called *Unweaving the Rainbow*. Now, this title is taken from a few lines by Keats. He says, "Shalt thou unweave the rainbow?" And it's a vaguely antiscientific theme. He's saying if you explain the rainbow, it is somehow making it less beautiful, by taking away the mystery from it. But everybody who knows anything about anything knows that the more you know, the more beautiful it is. And I think that is the theme of Dawkins's book—he's referring to Keats and saying, "No, it's a good idea to unweave the rainbow." I keep on meaning to catch Dawkins one day and interrogate him on how the rainbow is formed. Because I think if he's written a book called *Unweaving the Rainbow*, he should actually succeed in unweaving the rainbow. Maybe he does, I don't know, I haven't read his book. So maybe he knows how the rainbow is formed, but it's really quite conceivable that he doesn't, because so very few people do.

Seeking out Conway, seeking the end of the book, I had this rainbows consultation on my to-do list. Having covered that, he went on with his worrying, about another talk he was due to deliver at Queens College on the Hebrew calendar. His expertise on the Hebrew calendar developed out of his Doomsday shtick, which pertains exclusively to the Roman calendar. But doing this shtick in talks over the years, every now and then someone asked him what he could tell them about their Jewish birth date. The answer was nothing. This spurred him to expand his knowledge, and he worked out a rule for mentally converting between the Roman calendar and the Hebrew calendar, with its 4 postponements (he also devised a rule for converting to the Muslim calendar, but it is now mostly forgotten and in need of reconstruction). So he was worrying about this talk on the Hebrew calendar, worrying especially that there might be a few real experts—rabbis, that is—in attendance.

> I've been interested in all sorts of junk in my life. I don't know whether I ever told you about The Vow I made; I'm sure I have. Because I had this black period in my late 20s, and then suddenly I was tremendously successful. I was shot into international prominence—in mathematics, I'm not talking about in general. And I sort of wondered why it was that a few years ago I was depressed and now I was at the top. And I vowed to think on whatever I was interested in and not worry whether it was profound or whatever. And that has been quite important to me. Ever since, I've felt free and I've done all sorts of stuff and, you know, reached the top of the mathematical tree. And at the *same time*, I've reached the bottom.

That seemed rather like THE END.

Or at least a possible end. As good as any ending. Some writers know their ending right from the beginning—like intuiting the solution to a problem, and then all that's left is figuring out the path to the proof. I had trouble finding any such end point on the Conway horizon. The vanishing point kept moving farther off. Because Conway kept talking.

> I don't worry whether what I'm doing is important or deep or significant. And it's much nicer. The most fantastic thing is—it still impresses me every now and then—that by studying children's games I found a new collection of numbers, and a new way of dealing with the old numbers. Absolutely astonishing!

Then staring out the window, he revised.

> I suppose in some way it must still be hard for me to continue to be interested in these trivial things, otherwise I wouldn't still be going on about it. It's okay, of course, now that I've retired—it's okay for me to take an interest in whatever the hell I like. But in a way I don't feel I've retired.
>
> I was talking with Gareth some time ago—this doesn't follow immediately from the last sentence—but he was being very careful and saying, "You know, Dad, some people might think you are a bit autistic." And he was being *very careful* to make sure that it wasn't *he* who was included in

the some people. And I think, you know, he's a little bit worried. For instance, this day-of-the-week trick is one of the standard things that the people who used to be called *idiots savants* did. And it's never put me off. But several times I've met people who have said, "Aren't you scared of being thought of as an idiot savant?" And my standard response is "Why should I care what stupid people think?" But when I was talking with Gareth about that sort of opinion—well, I was suppose I was a little bit worried that he might start caring what stupid people think.

That reminded me: Gareth, it must be said, is as psyched about having a nerd for a father as any boy could be. Now 13, he has all of his dad's diplomas and awards and honorary doctorates hanging on his bedroom wall. And when he was off from school during a holiday, and his mom dropped him off to spend the day at the math department, Gareth asked her, "Is the university open today?" Yes, she said. "Good, I like it when people are there. I like hearing people talk with Dad about things, even if I don't understand them. It's cool."

That, too, seemed a good place to put THE END. But Conway meanwhile had circled back to his worries about his talk on the Hebrew calendar and offending the Orthodox Jews. He needn't have worried. As it turned out, the talk took place the night after that winter's biggest snowstorm and he still drew a decent audience of 40 people, about 35 Orthodox, and about half of those congregational rabbis. He talked for an hour, followed by 2 hours of questions. His friend Alex Ryba, the host, had to close down the proceedings just before midnight—he was worried about the roads icing up and people getting home safely. Before Conway left, the rabbis booked him for a follow-up talk to the really serious rabbis, the great scholars at Yeshiva University.

Oh by the way, when I was in Naomi's Kosher Pizza place the other day, with Bojana, an Orthodox mathematician at Queens College, this guy approached our table and said some Hebrew words with great solemnity. I hadn't the faintest idea what he was doing. Afterward, when he went away, Bojana said that what he was doing was pronouncing a blessing on me as a great secular scholar. She said there is a standard blessing for a great religious scholar. You give praise to God for letting this person into your presence, or something. But there is a parallel blessing for a great secular scholar. How he determined I was a great secular scholar I don't know, I don't have the faintest idea.

It occurred to me that Conway might have some ideas on how to conclude his biography. So I asked him: Is there anything that you think should be added at the end?

YOUR APOLOGIES!
God, I am scared of this book, you know. There was something I was just reading . . .

He'd been reading Nathaniel Hawthorne's *Twice-Told Tales*, fittingly enough, but he was referring to something else. He pulled out a recent issue of the *New York Review of Books* and turned to an essay about a new biography of American art historian Bernard Berenson. The piece opened with a quotation from Berenson that rang true.

It's a lovely quotation which tells you how I feel: "Why do I wriggle and toss at the idea of being biographied? It makes me uncomfortable and unhappy. Is it only because there are so many big and little episodes I wish forgotten? Of course, I have much behind me that I hate to recall. . . . Every kind of *lâcheté*"—I don't know what that is; I think *lâcheté* must mean laxity—"meanness, pettiness, cowardice . . . humiliations, furtiveness, ostrichism, etc. . . . How passionately one wants to forget! No—not these only or chiefly. I dread having my life written as the 'success story,' as it is bound to be. . . ."
Well, I'm not so sure I dread that.
It is funny, though. I've not the faintest idea what to expect. You'll have said good things and bad things about me, or other people will have said them. I'm also scared of something else, which is that people will think I dragooned you into writing it. Which is not the case, as you will remember. You wanted to write it initially and I tried to stop you.

I closed my notebook and put the damned recording device away. Conway, master of knowing it all, knew by now that this was his cue to stop talking, and he bade me his Shakespearean good-bye:

Okay, fare thee well.

Leaving the alcove, heading down the hallway, I looked over my shoulder. He was already back at it. Having entertained my endless questions, recounted his nth-told tales, unburdened himself of some worries, and cleared away the clouds of reality, he made a swift return to the abstract land where he finds solace and infinite unadulterated pleasure.

But Conway should of course get the last word. As he himself once simply put it:

Math was always there for me.

THE END.

On Morley's Trisector Theorem

JOHN CONWAY

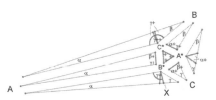

Figure 1. The seven puzzle-piece triangles.

Editor's Note: John Conway's simple and elegant proof of Morley's Theorem is legendary. That is, it's well known, and it's "out there," yet nowhere in print. We are pleased that he accepted our invitation to publish it, for the record, in The Mathematical Intelligencer. —M. S.

In their book *Geometry Revisited* Coxeter and Greitzer say

> One of the most surprising theorems in elementary geometry was discovered about 1904 by Frank Morley [...] Theorem: *The points of intersection of the adjacent trisectors of the angles of any triangle are the vertices of an equilateral triangle.*

The theorem was notorious throughout the 20th century as being difficult to prove. In the 21st century it has become easy! Here is the indisputably simplest

PROOF. Let the given triangle have angles $A = 3\alpha$, $B = 3\beta$, $C = 3\gamma$ and let $\theta+$ mean $\theta + 60°$ (and + by itself mean $60°$) Then there exist seven triangles with angles

$$\alpha + +, \beta, \gamma$$
$$\alpha, \beta + +, \gamma$$
$$\alpha, \beta, \gamma + +$$
$$\alpha, \beta +, \gamma+$$
$$\alpha +, \beta, \gamma+$$
$$\alpha +, \beta +, \gamma$$
$$+, +, +$$

because in each case these angles add to $(\alpha + \beta + \gamma)$ $+ + = 180°$. These triangles, so far determined only up to similarity, are illustrated in Figure 1. We can scale them so that the red lines in that figure all have the same length.

The red lines from A^* to BC are the two lines through A^* that make angle $\alpha+$ with BC, and are the same length since they form an isosceles triangle. (I call drawing such lines "dropping non-perpendiculars of angle $\alpha+$.") If one of the angles of ABC is obtuse—as is C in the figure—then the two angles at the feet of these non-perpendiculars (here $\gamma+$) are *exterior* angles of the isosceles triangle they form, rather than interior ones, but this does not affect the proof.

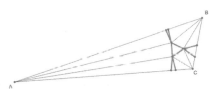

Figure 2. The assembled puzzle.

We shall show that these triangles fit together like a jigsaw puzzle to form a triangle with the required given angles $A = 3\alpha$, $B = 3\beta$, $C = 3\gamma$. For, the angles around A^*, B^*, C^* add up to $360°$; for example around C^* they are $\gamma + +, \alpha +, +, \beta+$ totalling $(\alpha + \beta + \gamma) + + + + + = 360°$. But also the two edges from A to B^*, say, must have the same length because the triangles AB^*C^* and AB^*X are congruent. (Their angles at A and B^* are α and $\gamma+$ and $B^*C = B^*X$, these being red lines.) Figure 2 shows the assembled puzzle that proves the theorem.

Department of Mathematics Queens College
CUNY
65-30 Kissena Boulevard
Flushing, NY 11367
USA

© 2014 Springer Science+Business Media New York
DOI 10.1007/s00283-014-9463-3

THE LEXICODE DICTIONARY

Giving his golden oldie talk, this is how Conway briefly describes the manner in which words amass in the Lexicode dictionary:

> So *a* comes before *b* comes before *c*, and so on, and *aa* comes before *ab* comes before *ac*, and they all come before *az*, and then come *ba*, *bb* …
> IT'S SPELLING!!!
>
> It's the way the words are in a dictionary. *Lexicon* is the Greek word for "dictionary," and it's still used in English occasionally. So here, it means that the words of the code are coming out in a lexicographic order.

For the code Conway was dealing in his talk, for any 2 words, the distance between those 2 words, or the number of digits by which those 2 words differ, must be at least 3—so the lexicode for this code, C3, has to satisfy minimal distance 3.

> With C3, if '… 000000' is the first word—by the way, all words begin with infinitely many 0s—then the earliest next word would be 000111. It could not be 000011 or 000010 or 000110, since neither of those words would satisfy minimum distance 3, they wouldn't differ from the initial word by the necessary 3 digits. The words in the code C3 would then proceed and accumulate as follows . . .

...000000
...000111
...000222
...000333
...000444
...000555
...000666

......

...000nnn

......

...001012
...001103
...001230
...001321
...001456
...001547
...001674
...001765

......

...002023

......

...010102

......

The wonderful Lexicode Theorem, then, asserts the following: "Digitwise" addition of any 2 words in the lexicode produces another word that must also be in the lexicode. Also, any scalar multiple of a code word must be in the lexicode. Which is to say, a bit more technically, that the lexicode is "closed" under addition, according to natural definitions of vector addition and scalar multiplication. This is easy to see, by taking two *nnn* words and adding them up:

000111
+ 000222
= 000333

Correct. If we check back to that list, 000333 is in the lexicode.

SURREALLY

Domineering is a good game for getting the gist of Conway's theory on surreal numbers, starting with a smaller version of a regular board.

The game goes like this. Players take turns placing dominoes to cover 2 squares. The first player, who we'll call Right, puts her domino in horizontally, and then Left puts his in vertically—we used to say "Lefty" or "Rita" since it's nice to be able to say "he" or "she." So Right might do this for her first move:

And Left might do that:

And then let's have Right make this move:

And then, when it's Left's turn, he has only 3 options, as you can see, so let's suppose he moves down there at the bottom middle . . .

That's how it goes.

Now with this microscale version of the game, currently about half-way through, Conway proceeds with some analysis.

What remains of this game is the sum of a number of smaller games—the L-shaped region, and the horizontal-shaped region of 2 squares, and the vertical-shaped region of 2 squares. And now let me show you what happens. Suppose we pull them apart and analyse these smaller games that remain.

If you think of the L-shaped region as a game unto itself, Left has 2 distinct moves:

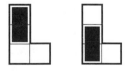

But if it's Right's turn, Right has only 1 move, she can only move like this:

And now, Left can still move like that . . .

And that ends that mini game in the L-shaped region. Right can't move. That gives you some sense of how a game breaks down into smaller games.

Similarly, in this mini game below, Right has 1 move, and Left would have no move.

And then in this mini game, Left has 1 move, and Right has no move.

That's a very simplified peek at how Conway studied games, broke apart bigger games into littler games, and in doing so noticed that certain games are equal to numbers.

And as Conway says, the games are logically prior to the numbers. So now for a simplified glimpse at the numbers.

Consider the smallest possible Domineering game, a lone empty square. Too small for even a single domino, this game allows neither player to move, and thinking back to Conway's {L | R} rules, this empty game generates the number 0.

$$\square = 0$$

When there are 2 vertical cells, this allows Right no moves, but Left 1 move. After Left moves, there are no squares remaining, so then again, neither player can move. Left's move is therefore called a "move to 0"— Left generates an endgame situation, and in Conway's notation this 2-cell vertical game is equal to 1.

$$\square = \{0 \mid \} = 1$$

Conway's surreal numbering system then proceeds as follows:

$$\boxed{} = \{\,|\,0\} = -1$$

$$= \{0, 1|\,\} = 2$$

$$= \{\,|-1, 0\} = -2$$

$$= \{-1, 0\,|\,1\} = \tfrac{1}{2}$$

$$= \{-1\,|\,0, 1\} = -\tfrac{1}{2}$$

$$= \{\tfrac{1}{2}\,|\,1\} = \tfrac{3}{4}$$

$$= \{-1\,|-\tfrac{1}{2}\,|\,\} = -\tfrac{3}{4}$$

And so on. But how do the fractions appear?

Quite. That is the Simplicity Theorem. Every surreal number is the simplest thing it can be. The simplest thing between $\tfrac{1}{2}$ and 1 is $\tfrac{3}{4}$. Whereas $\tfrac{2}{3}$ is not quite as simple, by my definition.

But what precisely is "simplest"?

It's very trivial. Each number is made using some previous numbers.

For instance, x is a simplest number with some "property"—if x has the property, and if no x^L or x^R has that property, it turns out, and it is a consequence of the simplicity theorem, in fact, that there is a unique simplest number that is greater than some numbers and less than other numbers.

It might help if you think of the property as being "green." Then x is the simplest green number if and only if 2 things happen: the first is that x is in fact green, and the second is that no x^L or x^R is green (and the second clause is just saying that nothing simpler is green).

Another great theorem in my theory is simply that certain games behave like numbers and can be thought of as numbers, and already we're doing that. We're creating a dictionary defining games as numbers, relating games to numbers according to the moves open to each player. With this dictionary of the mini games, the larger, more complicated game can then be defined inductively—that is, it can be defined as the sum of these simpler mini games, quite literally by adding up the component parts.

To go back to that game we had going before:

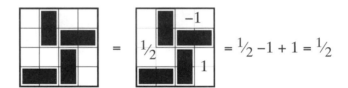

Now let me tell you what happens. Once you start assigning numbers to games, you notice certain patterns start to develop.

If you are playing a number, which is to say if you're playing a game whose value is a number—from now on if I say I'm playing a "number" I mean a "game," a certain kind of game that is equal to a number. So, if you're playing a number, whenever the number is positive, Left should always win if he plays optimally, and if the number is negative, Right should always win if she plays properly. And by "play properly," I mean that if Left has 2 options for a move, he will choose the better option, which will dominate over the smaller, weaker option.

So, if the number is positive, Left will win; if the number is negative, Right will win. And if the number is 0, whoever plays second will win. In any game 0—and there are many of them—since neither player has a legal move, the second player always wins. Here is the equipment for a game 0. Would you like to go first?

$$\square = 0$$

Another way to describe it is that Conway's surreal theory provides a barometer for who's winning at any given game—it provides an expression of the advantage the leading player has over his opponent. In that game 0, neither player is winning, because neither can make a move. And no one should be so foolish as to accept Conway's offer to go first in game 0. In the game 1, Left is winning. In the game –1, Right is ahead. This provides an application, of sorts, for the surreals theory, as Conway mentioned in an early lecture on the subject, "A Gamut of Game Theories.":

> The theories can be applied to 100s and 1000s of games—really lovely little things; you can invent more and more and more of them. It's especially delightful when you find a game that somebody's already considered and possibly not made much headway with, and you find you can just turn on these automatic theories and work out the value of [the game] and say, "Ah, Right is $\frac{47}{64}$ths of a move ahead, and so she wins."

AUTHOR'S NOTE

Writing *Genius at Play* was a decidedly collaborative effort. Conway sat for countless interviews, willingly (and sometimes unwillingly) revisiting well-worn inquiries, all of which combined in various permutations to inform the narrative and to form Conway's first-person presence throughout. This seemed like the only way to write a biography of Conway, with Conway speaking for himself. And so the book would not exist in its current shape had he not been game; were it not for his patience and magnanimity, which were close to unfaltering. That said, all errors—as well as what Conway might consider incorrect word choices and pedestrian metaphors, et cetera—are my own.

ACKNOWLEDGMENTS

I began this book in the fall of 2007 while a Director's Visitor at the Institute for Advanced Study in Princeton. This came about through the supreme generosity of then director Peter Goddard, who invited me to return in following years; one visit was supported with a science-writing grant to the institute from former trustee Peter Kann. The current IAS director, Robbert Dijkgraaf, kindly had me back for a final stay during the 2013–2014 academic year; this visit was supported by the Otto Neugebauer Fund. As well, Karen Cuozzo, Sharon Tozzi, Momota Ganguli, Judy Wilson-Smith, Nancy Kriegner, Helmut Hofer, Nicola Di Cosmo, and Piet Hut were instrumental in facilitating my many stints at the Institute.

A crucial year of writing and editing took place when I was a fellow at the Leon Levy Center for Biography at the CUNY Graduate Center in New York City—envisioned and founded by Shelby White, and expertly and engagingly run by program director Michael Gately and executive director Gary Giddins. A few fiddly details extended into my tenure in Berlin as writer-in-residence at Humboldt University's Institut für Mathematik and the Berlin Mathematics School at the behest of Jochen Brüning and John Sullivan. And over the course of writing the book I benefited from grants awarded by the Canada Council for the Arts and the Ontario Arts Council.

This book would not exist in the first place were it not for the great George Gibson, publishing director of Bloomsbury USA, who supported it through and through, even when things inevitably got a bit gonzo and wonky and experimental. And similarly, I am indebted to the patience and perseverance of the Bloomsbury team, editor Jacqueline Johnson, copy editor Emily DeHuff, managing editor Laura Phillips, art director Patti Ratchford, cover designer Natalie Slocum, interior designer Simon Sullivan, and publicist Summer Smith, as well as my agent Michelle Tessler. Along the way, the book was lucky enough to have several editors and readers (of the entirety or bits and pieces): Douglas Bell, Greg Villepique, Marjorie Senechal, Doris Schattschneider, Ian Pearson, Peter Goddard, Chaim Goodman-Strauss, Tim Rostron, John Bohannon, George Dyson, James Gleick, Don Knuth, Graham Farmelo, George Francis, Peter Doyle; as well as my fellow Leon Levy fellows (Peter Aigner, Susan Bernofsky, Langdon Hammer, Lauren Kaplan, Damion Searls), also Michael Gately, Gary Giddins, and LLCB deputy director John Matteson; and everyone at the BIRS Banff creative writing workshops, especially organizers Florin Diacu and Marjorie Senechal, Barry Cipra and John Bohannon, all of whom managed to contribute Conway stories.

The book was informed by many such stories, gleaned from interviews casual and formal, single and serial. There were too many to mention them all; everyone I encountered seemed to have at least a few. For the England era—special thanks to Conway's daughters, Susie, Rosie, Ellie, and Annie, as well as Eileen Conway, the late Joan Conway and Liz Fleming, Peter Evennett, and Conway's fellow Cantabrigians (at one time or another): Ben Garling, Pelham Wilson, Peter Johnstone, Jan Saxl, Ruth Williams, John Thompson, John Coates, Martin Rees, Peter Swinnerton-Dyer, Christopher Zeeman, Michael Atiyah, Ian Cassels, Tadashi Tokeida, Andrew Glass, Gordon Lord, Edward Welbourne, Clive Bach, David Benson, Mike Paterson, Stephen Bourne, Nigel Martin, David Bailin, Clive Rodgers, Robert Griess, Bernd Fischer, Richard Borcherds, Jim Roseblade, Peter Goddard, and particularly Conway's ATLAS sum chums Robert Curtis, Simon Norton, Richard Parker, Robert Wilson, as well as Conway's best friend, Mike Guy, Alexander Masters for his lovely book about Simon Norton, and Christopher Hum, Master of Gonville and Caius College, who generously hosted us during the research trip in Cambridge. I am also indebted and grateful to: Richard Guy and Elwyn Berlekamp, Donald Knuth, Roger Penrose, Bill Gosper, Robert Wainwright, Andrew Adamatzky, Neil Bickford, Adam Goucher, Daniel Dennett, Melanie Mitchell, Hans Moravec, Steven Weinberg, Edward Fredkin, William Poundstone, John Horgan, the late Martin Gardner, James Gardner, and Stephen Wolfram. For the America era—special thanks to Diana Conway and Gareth Conway, Simon Kochen and Joe Kohn, as well as Peter Sarnak, Eli Stein, Andrew Wiles, Robert Gunning, the late Ed Nelson, Alex Ryba, Avi Wigderson, George Dyson, Freeman Dyson, the late Bill Thurston, Peter Doyle, Jane Gilman, John Sullivan, Bob Freidin, Bernie Freidin, Graham Burnett, Ron Graham, Persi Diaconis, Gerald Alexanderson, Marjorie Senechal, Doris Schattschneider, Andrew Granville, Matthew Ferszt, Gale Sandor, Jill LeClair, David Gabai, Douglas Hofstadter, Colin Mallows, Neil Sloane, Hugh Montgomery, Brandon Fradd, Derek Smith, Jade Vinson, Jacob Tsimerman, Boris Alexeev, Stephen D. Miller, Francis Fung (who shared his tapes of Conway talking), Simon Fraser, Polly Shulman (who shared her interview tapes with Martin Kruskal and more of Conway talking), Josh Jordan, Simon Viennot, Tanya Khovanova, James Lepowsky, Dierk Schleicher, Erik Demaine and Martin Demaine, James Propp, Marc Pelletier, Robert Bosch, Tom Rokicki, Mark Mitton, the late Tom Rodgers and the G4G team, John McKay, Hitoshi Murayama at Kavli IPMU, Mathcamp's Mira Bernstein and Marisa Debowsky and crew and campers, Numberphile's Brady Haran, Allex Bellos, Ken Norman, Rex Jung, Tod Lippy, Hans Halvorson, Stephen Adler, Nima Arkani-Hamed, William Newsome, Chris Scott, Sandra Witelson, Asia Ivić Weiss, and Magnus Wenninger.

For encouragement and support in many forms I owe a debt of gratitute to John Bohannon, George Dyson, Graham Farmelo, Peter Galison, James Gleick, Andy Keen and Kelly Pullen, Shannon Black, Sarah MacLachlan and Noah Richler, Marjorie Senechal, Doris Schattschneider, my late mum, Anne, and my brother, Dylan. And my Douglas Bell.

With apologies to JHC.

A SELECT CONWAY BIBLIOGRAPHY

1955. "n-Dimensional Regular Polytopes." *Holt School Magazine*, Liverpool, March 1955, 11–13.

1956. "Science Society." *Holt School Magazine*, Liverpool, March 1956, 26–27.

1959. "Problems Drive" (with M. R. Boothroyd). *Eureka* 22:15 (solutions, 22–23).

1962. "π in four 4's" (with M.J.T. Guy). *Eureka* 25:18–19.

1964. "Mrs. Perkins's Quilt." *Proceedings of the Cambridge Philosophical Society* 60:363–68.

1967. "Four-Dimensional Archimedean Polytopes." *Proceedings of the Colloquium on Convexity, Copenhagen, 1965*. Copenhagen: University of Copenhagen Mathematics Institute, 38–39.

1968. "A Perfect Group of Order 8,315,553,613,086,720,000 and the Sporadic Simple Groups" (communicated by Saunders MacLane). *Proceedings of the National Academy of Sciences*, vol. 61, 398–400.

1968. "Sets of Natural Numbers with Distinct Sums" (with R. K. Guy). *Notices of the American Mathematical Society* 15:345.

1969. "Solution of a Problem of P. Erdös" (with R. K. Guy). *Colloquium Mathematicum* 20:307.

1969. "A Characterization of Leech's Lattice." *Inventiones Mathematicae* 7:137–42.

1969. "A Group of Order 8,315,553,613,086,720,000." *Bulletin of the London Mathematical Society* 1:79–88.

1970. "An Enumeration of Knots and Links, and Some of Their Algebraic Properties." *Computational Problems in Abstract Algebra* (John Leech, ed). Oxford: Pergamon Press, 329–58.

1971. *Regular Algebra and Finite Machines*. London: Chapman and Hall. New edition by Dover, 2012.

1972. "All Numbers Great and Small, Research Paper No. 149." Calgary: University of Calgary, Department of Mathematics and Statistics.

1972. "The Centre of a Finitely Generated Group" (with H.S.M. Coxeter and G. C. Shephard). *Tensor* 25:405–18.

1972. "Unpredictable Iterations." *Proceedings of the 1963 Number Theory Conference*. Boulder: University of Colorado, 49–52. (Also available in *The Ultimate Challenge: The 3x + 1 Problem*. Providence: American Mathematical Society, 2010, 219–24.)

1973. "Construction of the Rudvalis Group of Order 144,926,144,000" (with D. B. Wales). *Journal of Algebra* 27:538–48.

1973. "Tomorrow Is the Day After Doomsday." *Eureka* 36:28–31.

1973. "Triangulated Polygons and Frieze Patterns" (with H.S.M. Coxeter). *Mathematical Gazette* 57:87–94, 175–83.

1975. "All Games Bright and Beautiful, Research Paper No. 295." Calgary: University of Calgary, Department of Mathematics and Statistics.

1975. "A Group to Classify Knots" (with C. McA. Gordon). *Bulletin of the London Mathematical Society* 7:84–86.

1976. *On Numbers and Games.* London: Academic Press. Second edition, A. K. Peters, 2001.

1977. "A Headache Causing Problem" (with M. S. Paterson, and Moscow, U.S.S.R.). *Een Pak Met Korte Broek (A Suit in Short Trousers)*; P. van Emde Boas, J. K. Lenstra, F. Oort, A.H.G. Rinnooy Kan, and T. J. Wansbee, eds. See http://www.tnyakhovanova.com/BlogStuff/Conway/Headache.pdf.

1978. "A Gamut of Game Theories." *Mathematics Magazine*, vol. 1, no. 1 (January 1978), 5–12.

1979. "Monstrous Moonshine" (with S. P. Norton). *Bulletin of the London Mathematical Society* 11:308–39.

1979. "On the Distribution of Values of Angles Determined by Coplanar Points" (with H. T. Croft, P. Erdös, and M.J.T. Guy). *Journal of the London Mathematical Society* 19:137–43.

1980. "Monsters and Moonshine." *The Mathematical Intelligencer*, vol. 2, 165–71.

1981. "The Hunting of J_4." *Eureka*, no. 41 (Summer 1981), 46–54.

1981. "Fast 4- and 8-Dimensional Quantizers and Decoders" (with N.J.A. Sloane), *National Telecomm. Conf. Record – 1981*, IEEE Press, NY, 3, F4.2.1-F2.2.4.

1982. "Fast Quantizing and Decoding Algorithms for Lattice Quantizers & Codes" (with N.J.A. Sloane), *IEEE Trans. on Information Theory*, vol. IT-28, 227–32.

1982. *Winning Ways for Your Mathematical Plays* (with Elwyn Berlekamp and Richard Guy). London: Academic Press. New edition, in four volumes, A. K. Peters, 2004.

1982. "Message Graphs" (with M.J.T. Guy). *Annals of Discrete Mathematics* 13:61–64.

1983. "The automorphism group of the 26-dimensional even unimodular Lorentzian lattice." *Journal of Algebra*, vol. 80, no. 1 (1983), 159–63.

1983. "A Fast Encoding Method for Lattice Codes and Quantizers" (with N.J.A. Sloane), *IEEE Trans. Information Theory*, IT-29, 820–24.

1984. "A monster Lie algebra?" (with Richard Borcherds, Larissa Queen, and N.J.A. Sloane). *Advances in Mathematics*, vol. 53, 75–79.

1985. "A Simple Construction for the Fischer-Griess Monster Group." *Inventiones Mathematicae* 79:513–40.

1985. *Atlas of Finite Groups: Maximal Subgroups and Ordinary Characters for Simple Groups* (with R. T. Curtis, S. P. Norton, R. A. Parker, and R. A. Wilson). Oxford: Clarendon Press.

1985. "Decoding Techniques for Multi-Dimensional Codes (with N.J.A. Sloane). U.S. patent no. 4,507,648 (March 26, 1985).

1986. "Lexicographic Codes: Error-Correcting Codes from Game Theory" (with N.J.A. Sloane). *IEEE Transactions in Information Theory*, vol. 32, no. 3 (May 1986), 337–48.

1986. "Soft Decoding Techniques for Codes and Lattices, Including the Golay Code and

Leech Lattice" (with N.J.A. Sloane). IEEE Transactions on Information Theory, vol. 32, no. 1 (January 1986), 41–50.

1986. "The Weird and Wonderful Chemistry of Audioactive Decay." *Eureka*, vol. 46, January 1986, 5–18. Also available in *Open Problems in Communication and Computation*, T. M. Cover and B. Gopinath, eds. New York: Springer-Verlag, 1987, 173–88.

1987. "Fractran: A Simple Universal Programming Language for Arithmetic," in *Open Problems in Communication and Computation*, T. M. Cover and B. Gopinath, eds. New York: Springer-Verlag, 1987, 3–26. Also available in *The Ultimate Challenge: The 3x + 1 Problem*. Providence: American Mathematical Society, 2010, "FRACTRAN," 249–66.

1990. "Friezing Our Way into Summer." *Quantum*, May, 50.

1990. "Geometry and the Imagination" (with P. Doyle and B. Thurston). *Geometry's Future, Conference Proceedings*, Joseph Malkevitch, ed. Arlington: COMAP, 37–80.

1990. "Integral Lexicographic Codes." *Discrete Mathematics* 83:219–35.

1990. "Orbit and Coset Analysis of the Golay and Related Codes" (with N.J.A. Sloane). *IEEE Transactions on Information Theory* 36:1038–50.

1990. "Play it again . . . and again . . ." *Quantum*, Nov.–Dec., 30–31.

1991. "Calendar Calculations." *Quantum*, Jan.–Feb., 46.

1991. "Some Mathematical Magic." *Quantum*, Mar.–Apr., 28.

1992. "The Orbifold Notation for Surface Groups." *Groups, Combinatorics and Geometry: Proceedings of the L.M.S. Durham Symposium, July 5–15, Durham, U.K., 1990*, M. W. Liebeck and J. Saxl, eds. Cambridge: Cambridge University Press, 438–47.

1993. "Self-Dual Codes over the Integers Modulo 4" (with N.J.A. Sloane). *Journal of Combinatorial Theory, Series A*. 62:30–45.

1993. "Quaternary Constructions for the Binary Single-Error-Correcting Codes of Julin, Best and Others" (with N.J.A. Sloane). *Designs, Codes, and Cryptography* 4:31–42.

1995. "Sphere Packings, Lattices, Codes and Greed." *Proceedings of the International Congress of Mathematicians, ICM '94, August 3–11, 1994, Zürich, Switzerland*, vol. 1, S. D. Chatterji, ed. Basel: Birkhaeuser, 45–55.

1995. "What are all the best sphere packings in low dimensions?" (with N.J.A Sloane). *Discrete and Computational Geometry* 13:282–403.

1996. "The Angel Problem." *Games of No Chance* 29:3–12.

1996. *The Book of Numbers* (with Richard Guy). New York: Copernicus Books.

1996. "Budding Mathematician Wins Westinghouse Competition" (with A. Jackson). *Notices of the American Mathematical Society* 43:776–79.

1997. *The Sensual (Quadratic) Form* (with Francis Y. C. Fung). Washington, DC: Mathematical Association of America.

1997. "The Primary Pretenders" (with R. K. Guy, W. A. Schneeberger, and N.J.A. Sloane). *Acta Arithmetica* 78:307–13.

1998. "A Brief History of the ATLAS" (with R. T. Curtis and R. A. Wilson). *The Atlas of Finite Groups, Ten Years On*. Cambridge: London Mathematical Society Lecture Note Series no. 249, Cambridge University Press.

1998. "On Happy Factorizations." *Journal of Integer Sequences* 1, https://cs.uwaterloo.ca/journals/JIS/happy.html.

1998. *Sphere Packings, Lattices, and Groups* (with N.J.A. Sloane; third edition). New York: Springer-Verlag.

2001. "On Three-dimensional Orbifolds and Space Groups" (with Olaf Delgado Friedrichs, Daniel H. Huson, and William P. Thurston). *Contributions to Algebra and Geometry* 42(2): 475–507.

2002. "Calendrical Conundrums" (with Fred Kochman). *Puzzlers' Tribute* (Wolfe and Rodgers, eds.). Natick, MA: A. K. Peters, 191–204.

2002. "The Orbifold Notation for Two-Dimensional Groups" (with D. H. Huson). *Structural Chemistry* 13(3-4): 247–57.

2003. *On Quaternions and Octonions* (with D. Smith). Natick, MA: A. K. Peters.

2006. "The Free Will Theorem" (with Simon Kochen). *Foundations of Physics* 36:1441–73.

2008. "Counting Groups: Gnus, Moas, and Other Exotica" (with Heiko Dietrich and E. A. O'Brien). *Mathematical Intelligencer*, vol. 30, no. 2, 6–15.

2008. *The Symmetries of Things* (with Heidi Burgiel and Chaim Goodman-Strauss). Wellesley, MA: A. K. Peters.

2009. "The Strong Free Will Theorem" (with Simon Kochen). *Notices of the AMS* 56(2): 226–32.

2012. "The Pascal Mysticum Demystified" (with Alex Ryba). *Mathematical Intelligencer*, vol. 34, no. 3, 4–5.

2013. "Extending the Pascal Mysticum" (with Alex Ryba). *Mathematical Intelligencer*, vol. 35, no. 2, 44–45.

2013. "Extreme Proofs I: The Irrationality of √2" (with Joseph Shipman). *Mathematical Intelligencer*, vol. 36, no. 3, 2–3.

2013. "Fibonometry" (with Alex Ryba). *Mathematical Gazette*, vol. 97, issue 540, 494.

2013. "On Unsettleable Arithmetical Problems." *American Mathematical Monthly*, vol. 120, no. 3 (March 2013), 192–98.

2014. "All Solutions to the Immobilizer Problem" (with Ben Heuer). *Mathematical Intelligencer*, vol. 36, no. 4, 78–86.

2014. "A Characterization of Equilateral Triangles and Some Consequences." *Mathematical Intelligencer*, vol. 36, no. 1, 1–2.

2014. "On Morley's Trisector Theorem." *Mathematical Intelligencer*, vol. 36, no. 3, 3.

2014. "The Steiner-Lehmus Theorem Angle-Bisector Theorem" (with Alex Ryba). *Mathematical Gazette*, vol. 98, no. 542 (July 2014), 193–203.

Forthcoming. "The Extra Fibonacci Series and the Empire State Building" (with Alex Ryba).

Forthcoming. "Frenicle's 880 Magic Squares" (with Alex Ryba).

Forthcoming. *The Triangle Book* (with Richard Guy, Alex Ryba, and Steve Sigur). A. K. Peters.

Forthcoming. *The Free Theorem* (with Simon Kochen). Princeton University Press.

Forthcoming. *The Monster Book* (with Alex Ryba).

Forthcoming. *Pascal's "Hexagrammum Mysticum" and "The Mysticum Hexagrammaticum"* (with Alex Ryba).

Adamatzky, Andrew, ed. *Game of Life Cellular Automata*. New York: Springer-Verlag, 2010.

Albers, Donald. "John Horton Conway, Talking a Good Game." *Math Horizons*, vol. 1, no. 2 (Spring 1994), 6–9.

———. "A Conversation with Don Knuth: Part 1." *Two-Year College Mathematics Journal*, vol. 13, no. 1 (January 1982), 2–18.

———. "A Conversation with Don Knuth: Part 2." *Two-Year College Mathematics Journal*, vol. 13, no. 2 (March 1982), 128–41.

———. "Mathematical Games: Part I of an Interview with Martin Gardner." *College Mathematics Journal*, vol. 36, no. 3 (May 2005), 178–90.

———. "Mathematical Games and Beyond: Part II of an Interview with Martin Gardner." *College Mathematics Journal*, vol. 36, no. 4 (September 2005), 301–14.

———, and G. L. Alexanderson. *Mathematical People*. Boston: Birkhauser, 1985.

Alpert, Mark. "Not Just Fun and Games." *Scientific American*, April 1999, 40–42.

Amis, Kingsley. *Lucky Jim*. New York: New York Review of Books, 2012.

"Andrew Wiles: Working in an Attic Hideaway, He Cracked a Problem That Had Mystified Great Minds for Ages." *People*, December 27, 1993.

Applegate, D., G. Jacobson, and D. Sleator. "Computer Analysis of Sprouts." Carnegie Mellon University Computer Science Technical Report No. CMU-CS-91-144, May 1991.

Arnold, V. I. "Will Mathematics Survive? Report on the Zurich Congress." *Mathematical Intelligencer*, vol. 17, no. 3, 1995, 6–10.

Aron, Jacob. "First Self-Replicating Creature Spawned in Life Simulator." *New Scientist*, June 16, 2010.

Bak, Per. *How Nature Works*. New York: Springer-Verlag, 1996.

Barry, John. "The Game of Life: Is It Just a Game?" *Sunday Times*, June 13, 1974.

Bellos, Alex. "The 10 Best Mathematicians . . . Whose Revolutionary Discoveries Changed our World." *Observer*, April 11, 2010. http://www.theguardian.com/culture/2010/apr/11/the-10-best-mathematicians.

———. *The Grapes of Math*. Toronto: Doubleday Canada, 2014.

Berlekamp, Elwyn R. *The Dots-and-Boxes Game*. Natick, MA: A. K. Peters, 2000.

Beyers, Dan. "Complex Calculations Add Up to No. 1." *Washington Post*, March 11, 1996.

Borcherds, Richard E. "Sporadic Groups and String Theory." *First European Congress of Mathematics*, vol. 1, *Paris, 1992*. Basel: Birkhauser, 1994, 411–21.

———. "Monstrous Moonshine and Monstrous Lie Superalgebras." *Inventiones Mathematicae*, vol. 109 (1992), no. 2, 405–44.

———. "What is the monster?" *Notices of the A.M.S.* vol. 49, No. 9 October 2002, 1076–77.

Bouton, C. L. "Nim, a Game with a Complete Mathematical Theory." *Annals of Mathematics*, vol. 2, no. 3, 1902, 35–39.

Boyer, Carl B. *The Rainbow, From Myth to Mathematics.* New York: Thomas Yoseloff, 1959.

Brecher, K. "Spiral Galaxies from the Game of Life." *Bulletin of the American Astronomical Society*, vol. 24, 1992, 1168.

Brew, John M., and Ronald Shaw. "Svoyi Kosiri Is an Easy Game." *Eureka*, vol. 16 (1953), 8–12.

Broad, William J. "Seeker, Doer, Giver, Ponderer," *New York Times*, July 7, 2014.

Brodie, Josh. "Math Profs Link Particle Actions, Human Free Will." *Daily Princetonian*, November 24, 2004.

Browne, Malcolm W. "Intellectual Duel: Brash Challenge, Swift Response." *New York Times*, August 30, 1988.

———. "Puzzling Crystals Plunge Scientists into Uncertainty." *New York Times*, Sunday, July 30, 1985.

Burgess, D. A. "Harold Davenport," *Biographical Memoirs of Fellows of the Royal Society* 17 (1971), 159–92.

Burks, Arthur W., ed. *Essays on Cellular Automata.* Urbana: University of Illinois Press, 1970.

Cantor, Georg. *Contributions to the Founding of the Theory of Transfinite Numbers.* La Salle, IL: Open Court Publishing, 1941.

Carey, Benedict. "Where Did the Time Go? Do Not Ask the Brain." *New York Times*, January 5, 2010.

Carroll, Lewis. "Find the Day of the Week for Any Given Date." *Nature*, vol. 35 (March 1887), 517.

Chang, Kenneth. "In Math, Computers Don't Lie. Or Do They?" *New York Times*, April 6, 2004.

Chu-Carroll, Mark C. "Prime Number Pathology: Fractran." *Good Math, Bad Math*, October 27, 2006. http://scienceblogs.com/goodmath/2006/10/27/prime-number-pathology-fractra/.

Claesson, Anders, and T. Kyle Petersen. "Conway's Napkin Problem." http://arxiv.org/abs/math/0505080.

Cook, Mariana. *Mathematicians.* Princeton: Princeton University Press, 2009.

Cook, Matthew. "Universality in Elementary Cellular Automata." *Complex Systems*, vol. 15, no. 1, 1–40.

Coxeter, H.S.M. *Regular Polytopes.* New York: Dover, 1973.

———, and W. W. Rouse Ball. *Mathematical Recreations and Essays.* New York: Dover, 1987.

Coxeter Fonds, B2004-0024, University of Toronto Archives.

Crighton, Michael. *The Lost World.* New York: Ballantine Books, 2012.

Curtis, Robert, and R. A. Wilson, eds. *The Atlas of Finite Groups, 10 Years On.* Cambridge: London Mathematical Society Lecture Note Series no. 249, Cambridge University Press, 1998.

Danziger, Elon. "Freidin Involved with Polyhedra." *The Tower*, May, 1991.

Dauben, Joseph Warren. *Georg Cantor: His Mathematics and Philosophy of the Infinite.* Cambridge, MA: Harvard University Press, 1979.

Dawkins, Richard. *Unweaving the Rainbow.* New York: Houghton Mifflin, 2000.

Dawson, Jim. "Geometry, A 3-Ring Circus." *Star Tribune*, July 1, 1991.

Dehaene, Stanislas. *The Number Sense: How the Mind Creates Mathematics.* New York: Oxford University Press, 1997.

———. "What Are Numbers? A Cerebral Basis for Number Sense." *Edge*, October 27, 1997, http://edge.org/conversation/what-are-numbers-really-a-cerebral-basis-for-number-sense.

Demaine, Erik D., Martin L. Demaine, and David Eppstein. "Phutball Endgames Are Hard." *More Games of No Chance* 42, 2002, 351–60.

Dennett, Daniel. *Darwin's Dangerous Idea: Evolution and the Meaning of Life.* New York: Simon and Schuster, 1995.

———. *Elbow Room.* Cambridge, MA: MIT Press, 1984.

———. *Freedom Evolves.* New York: Penguin, 2003.

———. *Intuition Pumps.* New York: W. W. Norton, 2013.

———. "Real Patterns." *Journal of Philosophy*, vol. 88, no. 1 (January 1991), 27–51.

Doyle, Peter (with Conway). "How to Stare at a Brick Wall." Personal video, circa 1990.

Dunn, Ashley. "Predictably, the Game of Life Is Not Predictable." *New York Times*, July 16, 1997.

Du Sautoy, Marcus. *Symmetry.* New York: Harper Perennial, 2008.

Dyer, Geoff. *Out of Sheer Rage.* New York: Farrar, Straus and Giroux, 1997.

Dyson, Freeman. "Unfashionable Pursuits." *Mathematical Intelligencer*, vol. 5, no. 3, 1983, 47–54.

———. *Disturbing the Universe.* New York: Basic Books, 1979.

Dyson, George. *Turing's Cathedral: The Origins of the Digital Universe.* New York: Pantheon, 2012.

Einstein, Albert, B. Podolsky, and N. Rosen. "Can Quantum-Mechanical Description of Physical Reality be Considered Complete?" *Physical Review*, vol. 47, no. 10 (May 15, 1935), 777–80.

Einstein, Albert, and Alice Calaprice. *The Ultimate Quotable Einstein.* Princeton: Princeton University Press, 2011.

Eno, Brian. "The Limits of Intuition," in *This Explains Everything.* New York: HarperCollins, 2013, 210–11.

Epstein, Joshua M., and Robert L. Axtell. *Growing Artificial Societies.* Washington, D.C.: Brookings Institution, 1996.

Erven, C., et al. "Experimental Three-photon Quantum Nonlocality under Strict Locality Conditions." *Nature Photonics*, vol. 8 (2014), 292–96.

Fabre, Jean-Henri. *Insect Adventures.* New York: Dodd, Mead, 1917.

Farmer, Doyne, Tommaso Toffoli, and Stephen Wolfram. *Cellular Automata.* New York: North-Holland Physics Publishing, 1984.

Feeney, Mark. "Figured Out: We Don't Understand the Math, but Can We Get the Mathematicians?" *Boston Globe*, August 23, 2009.

"Flop of the Century?" *Time*, January 21, 1974.

Forney, G. David. "Review of *Sphere Packings, Lattices and Groups*, by J. H. Conway and N.J.A. Sloane." *IEEE Trans. Information Theory*, vol. 36 (July 1990), 955–56.

Francis, George K., and Jeffrey R. Weeks. "Conway's Zip Proof." *American Mathematical Monthly*, vol. 106 (May 1999), 393–99.

Frenkel, Igor, James Lepowsky, and Arne Meurman. *Vertex Operator Algebras and the Monster*. Boston: Academic Press, 1988.

Friendly, Jonathan. "A School of Theorists Works Itself Out of a Job." *New York Times*, June 22, 1980.

Gahres, Edward T. "Tongue Rolling and Tongue Folding, and Other Hereditary Movements of the Tongue." *Journal of Heredity*, vol. 43 (1952), 221–25.

Gannon, Terry. *Moonshine Beyond the Monster*. New York: Cambridge University Press, 2006.

Gardner, Martin. *The Annotated Alice*. New York: W. W. Norton, 2000.

———. *The Annotated Hunting of the Snark*. New York: W. W. Norton, 2006.

———. *Hexaflexagons and Other Mathematical Diversions*. Chicago: University of Chicago Press, 1988.

———. *Mathematical Carnival*. New York: Alfred A. Knopf, 1975.

———. *Mathematical Magic Show*. New York: Alfred A. Knopf, 1977.

———. *Penrose Tiles to Trapdoor Ciphers*. Washington, D.C.: Mathematical Association of America, 1997.

———. *The Universe in a Handkerchief*. New York: Springer Science, 1996.

———. *Wheels, Life, and Other Mathematical Amusements*. New York: W. H. Freeman, 1983.

Gardner Papers, Special Collections 647, Stanford University Libraries.

Gilder, Louisa. *The Age of Entanglement*. New York: Vintage, 2008.

Giovinazzo, Raife. "Eclectic Dialogue: John Conway." *Princeton Eclectic*, Fall 1994, 32–39.

Gleick, James. *The Information*. New York: Pantheon, 2011.

Goddard, Peter. "Algebras, Groups, and Strings." *ESI 2013*, 12–15.

———. "Interdisciplinarity and the Interplay Between Mathematics and Physics," unpublished talk, Kavli Institute for the Physics and Mathematics of the Universe Seminars 2014.

———. "The Work of Richard Ewen Borcherds." *Proceedings of the International Congress of Mathematicians*, vol. 1, Berlin, 1998. *Documenta mathematica* 1998, 99–108. http://www.math.uiuc.edu/documenta/xvol-icm/ICM.html.

Gödel, Kurt. "What Is Cantor's Continuum Problem?" *American Mathematical Monthly*, vol. 54, no. 9 (November 1947), 515–25.

Gödel Papers, C0282. Institute for Advanced Study, Shelby White and Leon Levy Archive Center. On deposit at Princeton University, Department of Rare Books and Special Collections.

Gonshor, Harry. *An Introduction to the Theory of Surreal Numbers*. London Mathematical Society Lecture Notes, Series 110, 1986.

Goodman-Strauss, Chaim. "Can't Decide, Undecide." *Notices of the American Mathematical Society*, vol. 57, no. 3 (March 2010), 343–56.

Gopnik, Alison, Patricia Kuhl, and Andrew Meltzoff. *The Scientist in the Crib*. New York: William Morrow, 2001.

Gorenstein, D. *The Classification of Finite Simple Groups*. New York: Plenum Press, 1982.

Gray, Lawrence. "A Mathematician Looks at Wolfram's New Kind of Science." *Notices of the AMS*, vol. 50, no. 2 (February 2003), 200–211.

Greer, Germain. *The Female Eunuch*. New York: McGraw-Hill, 1971.

Griess, Robert L. "The Friendly Giant." *Inventiones Mathematicae*, vol. 69 (1982), 1–102.

Grünbaum, Branko, and Geoffrey C. Shepard. *Tilings and Patterns*. San Francisco: W. H. Freeman, 1987.

———. "The Symmetries of Things by John H. Conway, Heidi Burgiel, and Chaim Goodman-Strauss." *American Mathematical Monthly*, vol. 116 (June–July 2009), 555–61.

Grundy, P. M. "Mathematics and Games." *Eureka*, vol. 2 (1939), 6–8.

Guy, Richard K. "Conway's Prime Producing Machine." *Mathematics Magazine*, vol. 56 (January 1983), 26–33.

———. "John Horton Conway: Mathematical Magus." *Two-Year College Mathematics Journal*, vol. 13, no. 5 (November 1982), 290–98.

———, and Cedric Smith. "The G-values of Various Games." *Proceedings of the Cambridge Philosophical Society*, vol. 52 (1956), 514–26.

Hadamard, Jacques. *An Essay on the Psychology of Invention in the Mathematical Field*. Princeton: Princeton University Press, 1945, app 1 137–41, app 2 142–43.

Halvorson, Hans. *Deep Beauty: Understanding the Quantum World Through Mathematical Innovation*. New York: Cambridge University Press, 2011.

Hardy, G. H. *A Mathematician's Apology*. New York: Cambridge University Press, 1985.

Hargittai, Istvan. "John Conway—Mathematician of Symmetry and Everything Else." *Mathematical Intelligencer*, vol. 23, no. 2 (2001), 6–14.

———, and Magdolna Hargittai. *Symmetry, A Unifying Concept*. Bolinas, CA: Shelter Publications, 1994.

Haseltine, Eric. "Discover Roundtable." *Discover Magazine*. October 2002.

Hawking, Stephen. *A Brief History of Time*. New York: Bantam, 1998.

Healy, Michelle. "Surreal Numbers Place First in Science Search." *USA Today*, March 11, 1996.

Hilbert, D., and S. Cohn-Vossen. *Geometry and the Imagination*. New York: Chelsea Publishing, 1952.

Hofstadter, Douglas. *Gödel, Escher, Bach*. New York: Basic Books, 1999.

———. Personal Papers. Letter to Conway, September 2, 1988.

Holt, Jim. "Numbers Guy, Are Our Brains Wired for Math?" New Yorker, March 3, 2008.

———. *Why Does the World Exist?* New York: W. W. Norton, 2012.

Horgan, John. "The Death of Proof." *Scientific American*, October 1993, 92–103.

Hoste, Jim, Morwen Thistlethwaite, and Jeff Weeks. "The First 1,701,936 Knots." *Mathematical Intelligencer*, vol. 20, no. 4 (1998), 33–48.

Huber-Dyson, Verena. "On the Nature of Mathematical Concepts: Why and How Do

Mathematicians Jump to Conclusions?" *EDGE*, February 15, 1998. http://edge.org/conversation/on-the-nature-of-mathematical-concepts-why-and-how-do-mathematicians-jump-to-conclusions.

Jackson, Allyn. "Borcherds, Gowers, Kontsevich, and McMullen Receive Fields Medals." *Notices of the AMS*, vol. 45, no. 10, 1358–60.

Jingrun, Chen, "Waring's Problem g(5)." *Acta Mathematica Sinica*, vol. 14 (1964), 715–34.

Johnson, George. "Mindless Creatures Acting 'Mindfully.'" *New York Times*, March 23, 1999.

———. "You Know That Space-Time Thing? Never Mind." *New York Times*, June 9, 2002.

Johnson, Samuel. "Rambler #60," October 13, 1750. http://www.samueljohnson.com/ram60.html.

Kaesuk Yoon, Carol. "Oozing Through Texas Soil, a Team of Amoebas Billions Strong." *New York Times*, March 23, 2009.

Kaiser, Walter. "The Passions of Bernard Berenson." *New York Review of Books*, vol. 16, no. 8 (November 21, 2013).

Kennedy, Juliette. "Can the Continuum Hypothesis Be Solved?" *IAS Letter*, Fall 2011. IAS; Gödel Archives.

Khovanova, Tanya. "Conway's Recipe for Success," March 6, 2010. http://blog.tanyakhovanova.com/?p=214.

———. "The Greatest Mathematician Alive," March 20, 2010. http://blog.tanyakhovanova.com/?p=218.

———. "The Sexual Side of Life," July 25, 2010. http://blog.tanyakhovanova.com/?p=260.

Knuth, Donald E. Personal Archives (1950–).

———. *Surreal Numbers: How Two Ex-Students Turned On to Pure Mathematics and Found Total Happiness*. New York: Addison-Wesley, 1974.

Kolata, Gina. "Mathematical Games: Are They Bona Fide Research?" *Science*, vol. 197, no. 4303 (August 5, 1977), 546.

———. "John H. Conway, At Home in the Elusive World of Mathematics." *New York Times*, October 12, 1993.

Konhauser, Joseph, Dan Velleman, and Stan Wagon. *Which Way Did the Bicycle Go?* Washington: Mathematical Association of America, 1996.

Kullman, David. "The Penrose Tiling at Miami University." Presented at the MAA Ohio Section Meeting, Shawnee State University, October 24, 1997. http://www.lib.miamioh.edu/epub/tilings/doc.html.

Lagarias, Jeffrey C., ed. *The Ultimate Challenge: The 3x + 1 Problem*. Providence: American Mathematical Society, 2010.

Landsman, Klaas, and Eric Cator. "Constraints on Determinism: Bell Versus Conway-Kochen." *Foundations of Physics*. http://arxiv.org/abs/1402.1972.

Lavin, Irving, and Marilyn Aronberg Lavin. *Truth and Beauty at the Institute for Advanced Study*. Princeton: Institute for Advanced Study, 2010.

Leech, John. "Some Sphere Packing in Higher Space." *Canadian Journal of Mathematics*, vol. 16, 657–82.

———. "Notes on Sphere Packings." *Canadian Journal of Mathematics*, vol. 19, 25167.

Lemoine, Julien, and Simon Viennot. "Numbers Are Inevitable." *Theoretical Computer Science*, vol. 462, 2012, 70–79.

———. "Computer Analysis of Sprouts with Numbers." *Games of No Chance 4*. MSRI Publications. Forthcoming.

Lepowsky, James. "The Work of Richard E. Borcherds." *Notices of the AMS*, January 1999, 17–19.

———, et al., eds. *Moonshine: The First Quarter Century and Beyond*. New York: Cambridge University Press, 2010.

Lévi-Strauss, Claude. *The Elementary Structures of Kinship*. Boston: Beacon Press, 1969.

———. "The Mathematics of Man." *International Social Science Bulletin*, vol. 6, no. 4 (1954), 581–90.

Lewis, Peter H. "Escapist Software." *New York Times*, July 9, 1985.

Lippy, Tod. "John Conway." *Esopus*, no. 6 ("Process"), 2006, 33–52.

Liverpool Daily Post. "Oxford and Cambridge Scholarship Awards," Saturday, December 17, 1955, 6.

Lurie, Jacob. "The Effective Content of Surreal Algebra." *Journal of Symbolic Logic*, vol. 63, no. 2 (1998), 337–71.

———. "A Question for Jacob Lurie." *New York Times*, April 7, 1996.

Malcolm, Janet. *Two Lives*. New Haven: Yale University Press, 2007.

Mallows, Colin. "Conway's Challenge Sequence." *American Mathematical Monthly*, vol. 98, no. 1 (January 1991), 5–20.

———. "Conway's Challenge, Mallows Replies." *American Mathematical Monthly*, vol. 99, no. 6 (June/July 1992), 563–64.

Margolus, Norman, and Tomasso Toffoli. *Cellular Automata Machines*. Cambridge: MIT Press, 1987.

Masters, Alexander. *Simon, The Genius in My Basement*. New York: Delacorte Press, 2011.

Matthews, Robert. "The Man Who Played God with Infinity." *New Scientist*, September 2, 1995, 36–40.

M.F.A. "Professor A. S. Besicovitch." *Eureka*, vol. 27 (October 1964), 26–28.

Mitchell, Melanie. *Complexity: A Guided Tour*. New York: Oxford University Press, 2009.

Moorehead, John. "How Simon Survives Being a Genius." *Daily Mail*, July 25, 1969.

Morales, Linda, and Hal Sudburough. "A Quadratic Lower Bound for Topswops." *Theoretical Computer Science*, vol. 411, no. 44–46 (October 2010), 396–70.

Moravec, Hans. *Mind Children*. Cambridge, MA: Harvard University Press, 1990.

Morgan, Frank. "Math Chat," October 6, 1997. https://www.youtube.com/watch?v=oe9 9rjLoJkk&feature=youtu.be.

"Mystery and Magic of Mathematics: Martin Gardner and Friends." *Nature of Things*, CBC, 1996.

Nasar, Sylvia. *A Beautiful Mind*. Toronto: Simon and Schuster, 1998.

Neisser, Ulric. "John Dean's Memory: A Case Study." *Cognition*, vol. 9, 102–15.

Nelson, Edward. "Warning Signs of a Possible Collapse of Contemporary Mathematics." https://web.math.princeton.edu/~nelson/papers.html.

O'Connor, John J., and Edmund F. Robertson. "John Horton Conway." MacTutor History of Mathematics Archive, University of St. Andrews. http://www-history.mcs.st-andrews.ac.uk/Biographies/Conway.html.

Osmundsen, John A. "2 Key Mathematics Questions Answered After Quarter Century; Proof Concerns Theory of Sets, Widely Used in Teaching Beginners." *New York Times*, November 14, 1963

Overbye, Dennis. "Did This Man Just Rewrite Science?" *New York Times*, June 11, 2002.

———. "Far Out, Man. But Is It Quantum Physics?" *New York Times*, March 14, 2006.

———. "Free Will: Now You Have it, Now You Don't." *New York Times*, January 2, 2007.

Penrose, Roger. *The Emperor's New Mind*. Oxford: Oxford University Press, 1999.

———. "Pentaplexity: A Class of Nonperiodic Tilings of the Plane." *Mathematical Intelligencer*, vol. 2 (1979), 32–37.

Perko, Kenneth A. Jr., "Remarks on the History of the Classification of Knots." Banach Center Publications, vol. 103 (2014), 241–50.

Petard, H. "A Contribution to the Mathematical Theory of Big Game Hunting." *American Mathematical Monthly*, vol. 45, no. 7 (Aug./Sept. 1938), 446–47.

Peterson, Ivars. "Computing in a Surreal Realm." *Science News*, March 18, 1996.

———. "Sprouts for Spring." *Science News*, April 5, 1997.

Pickover, Clifford A. *The Math Book*. New York: Sterling, 2009.

———. *Wonders of Numbers*. New York: Oxford University Press, 2001.

Point Foundation. *The Essential Whole Earth Catalog*. San Francisco: Main Street Books, September 24, 1986.

Postol, Michael. "Method for Storage and Reconstruction of the Extended Hamming Code for an 8-dimensional Lattice Quantizer." With the Director of the National Security Agency, Government of the United States. United States Patent No. 6,404,821 B1, June 11, 2002.

Poundstone, William. *The Recursive Universe: Cosmic Complexity and the Limits of Scientific Knowledge*. Chicago: Contemporary Books, 1985.

"Professor Harold Davenport, Leader of British School of Number Theory." *Times*, June 10, 1969, 12.

Revkin, Andrew. "Obama's Call to Create, Not Just Consume." *New York Times*, April 27, 2009.

Roberts, Siobhan, *King of Infinite Space*. New York: Walker, 2006.

———. "Strength in Numbers." *Globe and Mail*, August 16, 2003.

———. "Thank Einstein Almighty, They're Free at Last." *Globe and Mail*, March 19, 2005.

———. "Do the Math." *Walrus*, November 2005.

———. "The Cubic Connection," *Walrus*, April 2007.

———. "John Conway, Mathemagician," *IPMU News*, no. 3, September 2008.

———. "Number Nerds Get Pi-eyed for the Raddest Ratio." *Globe and Mail*, March 14, 2009.

———. "Finding Nirvana in Numbers: Mathcamp." *Simons Foundation*, December 21, 2010.

———. "Curiosities: Pursuing the Monster." *IAS Letter*, Fall 2013.

———. "Science Lives: John Conway." *Simons Foundation*, April 4, 2014.

Ronan, Mark. *Symmetry and the Monster*. Oxford: Oxford University Press, 2007.

Rota, Gian-Carlo. *Indiscrete Thoughts*. New York: Springer Science, 1997.

Rufford, Nick. "Numbers Man Hits $10,000 Jackpot." *Sunday Times*, September 11, 1988.

"Russia: A Bit of Fear." *Time*, February 25, 1966.

Schattschneider, Doris. "M. C. Escher's Classification System for His Colored Periodic Drawings." In *M. C. Escher: Art and Science*, H.S.M. Coxeter, M. Emmer, R. Penrose, and M. Teuber, eds. Amsterdam: North Holland, 1986, 82–96.

Schleicher, Dierk. "Interview with John Horton Conway." *Notices of the AMS*, May 2013, 567–75.

Science Service. "Einstein Attacks Quantum Theory." *New York Times*, May 4, 1935.

Seife, Charles. "Mathemagician: Impressions of Conway." *Sciences*, May/June 1994, 12–15.

———. "Impressions of Conway." Draft version of "Mathemagician," December 1993. http://www.users.cloud9.net/~cgseife/conway.html.

Senechal, Marjorie. "The Algebraic Escher." *Structural Topology*, no. 15, 1988, 31–42.

Shalizi, Cosma. "A Rare Blend of Monster Raving Egomania and Utter Batshit Insanity." October 2005. http://vserver1.cscs.lsa.umich.edu/~crshalizi/reviews/wolfram/.

Shannon, C. E., and J. McCarthy (eds). *Automata Studies*. Princeton: Princeton University Press, 1956.

Shulman, Polly. "Infinity Plus One, and Other Surreal Numbers." *Discover*, December 1995, 97–105.

———. "Infinity Plus One." Research interview tapes, 1995.

Siegel, Aaron N. *Combinatorial Game Theory*. Providence: American Mathematical Society, 2013.

Silva, Jorge-Nuno. "Breakfast with John Horton Conway." *Newsletter of the European Mathematical Society*, no. 57, September 2005, 32–34.

Simons Foundation. "Science Lives: John Conway." Interview by Alex Ryba, filming by George Csicsery, May 12, 2011.

"Simpson, Frederick Arthur." Oxford Dictionary of National Biography. http://www.oxforddnb.com/view/printable/31689.

Smale, Stephen. "On the Steps of Moscow University." *Mathematical Intelligencer*, vol 6, no. 2, 21–27.

Steen, Lynn Arthur. "What's in a Game?" *Science News*, vol. 113 (April 1, 1978), 204–6.

Steen, Stourton. *Mathematical Logic*. New York: Cambridge University Press, 1972.

Suzuki, David. "Mystery and Magic of Mathematics: Martin Gardner and Friends," *Nature of Things*, CBC, 1996.

Tandon, Neeru. *Feminism: A Paradigm Shift*. New Delhi: Atlantic Publishers and Distributors, 2008.

Taubes, Gary. "John Horton Conway: A Mathematical Madness at Cambridge." *Discover*, August 1984, 41–50.

Thomas, Rachel. "Games, Life and the Game of Life." *Plus Magazine*, May 1, 2002. http://plus.maths.org/content/games-life-and-game-life.

———. "John Conway: Discovering Free Will" (I, II, III). *Plus Magazine*, December 27, 2011. http://plus.maths.org/content/john-conway-discovering-free-will-part-i.

Thompson, J. G. "Some Numerology Between the Fischer-Griess Monster and the Elliptic Modular Function." *Bulletin of the London Math Society* 11 (1979), 352–53.

Thompson, Nicholas. "My Friend, Stalin's Daughter: The Complicated Life of Svetlana Alliluyeva." *New Yorker*, March 31, 2014, 30–37.

Thompson, Thomas. *From Error-Correcting Codes Through Sphere Packings to Simple Groups*. Washington, D.C.: Mathematical Association of America, 1982.

Thurston, William. "The Geometry and Topology of Three-Manifolds." Princeton University Lecture Notes, 1978–1981 (unpublished). http://library.msri.org/books/gt3m/.

Tierney, John. "Discovering the Virtues of a Wandering Mind." *New York Times*, June 28, 2010.

Turing, Alan. "Intelligent Machines" (1948). In *Collected Works of A. M. Turing, Volume 1*. New York: North Holland, 1992.

———. "On Computable Numbers." http://www.turingarchive.org/viewer/?id=466&title=01a.

Ulam Papers, American Philosophical Society Library.

Ulam, S. M. *Adventures of a Mathematician*. New York: Charles Scribner's Sons, 1976.

Von Neumann, John. *Theory of Self-Reproducing Automata*. Edited by Arthur W. Burks. Urbana: University of Illinois Press, 1966.

Wainwright, Robert. "Conway's Game of Life: Early Personal Recollections" In *Game of Life Cellular Automata*. New York: Springer-Verlag, 2010, 11–16.

Walker, Brian. *Hippie Philosophy and the Building of the Environmental Counterculture*. Forthcoming.

Weinberg, Steven. "Is the Universe a Computer?" *New York Review of Books*, October 24, 2002.

Welbourne, Edward et al. "Prelude." *Eureka*, vol. 46, January 1986, 4.

Wertheim, Margaret. "Hunting a Mathematical Snark." *Cabinet*, Issue 34 ("Testing"), Summer 2009, 53–56.

Weyl, Hermann. "Invariants." *Duke Mathematical Journal*, vol. 5, no. 3 (1939).

Witelson, S. F., D. L. Kigar, and T. Harvey. "The Exceptional Brain of Albert Einstein." *Lancet*, vol. 345 (June 19, 1999), 2149–53.

Wodehouse, P. G. *The Heart of a Goof*. New York: Overlook Press, 2006.

Wolfe, David, and Tom Rodgers. *Puzzlers' Tribute*. Natick, MA: A. K. Peters, 2002.

Wolfram, Stephen. *A New Kind of Science*. Champaign, IL: Wolfram Media, 2002.

Wright, Robert. "Did the Universe Just Happen?" *Atlantic Monthly*, April 1988.

PROLOGUE

xii **Lewis Carroll's walrus** Gardner, 2000, 185.

xii **"fiction of humility"** Malcolm, 13.

xiii **Baggins and Gandalf** Feeney.

xiii **"Prof or Hobo?"** http://individual.utoronto.ca/somody/quiz.html.

xiii **cell towers on the rooftop** Dyson, George, 37.

xiv **"famous brainchild"** Gardner, 1983, 214.

xv **"shock to the intuition"** Eno, 211.

xv *Grand Design* "The Meaning of Life," *Stephen Hawking's Grand Design*, http://www.youtube.com/watch?v=CgOcEZinQ2I&feature=share&list=FLwikA_t8e6TSJW-L-lAHkKw.

xv **military report** Interviews with Gardner, Gosper, Conway.

xvi **game theory** Game theory here pertains to Conway's type of game theory, combinatorial game theory (a name he finds clunky), not to be confused with John von Neumann's type of game theory, the subject of von Neumann's book with Oskar Morgenstern, *Theory of Games and Economic Behavior*. Says Conway: "That's the useful kind of game theory. I never did anything useful."

xvi **"lot of room up there"** Gardner, 1983, 214.

xvi **"infinite classes"** Gardner, 1997, 51.

xvi **top-10 lists** Bellos, 2010; Pickover, 2001, 87; Khovanova, 2010. Clifford Pickover, in *Wonders of Numbers*, devotes a chapter to "A Ranking of the 10 Most Influential Mathematicians Alive Today." Conway ranks ninth, while his Princeton colleague Andrew Wiles ranks first. A ranking of the same mathematicians according to Google hits, conducted by mathematician and blogger Tanya Khovanova, places Conway second, with Roger Penrose first.

xviii **as yet no luck** Although he has had no luck so far with the Abel Prize, Conway has won other big prizes, including the Berwick, Polya, Nemmer, and Leroy P. Steele prizes.

xviii **classical geometer** Roberts, 2006.

xix *The Cocktail Party* Dyson, George, 37.

xxiii **personal knowledge** Johnson.

xxiii **devilishness** Sketched by his friend the University of Toronto emeritus professor

Simon J. Fraser at a conference in Toronto, the cartoon came with a dedication: "In homage to a diabolical mathematician."

prologue in general   Roberts, 2014 (parts of the account of JHC in the alcove here and there were previously published in *Science Lives*, on the Simons Foundation website).

1. IDENTITY ELEMENTS

3   **name published**   *Liverpool Daily Post*, December 17, 1955.

4   **Free Will Theorem**   Conway and Kochen, 2009; the Free Will Theorem lecture series ran on Mondays from March 23 to April 27, 2009, and can be viewed at http://www.princeton.edu/WebMedia/lectures/. Roberts, 2005 (parts of the account of the Free Will Theorem throughout were previously published in the *Globe and Mail*).

6   **philandering ken**   Explaining himself as he waded into the lecture, Conway provided a selective survey of philosophers who had weighed in on free will, including Descartes, Hobbes, Locke, Kant, and Leibniz, but first, he cited the Roman Titus Lucretius, who observed, "Although many men are driven by an external force and often constrained involuntarily to advance or rush headlong, yet there is within the human breast something that can fight against this force and resist it ... So also in the atoms you must recognize the same possibility. Besides weight and impact, there must be a third cause of movement, the source of this inborn power of ours, since we see that nothing can come out of nothing. ... But the fact that the mind itself has no internal necessity to determine its every act ... this is due to the slight swerve of the atoms at no determinate time or place." The crucial point was those atoms; at indeterminate times and places they swerve. Says Conway: "I find it absolutely fantastic that somebody 2,000 years ago could have suggested that atoms actually, in some sense, have free will."

2. DAZZLING NEW WORLD

10   Joan Conway died in February 2015.

13   **"Everyone is acquainted"**   Coxeter, 1973, 1.

13   **"early history ... is lost"**   Coxeter, 1973, 13.

15   **"by direct observation"**   Coxeter, 1973, vi.

16   **"n-Dimensional"**   Conway, 1955, 11.

16   **Science Society**   Conway, 1956, 26.

3. GYMNASTICS

21   **Archimedean solids**   Conway, 1967.

26 **tongue tricks**   Gahres. Although nothing could be found in *Reader's Digest* on this subject, in 1952 the *Journal of Heredity* ran an article titled, "Tongue Rolling and Tongue Folding, and Other Hereditary Movements of the Tongue."

30 **11 or fewer crossings**   For some debate on this matter see Perko, "Remarks on the History of the Classification of Knots."

31 **untangle it**   Learning the history of knots at the Central Library in Liverpool, Conway read the first book on knots, published in 1848 and written in German by J. B. Listing, who proved a knot was indeed a knot and not untanglable. He also studied the work of Scottish mathematician and physicist Lord Kelvin, and Lord Kelvin's friend, Peter Guthrie Tait, also a Scottish physicist, as well as Kelvin's collaborator Thomas Penyngton Kirkman, a vicar and mathematician and member of the Royal Society. Conway undertook an intensive study of this literature and invented a notation that made it easier to tell the difference between knots, defining knots by breaking them apart into their component parts, which he called "tangles." He classified the tangles according to their orientation, and he described their orientation according to the compass points and quantified their total content according to their crossings. Says Conway: "It's very, very difficult to get ahold of why one knot is different from another one. The notation I invented made it a bit easier. It hasn't solved the problem completely—not all knots are good enough to have a notation in my system, and I don't know really what to do when they are not." See Conway, 1970.

33 **"mysteries of flexigation"**   Gardner, 1988.

33 **"Dear Sir"**   Coxeter Fonds, letter from Conway to Coxeter, March 1, 1957.

35 **"Murder Weapon"**   Roberts, 2006, 253.

41 **Proofs emerged**   In 1909 David Hilbert proved that the sum of powers could always be done, with the Hilbert-Waring theorem, and over the years mathematicians picked off proofs for more powers. Cubes fell in 1909 and sixth powers in 1940. For the fourths and higher, the Cambridge duo Hardy and Littlewood established an upper bound. All sufficiently large numbers are the sum of no more than 19 fourth powers. In the process they developed the Hardy-Littlewood method that became the definitive approach. Davenport, Littlewood's Ph.D. student (making Littlewood Conway's grandfather, mathematically speaking), carried on with a fundamental subset of the fourth powers problem, getting the bound down to 16—that is, every number is the sum of at most 16 fourth powers. Davenport proudly passed on the tradition in recommending that Conway prove the fifths.

42 **better solution**   Jingrun, 1964.

4. CALCULATE THE STARS

43 **"I frame no hypothesis"**   Cantor, 85.

45 **never reached**   That's Conway's paraphrasing. We Googled to get the exact quotation: "The use of an infinite magnitude (quantity) as a completed one is never permitted in mathematics. The infinite is only a *façon de parler*, while one really

speaks of limits which certain ratios approach as closely as one desires, while others are permitted to increase without limitation." Aristotle on the subject of the infinite also distinguished between "actual" and "potential."

50 **"funny thing"** Cook, 18.

52 **not a social construct** This is an idea Conway discussed with his late Princeton colleague Edward Nelson, who at times questioned the nature of the integers. See Nelson.

53 **logical foundation** As mathematicians played around with the science of infinity, paradoxes emerged, such as "the set of all sets." Cantor proved that given any set, there is always a strictly larger set. But what about the set that contains everything, including the universe? There can't be anything larger than that, because this set includes everything, even the infinite. "Don't say 'the infinite,'" says Conway. "This set contains everything, EVERYTHING. If we are talking in a non-mathematical way, it contains you and me and this walking stick. However, we don't need those for mathematical purposes. It contains all integers, all real numbers, all sets of real numbers, all everything, all mathematical objects. There can't be a set of mathematical objects larger than that. Well, that contradicts Cantor's theorem. Cantor's theorem says no matter what set you take, there is a larger set." The logic collapses in on itself, degenerates into a recursive cycle, like the ancient symbol Ouroboros, a snake eating its tail. Notwithstanding these predicaments— another was that set theory's axioms seemed to imply paradoxical things, for instance that you can divide a sphere into three congruent parts, A and B and C, all the same shape and size, but such that part A is the same size as parts B and C combined—despite predicaments like this, the mathematical establishment was unwilling to renounce the logical framework of set theory. Hilbert said, "No one shall expel us from the Paradise that Cantor has created." Instead, mathematicians tried to eliminate the paradoxes. They began pulling apart set theory, analyzing the founding principles and, with the German Ernst Zermelo leading the way, reorganizing the theory into a formal system. Over time, as mathematicians worked away trying to get at the root of the problem, suspicions fell on Zermelo's Axiom of Choice, formulated in 1904. In 1940, Kurt Gödel made a major breakthrough when he proved that the Axiom of Choice could not be disproved using the other axioms—he proved the consistency of the Axiom, showing that any flaw or contradiction that arose when mathematicians used the Axiom could also arise when they did not use the Axiom. Says Conway: "Had it been inconsistent that would have been terrible. Whenever you used it you would be in danger of getting a contradiction. When you get a contradiction this destroys mathematics. If you could prove every proposition and also its negative that would mean the axioms didn't really correspond to anything at all. It would all be nonsense. The whole idea of mathematics is you can't prove 2 propositions, 1 of which contradicts the other. If you could prove that 2 times 2 equals 4, and also that 2 times 2 equals 5, then you don't know what 2 times 2 is, and that's a bit sad." So Gödel removed the Axiom of Choice as the culprit. He still wondered whether the Axiom of Choice was also independent of the other axioms, or, conversely, whether it could be derived from

the other axioms. However, proving the independence of the Axiom of Choice was a much tougher nut to crack. See Osmundsen.

5. NERDISH DELIGHTS

59 **"vague intuitive ideas"** Steen, 1.
68 **invented Phutball** For some serious analysis on Phutball, see "Phutball Endgames Are Hard," by Erik Demaine, Martin Demaine, and David Eppstein, in which the authors proved that in Phutball "it is NP-complete to determine whether the current player has a move that immediately wins the game. In contrast, the similar problems of determining whether there is an immediately winning move in checkers, or a move that kings a man, are both solvable in polynomial time." Gardner Papers, 1974.
71 **"got your first parcel"** Gardner Papers, 1967.
71 **cut up letter** Naturally, Conway didn't date his letters, and he didn't keep copies. Gardner filed them all away, as well as drafts of his replies, and a good-sized collection resides among his papers at the Stanford University Archives. Though Gardner, too, had his idiosyncrasies as far as letters went. His tendency to cut up his correspondence and scatter original letters according to snippets of subject matter gives the archivist there a headache.
72 **first *Scientific American*** Gardner, 1975, 6–11.
73 **sproutology** Gardner Papers, 1967.
73 **Bell Labs trio** Appegate, Jacobson, Sleator.
73 **French duo** Lemoine, Viennot.
77 **"twisted mind"** Welbourne.
77 **"Look-and-Say"** Richard Guy came up with this name for the sequence.
78 **"Weird and Wonderful"** Conway, *Eureka*, 1986.
81 **befuddled biographer** This piece of wisdom comes courtesy of Geoff Dyer from his book *Out of Sheer Rage: Wrestling with D. H. Lawrence*: "I had often puzzled over the contradiction contained within these rival claims. . . . Taken on their own, individually, both would have been false; the truth lay in the contradiction."

6. THE VOW

83 **work of an alien being** In 1963, as Conway recalls, "Something terrible happened. Or no, actually, something marvelously good!" The American mathematician Paul Cohen, of Stanford, proved the independence of the Continuum Hypothesis, and as a sidecar he also proved that the Axiom of Choice was logically independent from the other axioms. There in one fell swoop Cohen had made 2 of the greatest advances in mathematics in the twentieth century. The *New York Times* gave the story feature treatment: "2 Key Mathematics Questions Answered After Quarter Century; Proof Concerns Theory of Sets"—1,604 words' worth of

mathematical news fit to print, plus diagrams. Conway looked up Cohen's paper and took a peek. Here, for him, the horror set in. Cohen's result looked like the "work of an alien being." The horror wasn't that Cohen had succeeded where Conway had failed in solving these big problems; the horror was more what Cohen had done and how he had done it. Cohen found a powerful method for answering questions as to whether or not such-and-such a set-theoretical statement implied another such statement. "Forcing," it was called, and as the name suggested, it required hard work. Mathematicians started writing 200-hundred-page papers applying this method. One could prove just about anything this way, it seemed, if one was willing to write a 200-hundred-page paper. Says Conway: "I don't like either writing or reading 200-hundred-page papers. It's not my idea of fun."

85 **Leech Lattice**   Du Sautoy; Ronan; Thomas Thompson.
85 **grand mathematical expedition**   Ibid.
89 **"youthful acrobatics"**   Conway, 1985, *Atlas of Finite Groups*, viii.
90 **unearthed a monograph**   Thomas Thompson.
91 **"manning a stall"**   Du Sautoy.
92 **On the first Saturday**   Thomas Thompson.
93 **"It was about 6"**   Ibid.
93 **"It wasn't entirely"**   Ibid.
93 **"The problem was"**   Ibid.
94 **"I said, 'Well now'"**   Ibid.
94 **"Well, how bloody"**   Ibid.
94 **"found a big group!"**   Conway, 1968 "Perfect Group"; 1969 "Group of Order."
98 **riff on the number**   Conway, 1996, *The Book of Numbers*, v–vi.

7. RELIGION

104 **"Cheshire cats and such"**   Gardner Papers, Conway letter to Gardner, November 1970.
108 **"the illusion of free will"**   Overbye, 2006, 2007.

8. CRITERIA OF VIRTUE

110 **didn't understand**   Persi Diaconis tells an almost identical story of listening to Conway (having been instructed to listen with an "unhearing ear"), and as it happens, at the time they were traveling by train en route to Gardner's house. But in Diaconis's telling, as he was listening he started to understand, so he asked Conway a question. Conway said, "No, no, no. Don't interrupt."
110 **"around for years"**   Gardner Papers, Conway letter to Gardner, March 1970.
111 *Automata Studies*   Shannon, 1956.
111 *Jugendtraum*   Following in the tradition of "Kronecker's Jugendtraum" (which is sometimes referred to as Hilbert's 12th problem).

111 **infinite memory**   Turing, 1948, 110.

112 **spirit of von Neumann**   Conway likely came upon this notion via Freeman Dyson's book *Disturbing the Universe* (see "Thought Experiments," 194–204), and Dyson in turn had been inspired by the work of Isaac Asimov.

113 *Theory of Self-Reproducing Automata*   Von Neumann.

114 **recipe for success**   Khovanova, March 6, 2010.

116 **FRACTRAN**   Conway, 1972, "Unpredictable Iterations"; 1987, "Fractran"; and 2013, "On Unsettleable Arithmetical Problems."

117 **very inefficient**   Simons Foundation, transcript of interview with Alex Ryba.

118 **like soap powder**   Conway, 1987, "Fractran." Minsky is a revisionist edit, since Conway always wished he'd included it in his original paper.

118 **fascinating bugger**   Chu-Carroll.

120 **"The Sexual Side of Life"**   Khovanova, July 25, 2010.

121 **stated the rules**   Gardner Papers, Conway letter to Gardner, March 1970.

124 **abandoned warehouse**   Schleicher; see also Thomas, 2002.

124 **press a button**   Thomas, 2002; see also Schleicher.

125 **force for the good**   Siegel, 479–81.

125 **games research**   Guy, 1956.

125 **considered pivotal** Siegel, 480.

126 **come over here**   Conway, *Winning Ways*, Volume 4, 931.

9. CHARACTER ASSASSINATION

130 **"book pay for itself"**   Gardner, 1975, viii–x .

132 **tribute to Gardner**   *Nature of Things.*

133 **"serious mathematician"**   Ibid.

138 **game called Nim**   Bouton. Also see Conway et al., 1982, *Winning Ways.*

141 **"impossible to tie a knot"**   *Nature of Things.*

143 **Minsky's MIT**   Gosper won Conway's $50 prize for discovering the glider gun together with a group of hackers at Marvin Minsky's Artificial Intelligence Lab at MIT, among them Robert April, Michael Beeler, Richard Howell, Rich Schroeppel, and Michael Speciner. When Gosper recently learned of Conway's retroactive preference for naming "gliders" "ants," Gosper in turn wondered: "Inflicting what caconym on my glider gun? Ant uneater? Formicator? Pismire pisser?"

144 **infinitely growing**   Gardner Papers, Conway letter to Gardner, April 1970; Poundstone.

144 **remaining deep problem**   Gardner Papers, Conway letter to Gardner, November 1970.

144 **Cambridge team**   Gosper's MIT team also proved Life's universality, though Conway and company (mostly with Norton's help) beat them to the draw by a slim margin—their letter arrived in Gardner's mailbox first.

144 **LIFE IS UNIVERSAL**   Gardner Papers, Conway letter to Gardner, mailed December 6, 1970.

145 **size of Monaco**   Poundstone, 228: "Displaying a 10^{13}-pixel pattern would require a video screen about 3 million pixels across at least. Assume the pixels are 1 millimeter square. . . . Then the screen would have to be 3 kilometers (about 2 miles) across. It would have an area about six times that of Monaco. . . .Perspective would shrink the pixels of a self-replicating pattern to invisibility. If you got far enough away from the screen so that the entire pattern was comfortably in view, the pixels (and even the gliders, eaters and guns) would be too tiny to make out. A self-reproducing pattern would be a hazy glow, like a galaxy."

145 **spiral galaxies**   Brecher.

145 **Conway's Presumption**   Goodman-Strauss. Stated in full: "If a system has enough complexity, the betting man should assume there are enough building blocks to encode arbitrary computation. At the very least the betting man is not likely to be contradicted! Examples abound, and it does not take much to lift off into computational universality—in some sense we might argue that this is the generic condition!"

146 **New Delhi, Tokyo**   "Flop of the Century?"

146 **Ulam relayed to Conway**   Ulam Papers, Ulam letter to Gardner, September 10, 1970; Ulam letter to Conway, October 6, 1970. Courtesy of Charles Greifenstein, via a tip from George Dyson.

146 **Ulam had devised**   Burks.

146 **"Ulam was the real founder"**   Gardner Papers, Conway letter to Gardner, November 1970.

147 **"practical applicaton"**   Gardner, 1983, 239–40.

147 **sent in by readers**   Gardner, 1983, 226–57. Deluged by the mailbag, Gardner suggested a book could and should be written, an *Encyclopedia of Life*, or a *Handbook of Life*, a record of extant Life-forms, thereby saving Lifenthusiasts the labor of rediscovery. Wainwright started a quarterly newsletter, *Lifeline*, a clearinghouse to ease Gardner's burden, addressing inquiries and adjudicating discoveries. After 11 issues, *Lifeline* ceased publication—it had become too much of a burden for Wainwright, intruding to much on work, family, life in general, especially after he got a computer up and running at home.

147 **Life legend**   Gardner, 1983, 223; "Flop of the Century."

148 **London's *Sunday Times***   Barry.

150 **"The Death of Proof"**   Horgan. Says John Horgan: "Many mathematicians were outraged by that article, and some of my sources claimed they were misquoted. But I taped all my interviews and provided exact quotes."

151 **addendum of an apology**   Wolfram Personal Papers, Conway letter to Horgan, undated (1993).

155 **a few things to learn**   Wolfram.

155 **describing Cook's proof**   The proof was subsequently published with Cook's sole authorship in Wolfram's journal *Complex Systems*, vol. 15, no. 1, 2004.

156 **"Is the Universe a Computer?"**   Weinberg.

156 **Google Books**   Searched on August 12, 2014; "Conway Game of Life" produced

"About 16,000" results while the same with no quotation marks got 8,450, and "Game of Life" got 189,000.

156 *The Lost World* In the acknowledgements, Crichton assures that the novel is fiction, but all the same he mentions indebtedness to the work and speculations of many: the Cambridge astronomer Fred Hoyle; the computer scientist Christopher Langton, who coined the term "artificial life" and in the 1980s devised the cellular automaton called Langton's ants; the Princeton theoretical physicist John Wheeler; and Conway. The book is divided by section into "configurations," each illustrated at the outset with what looks like a screenshot from the Game of Life. See Crichton.

157 **"evolutionary computation"** Mitchell, 149–51, 156.

157 **Stan Ulam and onward** In *Adventures of a Mathematician*, page 285: "An especially ingenious set of rules was devised by John Conway, a number theorist. The Conway Game of Life is an example of a game or pastime which, perhaps much like the early problems involving dice and cards, has led ultimately to the present edifice of probability theory, and may lead to a vast new theory describing the 'processes' which Alfred North Whitehead studied in his philosophy." In the index, Conway is listed as the "John B." Conway who wrote a book on being a department head (and there is also the mathematician John C. Conway, who wrote a well-regarded textbook on complex analysis).

157 *Cellular Automata Machines* Margolus, 10.

157 *How Nature Works* Bak, 107–12, 118, 142, 161.

157 *Growing Artificial Societies* Epstein, 17.

158 *Mind Children* Moravec, 151–58, 175–76.

158 **"large enough configuration"** Thomas, 2002.

159 *Hippie Philosophy* Walker, 89–91.

159 *Essential Whole Earth* Point Foundation, 24.

161 **nifty meme** Ibid., 166.

162 **known we were coming** Dyson, 1979, 250. To quote Dyson directly: "The more I examine the universe and study the details of its architecture, the more evidence I find that the universe in some sense must have known we were coming."

162 **"some self-reproducing"** Dennett, 175–76.

A New Kind of Science **reviews** Overbye, 2002; Johnson, 2002; Gray, 2003; Shalizi, 2005; and a compilation of reviews, http://shell.cas.usf.edu/~wclark/ANKOS_reviews.html.

164 **likens it to Bigfoot** Wright.

165 **"turtles all the way"** Hawking, 1; Holt, 131.

165 **"analogies with real life"** Conway et al., 2004, vol. 4, 960.

166 **"First Self-Replicating"** Aron; Bellos, 2014. The first self-replicating organism, a spaceship pattern, was devised by the Torontonian programmer Andrew J. Wade—he called it "Gemini." Other practicing Lifenthusiasts, known as "obsessive ultraspecialists," include the New Zealander Mike Playle, who devised "Snark"; Adam Goucher, a self-described "cellular automatist" at Trinity College, Cam-

bridge, who devised the π calculator; and Harvard's Noam Elkies, who proved the still life conjecture.

10. SNIP, CLIP, PRUNE, LOP

171 **"In the beginning"**   Knuth, 1974, 6.

172 **"astonishing feat"**   Gardner, 1977, 19.

172 **key to Conway's**   Conway, ONAG, 2001.

172 **contemplated "nothing"**   Gardner, 1977, 22–24.

172 **"Be fruitful"**   Knuth, 1974, 50.

176 **"Conway, oh boy"**   Knuth Personal Archives.

176 **"pop-it beads"**   Conway, 1970, "Enumeration of Knots and Links."

176 **"over Christmas"**   Knuth Personal Archives; Gardner Papers, Conway letter to Gardner, March 1970.

179 **Svetlana Alliluyeva**   Nicholas Thompson.

180 **Col . . . Snort**   Conway, ONAG, 91–96.

180 **Tribulations . . . Fibulations**   Conway et al., *Winning Ways*, vol. 4, 520, 535, 537.

180 **Sylver Coinage**   Ibid., 609–31, 635–40.

180 **Traffic Jams**   Conway, ONAG, 135.

180 **Domineering**   Conway, ONAG, 114–21; *Winning Ways*, vol. 1, 119–22.

181 **"fantastic surprise"**   Taubes.

182 **twin papers**   Conway, 1972 "All Numbers; 1975 "All Games."

182 **"snipping, clipping"**   "Simpson, Frederick Arthur."

182 **"blowing a trumpet"**   Guy, "Mathematical Magus," 292.

183 **"horrid compounds"**   Gardner Papers, Conway letter to Gardner, March 1970.

184 **"getting in the way of writing *Winning Ways*"**   Conway, ONAG, v.

184 **threatening legal action**   Conway, ONAG, vi; Berlekamp would disagree—he noted that his legal invocations, pertaining to a separate but related dispute with *Winning Ways*, never made an outright threat to sue, but were successful nonetheless. Siegel, 486–87.

185 **neither of them could ever prevail**   Siegel, 484. Siegel gives vivid portraits of the Conway-Guy-Berlekamp trio.

186 **"the filing cabinet!"**   Guy, "Mathematical Magus," 293.

186 **"genius is 1 percent"**   Ibid., 292.

187 **mastered the solutions**   With his Ph.D. student David Wolfe.

187 **had indeed been ill received**   Siegel, 487.

189 **"John, print it"**   Bunyan.

189 **recorded in his diary**   Knuth Personal Archives.

189 **"archaeological digging"**   Knuth, 1974, 5.

190 **"In the beginning"**   Knuth, 6–7.

191 **"Empire State Building"**   Conway, forthcoming.

193 **"sure gets around"**   Knuth, 1974, 11.

194 **"A Hair, they say"**   FitzGerald.

194 "What Are Numbers"   Dedekind.

197 "Everything is what it is"   Also attributed to Joseph Butler.

199 game called Hackenbush   Conway et al., *Winning Ways*, vol. 1.

208 something ephemeral   Polly Shulman's article gets this across whimsically.

208 "last theorem in this book"   Conway, ONAG, 224.

208 "Vintage Conway"   Gardner, 1997, 49.

208 "fantastic edifice"   Gardner, 1997, 56.

209 "of any use?"   Conway, 1972, "All Numbers," 13.

209 "on the boundary"   Taubes.

209 "really good play"   Kennedy. And Gödel archives.

210 Surprising Assertion   Gödel, 1947. Conway and I checked this paper, and a number of other sources such as Gödel's collected works, but were unable to find the surprising assertion. However, Kennedy seemed to think it was the sort of thing Gödel would speculate about—it sounded "vaguely Gödelian"—and she suggested it might have been transmitted to Conway via Tennenbaum.

210 "round trip on a rocket"   Gödel Archives, box 6c, 8b, 11b, 12.

211 conclusion was wrong   Kennedy, 2011.

212 discussions with Tennenbaum   Gödel Archives, box 3b, 14c.

212 illegible handwriting   The Gödel scholar Cheryl Dawson translated the relevant Conway passages but did not find anything more precise.

212 looked like "Conway"   Gödel Archives, box 3b, "Discussion notes: 1972–1974 01/186."

214 "creative mathematician"   Knuth Personal Archives.

215 "Wise to wrangle"   FitzGerald.

11. DOTTO & COMPANY

216 Physics and Mathematics of the Universe   Roberts, 2008 (parts of the account of the Japan research trip were previously published in *IPMU News*).

217 meeting, in 2004 in Edinburgh   Du Sautoy, 339–40, 348–52.

217 "applaud now"   Ibid., 339.

218 predicted the existence   Du Sautoy; Ronan.

218 "The Hunting of the Snark"   Wertheim.

218 snark was inadmissible and unimaginable   Gardner, 2006, 110.

218 best tools to wield   Gardner, 2006, 42.

219 interesting properties   Conway et al., 1998, "A Brief History," 288–93 (and all things *Atlas*).

220 went on and on   Conway, 1968, "A Perfect Group."

220 "cymbals of sunlight"   Camus.

223 Rudvalis group   Conway, 1973, "Construction of the Rudvalis Group."

226 christened "Atlantis"   Conway et al., 1998.

228 Find the Day   Carroll.

229 Doomsday Rule   Conway, 1973, "Tomorrow Is the Day"; and Conway, *Winning*

Ways, 191–204. For further details, see http://en.wikipedia.org/wiki/Doomsday_ rule or "What is Doomsday?" at http://www.mathaware.org/mam/2014/calendar/ doomsday.html as well as Gardner, 1996, 24.

230 **Penrose tiles**   Gardner, 1997, 1–30; Penrose.

231 **"ultimately simple"**   Roberts, 2006, 272.

231 **Gardner was also due**   Kullman.

237 **Numerology**   J. G. Thompson, "Some Numerology."

237 **Monstrous Moonshine**   Conway and Norton, 1979.

238 **"dancing Irish leprechauns"**   Ronan, 2.

238 **Rubik's Cube**   Conway et al., 1982, *Winning Ways* (2004 ed., vol. 4, 868–76).

12. TRUTH BEAUTY, BEAUTY TRUTH

241 **analyzing human**   Lévi-Strauss.

245 **mating algorithm**   Fabre.

246 **1970 international bestseller**   Greer.

246 **"saucy feminist"**   Tandon, 76.

248 **brilliant invention**   Taubes.

248 **707 digits**   Conway notes that he initially had 184 digits wrong, because the existing authoritative source at the time was later discovered to be wrong after digit 523.

249 **turned his attention**   Conway, 1981, "The Hunting of J_4."

249 **set his mind**   Griess's method was voluminous, using the "Griess algebra," a structure, a vector space, which he defined expressly for this purpose. Griess, 1982.

250 **Errors also infested**   Conway et al., 1998, *The Atlas of Finite Groups, 10 Years On*.

251 **"beginning of the end"**   Masters, 300.

251 **"The Thirty Years' War"**   Gorenstein formally announced the Classification Project in 1972, but he was backdating it by a couple of decades, if not more.

251 **"asked some time ago"**   Conway, 1980, *Monsters and Moonshine*, 165.

251 **"Among those who"**   Ibid.

252 **"Understand it all"**   Ibid., 170.

252 **"The Friendly Giant"**   Griess, 1982.

252 **"Unfashionable Pursuits"**   Dyson, 1983, 52–53.

254 **"John starts thinking"**   Taubes, 50.

254 **"To One Who Will Understand"**   Conway, 1985, "A Simple Construction"; Wodehouse, 204.

258 **"Conway Seal of Grudging Approval"**   Conway et al., 1998, 291.

258 **"resulting tour-de-force"**   Ibid., 292.

258 **"regard to errors"**   Conway et al., 1985, xxxi.

267 **"wondrous little spot"**   Einstein, 2011, 72.

13. MORTALITY FLASH

272 attention of the *New York Times*   Kolata, 1993.

275 "best survey of the best work"   Rota, 253.

275 Free Will Theorem   Roberts, 2005.

275 important to note   In 1965, simultaneously explored by John Bell, Kochen and Specker proved a theorem and applied it to show that a class of hidden variables can't exist using the Spin axiom. In 1970 Kochen showed that the class of local hidden variables can't exist using the Twin axiom. Conway and Kochen's work in 2006 showed that hidden variable theories that obey special relativity must be local theories.

276 EINSTEIN ATTACKS   Science Service, *New York Times*, 1935.

280 "Oozing Through Texas Soil"   Kaesuk Yoon.

14. OPTIONAL PROBABILITY FIELDS

282 mathematicians' styles   Shulman. "Infinity Plus One" interview tapes, 1995.

283 "I love my subject"   Browne, 1988.

283 "How to Stare at a Brick Wall"   Doyle, circa 1990.

285 "Deep inside"   Giovinazzo, 32.

285 "But with respect to teaching"   Ibid.

285 "wake people up"   Ibid, 33.

287 "I wasn't invited"   Seife, 14.

287 good buy after the fact   Hargittai, 7.

288 "almost revere him"   Shulman, 1995; Shulman interview tapes.

288 Kruskal devoted   Ibid.

288 infinite divergences   Matthews, 40.

288 "aesthetic sense better"   Matthews, 38–39.

289 alluring theory of the "soliton"   Kruskal discovered it together with Norman Zabusky.

292 "nice notation"   Conway, 2001, "On Three-dimensional Orbifolds."

292 "Geometry and the Imagination"   Conway et al., 1990.

292 book of the same name   Hilbert.

293 curiosity-driven fun   Curiosity- and games-driven learning is a movement gaining steam in the education world, in places like exhibit programming at the American Museum of Natural History and New York City's "Quest to Learn" public school.

294 back wheel   For more details, see Konhauser et al.

295 weigh the hypothesis   Doyle came up with the problem when his father-in-law pointed out a fallacy in Sherlock Holmes's reasoning in deciphering bicycle tracks in *The Adventure of the Priory School*.

295 "take the student out"   Dawson.

295 "let them exercise"   Ibid.

296 15,000 polygons   Danziger.

298 **"Barnum & Bailey"**   Ibid.

298 **"we call it a circus"**   Ibid.

298 **"We fight like hell"**   Ibid.

299 **"Conway jumped"**   Ibid.

299 **INTELLECTUAL DUEL**   Browne, 1988.

300 **"used to invent sequences"**   Ibid.

301 **"can't resist a challenge"**   Ibid.

301 **"Some Crazy Sequences"**   The to-do was also covered by London's *Sunday Times*; Rufford; also, for a more detailed accounting, see Mallows's "Conway's Challenge Sequence." Mallows notes that the confusion was compounded by the fact that at least one point during the lecture Conway said $\frac{1}{40}$ rather than $\frac{1}{20}$. He marveled at "how confused a top mathematician can get while talking about his own problem."

302 **"Dear Colin"**   Conway letter to Mallows (undated), courtesy of Mallows.

303 **"The concept is very general"**   Hofstadter, 1999, 127.

304 **numbers he called the Q-numbers**   Hofstadter, 1999, 137–38.

304 **"Let me close this letter"**   Hofstadter letter to Conway, September 2, 1988, courtesy of Hofstadter.

305 **$10,000 sequence**   See OEIS: http://oeis.org/A004001.

305 **"walking along"**   Seife, 1994, "Impressions of Conway," draft.

306 **"not really doing mathematics"**   Seife, 1994, "Mathemagician," 15.

306 **"expanding it"**   Ibid.

306 **"ceased being"**   Ibid.

306 **intellectual prowess**   Hardy.

306 **"passionate lament"**   Hardy (foreword by C. P. Snow), 9–57.

306 **"if it sits down"**   Schleicher, 567.

306 **"stay being 4"**   Math Chat video courtesy of Frank Morgan.

308 **proved Fermat's last**   *People* magazine, "Andrew Wiles."

308 **Fermat Fest**   http://www.msri.org/publications/video/forsale/fermat.html.

310 **"ordinary human man"**   Shulman, "Infinity Plus One," 1995.

310 **"I'm a Sybarite"**   Seife, "Impressions of Conway," draft, 1994.

310 **first heart attack**   It was likely circa 1992.

311 **"got very depressed"**   Shulman, "Infinity Plus One," interview tapes.

311 **Metaphorically it was true**   Ibid.

311 **"I tried to commit"**   Interviews with Miller.

314 **received U.S. Patent**   Conway and Sloane, 1985.

314 **patents assigned**   Postol.

15. LUSTRATION

322 **"here I am winging it"**   Conway, 1995, "Sphere Packings, Lattices, Codes and Greed," 45.

324 **"Will Mathematics Survive?"**   Arnold, 8–9.

325 **"conjecture was formulated"** Borcherd's Fields Medal citation also notes: "The Moonshine conjecture provides an interrelationship between the so-called 'monster group' and elliptic functions. These functions are used in the construction of wire-frame structures in two dimensions, and can be helpful, for example, in chemistry for the description of molecular structures.The Monster group, in contrast, only seemed to be of importance in pure mathematics." See http://www.cis.umac.mo/~fstitl/research/1998-fieldists.html.

326 **"get down to work"** Goddard, 1998.

327 **"Borcherds got his Fields Medal"** Lepowsky, 1999; Borcherds, 2002.

327 **the proof that I came up with** Borcherds, 1992, 1994.

328 **soul of all mathematical** Weyl, 500. The precise quote is: "In these days the angel of topology and the devil of abstract algebra fight for the soul of each individual mathematical domain."

329 *Vertex Operator Algebras And The Monster* Frenkel et al, 1988.

330 **Moonshine revival** The revival keeps a number of high-profile string theorists busy, among them Hirosi Ooguri at Kyto University, Jeff Harvey at the Enrico Fermi Institute in Chicago, Shamit Kachru at Stanford, and Miranda Cheng at Paris's L'institut de mathématiques de Jussieu.

332 **"has Monstrous Moonshine been explained?"** Gannon, 435.

the monster in general Roberts, 2013 (parts of the account of the Monster throughout were previously published in the *IAS Letter*); Goddard, 2013, an unpublished talk; Lepowsky, 1999, 2010; Du Sautoy; Ronan.

16. TAKE IT AS AXIOMATIC

334 **I first met Conway** Roberts, 2003, 2010 (parts of the accounts of visits to Mathcamp throughout were previously published by the *Globe and Mail* and the *Simons Foundation*).

336 **"tangles"** Conway, 1970.

339 **"Happy Pi Day!"** Roberts, 2009 (parts of the account of Pi Day were previously published in the *Globe and Mail*).

339 **rumors of his prowess** Japan holds the world records in reciting and calculating π. Akira Haraguchi, a retired engineer and mental health counselor, recited π to 1,000 digits in 16 hours in 2006. And over 94 days in 2013, π was computed to 12.1 trillion digits, using a program written by Alexander J. Yee and a desktop computer built by Shigeru Kondo.

341 **date to travel to Poughkeepsie** Roberts, 2007 (parts of the account of the visit to Poughkeepsie were previously published in the *Walrus*). George Odom died on December 18, 2010.

343 **"these cute terms"** Grünbaum, 2009, 557.

345 **more mathcamp** Roberts, 2010.

mathcamp in general The Mathcamp section, as noted in passing, is a composite of my three visits, in 2003, 2010, and 2013.

346 **Dots and Boxes**   Conway et al., 1982 (*Winning Ways*, 2003 edition, vol. 3, 541–84); see also Berlekamp, 2000.

17. HUMPTY DUMPTY'S PREROGATIVE

355 "restore science to its rightful place"   Revkin.

360 **Anderson . . . was more optimistic**   Brodie.

361 "**Conway and Kochen's argument exemplifies**"   Halvorson, 9.

361 "**in fact, what it seems**"   Brodie.

365 "**The Exceptional Brain of Albert Einstein**"   Witelson.

368 *An Essay on the Psychology of Invention*   Hadamard.

368 **Appendix I**   Ibid., 137–41.

368 **Appendix II**   Ibid., 142–43.

the brain generally   Neisser; Carey; Tierney; Holt, 2008; Dehaene, 1997.

the brain and free will   Conway attended a talk at Princeton during the FWT lecture run, "Of Neurons, Decisions, and Value: Probing the Unconscious Math of the Brain," by Stanford neuroscientist William Newsome. Newsome occasionally wades into these philosophical waters, with a variation of talk titles such as "Brain, Mind, and Free Will: Did My Neurons Make Me Do It?" and "Neuroscience, Explanation, and the Problem of Free Will." These talks evolved because in giving his usual technical talks on the brain and decision making, he noticed there was almost always a student in the audience who piped up with the question: "What about free will?" Conway was curious to talk to Newsome afterward, but in the end he was too hungry and he went off to get some dinner. Matter over mind.

EPILOGUE

376 "**working**" **harder than ever**   Conway, forthcoming.

377 "**simple but extravagant claims**"   Conway, 2013, "On Unsettleable Arithmetical Problems."

378 "**statements that are true but**"   Ibid., 192.

381 **Thrackle Problem**   aka the Conway Thrackle Conjecture. See Wikipedia.

384 **holyhedron . . . is a polyhedron**   Pickover, 2009, 502.

385 "**Science Lives**" **project**   Transcript of interview with Alex Ryba by George Csicsery. See also http://www.simonsfoundation.org/science_lives_video/john-conway/. Roberts, 2014 (parts of the account JHC in the alcove here and there were previously published in Science Lives on the Simons Foundation website).

386 "**rainbow has had hosts of admirers**"   Boyer, 7.

391 **quotation from Berenson that rang true**   Kaiser.

392 "**Math was always there for me.**"   Seife, 1994, "Mathemagician," 13.

ART CREDITS

Hand drawings throughout by John Horton Conway.

Line drawings throughout by Chaim Goodman-Strauss; knots by Rob Scharein.

Section breaks by Doris Schattschneider.

E_8 endpapers, courtesy of Brian Conrey, American Institute of Mathematics.

vi John "Horned" Conway caricature, courtesy of Simon J. Fraser.

16 n-Dimensional Regular Polytopes from *Holt School Magazine*, courtesy of John Conway.

26 Tongue tricks photos, courtesy of Ric Gemmell.

29 Water computer photo, courtesy of Peter Evennett.

55 Infinity spiral, Wikimedia Commons.

65 Conway family photo, courtesy of Eileen Conway.

70 Backgammon photo, courtesy of Pelham Wilson.

71 Sprouts game, courtesy of James Gardner, Martin Gardner Papers, Special Collections, Stanford University Libraries.

87 M.C. Escher's *Circle Limit IV* © 2015 The M.C. Escher Company – The Netherlands. All rights reserved. www.mcescher.com

116 Prime-producing machine, by David Logothetti, courtesy of Faith Logothetti.

123 Survey of Life-forms, courtesy of James Gardner, Martin Gardner Papers, Special Collections, Stanford University Libraries.

144 Life is Universal, courtesy of James Gardner, Martin Gardner Papers, Special Collections, Stanford University Libraries.

148 Conway at Life computer photo, by Kelvin Brodie, courtesy of *The Sun*/News Syndication.

173 M.C. Escher's *Symmetry Drawing E22* © 2015 The M.C. Escher Company – The Netherlands. All rights reserved. www.mcescher.com

179 Go games, courtesy of Jon Diamond, British Go Association.

192 Empire State Building, courtesy of Alex Ryba.

232 *Scientific American* cover, courtesy of Doris Schattschneider.

254 Baby Monster, courtesy of Ric Gemmell.

260 *The ATLAS*, courtesy of John Conway, Rob Curtis, Simon Norton, Richard Parker, Rob Wilson.

273 Conway in Princeton office photo, by Dith Pran, courtesy of Redux Pictures.

278 Free Will Theorem cube, courtesy of Frank Swenton.

278 M.C. Escher's *Waterfall* © 2015 The M.C. Escher Company – The Netherlands. All rights reserved. www.mcescher.com

439

314 Tennis balls, courtesy of Stephen D. Miller.
340 Gareth wins Pi Day, courtesy of Diana Conway.
355 Proof cartoon, courtesy of Sidney Harris.
393 *On Morley's Trisector Theorem*, courtesy of Marjorie Senechal, *The Mathematical Intelligencer.*

INDEX

Abel Prize, xviii

Adamatzky, Andrew, ed. *Game of Life Cellular Automata*, 159

Adams, Frank, 68–69, 256, 267

Adler, Stephen, 360

aesthetics, 264–65

Alephs (cardinal numbers), 45–47, 194

Alexander of Aphrodisias, 388

Alexander's dark band, 388

Alexeev, Boris, 327, 328

ALIFE 14, 381

Alliluyeva, Svetlana, 179

American Academy of Arts and Sciences, 305

Amis, Kingsley, 121

Anderson, Philip, 360

anthropic principle, 162

Appel, Kenneth, 231

Archimedean solids, 21–22, *21*

Archimedes, xvii, 22, 335

Archimedes palimpsest, 287n

Aristotle, 45

Arnold, Vladimir, 324

artificial intelligence, 111, 143, 144, 157–58

artificial life, 157, 158–59

Assassin, 351

asymptotic series, 288

AT&T Bell Labs, 73, 184, 282, 301

Atiyah, Sir Michael, 83, 214, 252, 266

ATLAS (of group theory), 225, 256

    character tables in, *260*, 261

    completed project, 259, 265, 329

    Conway's explanation of, 261–65

    creation of, 219–20, 221

    delays in, 230, 235, 254

    error book of, 250–51, 258

    guard book of, 226, 250–51

    introduction to, 258, 262

    in progress, 226–27, 228, 235, 241, 247, 258–59

    and simple groups, 258, 288

    and symmetry, 262, 263

    tenth anniversary celebrations, 258

Automata Studies, 111

automata theory, 147

Axiom of Choice, 46, 92

Axtell, Robert, and Epstein, *Growing Artificial Societies*, 157

backgammon, 69–70, *70*, 99, 114, 227, 254, 287, 357–58

Bacon, Francis, 48

Bailin, David, 30, 32

Bak, Per, *How Nature Works: The Science of Self-Organized Criticality*, 157

Baker, Alan, 40

Ball, W. W. Rouse, *Mathematical Recreations and Essays*, 13, 33

bar billiards, 125

Bar-Natan, Itai, 346

Basterfield, John, 32–33

beanstalks, 200, *200*, 203

Beaumont, Francis, 111

Beckett, Samuel, 119

Bell Labs:

    "Computer Analysis of Sprouts," 73

    Conway's lectures in, 282, 301

    and Dots and Boxes, 184

Benson, David, 235

Berenson, Bernard, 391

Berlekamp, Elwyn, 165, 184–89

Bernini, Gian Lorenzo, 66

Besicovitch, Abram Samoilovitch, 35–36

Besicovitch's Game, 36, 68, 179

Bevan, Edward, 105

Bhargava, Manjul, 327n

441